Strategic Marketing Management
Planning and Control, Analysis and Decision

Paul Fifield and Colin Gilligan

Published on behalf of
the Chartered Institute of Marketing

This book is dedicated to Jane, Rosie and Ben who, to paraphrase the immortal Bette Midler, are 'the wind beneath our wings'.

Butterworth-Heinemann Ltd
Linacre House, Jordan Hill, Oxford OX2 8DP

℞ A member of the Reed Elsevier plc group

OXFORD   LONDON   BOSTON
MUNICH   NEW DELHI   SINGAPORE   SYDNEY
TOKYO   TORONTO   WELLINGTON

First published 1995

British Library Cataloguing in Publication Data
A catalogue record for this book is available from the British Library

ISBN 0 7506 1990 2

Produced by **AMR**
Printed in Great Britain by Scotprint, Musselburgh, Scotland

Contents

Preface

The development by the Chartered Institute of Marketing of Syllabus '94 has led to a far greater emphasis at the Diploma level upon the strategic aspects of marketing, a move which is reflected not just in the refocusing of all four of the Diploma syllabuses, but also by the way in which the Planning and Control and the Analysis and Decision examinations are now linked under the heading of Strategic Marketing Management. In writing this workbook, we have therefore paid particular attention both to the strategic aspects of the subject and to an exploration of the very strong linkages that exist – and which students are expected to demonstrate – between the Planning and Control and Analysis and Decision examination papers.

However, it needs to be recognized from the outset that candidates for the Diploma are also expected to demonstrate the depth and breadth of their understanding of marketing and that a workbook is designed as a complement to and not a substitute for a far wider programme of reading and research. It is for this reason that throughout the text you will find references to two other books that you would do well to read. They are:

Strategic Marketing Management: Planning, Implementation and Control by Wilson and Gilligan with Pearson (1992), Butterworth-Heinemann

and

Marketing Strategy by Fifield (1992), Butterworth-Heinemann.

We wish you success in the examinations.

Paul Fifield
Colin Gilligan

Acknowledgements

The authors would like to thank Maggie Duncan, Janice Nunn and Catherine Lowe for wordprocessing the manuscript, and Jonathan Glasspool and Sandra Benko at Butterworth-Heinemann whose increasingly frequent, and seemingly desperate, phone calls to check on the progress of the manuscript eventually forced us to sit down and write it.

A quick word from the Chief Examiner

I am delighted to recommend to you the new series of CIM workbooks. All of these have been written by either the Senior Examiner or Examiners responsible for marking and setting the papers.

Preparing for the CIM Exams is hard work. These workbooks are designed to make that work as interseting and illuminating as possible, as well as providing you with the knowledge you need to pass. I wish you success.

Trevor Watkins
CIM Chief Examiner,
Deputy Vice Chancellor,
South Bank University

How to use your CIM workbook

The authors have been careful to structure your book with the exams in mind. Each unit, therefore, covers an essential part of the syllabus. You need to work through the complete workbook systematically to ensure that you have covered everything you need to know.

This workbook is divided into ten units. Each unit contains the following standard elements:

Objectives   tell you what part of the syllabus you will be covering and what you will be expected to know having read the unit.

Study guides   tell you how long the unit is and how long its activities take to do.

Questions   are designed to give you practice – they will be similar to those that you get in the exam.

Answers   give you a suggested format for answering exam questions. *Remember* there is no such thing as a model answer – you should use these examples only as guidelines.

Activities   give you the chance to put what you have learnt into practice.

Exam tips   are hints from the senior examiner or examiner which are designed to help you avoid common mistakes made by previous candidates.

Definitions   are used for words you must know to pass the exam.

Extending knowledge sections   are designed to help you use your time most effectively. It is not possible for the workbook to cover *everything* you need to know to pass. What you read here needs to be supplemented by your classes, practical experience at work and day-to-day reading.

Summaries   cover what you should have picked up from reading the unit.

Introduction

The Strategic Marketing Management component of the Diploma in Marketing consists of two interrelated modules: Planning and Control and Analysis and Decision. In the case of Planning and Control, the syllabus has been designed to provide you with a detailed understanding of the ways in which marketing activities in a variety of types and size of organization are capable of being planned, implemented and controlled. This is achieved by examining the nature of marketing and the key issues in the strategic marketing process. The syllabus is therefore made up of five interrelated parts (the figures in brackets indicate the relative weighting that should be given to each section).

Stage one: Introduction to planning and control (10%)

Stage two: Where are we now? – strategic, financial and marketing analysis (25%)

Stage three: Where do we want to be? – strategic direction and strategy formulation (25%)

Stage four: How might we get there and which way is best? – strategic choice and evaluation (30%)

Stage five: How can we ensure arrival? – strategic implementation and control (10%)

These questions and themes are then developed further and emphasis given to their application within the Analysis and Decision syllabus which culminates in the case study examination.

At the same time, the content of the two modules has been designed to complement the syllabuses for the other two Diploma papers, Marketing Communications Strategy and International Marketing Strategy (see Figure 1) and to build upon material at the Certificate and Advanced Certificate levels. In working your way through the book, you should therefore actively look for and think about the sorts of interrelationships that exist throughout the Certificate, Advanced Certificate and Diploma stages; an obvious example of the way in which this might be done would be to examine how approaches to market segmentation and targeting might be applied in overseas markets. Equally, you might think about how a communications strategy needs to reflect the stage reached on the product life-cycle.

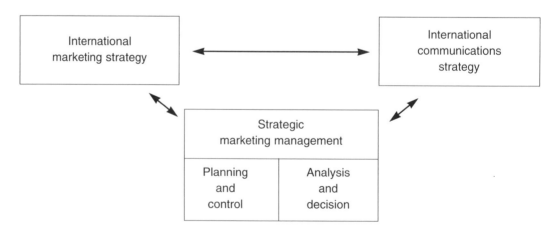

Figure 1   The diploma in marketing

Given this structure, and in particular the nature of the interrelationships between the two elements of Strategic Marketing Management, this workbook has been designed to provide you with a clear insight into the marketing planning and control processes and to the ways in which these can best be applied within the business and commercial world as well as, of course, to the CIM's Diploma examination papers.

In doing this, we give considerable emphasis to the three elements that underpin all of the CIM's syllabus: knowing, understanding and doing. Thus, in each of the units we outline and discuss the relevant concepts so that your knowledge and understanding is increased. We then address the issue of 'doing' by means of a series of exercises and questions and, of course, through the mini case study that forms Section 1 of the Planning and Control examination paper and the maxi case study of the Analysis and Decision examination.

It needs to be recognized from the outset, however, that a workbook cannot explore the complexity of concepts in the same way that a textbook can. For this reason, we make reference at various stages to two books that you may well find useful. These are:

Wilson, R.M.S. and Gilligan, C.T. with Pearson, D. (1992) *Strategic Marketing Management: Planning Implementation and Control*, Butterworth-Heinemann, and Fifield, P. (1992) *Marketing Strategy*, Butterworth-Heinemann.

The first of these, *Strategic Marketing Management*, was written specifically for the CIM's Planning and Control syllabus and was first published in 1992. A second edition by Professors Dick Wilson and Colin Gilligan is due for publication at the beginning of 1996. The references that we make within this workbook are therefore to the first edition. *Marketing Strategy* was written for a slightly different market and is part of Butterworth-Heinemann's 'Practitioner' series. Nevertheless, students of the CIM's Diploma will undoubtedly find it a very useful book, not least because of its very direct style.

Strategic Marketing Management: Planning and Control
We commented earlier that the Planning and Control syllabus focuses upon five key issues: these are illustrated in Figure 2.

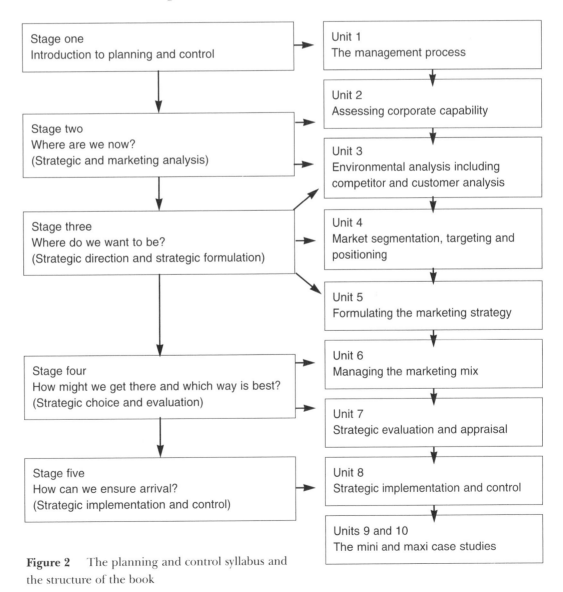

Figure 2 The planning and control syllabus and the structure of the book

In Unit 1 we examine a number of the dimensions of the management process and the role of marketing within this. Against this background, we then concentrate in Units 2–8 upon taking you through the most important dimensions of four major questions – Where are we now? Where do we want to be? How might we get there? and How can we ensure arrival? – as a prelude in Units 9 and 10 to an examination of the mini case study that forms the first part of the Planning and Control examination paper, and then the major case study that is the basis for the Analysis and Decision examination.

The first of the five stages of the Planning and Control syllabus is concerned with a series of background issues and, in particular, the nature of planning and the relationships that can – or should – exist between marketing management and corporate management. Unit 2 then focuses upon the various ways in which managers might identify their organization's current position and, in the light of a clear understanding of competitors and customers, assess its *true* level of marketing capability. For a variety of reasons, the assessment of capability can be seen to be one of the principal foundation stones of any strategic planning process, since it determines exactly what the organization is or should be capable of achieving. All too often, however, managers either overestimate levels of capability or fail to understand its various dimensions in sufficient detail.

Marketing capability by itself is, of course, only one part of the planning process and needs to be looked at against the background both of the organization as a whole and the nature and shape of the environment. It is for this reason that in Unit 3 we turn our attention to an analysis of the marketing environment in order to illustrate the sorts of changes that are taking place and the types of opportunities and threats that are emerging from this.

The juxtaposition of these two units is deliberate, since in recent years there has been a shift in management thinking away from the traditional idea that strategy should be environmentally-led to the view that it should be much more firmly capability-led. The two views should not, however, be viewed as bi-polar extremes, since in practice any strategy needs to reflect a clear and detailed understanding both of the environment and what the organization is capable of doing.

It is then against this background that in Unit 4 we turn to one of the other major foundation stones of any strategy, that of market segmentation, targeting and positioning. The ideas introduced within this section of the book are then developed further in Unit 5 in which we focus upon the various types of marketing strategy and how they can best be formulated. From here we go on to examine in Unit 6 the issues associated with the planning and management of the marketing mix. In Unit 7 we focus upon methods of control and appraisal and then, in Unit 8, the ways in which strategy might possibly be implemented.

Units 9 and 10 focus, in turn, upon the mini case that forms Section 1 of the Planning and Control examination and the maxi case that is the basis of the Analysis and Decision paper. In both units, we have included previous cases and solutions that are designed to provide you with a clear understanding of how you should approach the answer.

Approaching the Planning and Control examination

The syllabus for Planning and Control has a number of distinct aims and objectives and is designed to ensure that students:

- Are made aware of all the major aspects of the planning and control elements of the marketing management function.

- Have an understanding of and an ability to evaluate the contribution of marketing management to corporate management.

- Examine and are familiar with all aspects of the planning process and its application to marketing.

- Are able to use the tools of analysis and decision making in the preparation of marketing plans.

- Appreciate the characteristics and planning needs of organizations in a variety of sectors so that the marketing mix can be tailored in its detail to meet the wants/needs of identified market segments and achieve specified strategic and tactical objectives.

- Have an understanding of the issues associated with the effective implementation and control of marketing plans and how the principal barriers to implementation might possibly be overcome.

- Appreciate the need to understand the dimensions of the international environment within which marketing decisions are increasingly being made.

The learning outcomes that emerge from this mean that you should be able to:

- Understand a wide variety of marketing techniques and models.

- Apply these techniques/models to the marketing planning process in competitive and collaborative environments.

- Undertake comprehensive analyses of markets, customers and competitors.

- Conduct detailed marketing audits, both internally and externally.

- Determine marketing objectives and strategies.

- Prepare a straightforward marketing plan.

- Design appropriate marketing mixes for particular market segments.

- Initiate appraisal and control systems for marketing planning.

- Specify the marketing research needed to formulate effective marketing plans.

- Understand how the barriers to the effective implementation of marketing plans might be overcome.

What the examiners want ...	What the examiners all too often get ...	The solution
An answer to the *specific* question posed	Highly general answers that fail to tackle the specifics of the question and, instead, tell us everything that the student can vaguely remember	Read the questions and write an answer that addresses the *specific* question posed. Avoid putting down everything you know in a general and indiscriminate manner
A clear and distinct structure	Inadequate or non-existent structures and a series of generalized ramblings based on unrealistic and unsustainable assumptions	A strong and obvious structure with sub-headings and key points that have been highlighted
Answers that are written in the format that is specifically asked for, be it a report, memo, briefing paper, essay or marketing plan	Either a general essay or a series of bullet points which lack any elaboration or sense of perspective	An answer that adopts the format asked for
Examples to illustrate the points being made	A total absence of examples	Several brief, carefully chosen and appropriate examples
Reference to the appropriate literature and/or research findings	A lack of any evidence of reading or awareness of what is happening in the world of marketing	Evidence that you are aware of what has been written in the area and what is happening currently
A firm conclusion and, where asked for, an *evaluation* of the issue that is at the heart of the question	Answers that tail off or stop abruptly mid-sentence	Answers that conclude with a summary or evaluation of the key issues raised
Answers that illustrate that the candidate has a clear and detailed understanding of marketing and the marketing process	Answers that show far too little understanding of the subject	Read, practice on past papers, and THINK

Figure 3 The examinations and the scripts that we receive

EXAM TIP

After each examination the Senior Examiners write a report for the Chartered Institute in which they discuss how the students coped with the examination and highlight any particular problems that have been experienced. In looking back at the reports that I have written since taking over as the Senior Examiner for Planning and Control in 1991, there are several issues which I have referred to on almost every occasion; these, together with suggestions for the ways in which the problems might possibly be overcome are illustrated in Figure 3.

Note: Each year we are faced with several examination scripts that consist of half a page of writing and then a message to the examiner which invariably starts, 'Dear Examiner.' The message then typically goes on to say that, because of work and/or domestic pressures, the candidate has not been able to follow any sort of study programme or revise for the examination. Despite this, the candidate would be eternally grateful if the examiner could find it in his heart (author's note: never forget that we also have female examiners) to award a pass. Although examiners try to be sympathetic, you are far more likely to pass if you display real evidence of having studied the syllabus and understand the subject than if you make a plea for special treatment based on ignorance or laziness.

Approaching the Analysis and Decision examination

Unlike other Diploma subjects, the major case study paper has no formal syllabus. The examination is based on a full case study normally made up of 10–12 pages of narrative and 20–30 pages of charts, tables and appendices. The case study is sent to candidates four weeks in advance of the examination to allow time for individual and group analysis and discussion.

At the time of the examination additional information will be provided as well as three or four questions which will have to be answered in full. The examination is 'open book' which means that you will be able to take reference material with you into the examination room. You should note, however, that only material produced during the examination itself will be marked and any pre-prepared material appended to the script will be ignored by the examiner.

The major case study is designed to be a practical test of the candidate's ability to apply his or her marketing knowledge. Candidates who only reproduce theory or models which are not applied to the case situation will not gain a pass grade. Equally, the case is likely to draw from all areas of marketing and will test the candidate's ability to apply knowledge in international as well as domestic marketing strategy. Many aspects of the entire Certificate, Advanced Certificate and Diploma syllabus may be applicable and if you have been exempted from parts of the course you should familiarize yourself with the detailed course requirements.

The rationale for the paper is:

> To extend the practice of candidates in the quantitative and qualitative analysis of marketing situations, both to develop their powers of diagnosis and to create a firm basis in decision making.
> (Tutors' guidance notes CIM)

Tackling the major case

Questions applied in the case study do not have a standardized format; they may vary in number, may emphasize different points; but will always be directed towards strategy rather than tactics. Time management in the exam is crucial. Candidates are required to answer all the questions posed and in accordance with the mark allocation stated on the paper. In every case, the candidates have a role to play and they are expected to be able to relate their answer to this role.

There are two basic questions posed in any case, and your preparation should therefore reflect this guide:

1 What is wrong?
2 What are you going to do to put it right?

The second question is critical but cannot be answered without the first. Problem identification will certainly require the application of statistical and financial analytical techniques, an organizational and behavioural understanding and marketing knowledge. Having read your answer, the examiners must know:

- What these problems are.
- What alternative solutions have been considered.
- What solution has been chosen.
- Why it has been chosen.
- How it will be implemented.

The lack of imagination by the majority of candidates in this examination is a major weakness. Marketing is creative. It is one of the means by which companies distinguish themselves and their products/services from competition. On the rare occasions that examiners are offered a creative or different approach, marks tend to soar.

Marketing is about customers first, products second. Few candidates take a truly customer-led approach to the case study. When they do, marks tend to rise dramatically.

The rules to successful case study examinations are:

- Think customer.
- Think creative.
- Think practical.
- Think application, not theory.
- Think in the role given in the case.

One of the most common examination mistakes that candidates make is to ignore the specific question posed. Always identify as clearly as possible *precisely* what the examiner is asking for and never let yourself fall into the trap of giving a general 'let me tell you everything I know or can think of' sort of answer in the hope that the person marking the paper will put it into a more structured context; they will not.

Summary

Within this introduction we have discussed the structure and purpose of the Strategic Marketing Management syllabus and made reference to the sorts of interrelationships that exist with the other papers at Diploma level. As a check on your understanding of this, consider the following questions:

- What is the structure of the Planning and Control syllabus and what is the syllabus designed to achieve?
- In what ways does the Planning and Control syllabus provide a feed-in to the Analysis and Decision examination?

Introduction to planning and control: the management process

This first part of the syllabus has been designed to help you understand the managerial context within which marketing takes place. Having worked your way through this unit, you will understand:

- The relationships between marketing planning and corporate planning.
- The basis of planning and control, the cycle of control and the nature and role of strategic, tactical and contingency planning.
- The nature of management and marketing information systems and the contribution that market research is capable of making to each stage of the planning process.
- The implications for planning and control of organizational structures and managerial cultures.

It is essential that you do not look at marketing in isolation, but that you recognize instead the sorts of interrelationships that exist between marketing planning and corporate planning. In particular, you should be aware of the sorts of constraints within which many marketing decisions are made. Although this part of the syllabus accounts for only 10 per cent of the total, it is an important underpinning for what follows, since it should help you to develop a breadth of perspective. To help with this, you should read the business papers, looking for examples of how marketing decisions are influenced not just by what is happening in the environment, but also by decisions that have been taken in the past, the availability of resources, the culture of the organization, and so on. You should also talk to senior managers within your organization to gain a greater understanding of the sorts of issues that influence the marketing decisions that are taken.

In total, the unit should take you about 6 hours to complete. Suggestions for further reading appear at the end of the unit.

Although you will undoubtedly be familiar with a variety of definitions of marketing, we begin this unit by highlighting several key issues in their development.

Definitions of marketing

Definitions of marketing tend to fall into one of three distinct categories:

1. Those that focus on marketing's functional elements and activities.
2. Those concerned with marketing as a process.
3. Those that reflect the view that marketing is essentially a philosophy of how to do business.

For the most part, the functional definitions of marketing are now seen to be of little real value and so we will concentrate here upon the other two categories. In the case of process definitions, for example, it has been suggested that:

> Marketing is the process by which an organization relates creatively, productivity and profitability to the marketplace

and that:

> Marketing is a social and managerial process by which individuals and groups obtain what they need and want through creating, offering and exchanging products of value with others.

This process approach is also reflected in the definitions that have been put forward by the Chartered Institute of Marketing (CIM) and the American Marketing Association (AMA):

> Marketing is the management process for identifying, anticipating and satisfying customers profitably. (CIM)

> Marketing (management) is the process of planning and executing the conception, pricing, promotion and distribution of ideas, goods and services to create exchanges that satisfy individual and organizational objectives. (AMA)

These process views have been taken several steps further in recent years with the greater recognition that has been given to the role that *all* parts of the organization need to play in creating and maintaining high levels of customer satisfaction. The result has been a series of definitions which view marketing rather more as a philosophy of doing business, something which is reflected in the words of Peter Drucker in 1973:

DEFINITION 1.1

> Marketing is so basic that it cannot be considered a separate function on a par with others such as manufacturing or personnel. It is first a central dimension of the entire business. It is the whole business seen from the point of view of its final result, that is from the customers' point of view.

Although Drucker's definition is undoubtedly useful, since it highlights both the pivotal role of marketing within the organization and the need for managers to look at how they are operating from the customers' point of view (an outside-in approach), a series of other dimensions are typically now incorporated within any meaningful definition of the area. Perhaps the most significant of the changes that we have seen has been the far greater and more explicit recognition that is now given to the issue of *competitive position* (that is, that success comes not just from identifying customers' needs and wants, but from satisfying them more firmly than competitors) and to the broader *social role and responsibility of marketing*.

The first of these two additional dimensions is reflected in Kotler's suggestion (1991, page 16) that:

The marketing concept hold that the key to achieving organizational goals consists in determining the needs and wants of target markets and delivering the desired satisfactions more effectively and efficiently than competitors.

The second dimension – the issue of marketing's social responsibility – is then developed in what has been labelled the *societal marketing concept.*

The question of whether marketing managers should take account of the broader social implications of their decisions has been the subject of considerable debate, with advocates of the Chicago School of Economics such as Milton Friedman arguing that the primary – and sole – responsibility of business is to maximize the return to the organization's stakeholders. However, others argue that business has a distinct responsibility to the community and that decisions taken should therefore take full account of the consequences for society of their outcome. In developing this line of argument, Kotler (1991, page 25) has suggested that:

> In recent years, some people have questioned whether the marketing concept is an appropriate organizational philosophy in an age of environmental deterioration, resource shortages, explosive population growth, world hunger and poverty, and neglected social services. The question is whether companies that do an excellent job of sensing, serving, and satisfying individual consumer wants are necessarily acting in the best long-run interests of consumers and society. The marketing concept sidesteps the potential conflicts between *consumer wants, consumer interests,* and *long-run societal welfare.*

Because of this, he argues for the adoption of the societal marketing concept which:

> holds that the organization's task is to determine the needs, wants, and interests of target markets and to deliver the desired satisfactions more effectively and efficiently than competitors in a way that preserves or enhances the consumer's and the society's well-being.

Given the nature of these comments, there are two simple matrices that help to provide an insight to an organization. The first of these (see Figure 1.1) focuses upon the management team's orientation towards customers and competitors and illustrates how this orientation can range from a myopic and firmly inwardly-focused approach through to one that is truly market-driven with full account being taken both of competitors and customers.

		Low	High
The degree of customer focus	Low	Myopic and inwardly focused	Transfixed by one or more competitors
	High	Preoccupied by one or more customer groups	Market-driven

The degree of competitor focus

Figure 1.1   The management team's customer and competitor orientations

Taking an organization with which you are familiar, where in Figure 1.1 would you position the predominant managerial orientation? What sorts of factors contribute to this positioning? What are the implications of this for how the organization interacts with the marketplace?

ACTIVITY 1.1

The second matrix that helps to provide an insight to an organization focuses upon the legality of the marketing activity and the sorts of ethics and degree of social responsibility that is reflected in the management's decisions; this is illustrated in Figure 1.2.

	Illegal	Legal
Unethical	**Cell 1** Illegal and unethical	**Cell 3** Legal but unethical
Ethical	**Cell 2** Illegal but ethical	**Cell 4** Legal and ethical

Figure 1.2   The legal and ethical dimensions of marketing activity

Although Cell 4, in which decisions are both legal and ethical, is quite obviously the position which managers should aim for, competitive and other pressures may well force managers into other parts of the matrix.

ACTIVITY 1.2

Identify examples of products and/or services that fall into Cells 1, 2 or 3 of Figure 1.2. In what circumstances might a marketing decision be legal but unethical? Given the publicity that has been given to the apparent link between smoking and respiratory diseases, is the marketing of cigarettes ethical or unethical? Equally, is the sale of arms to a country with a civil war ethical or unethical? In what circumstances, if any, might you justify marketing an illegal product?

The relationship between marketing planning and corporate planning

It should be apparent from our comments on the ways in which definitions of marketing are changing, and in particular the emergence and acceptance of the societal marketing concept, that marketing decisions are not – or should not – be made in isolation, but with a full understanding of their consequences for a number of different stakeholder groups. At the same time, of course, marketing decisions need both to reflect and influence an organization's corporate decisions. So what then should be the relationship between marketing planning and corporate planning?

In answering this, we need to begin by clarifying what is meant by strategy and strategic decisions. In discussing this, Wilson et al (1992, pages 15–16) suggest that strategic decisions:

- Are concerned with the scope of an organization's activities, and hence with the definition of an organization's boundaries.
- Relate to the matching of the organization's activities with the opportunities of its substantive environment. Since the environment is continually changing it is necessary for this to be accommodated via adaptive decision making that anticipates outcomes – as in playing a game of chess.

- Require the matching of an organization's activities with its resources. In order to take advantage of strategic opportunities it will be necessary to have funds, capacity, and personnel available when required.
- Have major resource implications for organizations – such as acquiring additional capacity, disposing of capacity, or reallocating resources in a fundamental way.
- Are influenced by the values and expectations of those who determine the organization's strategy. Any repositioning of organizational boundaries will be influenced by managerial preferences and conceptions as much as by environmental possibilities.
- Will affect the organization's long-term direction.
- Are complex in nature since they tend to be non-routine and involve a large number of variables. As a result their implications will typically extend throughout the organization.

The Diploma syllabuses and examinations are concerned to a large extent with strategic issues. Far too many candidates confuse strategy and tactics and, as a result, lose marks. Make sure that you understand the difference between the two and that this is reflected in your answers.

The three levels of strategy

Strategic decisions are taken at three levels within an organization:

1 The corporate level.
2 The business unit or divisional level.
3 The functional level.

It follows from this that:

Marketing strategy (is) a process of strategically analysing environmental, competitive and business factors affecting business units and forecasting future trends in business areas of interest to the enterprise. Participating in setting business objectives and formulating corporate and business unit strategy. Selecting target market strategies for; the product-markets in each business unit, establishing marketing objectives, and developing, implementing and managing program positioning strategies for meeting target market needs.

Cravens

Strategic marketing management is the analytical process of seeking differential advantage through (1) The analysis and choice of the firm's product – market relationships with a view toward developing the best yield configuration in terms of financial performance; and (2) the formulation of management strategies that create and support viable product-market relationships consistent with the enterprise capabilities and objectives.

Kerrin and Peterson

Marketing strategy reflects the company's best opinion as to how it can most profitably apply its skills and resources in the marketplace. It is inevitably broad in scope. The plan which stems from it will spell out action and timings and will contain the detailed contribution expected from each department.

Marketing strategies are the means by which marketing objectives will be achieved and are generally concerned with four major elements of the marketing mix, as follows: Product, Price, Place, Promotion.

Formulating marketing strategies is one of the most critical and difficult parts of the entire marketing process. It sets the limit of success. Communicated to all management levels, it indicates what strengths are to be developed, what weaknesses are to be remedied, and in what manner. Marketing strategies enable operating decisions to bring the company the right relationship with the emerging pattern of marketing opportunities which previous analysis has shown to offer the highest prospect of success.

McDonald

The relationship between corporate planning and marketing planning is perhaps most easily understood if you think about them in terms of a hierarchy, with corporate planning and strategy at the top and marketing planning and strategy below this. Marketing decisions are not therefore taken in a vacuum but against the background of a series of guidelines and priorities that are determined by corporate management; this is illustrated in Figure 1.3.

Figure 1.3 The corporate planning and marketing planning hierarchy

The words 'objective', 'strategies' and 'tactics' are often used in a seemingly indiscriminate way. Before we go any further, we need to clarify what the terms really mean:

Objectives represents a statement of what the organization is trying to achieve. The guidelines for setting worthwhile objectives are straightforward and highlight the need for them to be quantifiable, mutually consistent, realistic and related to a specific timescale.

The *strategy* is then the broad statement of the way in which the organization sets out to achieve these objectives. Included within this would be a series of decisions on the markets in which the organization will operate, the type of products/services it will offer and the basis of the competitive stance.

The *tactics* follow on from this and represent the detailed and day-to-day dimensions of the strategic plan.

Influences upon strategy

In developing a strategy, irrespective of whether it is the corporate strategy or a marketing strategy, managers need to take account of a variety of factors, including:

- What is happening in the organization's external environment and how the environment is likely to develop both in the short and the long term.
- What the organization is *really* capable of achieving.
- The expectations of the organization's various stakeholders.

Because the first two points are discussed in some detail in subsequent units (Units 3 and 2 respectively), we will limit ourselves at this stage to a series of comments on the significance of the various stakeholders and how their expectations need to be taken into account and reflected in the marketing planning process.

Stakeholders are groups or individuals who have a stake in, or an expectation of, the organization's performance. They include employees, managers, shareholders, suppliers, customers and the community at large. (Johnson and Scholes, 1993, pages 156–157)

DEFINITION 1.4

The extent to which a stakeholder's expectations need to be taken into account in the marketing planning process depends in part on the planner's understanding of these expectations and his or her perception of the stakeholder's importance. Figure 1.4 illustrates an outline stakeholder map.

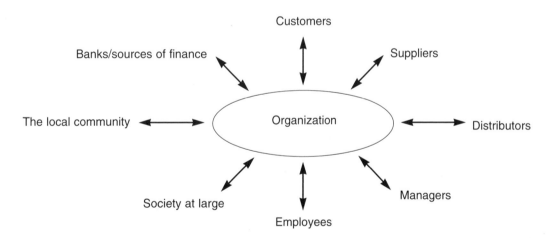

Figure 1.4 A stakeholder map

ACTIVITY 1.3

Using Figure 1.4 as your initial framework, draw a stakeholder diagram for an organization with which you are familiar. In doing this, list the principal expectations of each stakeholder as you perceive them. What scope for conflict exists between these expectations? How, if at all, does the organization currently attempt to manage these conflicts?

The difficulties of adopting a strategic perspective

Although the arguments for a long-term and strategic approach to marketing have an inherent logic, the reality is that in many organizations managers focus either very largely or exclusively upon the short term. There are several possible explanations for this, including the way in which relatively few managers are taught to think or act strategically and are instead measured very largely on the basis of short-term performance. Given this, there is an understandable temptation for managers to focus upon short-term and tactical issues rather than the longer-term strategic management of the marketing function. This temptation then tends to increase dramatically during periods of economic recession and when levels of competitive activity are particularly intense, and is reflected in an emphasis upon issues of *efficiency* rather than *effectiveness*.

Efficiency is concerned with how well an activity is performed, whilst *effectiveness* is concerned rather more with the appropriateness of the action. (See Figure 1.5.)

Strategic Management

		Ineffective	Effective
Operational Management	Inefficient	Decline quickly or die	Survive
	Efficient	Decline slowly or die	Prosper

Adapted from Christopher et al (1987, page 80)

Figure 1.5 Issues of efficiency and effectiveness

Making reference to the matrix in Figure 1.5, look at an organization with which you are familiar and plot its position. Having done this, think about the reasons for the organization being in this particular cell and, given the likely demands of the organization's marketing environment over the next few years, identify the probable consequences.

The relationship between marketing planning and corporate planning has been the focus of several examination questions over the past few years and the answers have tended to highlight the degree of confusion that exists in the minds of many students. Consider therefore the two questions on the next page:

(i) Evaluate the contention that marketing strategy and corporate strategy are one and the same activity (Marketing Planning and Control, December 1991, Question 4).

(ii) The arguments in favour of a strategic perspective to marketing have been well rehearsed, although research suggests that many managers still find the adoption of a strategic perspective to be difficult. Making reference to examples in either the private or the public sectors, comment upon the problems of developing a strategic approach to marketing and how these problems might possibly be overcome (Marketing Planning and Control, June 1991, Question 3).

The role of contingency and scenario planning

Given the nature of our comments so far, it should be apparent that *strategic plans* are concerned essentially with the long term and involve a series of interrelated decisions relating to the nature of the product or service that is to be sold, the market(s) in which the organization intends operating, and the competitive stance that is to be adopted. The *tactical plans* should emerge logically from the strategic plan and relate to how the organization operates on a day-to-day basis and how it responds to short-term environmental changes and pressures. However, almost regardless of how much environmental and corporate analysis underpins the strategic and tactical plans, conditions can change – sometimes dramatically – and demand a very different sort of response from the organization. Because of this, many organizations incorporate a contingency or scenario element into the planning process so that the dangers of responding in what is almost a knee-jerk fashion to the largely unexpected are reduced. The way in which this would be manifested is that, as part of the initial planning process, managers would think not just about the sort of environmental conditions that seem most likely to prevail, but also what else might happen and how the organization might respond. Scenario planning is the more extreme of the two approaches and based on the idea of 'what if ...?' thinking. Examples of this would be what if ...

- Energy prices rose by 30 per cent?
- There was a sudden change of government?
- Political factors led to the sudden closure of a major market?
- A major new competitor entered the market with a highly aggressive price-based strategy (an example of this would be the entry into various retail markets of the so-called 'category busters' who operate on a huge scale and who, by virtue of their enormous buying power and economies of scale, make the survival of all but the most efficient – and effective – competitors unlikely).

Scenario planning is therefore based very deliberately on the idea of thinking about the sorts of unexpected, sudden and dramatic changes which would demand a major response and possibly a significant change of direction on the part of the organization. The rationale for scenario planning is straightforward and based on the idea that, by thinking about the unexpected, deciding what alternatives are open to the organization and then having a plan ready, the likelihood of being stampeded into what might subsequently prove to be an ill-thought out response is reduced dramatically.

Contingency planning is somewhat less extreme than this and is designed for events that may possibly happen but which, on balance, the marketing planner feels probably will not occur. An example of this would be the entry to the domestic market of an organization that is currently operating in a series of international markets and which so far has shown no interest in further expansion. Other examples might be the sudden adoption of a price-based strategy by a competitor or the development by a competitor of a new approach to distribution. Although, as we comment above, the planner believes that these sorts of changes are unlikely, they remain a possibility and so a plan – possibly outline in nature – is developed in order to help cope with the situation if it should arise.

ACTIVITY 1.5

What contingency and/or scenario planning takes place within your own organization? What assumptions are these plans based on? What additional scenarios and contingencies might be incorporated within the process?

In the light of your findings, attempt the following question:

QUESTION 1.2

Explain what is meant by strategic, tactical, scenario and contingency planning.

The planning and control cycle

> To be effective, a strategic planning system must be goal driven. The setting of objectives is therefore a key step in the marketing planning process, since unless it is carried out effectively, everything that follows will lack focus and cohesion. (Wilson et al, 1992, page 137)

Using this quotation as the foundation, we can see that planning is designed to achieve several specific purposes, including:

- It helps to co-ordinate resources and direct them towards the achievement of goals.
- It encourages or forces managers to think about the future and in this way should reduce the likelihood of the organization being taken by surprise by previously unexpected events.
- It provides managers with a sense of direction.
- It provides a subsequent basis for control.

Although planning can never guarantee success, the planning proces – which involves looking in detail both at the environment and the organization's capability, as well as managerial and organizational expectations – should increase the chances of success, since it not only requires managers to identify their goals more explicitly, but also to identify and evaluate the courses of action that might lead to these goals being achieved.

Planning can therefore be seen to involve a series of decisions concerning:

- What are we trying to achieve?
- How might we achieve these objectives?
- Which strategy is the most appropriate?
- Who is to be responsible for it?
- Over what period of time and how is it to be implemented?

An important dimension of the planning process is the element of control. Having decided upon a set of objectives and how these might be achieved, the marketing planner needs to establish a series of control measures to ensure that the execution of the plan does not deviate from what was intended. These controls can be incorporated at various stages within the planning cycle, but are most obviously visible in terms of whether the goals that were set initially are ultimately achieved. However, for many organizations, and particularly those faced with an uncertain environment, this is too late a stage in the process and so a series of intermediate measures would typically be incorporated within the plan. This process of feedback is designed to provide managers with a regular update on performance and to highlight not just the extent to which the organization's performance is deviating from what was intended, but also – and very importantly – why. Given this information, managers can then decide whether corrective action is needed and, if so, what should be done; this is illustrated in Figure 1.6.

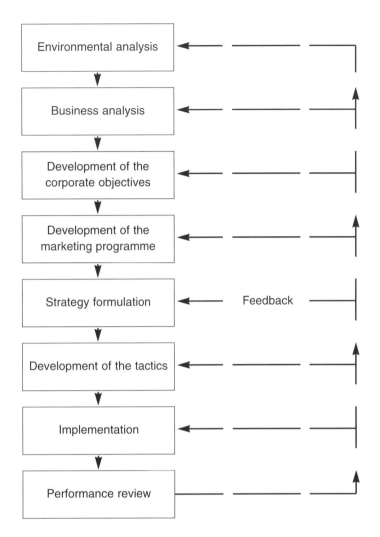

Figure 1.6 The planning and control cycle

If you were to draw the planning and control cycle for your own organization, in what ways would it differ from the cycle in Figure 1.6?

ACTIVITY 1.6

Is planning worthwhile?

Although the idea of planning has an apparent inherent logic, the value of planning as it has typically been conducted has been questioned in recent years. There are several reasons for this, the most obvious of which stems from the problems and difficulties of planning in ever more uncertain and volatile environments. However, in raising this question about the value of planning, we are not arguing for planning to be dispensed with completely, but rather that the traditional model of planning that appears in Figure 1.6 (this is sometimes referred to as the logical, sequential, rational approach) be replaced with a more flexible and open approach. Amongst those to have questioned the traditional planning processes are Stacey and Arthur. In their book *Managing Chaos* (1993), they suggest that anything useful about the long-term future is essentially unknowable and that because of this regular strategic planning meetings serve a ritual rather than a functional purpose. Effective strategies are derived therefore not from traditional approaches to planning, but from the politicking and informal lobbying that is a characteristic of organizational dynamics.

What approach to marketing planning predominates within your own organization? What do you see to be its strong and its weak points? In what ways do you feel it might be improved?

Recognition of the problems associated with traditional approaches to planning has also led to what is referred to as *freewheeling opportunism* in which opportunities are evaluated not within the formal structure of an overall corporate strategy, but are instead evaluated as they emerge and then either dropped or exploited. The benefits of this approach include:

- Opportunities are less likely to be lost as the result of the traditional planning framework.
- It is characterized by a higher degree of flexibility.
- It should lead to a higher degree of creativity amongst managers.

The obstacles to effective planning

The majority of organizations experience problems both in developing and implementing marketing plans. The most obvious causes of these problems include:

- A poor and unfocused environmental analysis that leads to the development of a plan that is based on faulty assumptions of the sort of environment the organization will face.
- An overestimation of the organization's marketing capability.
- Over-ambitious and possibly unattainable marketing objectives.
- Unrealistic timescales.
- Too much or too little detail.
- A set of objectives that are mutually inconsistent.
- An underestimation of the costs involved.
- A failure to recognize the implications of the plan for other parts of the organization and/or for distributors.
- A failure to think through in sufficient detail the issues associated with the plan's implementation.
- An 'ivory tower' syndrome in which the plan is developed by senior marketing management without making use of the knowledge and expertise of others in the marketing department. The result of this is not only that the plan fails to exploit the full spectrum of skills available, but also that others feel no real sense of ownership of or commitment to the plan.
- A failure to take sufficient note of feedback and a lack of willingness to review and modify the plan.

Look at your own organization and identify which of the obstacles to effective planning appears to exist. What are the apparent reasons for this and what appear to be the implications?

Management information systems and marketing information systems

An effective marketing programme is inevitably based on a clear and detailed understanding of the market. Management and marketing information systems are therefore designed to provide this information and are a fundamental part of the 'Where are we now?' element of the planning and control process.

In developing an information system, managers must begin with a view of what information is available currently, what information gaps exist, and what additional information would be of value. It is then against this background that a worthwhile marketing information system can be developed.

Kotler (1991, page 96) defines a marketing information system as a system which 'consists of people, equipment and procedures to gather, sort, analyse, evaluate, and distribute needed, timely, and accurate information to marketing decision makers.'

The structure of the marketing information system

In developing a marketing information system (MIS), McDonald suggests that managers need to go through four stages:

1 Identify all the data and information that are produced currently.
2 Get managers to list the decisions they have to make, together with the information that is essential to the making of these decisions.
3 Combine these two in the most logical manner, since it is likely that there will be information gaps, information duplication and information redundancies.
4 Begin organizing a focused and cost-effective system.

One of the most common problems in developing information systems is that they simply become too complex with the result that the information that is generated is not produced in the form that is really needed or is not passed to the people who need it most. Recognizing this, any information system needs to be evaluated on a regular basis to ensure that it is achieving the results that were hoped.

So what sorts of information do marketing managers need?

Although there is perhaps an understandable temptation to respond to the question by saying 'as much as possible', the reality is that managers face the very real problem of information overload. In developing an information system, considerable thought should therefore be given to the ways any information will be used. In discussing this, Brownlie (1987, pages 100–105) has highlighted the problems that are often associated with information collection and the development of a worthwhile database. All too often, he suggests, the information that organizations collect is:

- Poorly structured.
- Available only on an irregular basis.
- Often provided by unofficial sources.
- Qualitative in nature.
- Ambiguous in its definitions.
- Opinion based.
- Poorly qualified.
- Based on an insecure methodology.
- Likely to change.

Because of these and other problems, managers need to think in detail about their true information needs and then develop the MIS around these. In making this comment, we are not arguing that any information that falls outside these parameters should be ignored, but that if the information that is collected on a regular basis is of the type and in the form that managers feel they need, the likelihood of it being used – and used effectively – are increased.

Aguilar (1967) has suggested that managers' information needs can generally be classified under five headings:

1 *Market tidings* market potential, structural changes, competitor and industry changes, pricing, sales negotiations and customer information.
2 *Acquisition leads* mergers, joint ventures, and acquisitions.
3 *Technical tidings* new products, new processes and technology, product problems, costs, licensing and patents.
4 *Broad issues* general conditions, and government actions and policies.
5 *Other tidings* suppliers and raw materials, resource availability, and miscellaneous information.

Looking at your own organization, what market information is collected currently? How is this information used? Do you feel that it is used as effectively as it might be? What other types of information would be useful?

Developing the information system

It can be seen from Figure 1.7 that a marketing information system has four principal components:

1 *The internal records system* which includes information on orders received, prices, inventory levels, sales patterns, and so on
2 *The marketing intelligence system* which provides regular information on relevant developments in the marketing environment so that managers can monitor trends and more easily identify any unexpected changes.
3 *The marketing research system* which is concerned with the systematic collection and analysis of information that is relevant to specific marketing situations faced by the organization.
4 *The marketing decision support system* which Kotler defines as 'a set of statistical tools and decision models with supporting hardware and software available to marketing managers to assist them in analysing data and making better marketing decisions.' (Kotler, 1991, page 114).

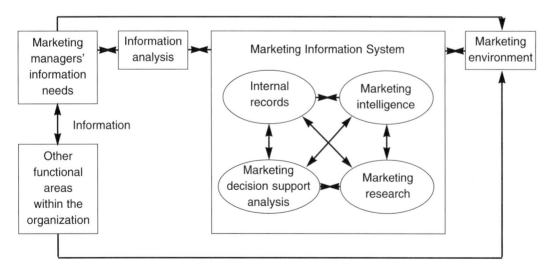

Figure 1.7 The marketing information system

As part of the *marketing intelligence* and *marketing research systems* (points 2 and 3 on page 14), managers will almost invariably need to make use of external as well as internal databases. A database is made up of files of information and data that are structured so that the user can gain access in a variety of different ways, depending upon his or her information needs. In recent years the number of commercial databases has increased enormously to the point at which virtually all product market sectors are now covered.

ACTIVITY 1.10

Go to your local business library and ask about the various databases that are available. In what ways might these databases currently supplement those used by your organization?

The characteristics of good information systems

The test of any information system must be the extent to which it contributes to the decision making process and helps managers to make better, faster and more informed decisions. The information that it contains must therefore be updated regularly, be easily accessible and in a form that managers find user-friendly. It is for this reason that we suggested earlier that in developing an information system the starting point must be a clear and detailed understanding of managers' information needs. Without this it is likely that the system will prove to be both unfocused and unwieldy. The essential ground rules that the designer of an information system needs to work with can therefore be summarized as:

- What do we need to know?
- How will the information be used?
- By whom?
- What is the preferred format?

QUESTION 1.3

Since taking over as the Senior Examiner of the Planning and Control examination in 1991, I have posed several questions on information systems and their various components. These include:

(i) What contribution might a well-structured Marketing Information System make to the successful implementation of a marketing plan?

(June 1993, Question 5)

(ii) It has been suggested that the sales force is a potentially valuable but frequently under-utilized source of marketing information. Given this, explain how a sales force might be used as a structured source of information. What types of information might they be expected to generate?

(December 1993, Question 3)

Marketing information systems were also the focus of the first of the two questions on the mini case study in the June 1994 examination; this case study (Watergate Pumps Ltd), the question and an outline answer appear in Unit 9.

The role and contribution of marketing research to effective planning

Returning for a moment to Figure 1.7 it can be seen that an important element of an MIS is the marketing research system. This is designed to provide information on specific aspects of the marketing process and as such can be seen to include:

- *Product research*   (the identification of product opportunities; customers' perceptions of existing and proposed products; comparative perceptions of competing products; positioning studies; test marketing; and packaging studies).
- *Pricing research*   (perceptions of price and quality; cost analysis; price and demand elasticities; and credit related issues).
- *Promotional research*   (the effectiveness of the various elements of the promotions mix; image studies; copy and media issues; sales effects; salesforce studies; and comparative studies of competitors' promotional techniques).
- *Distribution research*   (distributors' perceptions, attitudes and needs; and distribution alternatives).
- *Market studies*   (short- and long- term market forecasts).
- *Corporate research*   (consumers', competitors' and distributors' perceptions of the organization overall and others in the market).

The market research process

Market research studies can be conducted either by an organization's own specialist staff or by an outside agency. However, irrespective of which approach is used, the market research process is broadly the same; this is illustrated in Figure 1.8.

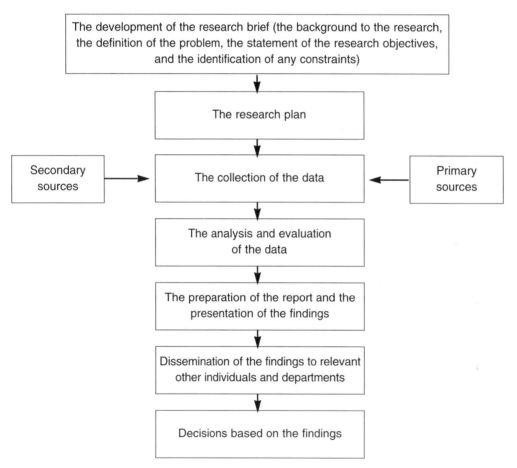

Figure 1.8   The marketing research process

In what ways might market research contribute to the effective development and management of the marketing process?

The use of secondary data

Because secondary data is generally so widely available and often relatively inexpensive, it is the obvious starting point in any data collection exercise. Although there are numerous sources of secondary information, we can identify the principal ones as being:

- Government publications
- Trade associations
- Professional and specialist journals
- Market research agencies
- Commercial publications (e.g. the Mintel and Euromonitor reports)
- Directories and yearbooks
- The national press
- Specialist libraries

There is, of course, often a trade-off involved when using secondary information in that, whilst it is generally available at a low cost, it may not be as up to date or indeed as detailed or as focused as you would like. It is because of this that secondary data often needs to be supported by more specific and focused primary data.

The use of primary data

Primary data can be collected in three main ways; these are illustrated in Figure 1.9.

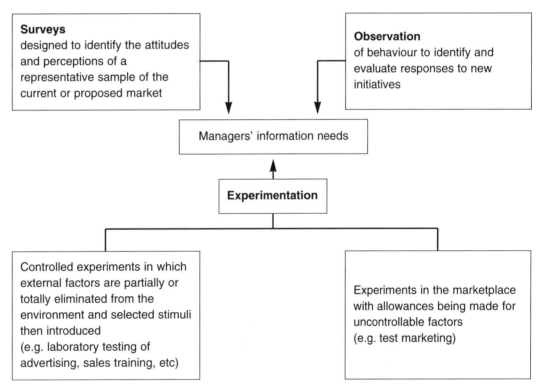

Figure 1.9 Approaches to collecting primary data

Using and choosing a market research agency

Market research can be conducted either by the organization's own specialist staff or by outside agencies. The benefits of using an outside agency are potentially significant and typically include:

- Greater specialist expertise.
- A different perspective upon the problem and, arguably, a greater degree of objectivity.
- Access to a network of other agencies.

There are several criteria that should be used in selecting an agency, the most significant of which are:

- The *type* of agency that is needed. Market research firms range from those that are capable of offering a wide range of services through to those that specialize by sector (e.g. industrial or consumer), type of market (e.g. foodstuffs, cars, drinks) and function (e.g. new product research, distribution research, advertising research). Equally, there are those that concentrate upon qualitative research and those that concentrate upon quantitative research. Others are international in their coverage, whilst some focus just upon the domestic market.
- The agency's size and the relative importance of the account to them.
- Their current and past client portfolio, since this will give an understanding not just of the breadth of their client range, but also the types of research work that they have undertaken in the past.
- Their understanding of the marketing problems faced and their views of the ways in which a programme of research might possibly contribute to their resolution.
- Their reputation.
- The nature of their pitch and the extent to which it appears to reflect an understanding of the organization and its market.
- The costs that are likely to be incurred.

An additional and possibly very important factor which should be taken into account is the *degree of empathy* which exists between the agency and the client, since it is essential that a fruitful and profitable relationship is developed. Other factors to which consideration might possibly be given include any areas of specialist expertise and their financial stability.

QUESTION 1.5

Your marketing director has decided to appoint an agency to carry out the market research work that previously has been conducted in-house. Prepare a short briefing paper identifying the criteria by which agencies pitching for the account should be shortlisted.

Organizational structures, managerial cultures and their influence upon approaches to planning

The way in which an organization develops and implements its plans is inexorably linked to its structure and managerial culture. These two elements are therefore fundamental determinants of organizational efficiency and effectiveness.

In structural terms, an organization consists of two interrelated dimensions:

- The formal structure.
- The informal structure.

The formal structure or formal organization relates to the authority hierarchy, the division of labour and to job specifications. The informal organization, which is sometimes referred to as the oil that makes or allows the wheels to go round, is rather more concerned with the social dimensions and relationships within the business.

The informal organization has been shown on numerous occasions to be a powerful basis both for getting things done and for creating obstacles. Any planning process should therefore recognize not just the formal structures that exist, but also the informal structures so that the two can be harnessed for maximum effect.

Take a diagram of your organization's formal structure and superimpose on this your understanding of some of the informal relationships and organizations that exist. What appears to be the overall effect of the informal organization? Is it generally beneficial or obstructive?

Influences upon the formal structure

Formal structures are influenced by a variety of factors, the most obvious of which are:

- The size of the business.
- The location of its markets.
- The type of staff and their abilities and skills.
- The age of the organization.
- The type of technology that it is dealing with.
- Patterns of managerial thinking (one of the major moves in organizational thinking is the early 1990s was that management hierarchies should be flatter so that patterns of communication would be faster and levels of creativity increased).
- Managerial cultures.

Against this background we can identify the three principal approaches to organization structure; these are illustrated in Figure 1.10.

Organization by:	Advantages	Disadvantages

1 Function	Logical
	Allows for a clear
	  division of work
	  on the basis of
	  specialisms
		Poor communication
		Tends to inhibit
		  creativity
		Limits the
		  development of
		  cross-functional teams

2 Product/brand	Direct accountability
	  for the performance
	  of individual products
	  and brands
	Cross-functional
	  activities can be
	  integrated
	Levels of specialism
	  can be increased
		Costs tend to be
		  higher than for 1
		Levels of complexity
		  increase

3 Territory or
  market sector
	More focused market
	  decision making
	Better local knowledge
	Stronger links and
	  relationships with customers
		Higher overheads
		Possible duplication
		  of effort

Figure 1.10   The advantages and disadvantages of different organizational structures

Given the nature of these comments, it should be apparent that, whilst each of the three approaches has certain advantages, there is no one best method of organization. In an attempt to overcome this, many organizations have developed *matrix structures* which are designed so that staff work in a multi-disciplinary and task-focused way. The claimed advantages of this are that it makes a far better use of the resources from across the organization and encourages a higher degree of flexibility, a stronger and more obvious market focus, better teamwork, higher levels of motivation, and an emphasis upon creativity.

There are, however, disadvantages to a matrix structure, the most common of which are that the pattern of dual authority can lead to conflict; individuals may find it difficult to report to two or more managers; and that the possibly greater ambiguity of roles can create tensions.

The significance of managerial culture

Perhaps the most commonly used and workmanlike definition of management culture is that 'it is the way in which we do things around here'. Although organizational behaviourists are critical of the definition because of the way in which it fails to come to terms with the full richness of culture, it has a certain value because of the way in which it highlights the significance of the organizational philosophy, practice and methods of working.

The culture of an organization is likely to be influenced by a variety of factors, including:

- The attitudes of the chief executive and the senior management team. What, for example, are their priorities? Are they risk averse or risk takers? What are their backgrounds? What are their perceptions of competitors, customers and the workforce?
- The leadership styles that exist.
- The nature of the market and the bases and intensity of competition.
- Previous cultures and work practices.
- Organizational structures and the emphasis given to rigidity or flexibility, the adherence to long-standing practices, perceptions of the importance of work creativity, and so on.
- The type of business and the technologies it is working with.
- Economic factors including expectations of economic trends.
- Past performance levels and the degree of success achieved.

The outcome of this is that several distinct managerial cultures can be identified:

1 *Highly bureaucratic cultures* in which structures and formality predominate, levels of flexibility and responsiveness to the market are low, and creativity and innovation is not encouraged.
2 *Highly entrepreneurial and individualistic cultures* in which the emphasis is upon getting things done, being innovative and moving on to the next task. Outputs are expected to be high and job roles are sketchy.
3 *Task cultures* which again have an emphasis upon getting the job done through the development of multi-functional teams.
4 Cultures in which considerable emphasis is placed upon *personal relationships*.

EXAM TIP

When tackling both the mini case study in the Planning and Control examination and the maxi case study in the Analysis and Decision examination, think about the type of managerial culture that exists and the implications for the marketing process. As an example of this, turn to Unit 9 and read the New Directions Plc case that was used in December 1992. As you will see, the organization had very different managerial styles and cultures during the two time periods that are referred to.

Summary

Within this unit we have attempted to highlight the key elements of the introductory elements to the Planning and Control process and syllabus. As a check on your understanding of these key concepts, consider the following questions:

1 What types of marketing definition can be identified? (See page 2.)
2 What major changes in definition have emerged over the past few years? What are the principal causes of these changes? (See pages 2–4.)
3 Should marketing managers take account of the implications for society of their decisions? If so, why? What are the possible consequences of ignoring these implications? (See page 4.)
4 In what, if any, circumstances might a marketing manager justify making a decision that is legal but unethical or illegal but ethical? Give examples of these sorts of decisions. (See page 4.)
5 What is or should be the relationship between marketing planning and corporate planning. Are they in fact the same activity? (See pages 4–5.)
6 What are the three levels of strategy? (See page 5.)
7 Define 'objectives', 'strategy' and 'tactics'. (See page 5.)
8 What is a stakeholder? How do (or should) stakeholders' expectations influence marketing decisions? (See page 7.)
9 What are the differences between efficiency and effectiveness? How might each be manifested in marketing? (See page 8.)
10 Explain what is meant by scenario planning and contingency planning. What role should each play in the overall marketing planning process? (See pages 9–10.)
11 Draw a model of the planning and control cycle. (See page 11.)
12 Is planning a worthwhile exercise? In what circumstances might it be seen to be a waste of time? (See pages 11–12.)
13 What are the principal obstacles to effective planning? (See page 12.)
14 What is a marketing information system? What contribution to planning should it be capable of making? (See pages 13–14.)
15 Draw a model of an MIS. (See page 14.)
16 What sorts of information do marketing managers need? (See page 14.)
17 What are the characteristics of good information? (See page 15.)
18 What contribution to planning can marketing research make? (See pages 15–16.)
19 In what circumstances would you use:
   (a) secondary data?
   (b) primary data?
   What are the pros and cons of each type? (See page 17.)
20 What criteria would you employ in selecting a market research agency? (See pages 17–18.)
21 What are the principal forms of organizational structure? (See page 19.)
22 What influences:
   (a) formal structures?
   (b) informal structures? (See pages 19–20.)
23 What is meant by managerial culture? Why is it typically seen to be so powerful an influence upon how an organization operates? (See page 20.)

EXTENDING YOUR KNOWLEDGE

Against the background of what has been said in this unit, you should look in detail at the trade and business press with a view to identifying how different organizations interpret the sorts of concepts that we have discussed here and how they operate. In particular, you should look at how effective their marketing appears to be *and why*.

Talk to the senior management within your organization, as well as to friends and contacts in other organizations, and get their views on some of the concepts that have been discussed here. Think about how practices differ between one organization and another (and why) and what you might learn from this.

In terms of further reading, you should turn to:

Wilson and Gilligan with Pearson, (1992), *Strategic Marketing Management: Planning Implementation and Control* – Chapter 1.

Fifield, *Marketing Strategy* – Introduction and Chapters 1 and 2.

Activity debrief

Question 1.1 (i):   Refer to the discussion on pages 4–6.

Question 1.1 (ii):   Refer to the discussion on page 8.

Question 1.2:   Refer to the discussion on pages 9–10.

Question 1.3 (i):   Refer to the discussion on pages 13–15.

Question 1.3 (ii):   The sales force needs to be told what sort of market information is needed and how it will be used. In terms of Figure 1.7 it would be part of the marketing intelligence system. The information that it could most easily collect would include general market movements, emerging opportunities and threats, and customers' and distributors' perceptions of the company's own products, prices and advertising, as well as those of competitors.

Question 1.4:   A clearer understanding of the market, including customers and distributors' perceptions; competitive behaviour, new product opportunities, pricing issues, promotion, short term promotions, and so on. (Refer also to pages 15–17.)

Question 1.5:   Refer to the discussion on pages 17–18.

Assessing corporate capability

This unit focuses upon the nature and sources of an organization's strategic capability and the ways in which meaningful measures of capability can be arrived at. Subsequent units will examine how the measures can be used in the development of an effective, competitive marketing strategy.

In this unit you will:

- Examine the nine step process that managers need to go through in developing an overall picture of an organization's strategic capability.
- Understand the need to examine capability both in an absolute and a relative sense.
- Appreciate how an understanding of strategic capability should underpin the development of marketing strategy.

By the end of the unit you will be able to:

- Undertake an assessment of corporate capability.
- Identify the factors that heighten or inhibit organizational capability.

This unit provides the framework for a section of the syllabus accounting for about 10–15 per cent of the total. Although this might appear to be a relatively small element, particularly when compared with some of the later units, its importance should not be underestimated, since any worthwhile marketing strategy must, of necessity, be based upon a clear and detailed understanding of what the organization is *really* capable of doing and achieving. Because of this, issues relating either directly or indirectly to the various dimensions of capability have been the basis of numerous examination questions in the past.

You should expect to spend about 6 hours working your way through the unit, although some of the activities could take considerably longer, depending upon the degree of co-operation that you are able to call upon. A number of the exercises, for example, require you to relate the material to your own organization and, in order to complete them fully, you will need to talk to people in a variety of functional areas. By the end of the unit you should have obtained a far clearer understanding of the sorts of factors that influence corporate capability and, in the case of your own organization, a greater insight to those elements which heighten or inhibit a manager's ability to achieve marketing objectives.

To help develop and broaden your understanding of the area, you should make a point of reading the quality and trade press with a view to identifying examples of good and bad practice in marketing – and the sorts of factors that contribute to this.

You should also support your study of the area by reading Chapters 2, 3 and 17 of *Strategic Marketing Management: Planning Implementation and Control* by Wilson and Gilligan with Pearson, and Chapter 2 of *Marketing Strategy* by Fifield; both books are published by Butterworth-Heinemann.

The changing thinking on strategy

A considerable amount of thinking in the 1980s on corporate and marketing strategy focused upon the nature and structure of organizational environments and upon the ways in which the environment is – or should be – the principal influence upon strategy formulation. More recently, however, it has been argued that the significance of the environment has been over-emphasized and that a more appropriate focus for strategy formulation would be the organization's resource base. By their very nature, resource-based strategies demand a clear understanding of the organization's strategic capability and it is this which provides the focus for this unit.

'A firm's *capabilities* relate to the distinctive competencies that it has developed to do something well and efficiently. A company is likely to enjoy a differential advantage in an area where its competencies outdo those of its potential competitors.'

Source: Dibb, Simkin, Pride and Ferrell (1994), *Marketing Concepts and Strategies*, (2nd European ed), Houghton Mifflin, page 538.

So what influences capability?

In coming to terms with strategic capability we need to examine the organization at various levels of detail. The starting point for this involves looking at the *broad issues of capability* which apply to the organization as a whole. In discussing this, Johnson and Scholes (1993, pages 115–116) comment that these:

> are largely concerned with the *overall balance* of resources and mix of activities. There are also assessments to be made of the quantity and quality of each *key resource area*, such as buildings, machines and people.

They go on to suggest that capability is 'fundamentally determined by the separate activities which it undertakes in designing, producing, marketing, delivering and supporting its products or services. It is an understanding of these various *value activities* and the *linkages* between them which is crucial when assessing strategic capability.'

It needs to be recognized, however, that in talking about capability we are not necessarily focusing only upon levels of *absolute* capability, but are instead, in many cases, rather more concerned with levels of *relative* capability. In other words, what do we do that is better (or worse) than our competitors? Equally, capability is not simply a function of an organization's internal resource base and how well or badly this is managed, but also of the way in which the organization interacts with the various parts of the chain that links it to its customers.

Looking at the industry or a market sector in which a part of your own organization operates, which competitors appear to be the most successful? What sorts of factors do you feel contribute to this? What dimensions of capability appear to be the most important?

There are therefore a number of elements which need to be examined when attempting to arrive at any realistic and worthwhile measure of corporate capability. These are illustrated in Figure 2.1 and include:

1   The nature and the quality of the internal and external resources that are available to the organization; these are most typically measured by means of a *resource audit*.

2   The *value chain* which is designed to highlight how the organization's resources are being used, controlled and linked together.

3   The way in which *resources are utilized.*

4   *Financial measures.*

5   *Comparative measures*, some of which may be *historical* (how has the organization's performance changed over time?), whilst others involve looking at *industry norms* (benchmarking) or *best practices* both within and outside the industry.

6   *Measures of balance* to ensure that the organization is not overly dependent upon particular geographic areas, parts of the product range, particular staff, particular processes, or specific customers.

7   The *performance-importance* grid.

8   A review of *marketing effectiveness.*

9   The identification of key issues in the form of a detailed *SWOT analysis* which summarizes the strategic insights gained from Stages 1–8.

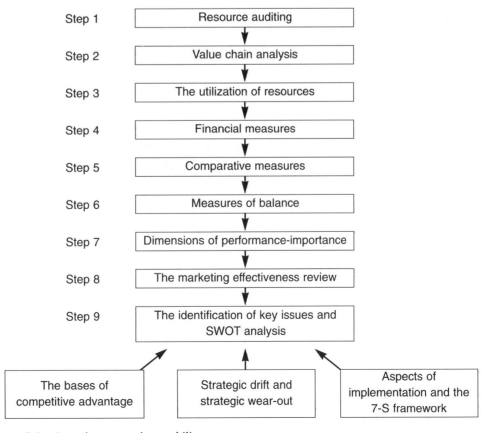

Figure 2.1   Assessing strategic capability

Many candidates, particularly in the mini and maxi case studies, make the mistake of making suggestions for action that would be far beyond the resource scope of the organization. In making suggestions, therefore, always think about issues of capability *and be realistic.*

Step one: the resource audit

The resource audit concentrates upon identifying and assessing the nature and strength of the internal and external resources that are available to the organization. These include:

- *Physical resources* such as the manufacturing capacity, the levels of production capability, retail outlets, and so on.
- *Human resources* including the appropriateness and mix of skills.
- *Financial resources* including the organization's capital base, its debtor/creditor ratio, and the sorts of relationships that it has with its shareholders and bankers.
- *Intangible resources* such as the image and reputation of the organization and the strength of its various brands.

In conducting the resource audit, several guidelines need to be borne in mind, one of the most significant of which is that resources and the resource base should be defined not just in terms of those that the organization owns in a legal sense, but also those to which the organization has access. Included within this will be distribution networks, political contacts, and individuals and organizations with which (strategically useful) relationships have been developed over the years.

ACTIVITY 2.2

Try conducting a straightforward resource audit for your organization. Identify clearly the sorts of information that you would need if the exercise was to be done in detail, where this might come from and the sorts of problems that might be encountered in its collection.

Step two: the value chain

Having conducted the initial resource audit, you need to think about the ways in which these resources relate to the organization's performance. In other words, *how* are these resources used as a means of gaining and maintaining a competitive advantage? One of the ways in which this can be done is by means of the value chain.

Although value analysis has its origins in accountancy and was designed to identify the profitability of each stage in a manufacturing process, a considerable amount of work has been done in recent years in developing the concept and applying it to measures of competitive advantage. Much of this work has been conducted by Michael Porter who suggests that an organization's activities can be categorized in terms of whether they are *primary activities* or *support activities*; this is illustrated in Figure 2.2.

The five primary activities that he identifies are:

1 *Inbound logistics* which are the activities that are concerned with the reception, storing and internal distribution of the raw materials or components for assembly.
2 *Operations* which turn these into the final product.
3 *Outbound logistics* which distribute the product or service to customers. In the case of a manufacturing operation, this would include warehousing, materials handling and transportation. For a service this would involve the way in which customers are brought to the location in which the service is to be delivered.

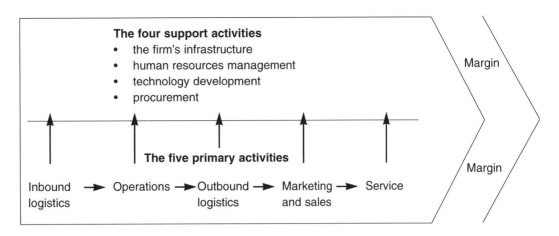

The four support activities
- the firm's infrastructure
- human resources management
- technology development
- procurement

The five primary activities

Inbound logistics → Operations → Outbound logistics → Marketing and sales → Service

Margin

Margin

Figure 2.2 The value chain. (Adapted from M. E. Porter (1985), *Competitive Advantage*, Free Press)

4 *Marketing and sales* which make sure the customers are aware of the product or service and are able to buy it.
5 *Service* activities which include installation, repair and training.

Each of these primary activities is, in turn, linked to the support activities which are grouped under four headings:

1 The *procurement* of the various resource inputs.
2 *Technology development,* including research and development, process improvements and raw material improvements.
3 *Human resource management* including the recruitment, training, development and rewarding of staff.
4 *The firm's infrastructure* and the approach to organization including the systems, structures, managerial cultures and ways of doing business.

Porter suggests that competitive advantage is determined to a very large extent by how each of these elements is managed and the nature of the interactions between them. In the case of inbound logistics, for example, many organizations have developed just-in-time systems in order to avoid or minimize their stockholding costs. In this way, the value of the activity is increased and the firm's competitive advantage improved. Equally, in the case of operations, manufacturers are paying increasing attention to lean manufacturing processes as a means of improving levels of efficiency. Porter's message is therefore straightforward. Managers, he suggests, need to examine the nature and dimensions of each of the nine activities with a view to identifying how the value added component can best be increased.

Carry out a straightforward value chain analysis of your own organization and try to identify how each of the four primary and five secondary activities might be managed differently in order to create competitive advantage.

ACTIVITY 2.3

He goes on to argue that value chain analysis should not simply stop with the manager's own organization, but in the case of a manufacturer should also include the suppliers and distribution networks, since the value of much of what an organization does will be influenced both by its *suppliers,* how they operate and the quality of their output, and the *distribution network* and how it interacts with the customer base, since this can either add or detract in a major way from the organization's marketing effort.

27

Step three: the utilization of resources

STUDY TIP

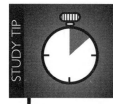

Refer back to page 8 of Unit 1 in order to refresh your memory of precisely what efficiency and effectiveness are and the sorts of factors that contribute to these.

Because of the much higher levels of competition that the majority of organizations now face, the search for ever higher levels of efficiency and effectiveness is something that preoccupies many managers. In many cases this has led to a fundamental questioning of exactly how organizational resources are used and whether changes might possibly lead to competitive advantage. At its most extreme, this search can be seen to have been manifested in business process re-engineering in which possibly radical changes are made to the way in which the organization operates. However, as an intermediate step, managers need to ask – and answer – a series of questions, including:

1   How are resources allocated currently?
2   To what extent does each stage of the value chain process actually add value?
3   In what ways might these value added elements be increased?
4   What are the critical success factors in each of the organization's market sectors?
5   How do *customers* perceive value and what are the implications for how the organization operates?
6   Which elements of the marketing programme sustain any competitive advantage(s) that the organization has?
7   In what areas is the organization operating sub-optimally? Are the stock levels too high, for example? Would it be better to sub-contract the distribution function? Is the organization working sufficiently closely with the distribution intermediaries? Is there scope for re-assessing the advertising effort?
8   What scope exists for collaborating with other organizations in order to improve levels of efficiency and effectiveness?

ACTIVITY 2.4

Take the eight questions listed above and discuss them with a senior manager within your organization.

This search for greater efficiency and effectiveness can also be seen in terms of the need to focus on a regular basis upon a variety of other factors including:

• Supply costs.
• Economies of scale in marketing and distribution, as well as manufacturing.
• Levels of productivity.

These three elements are, of course, measures of *efficiency* and are therefore capable of providing only a partial insight into the organization. To broaden this picture, we need also to focus upon issues of *effectiveness*, since it is these which illustrate the *appropriateness* of what the organization is doing. At the heart of any measure of effectiveness is the degree of fit that exists between what the organization is offering and what the customer wants. The sorts of questions that therefore need to be asked include:

1   Is the product/service that is offered what the customer *really* wants?
2   Do the support services meet customers' expectations?
3   Are any unique features and added value elements that are offered actually seen by customers to be important?
4   Do the pre- and post-sales services that are offered add value that is then reflected in the prices that are charged?

Take one part of your organization and, by speaking to the managers responsible for this area, identify the sorts of factors that contribute to the levels both of efficiency and effectiveness. How do these appear to compare with those of your direct competitors? What are the competitive consequences of any levels of efficiency and effectiveness that are lower than those of your competitors? What would be needed in order to improve these levels?

Step four: financial measures

The link between an organization's financial standing and its strategic capability is a strong one, since it is the availability of financial resources that is one of the principal determinants of a manager's freedom of action. But although it is typically the case that organizations generate considerable amounts of financial information, much of this is largely operational in nature and tends not necessarily to be viewed in strategic terms. If, however, a manager's assessment of strategic capability is to be at all meaningful, it is essential that the sort of strengths and weaknesses analysis that we discuss at a later stage in this unit reflects a strong strategic perspective.

Although there are a variety of financial measures that can be used to assess financial performance and financial standing, it is relatively easy to identify the financial expectations of the four principal groups of stakeholders:

1   *The banks* are most concerned with issues of risk and therefore focus upon the organization's capital structure, and especially the gearing ratio (that is, the ratio of debt to equity) since this is a measure of solvency.
2   *Suppliers and employees* are typically concerned with liquidity, since this determines whether short-term financial commitments such as invoices and wages can be paid.
3   *Management* tends to concentrate upon those measures which allow them to measure performance not just against the expectations of the shareholders, but also in relation to similar organizations (are we doing better or worse than our competitors?) and over time (are we doing better or worse than, say, twelve and twenty-four months ago?).
4   *Shareholders* who concentrate upon the wisdom of their investment and whether the capital growth and/or income is increasing.

Given these comments, we can identify a series of financial measures that can be used to build a picture of performance. Included within these are:

1   Profit margins: the ratio of profit to sales.
2   Asset turnover: the ratio of sales to the capital employed.

3   The return on capital employed (ROCE): the profit as a percentage of the capital employed (this is sometimes referred to as the primary ratio).
4   Earnings per share.
5   Gearing: the ratio of debt to equity.
6   Stock turnover: the time between raw materials being purchased and used.
7   The debt collection period: the time taken for customers to pay after a sale.
8   The creditor collection period: the time between taking delivery of materials and paying the supplier.
9   The current ratio or working capital ratio: the difference between current assets and current liabilities.
10 The quick ratio or liquidity ratio: the difference between current assets less stock and current liabilities.

Numbers 6–8 are often referred to as *operational ratios*, since they refer to the way in which cash is managed on a short-term basis. Numbers 9 and 10 are *liquidity ratios* and refer to the organization's ability to turn assets into cash in order to meet all of its possible payment demands.

Although this is by no means an exhaustive list of the dimensions that can be taken into account in a financial analysis (indeed, we have deliberately ignored issues such as advertising ratios, share price, sales margins, and so on), it illustrates the sorts of factors that provide a measure of capability.

ACTIVITY 2.6

What are the key financial measures within your own organization?

QUESTION 2.2

What use can be made of ratios in monitoring the implementation of marketing plans?

(Marketing Planning and Control, June 1991, Question 10.)

Step five: comparative analysis

We made the comment at an earlier stage that, in many cases, measures of strategic capability are best looked at in *relative* rather than *absolute* terms. In other words, what is it that the organization is better or worse at than its competitors *in the eyes of the customers*? This can be answered in several ways including:

- Historical analysis in which comparisons are made with the organization's performance in previous years. By doing this, the nature and significance of any changes across a variety of measures of performance, such as the absolute level of sales, the rate of sales growth (or decline), the mix of sales, geographic coverage and financial ratios can be assessed.
- Comparisons with industry norms.
- The analysis of best practice by means of competitor profiling and benchmarking.

Although a *comparison with industry norms* is capable of providing a useful insight into the relative performance of the organization, the results need to be treated with a degree of caution. It may be the case, for example, that whilst it appears that the organization is performing well against its direct competitors in terms of, for example, sales, R&D spend, cost levels and so on, little or no account is being taken of other organizations which may be capable either currently or in the future of satisfying the same need. Equally, the comparison may fail to take account of the industry norms of similar companies in other countries.

For this reason, comparative analysis should also take account of both *competitors' profiles* and *benchmarks* as a means of gaining a greater understanding of *best practice*.

Competitor profiling, which is discussed in greater detail in Unit 3, involves building a detailed picture of each competitor with a view to understanding the depth and breadth of their strategic capability. In doing this, attention needs to be paid to their resource base, what they are good at, what they are bad at, what their priorities are, the level of commitment that they have to each market and their managerial cultures. Included within this is the analysis of their *marketing assets*.

'*Marketing assets* highlight the capabilities that managers and the marketplace view as beneficially strong. These capabilities can then be stressed to the company's advantage. Customer-based assets include brand image and reputation; distribution-based assets may involve density of dealers and geographic coverage; internal-marketing assets include skills, experience, economies of scale, technology and resources.'

(Source: Dibb, Simkin, Pride and Ferrell (1994) *Marketing: Concepts and Strategies* (2nd European ed), Houghton Mufflin, pages 538–539.)

DEFINITION 2.2

The second dimension of best practice analysis involves *benchmarking* and the development of key performance targets for those activities which are seen to be crucial to success.

Benchmarking is an analytical process through which an enterprise's performance can be compared with that of its competitors. It is used to:

- Identify key performance measures for each business function
- Measure one's own performance as well as that of competitors
- Identify areas of competitive advantage (and disadvantage) by comparing performance levels
- Design and implement plans to improve one's own performance on key issues relative to competitors'

(Source: Wilson and Gilligan with Pearson (1992) *Strategic Marketing Management: Planning, Implementation and Control*, Butterworth-Heinemann, page 610.)

DEFINITION 2.3

Although there are several ways of establishing benchmarks, the most common involves identifying the levels at which market leaders are operating and then attempting to achieve or improve upon these.

Although the idea of benchmarking has an apparent inherent logic, it has been subject to a certain amount of criticism in recent years. There are several reasons for this, although perhaps the most meaningful is that benchmarking is typically limited to the 'hard' factors of management; an example of this would be the productivity or wastage levels being achieved by a competitor. What is arguably more important in measuring yourself against competitors are the 'soft' factors and, in particular, the managerial cultures and levels of expertise that competitors possess, since it is these which ultimately determine how they behave and the levels of long-term performance that are likely to be achieved. Equally, much benchmarking can be criticized for the way in which comparisons are drawn between organizations within the industry rather than with *best practice* in similar, and also possibly very different, industry sectors. As an example of this, it is a relatively easy but ultimately limited exercise to benchmark and draw comparisons between the catering functions of different hospitals. What might be a more useful (additional) exercise, would be to benchmark against different types of hotel or other catering suppliers.

Step six: issues of organizational balance

Having focused upon the individual elements of the organization and its resource base, attention needs then to shift to issues of organizational balance and the extent to which specific aspects of the resource base complement each other. In doing this, thought needs to be given to issues of flexibility and adaptability; the balance of skills that exists; and the extent to which the elements of the product/service portfolio are complementary.

In assessing *flexibility and adaptability*, the marketing planner is attempting to arrive at a measure of the organization's ability to cope with any changes that take place in the organization's environment. The most obvious – and straightforward – way of doing this simply involves listing those changes which can be foreseen, determining the organization's ability to cope with each of these, and then assessing the significance of any gaps that exist.

As part of this, thought needs also to be given to the demands that the environment is placing currently and will place in the future upon *managerial and workforce skills*. Is it the case, for example, that the sorts of individual and team skills that are increasingly being demanded by the environment actually exist within the organization to the depth and breadth that is needed?

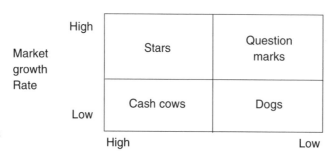

What degree of flexibility and adaptability appears to exist within your own organization? What sorts of factors do you feel contribute to this? What would be needed for higher levels of flexibility and adaptability to emerge? How important do you think that these two dimensions will become in future years?

The third dimension of balance relates to the extent to which the various parts of the *product portfolio* balance each other. Although a variety of frameworks for portfolio analysis have been developed (these are discussed in greater detail in Unit 5), probably the most useful at this stage is the Boston Consulting Group's growth-share matrix. The matrix involves plotting the organization's portfolio of strategic business units (SBUs) against two dimensions: the market's annual growth rate and the SBUs' relative competitive position; the matrix is illustrated in Figure 2.3.

	High		
Market growth Rate		Stars	Question marks
	Low	Cash cows	Dogs
		High	Low
		Relative competition position	

Figure 2.3 The Boston Consulting Group's growth-share matrix

The thinking that underpins the matrix is straightforward and based on the idea that SBUs should not be looked at in isolation but as parts of an interdependent portfolio. Thus, the cash generated by the cash cows should be used to fund the growth, and possibly the strengthening of the competitive position, of the stars, the question marks and, in certain circumstances, the dogs. In doing this, the marketing planner is aiming for an optimal balance between the nature, shape and health of today's portfolio and the nature, shape and health of tomorrow's portfolio.

QUESTION 2.3

You will undoubtedly have come across models of portfolio analysis such as the Boston Consulting Group's growth-share matrix in the past. Given this, what sorts of factors contribute to a healthy and an unhealthy portfolio?

Step seven: the performance–importance grid

Given the nature of our comments so far, it should be apparent that, although within this part of the workbook we are concerned principally with issues of *marketing* capability, only rarely can we look at elements of marketing capability in isolation. The reason for this is of course that, almost invariably, marketing issues – particularly at the strategic level – interact with a whole series of other elements within the organization and it is the interplay of these that influences or determines the organization's levels of capability. Because of this, any assessment of corporate capability needs to take account of at least four principal dimensions:

- Marketing specific factors.
- Financial elements.
- Manufacturing issues.
- Organizational factors such as managerial culture, organizational structures and staff capabilities.

These four areas can be brought together in one of a number of ways although one of the most useful tools for this is the performance–importance grid; an example of this appears in Figure 2.4. To use the grid you begin by giving a rating to your organization's performance ranging from a fundamental strength to a fundamental weakness for each of the forty-two dimensions running down the left-hand side of the grid. Having done this, you then give thought to the significance or importance of each of these elements. In the case of market share, for example, just how important or necessary is the possession of a high share in your industry? Equally, how important are product quality and the after-sales service? Having identified the importance of each of the elements you should have a far clearer *first* picture of capability. You can then expand upon this by going through the same exercise for each of your principal competitors. Having done this, you end up with a comparative picture which not only illustrates areas of absolute and relative strengths and weakness, but which also highlights those areas to which the greatest attention needs to be paid.

ACTIVITY 2.8

Using Figure 2.4, carry out a performance–importance analysis for your organization and its two principal competitors. Having done this, identify the areas of significant strength and weakness and consider the implications for marketing strategy.

	Performance					Importance		
Strengths	*Major strength*	*Minor strength*	*Neutral*	*Minor weakness*	*Major weakness*	*High*	*Medium*	*Low*
Marketing factors								
1 Market share	—	—	—	—	—	—	—	—
2 Image and reputation	—	—	—	—	—	—	—	—
3 Previous performance	—	—	—	—	—	—	—	—
4 Competitive stance	—	—	—	—	—	—	—	—
5 Customer base	—	—	—	—	—	—	—	—
6 Depth of customer loyalty	—	—	—	—	—	—	—	—
7 Breadth of product range	—	—	—	—	—	—	—	—
8 Depth of product range	—	—	—	—	—	—	—	—
9 Product quality	—	—	—	—	—	—	—	—
10 Programme of product modification	—	—	—	—	—	—	—	—
11 New product programme	—	—	—	—	—	—	—	—
12 Distribution costs	—	—	—	—	—	—	—	—
13 Size of dealer network	—	—	—	—	—	—	—	—
14 Dealer loyalty	—	—	—	—	—	—	—	—
15 Dealers' geographical coverage	—	—	—	—	—	—	—	—
16 Sales force, size and expertise	—	—	—	—	—	—	—	—
17 After sales service	—	—	—	—	—	—	—	—
18 Manufacturing costs	—	—	—	—	—	—	—	—
19 Manufacturing flexibility	—	—	—	—	—	—	—	—
20 Raw material advantages	—	—	—	—	—	—	—	—
21 Pricing	—	—	—	—	—	—	—	—
22 Advertising	—	—	—	—	—	—	—	—
23 Unique selling propositions	—	—	—	—	—	—	—	—
24 Structure and intensity of competition	—	—	—	—	—	—	—	—
Financial factors								
25 Cost of capital	—	—	—	—	—	—	—	—
26 Availability of capital	—	—	—	—	—	—	—	—
27 Profitability	—	—	—	—	—	—	—	—
28 Financial stability	—	—	—	—	—	—	—	—
29 Margins	—	—	—	—	—	—	—	—
Manufacturing factors								
30 Production facilities	—	—	—	—	—	—	—	—
31 Economies of scale	—	—	—	—	—	—	—	—
32 Flexibility	—	—	—	—	—	—	—	—
33 Workforce	—	—	—	—	—	—	—	—
34 Technical skill	—	—	—	—	—	—	—	—
35 Delivery capabilities	—	—	—	—	—	—	—	—
36 Supplier sourcing flexibility	—	—	—	—	—	—	—	—
Organizational factors								
37 Culture	—	—	—	—	—	—	—	—
38 Leadership	—	—	—	—	—	—	—	—
39 Managerial capabilities	—	—	—	—	—	—	—	—
40 Workforce	—	—	—	—	—	—	—	—
41 Flexibility	—	—	—	—	—	—	—	—
42 Adaptability	—	—	—	—	—	—	—	—

Figure 2.4 The performance–importance grid. (Source: adapted from Kotler, 1988, page 53)

The analysis can also be helped by identifying where in the matrix that is illustrated in Figure 2.5 each of the dimensions that is highlighted in Figure 2.4 lies. Those which fall into Cell 1 are, of course, the areas of highest priority, whilst those in Cell 4 are the areas to which perhaps too much (unnecessary) attention has been paid in the past.

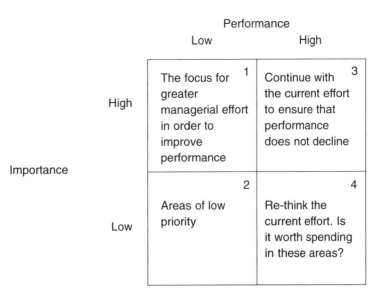

Figure 2.5   The performance–importance matrix

The table shown in the figure:

| | Performance | |
	Low	High
High Importance	1. The focus for greater managerial effort in order to improve performance	3. Continue with the current effort to ensure that performance does not decline
Low	2. Areas of low priority	4. Re-think the current effort. Is it worth spending in these areas?

Step eight: reviewing marketing effectiveness

Another way of assessing capability involves reviewing the organization's marketing effectiveness. Although there are several ways in which this can be done, including analysing sales and profit performance; market share levels and movements; levels of absolute and relative customer satisfaction; and new products success rates, the marketing effectiveness review (MER) typically concentrates upon arriving at a measure of the organization's performance or standing under five main headings:

1   The extent to which management practice reflects a customer-oriented philosophy.
2   Whether there is an integrated marketing organization.
3   The adequacy of the marketing information that exists.
4   The firm's strategic orientation.
5   The levels of operational efficiency.

A detailed framework for reviewing marketing effectiveness appears on pages 30–32 of *Strategic Marketing Management* and you might usefully refer to this. However, in the absence of this, identify the sorts of questions that would help you to gain an insight into each of the five dimensions of marketing effectiveness that are referred to above.

ACTIVITY 2.9

Step nine: the identification of key issues by means of SWOT analysis

Although SWOT analysis is a particularly well-known and a frequently used management tool, evidence suggest that far too many managers carry out SWOT analyses which are generally too bland to be of real value. There are several reasons for this, the most common of which is that managers simply list strengths and weaknesses and then the opportunities and threats without paying any or sufficient attention to their real significance. The result is what is sometimes called 'a balance sheet approach,' with managers taking comfort from the way in which the organization's strengths seemingly outweigh the weaknesses, but failing to recognize that one or more of the weaknesses may well cancel out all or most of the strengths; an example of this would be an impending cash flow crisis which undermines any strengths and limits managerial action.

The second major failing of many analyses of strengths and weaknesses is that they are carried out internally without sufficient attention being paid to market perceptions. In assessing an organization's strengths and weaknesses, detailed attention *must* be paid to the organization's strengths and weaknesses *as perceived by customers and competitors*. To illustrate this Nigel Piercy (1991, page 261) makes reference to two of the most commonly identified strengths:

- We are an old established firm.
- We are a large supplier.

Whilst it may well be the case that the organization is large and long established, these may not necessarily be seen as strengths in the marketplace. Instead, Piercy suggests, they may be seen by customers as indicators of an organization that is inflexible, old fashioned, lacking in innovation and overly bureaucratic. The lesson therefore is always to look at the strengths and weaknesses from the market's point of view.

A third failing of many SWOTs is that they are not sufficiently focused, the obvious consequence of which is that they end up as bland generalizations. Recognizing this, any SWOT analysis needs to be based on a clear and detailed definition of the area that is being evaluated. This can be done by focusing upon specific:

- Products and markets.
- Customer segments within a given market.
- Distribution systems for particular customer groups.
- Promotional activities within specific market sectors that are targeted at different customer groups and decision-making units.
- Pricing policies in specific markets.
- Product policies in given markets.
- Named competitors or groups of competitors.

The fourth limitation of many SWOT analyses is that, having conducted the exercise, managers do not then go on to examine in sufficient detail the implications of the analysis for future strategies. To help with this, Figure 2.6 illustrates the ways in which action should be taken to convert weaknesses into strengths, threats into opportunities, and how strengths are only meaningful when used to capitalize upon opportunities.

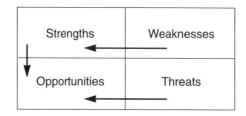

Figure 2.6   The SWOT framework

ACTIVITY 2.10

Conduct a *detailed* SWOT analysis for one of your organization's products or services. What implications for future strategy emerge from the analysis?

Against the background of these comments it should be apparent that SWOT analysis is not necessarily quite as straightforward as it often appears or indeed is often made out to be. Before going on to conduct a SWOT, there are several points that might usefully be borne in mind, including in the case of any opportunities and threats that are identified that:

they can never be viewed as 'absolutes'. What might appear at first sight to be an opportunity may not be so when examined against the organization's resources, its culture, the expectations of its stakeholders, the strategies available, or the feasibility of implementing the strategy. At the risk of oversimplification, however, the purpose of strategy formulation is to develop a strategy which will take advantage of the opportunities and overcome or circumvent the threats.

(Johnson and Scholes, 1988, page 77.)

Turn to Unit 9 of the Workbook and read the New Directions case study.

This case, which focuses upon a retail organization, was used as the mini case study for the Marketing Planning and Control examination in December 1992 and required candidates to conduct two SWOT analyses – one for the period before a takeover and one for the period following the takeover – as a prelude to examining the implications for planning and control. Using the knowledge that you have gained from the unit so far, conduct the SWOT analyses and then compare the results with the outline answer that appears on page 186.

ACTIVITY 2.11

(i) What practical contribution is SWOT analysis capable of making to the marketing planning and control processes? (Marketing Planning and Control, June 1993, Question 10.)
(ii) What problems might be encountered in carrying out a worthwhile SWOT analysis?

QUESTION 2.4

Strategic capability and the bases of competitive advantage

A considerable amount of marketing thinking is based on the identification, pursuit and exploitation of competitive advantage. A competitive advantage can be gained in a variety of ways, although the three principal categories of advantage can be seen to be:

1 Organizationally-related advantages (e.g. economies of scale, issues of flexibility, size, financial strengths, image, reputation and managerial cultures).
2 Departmental and functional advantages (e.g. strengths in marketing, R&D, production and personnel).
3 Advantages that are based on relationships with external bodies (e.g. customers, distributors, politicians, competitors and suppliers).

These are illustrated in Figure 2.7.

In assessing and coming to terms with an organization's strategic capability, you should therefore take each of these in turn with a view to identifying, firstly, its significance within a particular market and then, secondly, the extent to which the advantage either exists currently or might possibly be developed in the future.

Strategic drift and strategic wear-out

We have made the comment at several stages that, for a variety of reasons, corporate capability should be viewed in relative rather than absolute terms. By the same token, managers need to recognize that a high level of strategic capability often proves to be a transitory phenomenon. There are two inter-related reasons for this: the first is illustrated by the notion of *strategic drift*, the second being *strategic wear-out*.

The idea of strategic drift is straightforward and is a reflection of the way in which as the environment changes, so strategies need to be modified to take account of the newly emerging

The sources of a sustainable competitive advantage can be categorized as:

1 Organizational advantages

- Economies of scope and scale.
- Levels of flexibility.
- The appropriateness and proactivity of competitive stance.
- The size and power of the organization.
- The ability to identify and exploit opportunities.
- Past performance and size of the resource base.
- Financial strengths.
- Patterns of ownership and influence.
- Image and reputation.
- Managerial cultures.

2 Departmental and functional advantages

Marketing
- The size and loyalty of the customer base.
- Detailed knowledge of customers.
- New product skills.
- Pricing strategies.
- Communication and advertising.
- Distribution strategies.
- Sales force.
- Services support.
- Reputation.
- Detailed knowledge of competitors.

Research and Development
- Product technology.
- Patents.

Production
- Technology.
- Process efficiency.
- Economies of scale.
- Experience.
- Product quality.
- Manufacturing flexibility.

Personnel
- Management-worker relations.
- Workforce flexibility.

3 Advantages based on relationships with external bodies

- Customer loyalty.
- Channel control.
- Preferential political and legislative treatment.
- Government assistance.
- Beneficial tariff and non-tariff trade barriers.
- Cartels.
- Intra-organizational relationships.
- Access to preferential and flexible financial resources.

Figure 2.7   Competitive advantage.
(Adapted from Wilson and Gilligan with Pearson, 1992, *Strategic Marketing Management: Planning, Implementation and Control,* Butterworth-Heinemann, page 34.)

opportunities and threats. All too often, however, strategic reviews take place too infrequently or too superficially and the growing gap between what the market wants and what the organization is offering only then becomes apparent at a late stage (see Figure 2.8).

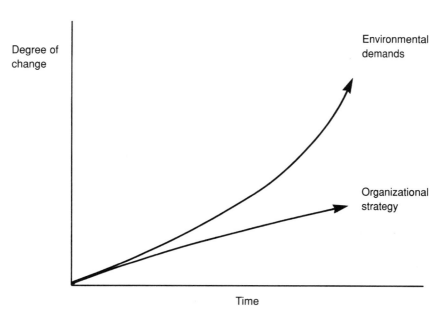

Figure 2.8   Strategic drift

These problems are then compounded by the *wear-out* or tiredness that almost inevitably eventually affects how an organization operates. In commenting on this Wilson et al (1992, page 271) suggest:

> The need for change often becomes apparent only at a later stage when the gap between what the company is doing and what it should be doing increases to a point at which performance and prospects begin to suffer in an obvious way. It is by this stage that an observant and astute competitor will have taken advantage of the company's increased vulnerability. The argument in favour of regular environmental and strategic reviews is therefore unassailable. Specifically, the sorts of factors which contribute to strategic wear-out include:

- Changes in market structure as competitors enter or exit.
- Changes in competitors' stances.
- Competitive innovations.
- Changes in consumers' expectations.
- Economic changes.
- Legislative changes.
- Technological changes; these include in some instances, the emergence of a new technology which at first sight is unrelated or only indirectly related to the company's existing sphere of operations.
- Distribution changes.
- Supplier changes.
- A lack of internal investment.
- Poor control of company costs.
- A tired and uncertain managerial philosophy.

Take three separate industries or market sectors and identify examples – and the consequences – of strategic wear-out. To what extent do you think that this wear-out might have been avoided?

Evidence suggests that many marketing programmes continue to be pursued long after their effectiveness has diminished. Explain why this is so and suggest how the strategic and tactical wear-out of a marketing programme might possibly be identified and avoided. (Strategic Marketing Management: Planning and Control, December 1994, Question 4.)

Corporate capability and issues of implementation

One of the biggest and most frequently recurring problems faced by managers is not that of planning but rather that of implementation. All too often, plans that seemed in the early stages to promise a great deal prove to be disappointing in that they fail to deliver what was hoped for. In many cases this is due to too little attention having been paid to the implementation phase, with the cost, time or resource implications having been underestimated. It is because of this that the issue of exactly *how* an organization implements its plans can be a major influence upon corporate capability. With this in mind, we can categorize the dimensions of planning and implementation in terms of a simple matrix; this is illustrated in Figure 2.9.

Marketing Planning

		Bad (inappropriate)	Good (appropriate)
Marketing Implementation	Bad (ineffective)	1 **Failure** The marketing programme fails to exploit environmental opportunities and build upon the resource base	2 **Trouble** The answer lies in focusing upon issues of implementation
	Good (effective)	3 **Trouble** The plan is flawed and any attempt at implementation is therefore of little value	4 **Success** The marketing programme achieves its objectives

Figure 2.9 The planning and implementation matrix. (Adapted from Bonoma, T, 1985, *The Marketing Edge: Making Strategies Work*, Free Press.)

Looking at your own organization, where in Figure 2.8 would you place it? Assuming that it is not in Cell 4, what appear to be the principal problems? What would be needed in order to overcome these?

'Marketing planning is generally a straightforward exercise; the marketer's real problems are those of effective implementation.' (Anonymous)

Identify the nature of the barrier to effective implementation that marketers typically encounter and suggest how, if at all, these barriers might be reduced. (Marketing Planning and Control, December 1992, Question 7.)

Corporate capability and the 7-S framework

Even when an organization has developed a clear – and appropriate – strategy that is supported both by the necessary systems and managerial structures, it may still fail to achieve its objectives. The sorts of problems that can cause this were touched upon in the previous section but are taken a step further in the McKinsey 7-S framework. The model, which was developed initially by Peters and Waterman as the result of their study of excellently managed and high performing companies, illustrates that capability is influenced not just by the three traditional 'hard' areas of management – strategy, structure and systems – but also, and in some cases more significantly, by the four 'soft' elements of *style* (the employees' style of behaving and thinking); *skills* (those needed to carry out the company's strategy); *staffing* (the extent to which staff have been trained well and assigned to the tasks which best match their talents); and *shared values* (the employees' understanding of and commitment to the same guiding values and missions). Refer also to pages 148–9.

Looking at your own organization, to what extent does there appear to be a conscious and well thought out process for managing the soft elements of the 7-S framework?

Summary

Within this unit we have attempted to identify the principal dimensions of corporate capability and highlight the range of factors that influence it. As a check on your understanding of the material, consider the following questions:

1. In what way is thinking on strategy changing? (See page 24.)
2. What is meant by 'capability'? (See pages 24–5.)
3. What are the principal influences upon corporate capability? (See pages 24–5.)
4. What is involved in conducting a resource audit? (See page 26.)
5. Explain what is meant by the value chain and how it can contribute to planning and control. (See pages 26–7.)
6. What is meant by 'efficiency' and 'effectiveness'? Which, if either, is the more important of the two concepts? (See pages 8, 28–9.)
7. Why is a comparative analysis of capability so important? (See pages 30–2.)
8. What is 'benchmarking'? (See pages 31–2.)
9. What are the possible limitations of benchmarking as it has traditionally been practised? (See pages 31–2.)
10. Explain what is meant by organizational flexibility and adaptability (See page 32.)
11. How might portfolio analysis be used to arrive at a measure of organizational balance? (See pages 32–3, 97–9.)
12. What are the key dimensions of the performance-importance matrix for your organization? (See pages 33–4.)
13. What financial measures should be used to arrive at a measure of capability? (See pages 29–30.)
14. What is meant by an 'opportunity' and a 'threat'? (See pages 35–7.)
15. What are the principal bases of competitive advantage? (See page 37.)
16. What are the causes of strategic drift and strategic wear-out? (See pages 37, 39.)
17. Why is implementation so frequently a problem for organizations? (See pages 40, 145–57.)
18. What contribution is the 7-S framework capable of making to our understanding of the determinants of good and bad implementation? (See pages 41, 148–9.)

Because an understanding of capability is so fundamental to the development of an effective strategy, it is essential that you come to terms with the sorts of factors that encourage – and inhibit – *true* capability. Although we have already made reference in the study guide at the beginning of the unit to the need to read Chapters 2, 3 and 17 of *Strategic Marketing Management* and Chapter 2 of *Marketing Strategy*, it is perhaps worth emphasizing the importance of these yet again. You should also extend your knowledge by spending time with your senior managers and asking how they perceive areas of strength and weakness within the organization, and hence organizational capability.

Activity debrief

Question 2.1: Refer to the discussion on pages 26–7.

Question 2.2: Refer to the discussion on pages 29–30.

Question 2.3: Turn to pages 97–9 in Unit 5.

Question 2.4 (i): A far more detailed view of organizational capability and environmental opportunities and threats. This should lead to a greater degree of objectivity in decision making; more frequent recognition and exploitation of market opportunities; a reduced likelihood of being taken by surprise; and a general strengthening of the competitive position. There are, however, problems with SWOT analysis (see pages 35–6) and these can detract from the value of the exercise.

Question 2.4 (ii): Refer to the discussion on pages 35–6.

Question 2.5: Refer to the discussion on page 38.

Question 2.6: Refer to the discussion on pages 39–40 and to Unit 8 (pages 145–57).

Environmental analysis

In this unit you will examine the nature and structure of the marketing environment. As a result of this you will understand:

- Why a regular analysis of the environment is strategically and tactically important.
- How managers go about analysing and interpreting the environment.
- The principal environmental changes that have taken and are taking place.
- The key elements of an environmental scanning system and marketing information system.
- The key dimensions of competitor and customer analysis.

By the end of this unit you will:

- Appreciate how the environment influences and needs to be reflected in an organization's marketing strategy.
- Be aware of the interrelationships that exist between an organization and its environment.
- Be capable of analysing competitors and customers.
- Understand the principal dimensions of an environmental monitoring system.

This unit covers a selection of material from Stages 2 and 3 of the Planning and Control syllabus. As such it accounts for approximately 25 per cent of the syllabus and, together with the supporting reading, should take you about 9 hours. The additional activities may, of course, increase this significantly, depending upon the help that you are able to call upon.

Because the marketing environment is the ultimate determinant of an organization's performance, it is essential that a marketing manager has a clear and detailed understanding of its constituents, the nature of the interrelationships that exist, and of the ways in which the environment is changing currently and how these patterns of change are likely to develop in the future. It is therefore essential that in your study programme you make sure that you relate the course material to market developments. One way of doing this is to acquire the habit of scanning both the quality press and the trade press for up-to-date articles, surveys and reviews that relate businesses to their environments. You should, in turn, supplement this by listening to and watching business programmes on the radio and television. As you will see from the exam tip that appears later, many of the questions require you to apply your knowledge and to give examples.

Because of the pivotal importance of the environment to the marketing planner, particular elements of the environment are introduced and discussed in all four modules of the Diploma. You should therefore make a conscious effort to explore the ways in which these dimensions combine to paint a complete picture of the environment within which marketing managers have to operate. Given this, it is perhaps understandable that the area has in the past proved to be a fertile ground for exam questions. In some instances these questions have required candidates to focus upon particular elements of the environment (approaches to customer or competitor analysis would be an obvious example) whilst others have been rather more general in their nature and relate to the ways in which environmental factors might possibly influence the development of a marketing strategy (this would typically emerge in the mini and maxi case studies).

As with the other units in this workbook, we have concentrated upon identifying the principal elements that you should focus upon against a background of a more detailed programme of reading. Included within this should be:

Wilson and Gilligan with Pearson (1992) *Strategic Marketing Management: Planning, Implementation and Control,* Butterworth-Heinemann, Chapters 4, 5 and 7.
Fifield (1992), *Marketing Strategy,* Butterworth-Heinemann, Chapter 3.

The marketing environment

In discussing the nature and significance of the marketing environment Wilson et al (1992, page 163) have commented that:

> Strategic marketing is ... an essentially iterative process. It is iterative for a number of reasons, the most significant of which is that as the company's external environment changes so opportunities and threats emerge and disappear only to re-emerge perhaps in a modified form at a later stage. Because of this, the marketing strategist needs to recognize the fundamental necessity both for an environmental monitoring process that is capable of identifying in advance any possible opportunities and threats, and for a planning system and organizational structure that is capable of quite possibly radical changes to reflect the environment so that the effects of threats are minimized and that opportunities are seized.

This comment goes some way towards highlighting the significance of the environment and illustrates the need for marketing planners to understand its various dimensions and interrelationships in some detail. Without this knowledge, marketing decisions will be made in something of a vacuum and almost inevitably will fail to achieve the expected or hoped for impact. It follows from this that there is a need for managers to adopt a strong external focus in which detailed consideration is given to analysing and interpreting what is happening in the environment currently and to forecasting what changes are likely to occur in the future. One way of doing this involves developing an environmental monitoring system. However, before we discuss the nature and structure of the environment and how an environmental monitoring system might best be developed, complete the following activity.

Given our comments above, identify two examples of organizations which have failed to monitor the environment sufficiently and which, as a consequence, have been taken by surprise by changing market structures (this might include the emergence of new competitors, a different market approach by the firm's current competitors, new customer demands, and so on).

Kotler (1991, page 129) defines a company's marketing environment as being

'made up of the actors and forces that affect the company's ability to develop and maintain successful transactions and relationships with its target customers.'

This environment, which is illustrated in Figure 3.1, consists of two distinct components:

- The macro environment.
- The micro environment.

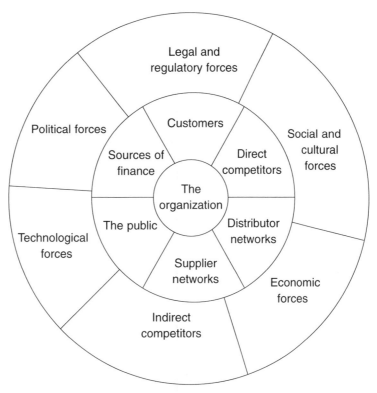

Figure 3.1   The marketing environment

The *micro* environment is the closer of the two to the organization. It is that part of the environment with which the organization interacts most immediately. Included within this are suppliers, customers, competitors, the public at large and the distribution network.

The *macro* environment consists of the rather broader set of forces that surround the organization including political, economic, social, cultural, demographic, technological and legal factors. These elements make up what are often referred to as the non-controllable elements of marketing and represent the framework within which most marketing decisions are made; this is illustrated in Figure 3.2. Although the elements on the left-hand side of the diagram are generally labelled as non-controllable, in practice it is often the case that at least some control can be exerted over several of the elements in the medium to long term. In the case of competitors, for example, strategic alliances might be developed, mergers might take place, and cartels – although often illegal – might be established, all of which have the effect of allowing for a degree of control to emerge. Equally, in the case of the legal environment, an organization's trade association might lobby Government in an attempt to have legislation passed that will be of benefit to member organizations; the

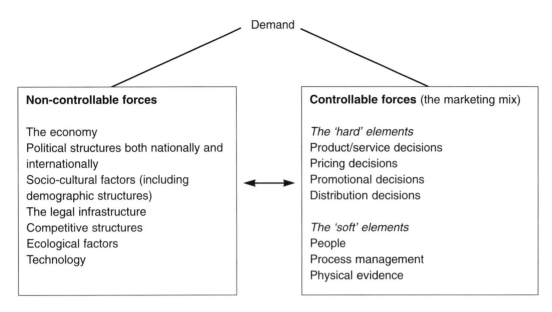

Figure 3.2 The marketing framework

immensely powerful tobacco lobby in Japan which has managed to limit severely the volume of western tobacco and cigarettes that can be imported into the country is an example of this. In the case of the political and economic dimensions, although the influence that can be exerted is perhaps less obvious, an organization – particularly a multinational – is likely to direct its investment patterns and marketing actions towards those parts of the world in which inflation rates are low, levels of political stability are high, and levels of consumer and organizational spending are buoyant. It is in this way that non-controllable factors become at least partially controllable.

Select two market sectors and identify the principal non-controllable elements in the macro environment. Having done this, identify how firms try to 'manage' these non-controllable elements in an attempt to reduce their impact or unpredictability. What success do they appear to have had?

The purpose of environmental analysis

The essential purpose of environmental analysis is to provide managers with a clear and detailed understanding of their current and future environments. Given this knowledge, managers should then be in a far stronger position to match the demands of the environment with the sorts of organizational capabilities that we referred to in Unit 2. However, while this might appear at first sight to be a relatively straightforward exercise, there are potentially a series of difficulties in doing this. This is partly because of the complexity of most environments, but also because there is often a degree of uncertainty as to how the environment *really* influences the organization. There are therefore two questions which the marketing planner needs to consider:

1   To what extent does or should the environment affect an organization's corporate strategy?
2   In what ways might organizational strengths and capabilities then best be related to the demands of the environment?

Environmental types

A number of writers have proposed methods for categorizing environments. Among the best known of these is the framework developed by Miles (1980) who advocates an approach based on the answers to six questions:

1 What degree of complexity exists in the environment?
2 How standardized or routinized are the organization's interactions with the environment?
3 What interconnections exist between the various dimensions of the environment?
4 What degree of dynamism and unpredictability exists in the environment?
5 To what extent is management receptive to the ways in which environmental pressures affect the organization's input and output processes?
6 What degree of flexibility does the organization possess in responding to the environment?

It is the answers to these questions which enables us to categorize environments as being:

- Simple/static.
- Dynamic.
- Complex.

Depending upon the type of environment faced by the organization, so the implications for approaches to environmental analysis – and subsequently the management of the organization – will vary. Remember, though, that particular problems emerge when an environment that previously has been relatively stable suddenly becomes far more volatile and complex.

Identify examples of each of the three environmental types referred to above. What are the marketing implications of each type for how an organization might operate?

ACTIVITY 3.3

In thinking about environmental types and the implications for management, Figure 3.3 should be of some help. In this, we move from the three forms referred to by Miles to four.

The first two of these – stability and incremental change – are both relatively straightforward, although stability is an environmental form which few organizations today experience. However, in both stages any changes that do take place are likely to be predictable and easy to manage. Rather bigger problems begin to emerge in Stage Three where the nature and magnitude of the changes increases, possibly fairly dramatically. For the marketing strategist there are two principal difficulties associated with this: firstly, that of forecasting what is likely to happen in the future, and then secondly, developing and implementing plans that are able to cope with these higher rates of change. These difficulties are then magnified further in Stage Four which we have labelled 'crazy days,' a

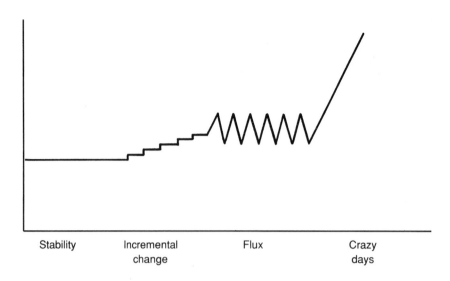

| Stability | Incremental change | Flux | Crazy days |

Figure 3.3 Patterns of environmental change

phrase which is taken from Tom Peters' book *Liberation Management*. In this, Peters argues that in the mid to late 1990s environmental uncertainty is the only certainty. Recognition of this and of the crazy days in which environmental structures change dramatically – and possibly increasingly malevolently – demands, he suggests, the far more innovative responses that he labels 'crazy ways'.

ACTIVITY 3.4

Look at the environment in which your organization operates and compare it with the sort of environment that existed ten years ago. In what ways has it changed? What problems have been experienced by the organization and its managers in coming to terms with the new environment? In what ways does it seem that the environment will change over the next few years? To what extent do you think that the organization's existing strategies, structures, systems and people will be able to cope with this?

QUESTION 3.1

Identify the principal strategic challenges that marketers are likely to face over the next decade and comment upon their implications for approaches to marketing planning.
(Planning and Control, December 1992, Question 3.)

The five stages of environmental analysis

Any analysis of the environment needs to be structured and detailed. It is therefore essential not only that environmental analysis takes place on a regular basis, but that it also has a clear focus and the results are then fully analysed, distributed to the appropriate people in the organization, and used subsequently in the development of strategies and tactics. Although a variety of approaches to environmental analysis exist, the most common involves a series of increasingly focused steps of the sort illustrated in Figure 3.4. The sequence, which was proposed by Johnson and Scholes (1993, page 76), is designed to provide the marketing planner with a clear understanding not just of the current state of the environment, but also how it is most likely to develop. In this way a picture of the principal opportunities and threats can be built up and a series of decisions then made about the strategic stance that the organization should adopt.

ACTIVITY 3.5

Making use of Figure 3.4, use Stages 1–3 to analyse your organization's environment. What picture emerges from this?

Stage 1

Audit the environment to identify:

- the factors that have influenced the organization's development and previous performance
- the probable direction in which the environment will develop
- the likely key influences

Stage 2

Assess the nature of the environment and the degree and source of any uncertainty that is likely to exist

Stage 3

Examine specific environmental factors including the nature and structure of each market sector the organization operates in

Stage 4

Analyse the firm's strategic position by means of:

- strategic group analysis
- market share analysis

Stage 5

Identify in detail how environmental forces will affect the organization and the sorts of opportunities and threats that will emerge

Stage 6

In the light of Stages 1–5, **decide upon the future ideal strategic position** and determine the implications for strategies, structures and systems

Figure 3.4   The five stages of environmental analysis.
(Adapted from Johnson and Scholes, 1993, *Exploring Corporate Strategy*, 3rd ed, page 76.)

The PEST framework

The general audit of environmental influences (Stage 1) represents the first stage of any environmental analysis and is designed to provide the strategist with an understanding of what is happening in each of the four principal dimensions of the environment: the political, economic, social and technological arenas. This analysis is typically referred to as PEST analysis and is illustrated in Figure 3.5.

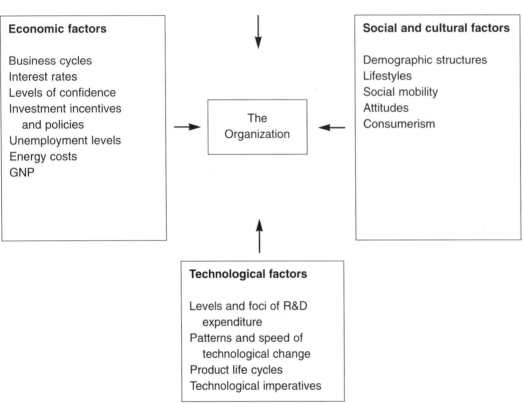

Political/legal factors

Legislative structures
Political structures
Government stability
Political orientations
Taxation policies
Employment legislation
Pressure groups
Trades Union power
Relationships with foreign governments
Foreign trade regulations
Competitive behaviour legislation

Economic factors

Business cycles
Interest rates
Levels of confidence
Investment incentives
    and policies
Unemployment levels
Energy costs
GNP

The Organization

Social and cultural factors

Demographic structures
Lifestyles
Social mobility
Attitudes
Consumerism

Technological factors

Levels and foci of R&D
    expenditure
Patterns and speed of
    technological change
Product life cycles
Technological imperatives

Figure 3.5 The PEST framework

ACTIVITY 3.6

Take two market sectors and identify the principal environmental forces currently and how they appear to be reflected in the marketing strategies that firms are pursuing. In what ways do you think these pressures might change over the next few years? What are the implications of this for approaches to marketing planning and control?

Developing an environmental monitoring system
Evidence suggests that the majority of firms have only poorly developed environmental monitoring systems, something which is reflected in a comment by Wilson et al (1992, page 170):

Recognition of the potential significance of environmental change highlights the need for a certain type of organizational structure and culture which is then reflected in both a balanced portfolio of products and in an adaptive management style supported by a well-developed intelligence and information monitoring system. Without this, the likelihood of the firm being taken unawares by environmental changes of one sort or another increases dramatically. Against the background of these comments, the need for environmental analysis would appear self-evident. All too often, however, firms appear to pay only lip service to such a need.

However, when organizations do recognize the need for a structured approach to environmental analysis, it appears that they move through a three-stage process in developing an environmental monitoring system:

1 *An appreciation stage* in which there is a general recognition within the company of the need to monitor the environment.
2 *An analysis stage* in which these approaches are formalized, the search for information is widened and greater attention is paid to the evaluation of information.
3 *An application stage* in which the process is formalized yet further with information evaluations being incorporated within strategies and plans.

What types of information should be collected as part of an environmental monitoring system? Is there a danger of collecting too much information with the result that managers are overwhelmed by the sheer volume of information available? Assuming that this is the case, how might you develop a truly user-friendly system?

The changing PEST environment

Perhaps the most obvious characteristic of the majority of today's markets is the degree of change that is taking place. Included within these changes are:

The political and legal environments

- A growing body of legislation that is designed to protect consumers from organizations abusing their power; legislation designed to limit large companies harming smaller ones; and legislation that protects society at large.
- The greater degree of influence that is being exerted by bodies such as the European Union.
- An upsurge in environmental and ecological issues.

The economic and competitive environments

- Possibly higher levels of economic uncertainty.
- A shift in economic and competitive power from Europe and the United States to Japan, the Pacific Rim and the industrializing nations.
- More intensely competitive markets with a greater emphasis upon new forms of competition.

The socio-cultural environments

- Changing demographic structures.
- Changing family structures.
- Shifting values.
- Major lifestyle changes.
- A greater willingness to accept technology.
- A greater emphasis upon value for money.
- Changing family roles.

The technological environment

- A seemingly ever-faster rate of technological change.
- Shorter product life cycles.

Quite obviously, the points that we have identified here do little more than simply scratch the surface. You should therefore think in detail about how each of these four elements is likely to change over the next few years and the probable implications for how organizations are likely to have to operate.

The June 1994 Planning and Control mini case study focused upon a firm of pump manufacturers who had been severely affected by a series of changes in their market. Question 1 put candidates in the position of the company's newly-appointed market analyst who had been given the responsibility for developing an environmental monitoring system. You might therefore find it useful at this stage to turn to the Unit 9, read the Watergate Pumps case study and attempt Question 1.

For a detailed discussion of approaches to market and environmental analysis, turn to Chapter 7 of *Strategic Marketing Management* by Wilson and Gilligan with Pearson, and to Chapter 3 of *Marketing Strategy* by Fifield.

Approaches to competitor analysis

In discussing issues of competition and approaches to competitor analysis, Wilson et al (1992, page 78) comment:

> Although the vast majority of marketing strategists acknowledge the importance of competitive analysis, it has long been recognized that less effort is typically put into detailed and formal analysis of competitors than, for example, of customers and their buying patterns. In many cases this is seemingly because marketing managers feel that they know enough about their competitors simply as the result of competing against them on a day-to-day basis. In other cases there is almost a sense of resignation with managers believing that it is rarely possible to understand competitors in detail and that as long as the company's performance is acceptable there is little reason to spend time collecting information. In yet others, there is only a general understanding of who it is that the company is competing against. The reality, however, is that competitors represent a major determinant of corporate success and any failure to take detailed account of their strengths, weaknesses, strategies and areas of vulnerability is likely to lead not just to a less than optimal performance, but also to an unnecessarily greater exposure to aggressive and unexpected competitive moves. Other probable consequences of failing to monitor competition include an increased likelihood of the company being taken by surprise, its relegation to being a follower rather than a leader, and to a focus on the short term rather than on more fundamental long-term issues.

Given the significance of this comment, they then went on to suggest that there is a need for marketing managers to pose five questions:

1. Who is it that we are competing against?
2. What are their objectives?
3. What strategies are they pursuing and how successful are they?
4. What strengths and weaknesses do they possess?

5 How are they likely to behave and, in particular, how are they likely to react to offensive moves?

It is the answers to these questions that enable the marketing planner to gain a greater understanding of the competitive environment (see Figure 3.6) and, ultimately, a far clearer idea of each competitor's probable response profile (see Figure 3.7).

ACTIVITY 3.8

Using your own organization or one with which you are familiar, complete Figure 3.6.

Your organization's products/services	The principal competitors	Your organization's market position	The intensity and bases of competition	The likelihood of new entrants to the sector	Your core marketing strategy
1					
2					
3					
4					

Figure 3.6 Coming to terms with the competitive environment

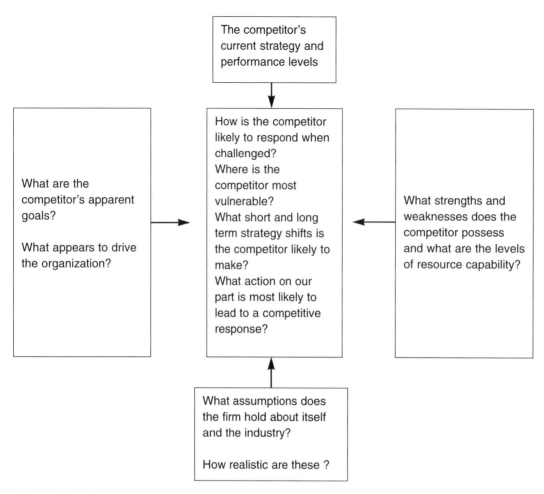

Figure 3.7 Identifying a competitor's response profile

One of the most significant contributions over the past few years to our understanding of competitive structures and of how competitive environments influence strategy has been made by Michael Porter.

DEFINITION 3.2

Michael Porter suggests that:
'Competition in an industry is rooted in its underlying economics and competitive forces that go well beyond the established competence in a particular industry.'

Coming to terms with existing and new competitors

If business history teaches us anything at all, it has to be the extent to which many organizations have failed to identify or recognize the significance of the competitive threats posed. All too frequently, managers either underestimate what an existing competitor is capable of doing, fail to react to competitive moves until considerable damage has been done, or are taken by surprise by a new entrant to the market. In many cases the reasons for this can be traced to the unnecessarily narrow ways in which managers define and perceive their competition. One of the first to comment upon this in detail was Theodore Levitt who in his now classic article 'Marketing Myopia' highlighted the almost inevitable consequences of adopting what is now usually referred to as 'an industry perspective of competition'. This perspective tends to lead to competitors being viewed in terms of those organizations which offer a broadly similar product or service. Because of this, the products are seen to be close substitutes for one another and the cross-elasticity of demand is therefore high; one of the most obvious and commonly cited examples of this is the market for butter. When the price of butter rises and/or a series of health concerns emerge about the fat content of butter, consumers switch to margarine.

The alternative to this involves adopting a far broader perspective of competition and, at its most extreme, defining it in terms of any product or service that might possibly attract consumers' spending power (this is referred to as 'the market perspective of competition'). In practice, of course, this extreme view is of little real value and so something more manageable is needed. In discussing this, Levitt refers to several examples, including the American railways system whose operators for many years made immense profits. Subsequently, however, the system has contracted enormously as 'new' competitors emerged in the form of airlines, transport companies, long-distance bus services and, of course, far higher levels of car ownership. Faced with this, the railways at first failed to recognize the threat but then underestimated its significance until it was too late to respond in any meaningful way. The result has been the virtual collapse of the industry.

The question that this raises is whether managers within the industry might possibly have identified the nature and significance of the threat at an early enough stage and then responded in such a way that the impact upon the railway companies might have been avoided altogether or, perhaps more realistically, minimized. The answer to this *has* to be that if the threat had been recognized as it emerged and grew, then a series of moves might have been made which would very largely have avoided the sorts of problems that the industry ultimately faced.

In the light of the comments above, what strategies might the railway companies have pursued that would have helped them come to terms with the growing competition?

In thinking about this question, you need to identify the alternatives that were open to the railway companies. Included within these were ignoring or failing to recognize the growing threat (this is broadly what they did); adopting the 'bunker mentality' by battening down the hatches in the hope that the threat would eventually go away; improving their levels of service (this is likely to be of only short-term value); and coming to terms with the threat by developing alliances with the new competition.

The fourth of these four alternatives involves recognizing several essential truths about competition:

- Competitive threats and challenges can come from unexpected as well as expected sources.
- New competitive threats can change market structures in a number of significant and far-reaching ways.
- In responding to competitors, a series of unorthodox, and often unpalatable, changes might be needed.
- Competitive arrogance is one of the most common reasons for organizations suffering a decline in their market position.

Look at your own organization and consider the following questions:

- Which competitive perspective – the industry perspective or the market perspective – predominates?

- What sorts of competitive changes are occurring in each of your major markets?
- Are these changes being led by your own organization or by another firm?
- To what extent does it appear that the full significance of any threats is recognized?
- How well equipped to cope with major competitive changes does the organization appear to be?
- Can you find any examples of the organization having been taken by surprise by competitors in the past? If so, what were the causes of this and what, if any, lessons have been learned from the experience?

Against the background of our comments so far, turn to the activity below.

ACTIVITY 3.10

Using Figure 3.7, develop a response profile for one of your principal competitors. What picture emerges from this and what are the implications for the way in which you should try to 'manage' the competition?

The need to have a clear understanding of who exactly your competitors are and the nature of their strengths and weaknesses is also illustrated in Figure 3.8. In this, we list some of the alternatives to aluminium. Although not all of the materials listed in Column One are alternatives in each and every situation in which aluminium is used, the table goes some way towards illustrating how an overly narrow competitive perspective could well lead to an organization being taken by suprise as customers switch to the alternatives.

Material	Advantages	Drawbacks
Mild steel	Very cheap Widely available	Weight Rusts easily
Low chrome ferritic stainless steel	Similar price Widely available	Weight Rusts in sea water
Titanium	Strength (especially at temperature) Corrosion resistance	Cost Processing (not easily extrudable)
Magnesium	Very light weight	Vulnerable to fire
Polystyrene unplasticated PVC	Light weight Reasonably cheap	Low strength No temperature/fire resistance
ABS, nylon engineering plastics	Light weight Strong	Cost
Wood	Cheap Widely available	Variable quality Rots
Composites		
Aluminium MMC's	Stiffer Stronger Harder	Extra cost Processing difficulties
Fibre reinforced plastics	Lighter for quality stiffness/strength	Can lack toughness Extra cost

Figure 3.8 Substitutes for aluminium

Competitive relationships

In trying to understand how firms compete, there is a need to consider four questions:

1 What is each organization's existing strategy?
2 What performance levels are they achieving currently?
3 What strengths and weaknesses do they possess?
4 What might we expect of each competitor in the future?

What information might a marketing manager need in order to understand a competitor? Where might this information come from? What problems might be encountered in collating this information?

A variety of approaches can be used to examine competitive relationships, including the idea of strategic groups; an example of this appears in Figure 3.9. The thinking behind strategic grouping is straightforward and based on the idea that in the majority of industries competitors can be categorized on the basis of the similarities and differences that exist in the type of strategy being pursued; in Figure 3.9 this is done on the basis of the breadth of each firm's geographic coverage of the market and the extent to which the product range is broad or narrow. Having plotted the market's strategic groupings, the marketing planner needs then to focus upon each firm's strengths and weaknesses, its market position (leader, challenger, follower or me-too), and its probable response to market changes. The question of how to go about analysing strengths and weaknesses was discussed in Unit 2 and it may be worth referring back to this in order to refresh your memory.

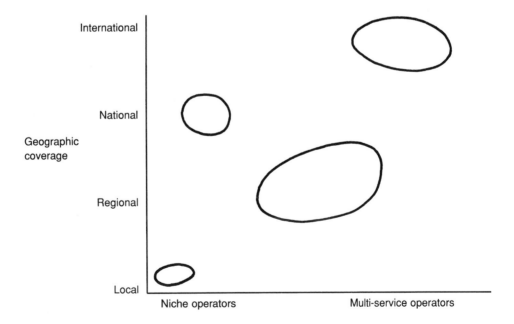

Figure 3.9 Strategic groups

With regard to the issue of market position, several frameworks have been developed. Two of the most useful involve categorizing firms on the basis of their relative position *within* a strategic group (is it the case for example that the firm's position is dominant, strong, favourable, tenable, weak or non-viable?); and focusing upon each organization's competitive status along the lines of the example in Figure 3.10.

Level	Competitive Status	Examples
1	One or a number of significant competitive advantages exist and are fully exploited	
2	A number of relatively small advantages exist that together give the organization a significant advantage	
3	Meaningful advantages either do not exist or are not recognized or exploited by the management team	
4	No real advantages exist	
5	Competitive disadvantages exist	

Figure 3.10   The five levels of competitive status (Adapted from Davidson, 1987, page 160.)

ACTIVITY 3.11

Turn to Figure 3.10 and identify examples for each of the five levels of competitive status. Where within this would you put your own organization?

So what do you need to know about your competitors?

Marketing strategy must, of necessity, be based upon a clear and detailed understanding of each competitor's strengths and weaknesses. As a first step, therefore, the marketing planner needs to collect information under a number of headings as a prelude to a full comparative assessment of the principal competitors. In discussing this, Wilson et al (1992, page 92) suggest that the information that is typically needed includes:

- Sales.
- Market shares.
- Cost and profit levels and how they appear to be changing over time.
- Cash flows.
- Return on investment.
- Investment patterns.
- Production processes.
- Levels of capacity utilization.
- Organizational culture.
- Products and the product portfolio.
- Product quality.
- The size and pattern of the customer base.
- The levels of brand loyalty.
- Dealer and distribution channels.
- Marketing and selling capabilities.
- Operations and physical distribution.
- Financial capabilities.
- Management capabilities and attitudes to risk.
- Human resources, their capability and flexibility.
- Previous patterns of response.
- Ownership patterns and, in the case of divisionalized organizations, the expectations of corporate management.

Quite obviously, collecting such a depth and breadth of information on any single competitor is likely to prove difficult, time-consuming and expensive. For multiple competitors, the problems are of course confounded. It is for this reason that the majority of firms adopt a generally pragmatic approach by focusing upon those organizations which they perceive to be their most immediate or significant competitors and which, therefore, appear to pose the most obvious threat, and then collecting information under a rather more limited number of headings than appears in the list above.

Who are your organization's three principal competitors? How much detailed information exists on each of these? What other information would be of value?

However, even when large amounts of competitive information are readily available, managers still face the problem of making use of this in an effective way. Only rarely is competitive information available in the form that managers really want and so they are often faced with the task of interpreting and coming to terms with ambiguity and having to second guess the implications of the sorts of pictures that emerge. Because of this, there are major benefits to be gained from developing a *structured* information system that, on a regular basis, pulls together the information that managers see as being the most strategically and tactically useful and significant.

The potential sources of this information are discussed in rather greater detail in the next section, but would generally include customers, distributors, the trade press, trade shows, and the company's own staff.

The interpretation and assessment of information is a problem that many managers face and it is for this reason that it is often worth developing comparative profiles that take account of customers' principal buying factors. One of the ways in which this can be done is by means of the sort of framework that appears in Figure 3.11 and, returning for a moment to Unit 2, Figure 2.4 on page 34.

Using Figure 3.11, prepare a comparative assessment of your organization's performance against its three principal competitors (the guidelines for how the figure should be completed appear at the bottom of the figure).

The sources of competitive information

Information on competitors is typically available from a large number of sources. The task faced by the planner can therefore be seen in terms of identifying in detail what sorts of competitive information would be the most valuable and then developing the systems that will ensure that this information is collected in a regular and systematic way.

It has been suggested that the sales force is a potentially valuable but frequently under-utilized source of marketing information. Given this, explain how a sales force might be used as a structured source of information. What types of information might they be expected to generate? (Planning and Control, December 1993, Question 3.)

Customers' buying factors	Our organization	Performance of competitors		
		1	2	3
Products				
Design				
Quality				
Performance				
Value for money				
Add-ons				
Running costs				
Reliability				
Breadth of the product range				
Depth of the product range				
Prices				
Price levels				
Volume discounts				
Promotion				
Levels of advertising				
Apparent effectiveness				
Product literature				
Performance at exhibitions and trade shows				
Sponsorship				
Selling and distribution				
Sales force calibre				
Experience				
Geographic coverage				
Sales force – customer relations				
Service				
Servicing costs				
Flexibility				
Speed				
Service levels				
Overall product performance				
Performance against promise				

Notes: In completing this, you should rate each dimension for each organization as Excellent, Good, Equal, Fair or Poor. In doing this you should not rely upon preconceived (and possibly misconceived) notions, but instead make use of marketing intelligence studies of current and potential customers, suppliers and distributors.

Figure 3.11 The comparative assessment of firms
(Adapted from Wilson and Gilligan with Pearson, 1992, *Strategic Marketing Management*, page 93.)

There are, in essence, three major sources of competitive data:

1 *Recorded data* such as primary market research; secondary sources such as the Mintel reports, the trade press, government reports, public documents, the daily press and technical journals; and company annual reports.
2 *Observable data* including competitors' price levels and shifts, their advertising campaigns, sales-force feedback, and product comparisons.
3 *Opportunistic data* such as that which emerges from trade shows, discussions with raw material suppliers, distributors, sub-contractors, packaging suppliers, company newsletters, conferences, new recruits, and a competitor's disgruntled employees.

Together, these are – or should be – capable of providing an increasingly detailed picture of competitors, although ultimately, of course, their value depends upon the interpretations that are put upon them (that is, the way in which the raw data are turned into useable information) and, subsequently, how the information is used. All too often, for example, information comes into an organization and is not then either evaluated properly or channelled to the most appropriate people.

QUESTION 3.6

How would you go about establishing an effective competitive monitoring system within an organization? What sort of competitive monitoring system does your own organization have? How effectively does it appear to work? What changes would you suggest be made to improve its effectiveness? How well do you think each of your competitors understands your organization?

EXAM TIP

Although we are focusing here upon the *competitive* information system, you should not look at the CIS in isolation, but should instead see it as an integral part of an *overall* environmental monitoring system. The mini case study that was used for the June 1994 exam paper was based on Watergate Pumps, an organization which was being hit hard by a series of environmental changes. You might therefore turn to Unit 9 and read both the mini case and the suggested solution.

The different types of competitor

In Figure 3.7 we outlined how competitors' response profiles might possibly be developed. With this information, competitors can be categorized in various ways. Kotler (1988, page 247), for example, identified four types:

1 *Laid back competitors*   who only rarely react quickly or aggressively.
2 *Selective competitors*   who respond to certain types of initiative such as a price cut, but not to others such as an increase in advertising levels.
3 *Tiger competitors*   who respond quickly and aggressively, irrespective of the type of competitive move.
4 *Stochastic competitors*   who exhibit unpredictable reaction patterns. In some cases these firms will respond aggressively to a competitor's move whilst on other occasions they will ignore broadly similar moves.

ACTIVITY 3.14

How would you categorize each of the organizations that you are competing against? How would you categorize your own organization?
  What are the implications of each type of competitor for how you might best handle them?

As an alternative to Kotler's approach, you might also think about Michael Porter's classification of firms as 'good' or 'bad' competitors. A 'good' competitor, he suggests, sticks to the industry's unwritten rules, avoids upsetting the status quo, avoids aggressive price changes, and generally works towards maintaining the balance of a healthy industry. 'Bad' competitors, by contrast, typically pursue unnecessarily aggressive moves, slash prices and, by virtue of their actions, force others in the industry to take high risks.

What makes a competitor vulnerable?

Any analysis of competitors needs to identify their areas of vulnerability. There are various factors that contribute to organizational vulnerability, including:

Financial factors
- A shortage of cash.
- Low margins.
- High operating costs.
- Inflexible cost structures.

Market factors
- An over-dependence upon one market.
- An over-dependence upon one account.
- A low market share.
- A high market share which leads to organizational complacency.
- Premium pricing.
- A dependence upon low-growth markets.
- A predictable strategy and response pattern.
- A poorly defined competitive stance.

Product factors
- Poor product quality.
- High servicing costs.
- Product obsolescence.

Organizational factors
- Bureaucratic structures.
- Complacent managerial attitudes.
- Low levels of staff skills.
- Poor training.
- A short-term focus.
- A lack of planning and foresight.
- Poor labour relations.
- Organizational myopia.
- Competitive arrogance and a belief that the organization's current position can not be eroded.
- Organizational inertia.

QUESTION 3.7

What is the underlying cause of organizational vulnerability? (In thinking about this, recognize that the factors that we have listed are the result of something more fundamental within an organization.)

Setting up a competitive information system (CIS)

It should be obvious from our discussion so far that the benefits of a competitive monitoring, intelligence and information system are potentially significant. Equally, it should be apparent that the consequences of *not* having such a system are likely to be reflected in the organization being taken by surprise and being forced ever more frequently into a reactive posture. Given this, we can identify several straightforward guidelines for establishing a CIS:

- Deciding in detail what information is needed.
- Collecting the data.
- Analysing and evaluating the data.
- Disseminating the information to the appropriate managers throughout the organization.
- Developing strategies based upon the information.
- Feeding back the results in order to monitor and improve the system.

These ideas have been discussed by Davidson (1987, page 34) who, in commenting on the mechanics of a CIS, highlights the need for the following:

- A focus upon three or four key competitors.
- Selecting and briefing data collectors in each department.
- Allocating the responsibility for chasing, co-ordinating and evaluating the data that emerge to a single person and ensuring that this is seen as an integral and important part of that person's job.
- Ensuring that the data collectors also know that it is an integral part of their job rather than an additional and dispensable activity, and that they provide regular and detailed data flows.
- The publication of regular tactical and strategic reports.

To this we can add the need for the reports to be presented in a way that the users find meaningful and that the system is driven by a member of the senior management team who is fully committed to it. Without this, it is likely that the system will be seen to be of little real value. (Again, you might find it useful to refer to Unit 9 and the Watergate Pumps mini case and suggested solution.)

For a detailed discussion of approaches to competitor analysis, turn to Chapter 4 of *Strategic Marketing Management* by Wilson and Gilligan with Pearson, and to pages 57, 64–6 and 82 of *Marketing Strategy* by Fifield.

EXTENDING YOUR KNOWLEDGE

Understanding customers

In discussing approaches to customer analysis, Wilson et al (1992, page 101) have suggested that:

It has long been recognized that marketing planning is ultimately driven by the marketing strategist's perception of how and why customers behave as they do and how they are likely to respond to the various elements of the marketing mix.

In the majority of markets however, buyers differ enormously in terms of their buying dynamics. The task faced by the marketing strategist in coming to terms with these differences is consequently complex. In consumer markets, for example, not only do buyers typically differ in terms of their age, income, educational levels and geographic location, but more fundamentally in terms of their personality, their lifestyles and their expectations. In the case of organizational and industrial markets, differences are often exhibited in the goals being pursued, the criteria employed by those involved in the buying process, the formality of purchasing policies, and the constraints that exist in the form of delivery dates and expected performance levels.

Despite these complexities, it is imperative that the marketing strategist understands in detail the dynamics of the buying process since the costs and competitive implications of failing to do so are likely to be significant.

Understanding buyer behaviour – the first step

The first step in any analysis of consumer or organizational buyer behaviour involves posing – and answering – seven questions:

1 Who is in the market and what degree of power do they have?
2 What do they buy?
3 Why do they buy?
4 Who is involved in the buying process?
5 How do they buy?
6 When do they buy?
7 Where do they buy?

Because an understanding of buyers and their motives is so fundamental a part of the marketing process, a considerable amount of time and effort has been directed towards the development of frameworks and models that will help in this. The first and most basic of these takes the form of what is referred to as a black box model, an example of this is illustrated in Figure 3.12. Although within a black box model we understand the inputs and the outputs, we do not understand exactly *how* the buyer evaluates and processes the inputs and arrives at a decision. Because of this, a considerable amount of research work in recent years has concentrated upon trying to improve our understanding of the evaluation process.

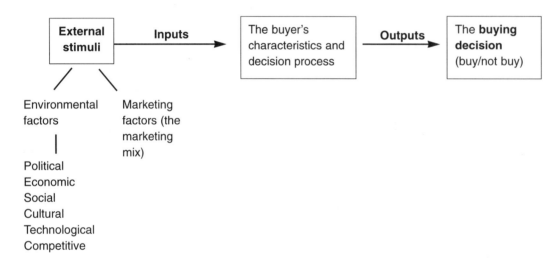

Figure 3.12   A black box model of the buying process

The differences between customers and consumers

Before going any further, we need to make a distinction between customers and consumers. The customer is the buyer of the product or service but may not necessarily also be the user. Instead, it is the user of the product who is the consumer. In the case of industrial products, for example, the customer may be the purchasing department which is operating to a series of distinct and written purchasing guidelines. The consumer or user might be a secretary or a machine operator. In the case of consumer goods, a parent might be the customer in that he or she buys the product, whilst the product is then consumed, or used, by the child. In both instances we need to recognize the possible different expectations of the customer (value for money, reliability, credit terms, and so on) and the consumer (image, range of features, immediate availability, and so on) and subsequently how these need to be reconciled and reflected in the marketing campaign.

The four types of buyer behaviour

Because products vary considerably in terms of their complexity, their prices and what we expect of them, we need to think about how they can be categorized so that approaches to analysing buyers reflect these differences. One way of doing this involves focusing upon two principal dimensions:

- The degree of involvement that the customer has with the product.
- The extent to which the buyer sees differences between the product or brand alternatives to be significant.

Using these two dimensions enables us to develop a simple matrix of the sort in Figure 3.13.

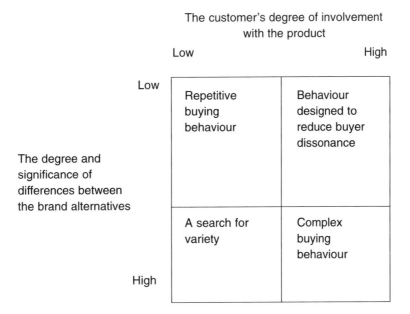

Figure 3.13 The four types of buying behaviour. (Source: adapted from Assael, 1987, page 87.)

Using Figure 3.13, find examples of the four types of buyer behaviour and consider the implications for marketing behaviour.

ACTIVITY 3.15

Influences on consumer behaviour

It is generally acknowledged that there are four main influences upon consumers:

1 *Cultural factors* such as:

- The culture of the society in which the individual grows up.
- Sub-cultures including nationality groups, religious groups, racial groups and geographical areas, all of which exhibit degrees of difference in ethnic taste, cultural preferences, taboos, attitudes and lifestyle.
- Social stratification and, in particular, social class.

2 These cultural factors are then influenced by a series of *social factors* including:

- Reference groups.
- The family.
- Social role.
- Status.

3 The third category consists of *personal influences* on behaviour such as:

- Age and life cycle stage.
- The person's occupation.
- Economic circumstances.
- Lifestyle.
- Personality.

4 The final set of influences are *psychological* and include:

- Motivation.
- Perception.
- Learning and beliefs.
- Attitudes.

These are illustrated in Figure 3.14 and highlight the typically broad or general influence exerted by cultural factors and the increasingly specific influence of the other three dimensions as you move through the model towards the buyer.

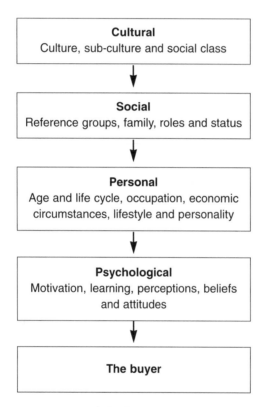

Figure 3.14 Influences upon consumer behaviour

How might the model that is illustrated in Figure 3.14 be used to increase our understanding of consumer buying patterns for:

- Foodstuffs?
- Cigarettes?
- Brands of alcohol?
- Cars?

Which are the seemingly most important influences upon consumer choice in each case? What are the implications for the marketing planner?

Making reference to a product or organization of your choice, identify the principal socio-cultural characteristics that appear to influence buyer behaviour. What are their implications for marketing planning? (Marketing Planning and Control, June 1993, Question 4.)

The buying decision process

With an understanding of the factors which influence behaviour, the marketing planner needs then to turn to the buying process. In doing this there is a need to focus upon:

- The types of buyer behaviour.
- The various buying roles within the decision making unit.
- The decision process.

We have already made a brief reference to the first of these three areas and it may therefore be worth returning for a moment to Figure 3.13 and the accompanying activity.

With regard to *buying roles*, we can distinguish between those circumstances in which identifying the buyer is a relatively easy exercise and those in which a number of people are involved. In the case of the family holiday or a car, for example, there are five clear roles:

1 The *initiator* who initially suggests buying the product or service.
2 The *influencer* or *influencers* who are capable of affecting the decision that ultimately is made.
3 The *decider* who makes the buying decision.
4 The *buyer* who physically makes the purchase.
5 The *user* or *users* who consume the product.

Taking the example of a family holiday, identify who might play each of the five buying roles and how the decision might be arrived at. What, if any, trade-offs might occur within the process? In what ways might a holiday company influence the decision and at whom should the message(s) be aimed?

It should be apparent from this that there is a very real need to understand the buying decision process in considerable detail, since it is this understanding which allows the marketing effort to be focused at the appropriate individual and the message tailored to fit their information needs. To help in this, it is useful to think about the stages which people typically go through in arriving at a decision; these are illustrated in Figure 3.15.

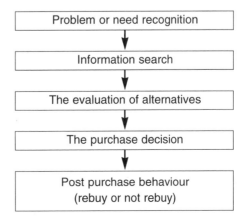

Figure 3.15
The five stages of
the buying process

Although sequential models of this type have been heavily criticized for their rather simplistic nature and failure to take account both of the richness and complexity of the decision process, they have a useful role in highlighting the principal stages through which buyers move either explicitly or implicitly.

It can be seen from Figure 3.15 that the process begins with the *recognition of a problem or need*. This can be sparked off in one of several ways including an advertisement, a friend or colleague's comment, the increasing unreliability of a car (and therefore the need for a new model), or changing food tastes.

The second stage involves the *search for information* and can range from the casual reading of an advertisement through to the detailed analysis of brochures, the specialist press, discussions with experts, and so on. The outcome of this is that the consumer's awareness, knowledge and understanding of the brand alternatives is increased dramatically and leads to an *evaluation of the alternatives* and a reduction in the number of brands that are seen to be serious candidates for purchase; this filtration of brands is illustrated in Figure 3.16.

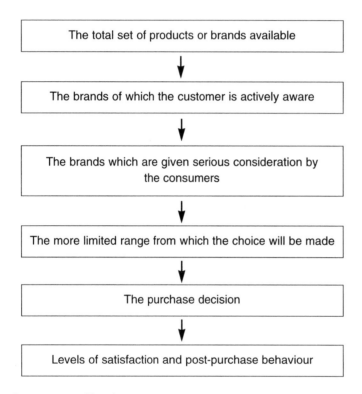

Figure 3.16   The consumer filtration process

The criteria which will be used in the ultimate choice will, of course, vary from one product to another and one consumer to another. It has been suggested, for example, that consumers can be categorized in terms of whether they are *deliberate* buyers in that they search actively for considerable amounts of information which they then carefully process, or whether they are *compulsive* buyers. Equally, consumers differ enormously in terms of their susceptibility to particular dimensions of the marketing programme such as price, advertising appeals, the type of distribution outlet, packaging, special offers and even country of origin. However, underpinning this is one simple fact that marketing planners should never lose sight of. It is that:

Customers do not buy products, they buy the benefits that the product or service delivers.

This has been discussed in some detail by Malcolm McDonald who argues for the 'which means that' test in order to link a product's features with the benefits that these features deliver. Amongst the examples that he gives to illustrate this is 'Maintenance times have been reduced from 4 to 3 hours *which means that* most costs are reduced by ...'

Think about a product or service offered by your organization and list the various benefits that it offers and then apply McDonalds '*which means that*' test. To what extent does the marketing programme really give emphasis to these? What benefits do competitors offer and stress? What benefits do customers really want?

So how does the consumer buying process work?

In coming to terms with buyer behaviour, marketing managers need to understand not just the sorts of factors that influence behaviour, but also how these influences are then reflected in the buying process. Is it the case, for example, that buyers consistently exhibit high degrees of brand loyalty and almost irrespective of what other organizations offer would not be swayed, or is it the case that in buying terms they exhibit a high degree of brand promiscuity? Amongst the other sorts of questions that therefore need to be answered are:

- How important is price?
- What role does advertising play?
- How much information do customers need?
- How significant is the product's country of origin?
- Do customers need the help of store assistants?

Knowing in detail *how* customers buy is therefore an important dimension of the marketing process. Because of this, researchers have proposed a variety of models in an attempt to understand more fully the buying process and hence how customers' behaviour patterns might most readily be influenced.

The earliest of these was proposed by Marshall, an economist, who developed the idea of 'economic man'. 'Economic man', he suggested, acts in a wholly rational manner and attempts to maximize the utility of any purchase. Although the model provides a potentially useful conceptual underpinning for any analysis of buyer behaviour, it is quite obviously a far from accurate reflection of how people behave in practice. Because of this, a number of models that gave a greater and more explicit recognition to the consumer's psychological state before, during and after the purchase began to be developed in the 1960s. The best known of these models were developed by Nicosia (1966), Engal, Kollat and Blackwell (1968), and Sheth (1969). Labelled the 'comprehensive models of consumer behaviour', they attempted to illustrate the breadth of the inputs to the decision process, the complexity of the information processing, and the ways in which the outputs need to be seen not just in terms of the purchase decision, but also in terms of the implications for perception and learning.

EXTENDING YOUR KNOWLEDGE

For a discussion of the structure of these models, refer to page 117 of *Strategic Marketing Management* by Wilson and Gilligan with Pearson.

Although these – and other – models have undoubtedly helped in our understanding of how buyers' behaviour patterns are influenced, they have been subjected to considerable criticism in recent years. Foxall (1987, page 128), for example, has suggested that:

1 The models assume an unrealistic degree of consumer rationality.
2 Observed behaviour often differs significantly from what is described.
3 The implied decision process is too simplistic and sequential.

4   Insufficient recognition is given to the relative importance of different types of decisions – each decision is treated by comprehensive models as significant and of high involvement, but the reality is very different and by far the vast majority of decisions made by consumers are relatively insignificant and of low involvement.

5   The models assume consumers have a seemingly infinite capacity for receiving and ordering information – in practice, consumers ignore, forget, distort, misunderstand or make far less use than this of the information with which they are presented.

6   Attitudes towards low involvement products are often very weak and only emerge after the purchase and not before as comprehensive models suggest.

7   Many purchases seem not to be preceded by a decision process.

8   Strong brand attitudes often fail to emerge even when products have been bought on a number of occasions.

9   Consumers often drastically limit their search for information, even for consumer durables.

10 When brands are similar in terms of their basic attributes, consumers seemingly do not discriminate between them but instead select from a repertoire of brands.

ACTIVITY 3.18

Take two different types of purchase that you make (e.g. a low cost and frequent purchase and a much higher cost and less frequent purchase) and attempt to construct a model that not only explains the thinking processes that you go through but which would also enable someone else to predict how you are likely to behave in the future.

Organizational buying behaviour

DEFINITION 3.3

Webster and Wind (1972, page 2) define organizational buying as 'the decision-making process by which formal organizations establish the need for purchased products and services, and identify, evaluate and choose among alternative brands and suppliers.'

Although organizational and consumer buying processes have numerous points of similarity, there are also many areas in which they differ. In discussing this, Kotler (1988, page 208) highlights the way in which:

- Organizations buy goods and services to satisfy a variety of goals: making profits, reducing costs, meeting employee needs, and meeting social and legal obligations.
- More persons typically participate in organizational buying decisions than in consumer buying decisions, especially in procuring major items. The decision participants usually have different organizational responsibilities and apply different criteria to the purchase decision.
- The buyers must heed formal purchasing policies, constraints, and requirements established by their organizations.
- The buying instruments, such as requests for quotations, proposals, and purchase contracts, add another dimension not typically found in consumer buying.

The strategic importance of organizational buying has been referred to by a growing number of writers in recent years, all of whom have emphasized the sort of comment made by Turnbull (1987, page 147) when talking about the telecommunications market:

Some telecommunications equipment manufacturers now buy in items accounting for up to 80 per cent of total cost. Thus even a 2 per cent procurement saving can have a marked effect on profitability or give the company a significant price advantage in the marketplace.

ACTIVITY 3.19

Look at the purchasing process within your organization and think about the following questions:

- How is the purchasing process organized?
- How influential within the organization is the person who has overall responsibility for purchasing?
- How often are suppliers reviewed?
- What sort of criteria are used for this?
- What evidence is there that purchasing is viewed *strategically* and as a potential source of competitive advantage?

The differences between consumer and organizational markets

We have already made the comment that organizational and consumer markets have a number of points both of similarity and difference. These differences have been summarized by Wilson et al (1992, pages 118–119) as:

1. The existence of a smaller number of buyers each of whom typically buys in larger quantities than is the case in consumer markets.
2. A (high) degree of buyer concentration, with a limited number of buyers often accounting for the bulk of purchasing within the industry.
3. Geographical concentration.
4. Close relationships between suppliers and customers, with products often being modified to fit the specific needs of the customer.
5. Inelastic demand, particularly in the short term.
6. Demand is generally derived, with the result that the strategist needs to examine the secondary markets which influence the demand for the primary products.
7. Professional purchasing which is performed by buyers who often work as part of a buying team and who, in attempting to satisfy particular performance of quality criteria, employ a greater degree of overtly rational thinking than is generally the case in consumer markets.
8. Reciprocal trading patterns often exist, making it difficult for new suppliers to break the market.

EXAM TIP

Exam questions sometimes require you to focus specifically upon either a consumer or an organizational market. Never forget that the two sectors can be very different and that the implications for your answer can be significant. Far too many candidates make the mistake of treating them in the same way.

However, despite these differences, the process for coming to terms with organizational markets is broadly the same as for consumer markets, with the strategist needing answers to several key questions:

- *Who* makes up the market?
- What *buying decisions* are made?
- *Who is involved* in the buying process?
- What are *the key influences* upon the buyer?
- What *organizational buying policies* and priorities exist?
- What *procedures are followed* in arriving at a buying decision?

The different types of buying decision

In 1967, three American researchers, Robinson, Faris and Wind, put forward a framework for categorizing buying situations, each of which demands a particular form of behaviour on the part of the supplier. These situations or buy classes are:

- The straight rebuy.
- The modified rebuy.
- The new task.

These terms are for the most part self-explanatory and their significance needs therefore to be seen in terms of the buyer's familiarity or unfamiliarity with the situation and how he or she tries to come to terms with this by searching for information in order to minimize risk.

ACTIVITY 3.20

Identify examples of each of the three types of buying situations within your organization. What sort of criteria are employed in each case when purchasing decisions are taken? Who is involved at each stage?

Who is involved in the buying process?

The majority of organizational buying decisions are taken by a group of individuals working to a pre-determined set of purchasing criteria. This group is known both as the buying centre and the decision-making unit (DMU).

DEFINITION 3.4

The DMU is 'those individuals and groups who participate in the purchasing decision-making process, who share some common goals and the risks arising from the decision.' (Webster and Wind, 1972, page 6.)

There are typically six roles in this buying process:

1 *The users* of the product who possibly initiate the buying process and who in some circumstances may be involved in defining the specification of the product or service.
2 *The influencers* who make an input into the process of evaluating the alternatives available.
3 *The deciders* who decide upon the final product specification and the supplier(s).
4 *The approver(s)* who authorize the purchase proposal.
5 *The buyer(s)* who negotiate the purchase terms.
6 *The gatekeeper(s)* who in one way or another are able to stop or inhibit sellers from reaching individuals in the DMU. Included within these are secretaries, receptionists and purchasing agents.

What sort of buyers do you have in your organization?

In their book *Strategic Marketing Management*, Wilson et al (1992, page 121) make reference to a piece of research conducted in the US in 1967 by Dickinson in which seven types of buyer were identified:

1 *Loyal buyers*   who remain loyal to a source for considerable periods.
2 *Opportunistic buyers*   who choose between sellers on the basis of who will best further his long-term interests.
3 *Best deal buyers*   who concentrate on the best deal available at the time.
4 *Creative buyers*   who tell the seller precisely what they want in terms of the product, service and price.
5 *Advertising buyers*   who demand advertising support as part of the deal.
6 *Chisellers*   who constantly demand extra discounts.
7 *Nuts and bolts*   buyers who select products on the basis of the quality of their construction.

Speak to those people within your organization who have responsibility for purchasing and try to identify what sort of buyer(s) they are.

Influences upon the organizational buying process

Much of the thinking that underpinned the earliest research on organizational buying reflected the idea that industrial buyers are wholly rational in their behaviour patterns. More recently, however, a considerable amount of research has highlighted the naivety of this and illustrated that a variety of other factors need to be taken into account. Harding (1966, page 76), for example, has suggested that:

> Corporate decision-makers remain human after they enter the office. They respond to 'image'; they buy from companies to which they feel 'close'; they favour suppliers who show them respect and personal consideration, and who do extra things 'for them'; they 'over-react' to real or imagined slights, tending to reject companies which fail to respond or delay in submitting requested bids.

The significance of this is also apparent in Figure 3.17 on page 74, which shows the four types of influence upon the ways in which buyers behave.

Arriving at a buying decision

In discussing consumer buying behaviour at an earlier stage in the unit, we suggested that buyers move through a five-stage process, beginning with the recognition of a problem and culminating in post-purchase behaviour; this was illustrated in Figure 3.15 on page 67. In the case of organizational buying, the pattern of thought is generally very similar, although Robinson, Faris and Wind extend the thinking slightly by identifying a further three steps. They then linked these to the three types of buying decision to form what is referred to as the *buy-grid framework*; this is illustrated in Figure 3.18 on page 74.

Product selection criteria

As you might expect, the sorts of criteria that buyers use to choose between possible suppliers varies enormously depending upon the type of purchase that is being made. These have been summarized by Lehmann and O'Shaugnessy (1974) in terms of:

*   *Routine orders* (straight rebuy)   delivery, price, reputation and reliability.
*   *Procedural-problem products*   such as office equipment: technical service, flexibility and product reliability.

73

- *Political-problem products* which might lead to arguments within the organization about their suitability: price, supplier regulation, product and service reliability, and supplier flexibility.

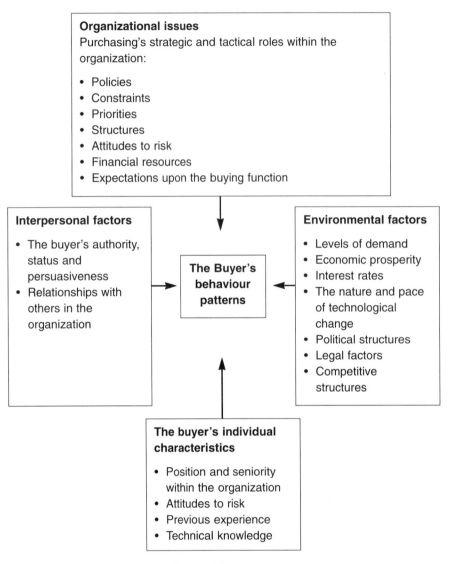

Figure 3.17 Influences upon the organizational buyer

Buy phases	Buy classes		
	Straight rebuy	Modified rebuy	New task
1 The recognition of the problem	N	Possibly	Y
2 The determination of the general need	N	Possibly	Y
3 The specific description of the required product	Y	Y	Y
4 The search for potential suppliers	N	Possibly	Y
5 The detailed evaluation of suppliers	N	Possibly	Y
6 The selection of a supplier	N	Possibly	Y
7 The establishment of an order routine	N	Possibly	Y
8 Performance review and feedback	Y	Y	Y

Figure 3.18 The Buy-grid matrix (Source: adapted from Robinson, et al,1967.)

Identify two examples of each of the three types of purchase within your own organization and compare the buying criteria that are used with those identified by Lehmann and O'Shaugnessy.

Models of organizational buying behaviour

For a more detailed discussion of organizational buying models, turn to page 123 and 130 of *Strategic Marketing Management* by Wilson and Gilligan with Pearson.

There are, in essence, four types of organizational buying behaviour models:

1   *Task-related models* which are similar in concept to the idea discussed earlier, of Marshallian economic man, in that the rationality of the purchasing behaviour and process is emphasized.
2   *Non-task related models* which give explicit recognition to the personal dimensions and interests of the decision maker. Included within these are issues such as the desire to avoid risk, develop relationships inside and outside the organization, and personal advancement.
3   *Complex and multi-disciplinary models* which incorporate a spectrum of social, cultural, psychological and economic factors.
4   *Interactive models* which emphasize the nature of the buying process and the relationships which develop within and between the buying and selling organizations.

The interactive approach has been the foundation of the work conducted by Hakansson and the IMP (International Marketing and Purchasing of Industrial Goods) group and has led to a far greater recognition of the way in which industrial buying and selling is typically concerned with the development and management of relationships. This has, in turn, led to the idea of relationship marketing.

The growth of relationship marketing

It has long been recognized that the costs of gaining a new customer, particularly in mature and slowly declining markets, are often high. Given this, it is argued, the marketing planner needs to ensure that the existing customer base is managed as effectively as possible. One way of doing this is to move away from the traditional, and now largely outmoded, idea of marketing and selling as a series of activities concerned with transactions, and to think instead of them being concerned with the management of long(er) term relationships; this is illustrated in Figure 3.19, on page 76.

What approach to marketing does your organization reflect – a transactional approach or a relationship approach?

Transaction marketing	Relationship marketing
Focus on single sales	Focus on customer retention and building customers loyalty
Emphasis upon product features	Emphasis upon product benefits that are meaningful to the customer
Short timescales	Long timescales recognizing that short-term costs may be higher, but so will long term profits
Little emphasis on customer retention	Emphasis upon higher levels of service that are possibly tailored to the individual customer
Limited customer commitment	High customer commitment
Moderate customer contact	High customer contact with each contact being used to gain information and build the relationship
Quality is essentially the concern of production and no one else	Quality is the concern of all and it is the failure to recognize this that creates minor mistakes that lead to major problems

Figure 3.19   Transaction v relationship marketing.
(Adapted from Christopher, Payne and Ballantyne, 1994, *Relationship Marketing,* page 9.)

The potential benefits of this are considerable and can be seen not just in terms of the higher returns from repeat sales, but also in terms of the opportunities for cross-selling, strategic partnerships and alliances. In developing a relationship marketing programme, there are several important steps:

- Identify the key customers, since it is these, particularly in the early stages, that the most profitable long term relationships can be developed.
- Examine in detail the expectations of both sides.
- Identify how the two organizations can work more closely.
- Think about how operating processes on both sides might need to be changed so that co-operation might be made easier.
- Appoint a relationship manager in each of the two organizations so that there is a natural focal point.
- Go for a series of small wins in the first instance and then gradually strengthen the relationship.
- Recognize from the outset that different customers have very different expectations and that these need to be reflected in the way in which the relationship is developed.

Your managing director has returned from a seminar at which reference was made to 'relationship marketing'. Prepare a briefing paper explaining what relationship marketing entails and what the implications for marketing planning might be. (Strategic Marketing Management: Planning and Control, December 1994, Question 5.)

Summary

Within this unit, we have discussed in some detail the various dimensions of the environment and how an analysis of the environment, including competitors and customers, might be conducted. As a check on your understanding of the material, consider the following questions:

1 Why is a detailed understanding of the environment so necessary for marketing planners? (See pages 44–9.)

2 What makes up the micro and macro marketing environments? (See page 45.)

3 Identify the three environmental types outlined by Miles. (See page 47.)

4 What do we mean by 'crazy days, crazy ways?' (See pages 47–8.)

5 What are the five stages of environmental analysis? (See pages 48–9.)

6 What specific factors would you include within a PEST analysis? (See pages 50.)

7 What are the three stages that organizations generally move through in developing an environmental monitoring system? (See page 51.)

8 What do you see to be the major changes that are likely to take place over the next few years in each of the four PEST dimensions? (See pages 51–2.)

9 What five questions should managers pose when analysing competitors? (See pages 52–3.)

10 What do we mean by a 'competitor's response profile?' (See pages 52–3.)

11 What was the essential message of Levitt's 'Marketing Myopia'? (See page 55.)

12 What are the four essential truths about competition? (See page 55.)

13 Distinguish between the industry perspective and the market perspective of competition. (See pages 54–5.)

14 How would you go about developing a strategic grouping for an industry? (See page 57.)

15 What are the five levels of competitive status? (See page 58.)

16 What information do you need to know about your competitors? (See page 58.)

17 What are the principal sources of competitive information? (See pages 59–61.)

18 Identify the four types of competitor. (See page 61.)

19 What does Porter mean by 'good' and 'bad' competitors? (See pages 61–2.)

20 What makes a competitor vulnerable? (See page 62.)

21 What seven questions is any understanding of buyer behaviour based upon? (See page 64.)

22 Distinguish between customers and consumers. (See page 64.)

23 What are the four types of buyer behaviour? (See page 65.)

24 What factors influence consumer behaviour? (See pages 65–6.)

25 What five roles need to be played in the consumer buying process? (See page 67.)

26 What is the difference between and significance of features and benefits? (See pages 68–9.)

27 What is meant by 'economic man?' (See page 69.)

28 What are the principal differences between consumer and organizational markets? (See pages 70–1.)

29 What are the three types of organizational buying decision? (See page 72.)

30 What roles are played in organizational buying? (See page 72.)

31 What sorts of factors influence the organizational buying process? (See pages 73–4.)

32 What is the buy-grid framework? (See pages 73–4.)

33 Identify the four types of model of organizational buying behaviour. (See page 75.)

34 What is relationship marketing? Why is it becoming increasingly important? (See pages 75–6.)

Against the background of what has been said in this unit, think in detail about how much – or how little – your organization appears to know about its environment generally and its competitors and customers specifically. Find examples of organizations that exhibit the principles of good practice in these areas and try to identify how and why they have a detailed knowledge of their environment. Think about the lessons that might be learned from how they operate. Having done this, turn to Chapters 4, 5 and 7 in *Strategic Marketing Management* and Chapter 3 in *Marketing Strategy*.

Activity debrief

Question 3.1: The sorts of issues that you need to think about include more demanding and more discriminating customers, increasingly aggressive and innovative competitors; more legislation; newer technologies; more volatile economic conditions; social changes (including different demographic patterns); cultural changes; and a faster pace of innovation. The implications include a need for greater flexibility; an improved environmental monitoring system; a clearer competitive stance; better (more precise) segmentation; more innovative advertising; and so on.

Question 3.2: Refer to Figure 3.5.

The danger of too much information would be reflected in information overload and managers ignoring some information and/or being more confused and uncertain than if the information was not available. With regard to a user-friendly system, refer to pages 62–3.

Question 3.3: What about investing in the growing industry or developing strategic alliances?

Question 3.4: Refer to Figure 3.7 and pages 53–62. The problems of collecting the information are the normal problems of information collection: where can we get it from? how accurate is it? what gaps exist? how can these gaps be filled? will the costs be too high?

Question 3.5: Refer back to the answer to Question 1.3 on pages 13–15.

Question 3.6: Refer to the specimen answer for the Watergate Pumps mini case that appears in Unit 9 (pages 196–9).

Question 3.7: Refer to the discussion on pages 37–9, 62, but think also about the significance of the underlying managerial culture. If this is complacent, myopic and competitively arrogant, vulnerability increases enormously.

Question 3.8: Levels of understanding can be increased by focusing upon the buyer's expectations of the product and then analysing the influence that is exerted by each of the principal elements in Figure 3.14. In the case of cars, brands of alcohol and cigarettes (whether the person smokes and what brands), the principal influences are likely to be social, personal and psychological.

Question 3.9: Refer to Figure 3.14 and pages 65–6.

Question 3.10: Refer to the discussion on pages 75–6.

Market segmentation, targeting and positioning

Segmentation, targeting and positioning are key strategic issues. They enable you to understand the nature of the organization's marketplace and to select the marketing programmes that will be profitable for the organization.

In this unit you will:

- Understand how to segment markets.
- Decide what makes a robust market segment.
- Explore ways of marketing to these segments.
- Consider how to position a company in its marketplace.

By the end of this unit you will be able to:

- Appreciate the characteristics and planning needs of organizations in a variety of sectors so that the marketing mix can be tailored to meet the needs/wants of identified market segments.
- Understand how positioning the organization has a powerful effect upon the development of the marketing mix.
- Differentiate between those segments of the market that an organization should target and those which should be avoided.

This unit is critical to Marketing Strategy. Although it only represents a small part of the syllabus, decisions taken on segmentation, targeting and positioning can be the key to a pass mark in the major case study.

Segmentation will often be a key factor to understanding the different market needs so being able to identify the opportunities open to the organization. Many of the past Planning and Control papers have included a question on segmentation and it accounted for 30 per cent of the marks on the ATC case study in the Analysis and Decision paper (December, 1994).

Company positioning, once correctly identified, will point the way for deciding the marketing mix which forms the basis of the marketing plans.

As you work through this unit remember that good strategy must be thought out carefully. The market, as always, must be the inspiration for good marketing. The better you know and understand the market and its needs, the better quality your marketing will be.

After you have completed this unit, review the press adverts in your usual papers. Can you identify what segments the advertisers are aiming their offerings at?

From a review of TV or trade press, can you find examples of good and bad practice.

What can you see of good and bad:

- Targeting?
- Positioning?

What are the consequences of bad decisions in these two areas?

What is segmentation?

Segmentation as a marketing tool came to the fore in the 1980s and looks set to be of critical importance to marketing strategy and strategists in the 1990s. There are two principal reasons for this increased interest in market segmentation. First, after so many years of recession, many companies have simply run out of cost savings that they can make and are now starting to look harder at how they can improve the effectiveness of their marketing spend.

Secondly, the interest in segmentation is directly related to the evolution of most western markets. If the 1960s and 1970s were typified by mass production and volume sales, the 1990s will be typified by people's search for a greater sense of individualism and for identity. People today are much more demanding and discriminating and much less ready to settle for a mass-produced standard item, be it a consumer or industrial product or service. Today's search is for something special, something different, something which reinforces the buyer's own sense of identity as a person, as an individual, as someone separate from the herd. The 1990s product offer stands witness to this ever-growing demand for wider and wider choice.

The net result for most organizations in most markets (except those still artificially regulated or protected) is that segmentation is no longer an option – it is a requirement. Customized marketing is re-emerging as the way to make money in the nineties.

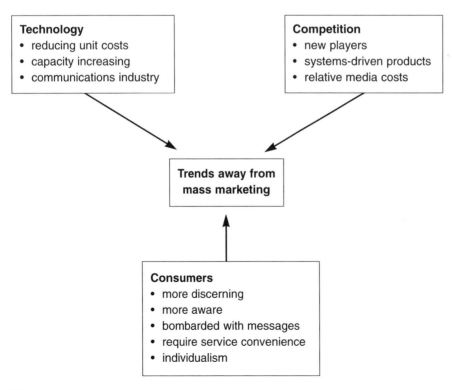

Figure 4.1

In some markets, such as luxury cars or bespoke tailoring, the providers can deal with each and every buyer as an individual and tailor the product accordingly – they can afford to pay for it. In other markets this is not possible – at least not at a price the market is happy to pay. So we have to look for a profitable compromise between the standardized product and the individually tailored. Enter the market segment.

Making reference to examples, discuss how lifestyle and geodemographic approaches to market segmentation might be used by a marketing manager to develop a detailed understanding of a market.
December 1994

(**See** Activity debrief at the end of this unit.)

Unfortunately, for a term that is so frequently used, market segmentation is one of the least understood of all marketing terms. However, used correctly it can be the source of significant competitive advantage.

Market segmentation is the sub-dividing of a market into homogeneous sub-sets of customers, where any sub-set may conceivably be selected as a market target to be reached with a distinct marketing mix.

(Kotler)

From this quite precise definition we can see that market segmentation is all about the identification of 'homogeneous sub-sets of customers', that is, customers who are alike in some way or other. Where any one of these groups 'may conceivably be selected as a market target' in other words we can go for one or all of these groups but we can treat them as a stand alone market target. The final implication, 'a distinct marketing mix', is that the segments, once identified, may each actually demand something different from us as a producer; in other words, the marketing mix is likely to be different from segment to segment. Such a breaking up of our marketing into a number of different mixes is obviously more costly in terms of marketing investment and control. The argument goes that with a more appropriate mix you should improve your penetration of a given market segment and the increased volume in sales would more than pay for the additional costs incurred.

Segmentation needs to be clearly integrated into the strategic process. The steps the marketer might follow are:

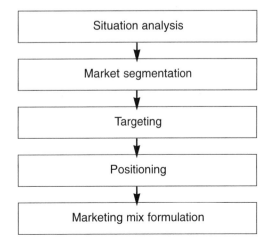

Figure 4.2

Take the example of Johnny Walker. A review of the marketplace obviously showed potential for more than just one type of Scotch whisky. In some duty free shops you can now find up to seven different brands of Johnny Walker – from 'Red Label' at £9 per bottle to 'Honour' at £130 per bottle. Johnny Walker Honour is targeted at the Japanese market and has been positioned as a prestige gift product rather than just an alcoholic drink.

ACTIVITY 4.2

Can you identify a company which has followed this process? How has segmentation led to targeting and then led to positioning? How do the final marketing mixes differ for the eventual product–market matches?

Segmentation bases

How can markets be segmented? Historically, the list is practically endless. Think of a segmentation base and someone somewhere has tried it and probably someone else will swear that it is the only possible way to segment their particular marketplace. Markets are normally broken up by:

- *Geography*   national, international markets, regions, county, town, even by street and house.
- *Demographics and socioeconomics*   by age, sex, family life stage, income, occupation, or education.
- *Psychographics*   social class, lifestyle and personality.
- *Behavioural*   product usage, benefits sought, store usage, usage rate, price sensitivity, user status, loyalty status and critical events.

These and other bases are covered in greater depth in Wilson and Gilligan with Pearson, pages 200–215.

Probably one of the most useful bases for segmentation is that of benefits sought. Benefit segmentation is not new – as a concept it has been around for almost thirty years, nevertheless it still forms the basis for most segmentation, certainly in consumer markets. The past four years have seen a number of developments in the area of segmentation. Much work has been carried out in the area of demographic and geodemographic segmentation. One operation (MOSAIC) is soon to incorporate the VALS typology into its surveys. These developments are in response to organizations' needs to understand more fully their customers' needs, wants and behaviour. Both the Planning and Control and Analysis and Decision papers are asking questions more frequently in the area of segmentation and students need to have a good grasp of the variables involved in strategic segmentation decisions.

One of the most powerful aspects of benefit segmentation is that, by focusing on purchase motivation, it forces the marketer to understand a fundamental truth about market segmentation. The marketplace segments itself. The terminology used in segmentation (both in the literature and company practice) always seems to imply that the organization or the marketer is actually doing something to the marketplace. This is a dangerous misconception. People, by their actions, fit themselves into particular market segments – and out of others. The concept of marketers forcing their customers into pre-determined groups for administrative convenience is seriously outdated. The job for marketers today is simple: identify how the market has divided itself up and package and present the marketing mix(es) accordingly.

Many marketing managers acknowledge that lifestyle approaches to segmentation become increasingly necessary as individuals progress through the hierarchy of needs. By reference to examples, identify the extent to which lifestyle segmentation might be used to improve our understanding of consumers.

June 1991

(**See** Activity debrief at the end of this unit.)

So, the question really becomes 'How can we identify relevant segments in our marketplace?'

ACTIVITY 4.3

- How does your organization segment its markets?
- Can you count more than one approach?
- How well does your organization use its segmentation approach to improve customer satisfaction?
- How do your competitors segment the market?
- Is segmentation used as a strategic tool?

Segmenting industrial markets

Although most of the work in recent years on segmentation has been applied to consumer markets, segmentation is becoming more and more important in the industrial and business-to-business markets too. Industrial buyers, like consumers, rarely buy on price alone and are constantly seeking value added for themselves and their organizations when they make their 'rational' purchases.

Typical segmentation bases which have been used for industrial markets include:

- *Demographic*   classification by industry, by type and size of company, by location.
- *Operating variables*   by principal form of technology which the customers use, user status (high, medium, low user), customer capabilities (broad or narrow range of needs).
- *Purchasing approaches*   buying criteria (quality, service or price), buying policies (purchase, lease, lowest bid), current relationships (new or existing customers).
- *Situational factors*   urgency (speed of delivery), size of order (large or small), applications (general or specific).
- *Personal characteristics*   loyalty, attitude to risk, organizational culture, status of the buyer in the organization.

QUESTION 4.3

Evaluate the proposition that our knowledge of how to segment industrial markets effectively now lags a considerable way behind how this might be done in consumer markets.

December 1992

(**See** Activity debrief at the end of this unit.)

It has been the trend over recent years for many industrial businesses to organize their markets in terms of 'vertical markets' and thereby divide their markets into commercial types such as banking, transportation, manufacturing, financial services etc. As long as this mode of classification produces groups of customers and prospects have more in common than, say, a collection of 'risk averse' organizations from different industries then the organization has a segment.

Tests of segmentation

There are a number of ways in which we can test potential market segments. Taking the best from the theorists, the questions you should be asking yourself are:

- *Is the segment homogeneous?* The most important question, will all the members of the segment act in a uniform manner and respond in the same way to the marketing input that they receive? If not, then you probably have a 'classification' but not a segment.
- *Is the segment measurable?* Do we know where it is, how big it is, and exactly how it differs from the market at large and other segments in particular?
- *Is the segment accessible?* There could be a perfect segment in the marketplace but if we can't get to it with our communication, or our delivery channels then that segment remains of purely hypothetical value.
- *Is the segment substantial?* Is it big enough for us to make profit out of? We must bear in mind the extra expense incurred in managing more than one marketing mix into our market segments and of course people's willingness to pay a premium price.
- *Is the segment exclusive?* Maybe a little purist, but will the segment understand and relate to messages directed at it and be turned off by messages originally aimed at another segment?
- *Is the segment recognized by the customers themselves?* If they don't identify with the segment, not only will they not understand or identify with the promotion or communication aimed at them, they may actually reject this enforced membership and wreak their vengeance upon your product offering.
- *Is the segment recognized by the intermediaries in the channel?* If they don't, they are unlikely to co-operate in the marketing activity making it unlikely that you and your organization will be able to satisfy properly the segment's needs.
- *Will the products or services be premium priced?* If not, why are you doing this? It is difficult for an offering to be seen as really different if you charge a standard price.
- *Will the segment offer above-average returns?* Not just desirable, but mandatory. You will be looking for profit from a smaller overall market – it must offer good returns.

These commonsense questions need to be answered if you are to be sure of having a potentially profitable segment on your hands.

ACTIVITY 4.4

Applying these tests to your own organization, how robust is your segmentation approach?

What changes (if any) would you recommend?

Problems with segmentation

The key problems with segmentation as currently implemented in many organizations can be summed up from the following diagram.

Past	Future
Correlation	Causality
Description	Motivation

Most organizations talk about segmentation in terms that relate to the words in the left-hand column rather than the words on the right.

- *Past and future*   When asked how they segment and what they are doing in the area, invariably people will start to describe their past experiences with customers; how people reacted; what they did and even an analysis of where the last three years' sales have come from. As we all know, the future is unlikely to be a straight-line extrapolation from the past, much as we would like it to be so.

    As marketers trying to put together a marketing strategy which will deliver what the business needs, our concerns must be for the future. Our attention must centre on where we should invest our marketing spend and our energy for both short and long-term returns from the marketplace. The past has gone. There is some value to be gained from understanding the lessons of the past but only if they can improve our future activity.

- *Correlation and causality*   The second problem is that when you press people to explain the rationale behind their segments you are often presented with a whole series of correlations. What we need to uncover is some degree of causality. There may be some relationships which an in-depth study of our existing customers could expose, however it is dangerous to build a strategy on relationships which lack an identifiable cause. In other words, is there an underlying motivational reason why people act in a certain way that we can understand from their circumstances?

3 *Description and motivation*   Finally, there is a general misunderstanding between description and motivation. An in-depth description of our existing customer base and our existing 'segments' in terms of age profiles, sex, income, occupation, education, family life stage or even socio-economic grouping is only really valid if we believe that these characteristics are motivational. Descriptors tend to come from the past. 'This is how last year's customers looked.' Only very rarely will a customer group described in these terms surprise us by acting in a way unique from the rest of the market.

    The only thing we know for sure about the future is that our ideas and predictions will be wrong; but it is still worthwhile working to reduce the margin of error. It is our job to ensure that we make the best possible return on the money which the organization invests in its markets. Returns are based upon informed judgement of how a segment will respond to our offer and what will motivate it to buy.

Once proper behavioural segments have been identified in the marketplace, the next important job is to describe these segments in such a way that practical operational marketing can be brought to bear on them. This is the point at which terms such as demographics, lifestyles, usage patterns and socio-economic groupings can properly be brought into play as targeting methods. As long as we remember that these are descriptive terms and not the reason why people will buy the product or service offered, they can be a useful shorthand way of enhancing general understanding of the segments.

Making reference to examples, discuss the extent to which developments in approaches to market segmentation over the past decade have advanced our understanding of consumer markets.

December 1991

(**See** Activity debrief at the end of this unit.)

QUESTION 4.4

Market targeting

Marketing is not only about satisfied customers today. It is about the longer term. It is about profits. It is about matching the organization's resources to market needs – it is about planning. If we have segmented our markets properly we will have identified different areas of need. We will also know where these groups are, how big they are and what it is they want from us.

This section will look at the key decisions that the marketer must take now. What is the future for the identified segments? Which segments should we approach and which should we leave? How do we market to the selected segments?

Market segmentation is – or ought to be – about improving the organization's return on its marketing investment. Segmentation will normally appeal more to the longer-term thinker than the 'quick buck' marketer because it involves an initial outlay in costs to adapt our marketing offer to the precise need(s) of the identified segment(s). If we are interested in tomorrow's returns on today's investments, then we need to have some idea about where the segments are going.

- *Is the segment growing or declining?* Here we are interested in two broad aspects of growth and decline. What is the projected future of the segment in terms of volume sales and profitability? Despite much argument to the contrary there need not be a link between volume sales and profit. Declining volumes in certain market segments can still be extremely profitable for the organizations which service them. It's often more a question of how the segment is managed rather than what the segment is doing.

ACTIVITY 4.5

Looking at your organization and its markets, can you identify emerging segments – the segments where tomorrow's money will be made?

- *Is the segment changing?* There are three aspects to this question of change. First, we need to try and get a feel for how the structure and make-up of the segment is likely to change over time. Is the segment starting to attract new and slightly different members to its centre? What effect will this have on the segment's needs?

   The second aspect of change relates to the nature of the products and services which we would expect this segment to be demanding in the future. In other words, do we see any significant change in the way in which the members of the segment are likely to translate their needs into buying behaviour? Will they want different products or services in three years time?

   The third area of segment change must consider the movements of the segments over time. For example, do we see the overall array of segments changing? There are two ways in which this structural change can occur. Segments may merge and combine to create larger more 'shallow' segments. Larger segments may fragment over time into smaller more precise market targets for the organization to approach.

Which segments should we enter?

Just because they are there doesn't mean that you have to be competing actively in each and every segment.

- *What does our strategy tell us?* This is the point at which you must touch base with your organization's business objectives and corporate positioning. Market segments ought to be selected according to the broader strategic decisions taken by the company. For example, the organization aiming for a 'differentiated' position in the marketplace will need to retain a certain degree of flexibility which will allow it to operate in a number of related market segments while still retaining its differentiated market position. The 'focused' organization on the other hand will necessarily have to get much, much closer to its fewer market segments, and will have to predict fragmentation and merging long before this phenomenon arises. It must be prepared and be able to continue to service changing segment needs as they arise. Failure to do this by the focused organization will leave it very vulnerable to competitive attack in its core markets.

- *And what about our resources and capability?* As well as identifying those segments which 'fit' our broader strategic aspirations, we ought to consider how well we are able to meet the identified needs of the various segments. It is wise to concentrate on those segments where your organization has the capability and resources to satisfy customer needs.

Ordering the segments

Now that we have identified the market segments and the likely evolutions of those segments over the next few years, we need to decide what to do with this information. Again, this doesn't mean hitting everything that moves, it means being selective. There are two reasons why selectivity should be considered.

First, marketing and business resources are necessarily limited, therefore we must choose where to invest our resources for the right level of returns. The second reason why selectivity is important concerns customer perceptions. In the 1960s and 1970s the large conglomerates could lay claim to being in a variety of different businesses. Their size was a major factor in this argument and customers accepted the claim that an adequate product and service could come from a large, non-specialist organization. The 1980s and the 1990s are seeing this claim being less readily acceptable in the marketplace. Quality, it is perceived, is more likely to come from specialization. The organization should then select market segments which will reinforce this image in the marketplace.

Unfortunately, marketing resources are normally limited so we have to consider approaching market segments in some ordered fashion. We can do this by looking at a number of quite clearly defined criteria as shown in Figure 4.3

Criteria	Weight	Segments				
1 Long-term volume growth 2 Long-term profit growth 3 Short-term volume growth 4 Short-term profit growth 5 Organizational image 6 Offensive strategic reasons 7 Defensive strategic reasons 8 Internal resource/capability 9 Relative competitive strength 10 Other ... 11 12						
Total						
Priority						

(Ratings 1–10, 10 = highly attractive)

Figure 4.3

The order depicted here need not necessarily be the one that you should follow; the order will largely depend upon the circumstances depicted in the examination case or question. There will also be additional criteria to be included that are specific to the market situation described in the paper.

A simple and convenient (although not mathematically accurate) analysis of market/segment attractiveness can be carried out with the diagram shown. After listing all the relevant criteria and the market segments in question, you can attempt to rate – using points out of 10 – each segment against each criteria.

1 *Long-term volume growth potential* These are typically the growing market segments which will generate large amounts of tomorrow's volume.

2 *Long-term profit growth* Profit growth and volume growth need not necessarily be contained in the same segment. Long-term profit growth could come from a declining segment where competition is vacating the segment and leaving more profit opportunities for our organization.

3 *Short-term volume growth* As we all know, long-term vision and strategy is essential for the survival of the organization. Nevertheless, it is important that the organization lives long enough to realize the potential coming from its future markets. In other words, we have to generate volume sales today if for no other reason than to make sure we are around tomorrow.

4 *Short-term profit growth* Short-term profits are as important as long-term profits. It is short term profits which allow us to invest in the future. These segments should be identified and should be carefully nurtured. They should not, however, be the only segments that we attack.

5 *Organizational image* There are things in life other than profit, at least more important than directly attributable profit. In the same way that the men's wet shaver market has used the concept of selling razors at a low price and making the margin on the blades, so we can extend this idea into strategic terms. There may be segments within which the organization must be a major or at least an active player if its strategic market position is to be credible in the marketplace. It may be that these segments produce no profit of their own but by being in this segment we are allowed to be in another segment where profit is generated. Combined segment profitability must be positive over the long term but individual segment losses need to be watched very carefully indeed.

6 *Offensive strategic reasons* The organization's business strategy may involve the development of new segments or the creation of bridgehead segments which in themselves hold no intrinsic value for the organization, but which will allow the achievement of the organization's business objective over the longer term.

7 *Defensive strategic reasons* These are segments which may appear to be much less attractive to the organization in terms of volume or in terms of profits or maybe even in terms of image and company positioning. However, falling out of the initial research in competitor analysis and competitive opportunities, it may become apparent that our competitors' strategies might take them into certain market areas which could, in the long term, prove quite dangerous for our organization's position.

8 *Internal resource/capability reasons* There will always be segments which we could tap purely because we happen to be good at producing the products and services that the segment demands; however, just because we have the internal ability and maybe the short-term profit looks attractive, this does not necessarily mean that we should be attacking these segments.

9 *Relative competitive strength* As above, there will also be segments where your organization has definite competitive strength and advantage over the competition. Again, it may or may not be a wise decision to attack these segments. Always look to the long term and the strategic rather than the tactical issues involved.

10 *Other* The industry or organization depicted in the examination question will probably have its own special criteria for what makes an attractive segment. But before you add extra measures make sure that you are not just dealing with conventional wisdom or industry 'myth'.

Once you have rated and weighted for various segments you can see what order of priority the segments are in. You should consider whether those lowest on the list need to be approached at all.

Look at your organization. Can you apply these tests to the segments that you have identified? What does this imply for the way that you organize your marketing to the various segments?

After having considered segmentation in one part of your answer (especially the major case study) use the conclusions of your work when answering further questions. For example, show how different mixes and marketing approaches can better target different segments.

Marketing to the segments

Having discovered now that your market is made up of a number of different segments, each with their own needs, doesn't automatically mean that you have instantly to modify all your marketing activities for each segment. You have three choices.

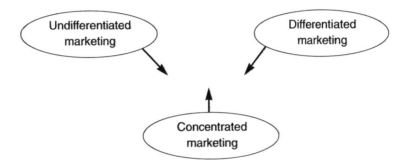

Figure 4.4

1   *Undifferentiated marketing*   Your know your market is made up of a number of different segments but you decide not to differentiate your marketing approach by segment. Maybe your competition is not particularly strong, or the needs among the segments are not particularly different. In any event you must keep a close eye on the segments and their development over time. Supporting more than one marketing platform can be expensive and the returns from the market need to justify this. Also, if there is no pressure from competition to segment your marketing why rush?

2   *Differentiated marketing*   You have identified the segments that make up your market and decide to offer a range of marketing offers to match the different needs. Under this scenario, you have decided to differentiate your marketing to better match the segment's needs. How far you move from a single, undifferentiated offer is, of course, up to you.

   You should bear in mind though that your branding policy is important too. Differentiated offers under the same brand can be confusing for customers and can dilute recognition of what the brand stands for. Multi-brand strategies avoid this problem but are quite expensive to maintain.

   Lastly, there is the management aspect. Keeping control of different marketing propositions so that each is clear and credible to the target market is not an easy task. Managing the propositions, especially where this 'overlap' occurs, takes time and effort – make sure that the market response makes this extra effort worthwhile.

3   *Concentrated marketing*   You have decided to concentrate your marketing effort on one or more of the segments that you have identified – and specifically not to market others. The concentration and specialist nature of your marketing should be clear for everyone to see. If you are going to profit from this approach, typically we would

expect to see a more tailored offer than other companies, better targeted than other companies, greater choice (within the target market) than other companies and higher prices than other companies.

ACTIVITY 4.7

Which of these three approaches is used by your organization?

Strategic positioning

Most readers will be well aware of Porter's work in the area of competitive strategy and his description of the three generic competitive strategies, cost leadership, differentiation and focus (see also Unit 5). Leaving aside discussion on the cost leadership strategy which is discussed in another section, focus and differentiation strategies both depend upon a successful positioning strategy by the organization to be successful. Porter's work in this area should always be read alongside the important article by Levitt – 'Differentiation – of anything' (*Harvard Business Review*, January/February 1980).

Both Porter and Levitt assert that in today's highly competitive marketplaces an organization (and its products or services) need to be seen by the marketplace and their customers as offering something different or unique from every other organization. This way lies profits. In deciding the organization's market position, the marketer will be stating to customers what the company stands for and how its products differ from current and potentially competing products.

Positioning is therefore the process of designing an image and value so that customers within the target segment or segments understand what the company or brand stands for in relation to its competitors. It should be readily apparent from this that company positioning is a fundamental element of marketing strategy, since any decision on positioning has direct and immediate implications for the whole of the marketing mix. In essence, therefore, the marketing mix can be seen as the tactical details of an organization's positioning strategy.

This being the case, it is then the marketing strategist's job to decide, in detail, the basis of the differentiation which it will hold in its own competitive arena. In other words the organization must identify and build a collection of competitive advantages that will appeal to the target market and then communicate these effectively.

EXTENDING YOUR KNOWLEDGE

Essential reading for any would-be strategist is the mould-breaking article 'Marketing Myopia' by Levitt (*Harvard Business Review*, 1960). Positioning the organization, in customer terms, will be essential for good grade passes in the major case study.

The process of positioning

The process of strategically positioning an organization can be described in a number of sequential steps:

1 Identify the total target marketplace and the manner in which the marketplace segments itself (see above).
2 Assess the organization's resources and capabilities and identify the possible alternative competitive advantages which the organization may decide to capitalize on in its target marketplaces.

3 Comparing 1 and 2, identify possible matches of competitive advantage to target market needs.

4 Select a particular emphasis (strategic market position) for the organization to pursue over the longer term planning period.

5 Implement the positioning strategy in market terms. This process will require a careful analysis of which market segments to target (see above), which products and product ranges need to be developed and marketed to support the agreed market position in the marketplace, and the branding policy which is required to support the positioning strategy.

6 Communicate the identified position to the target marketplace in such a way that the customers understand how the organization and its product or service offering is different from the competition and the nature of the additional value they will gain from purchasing from the organization.

'Market niching' is the term used to describe those organizations, usually small firms, who prosper by specializing in parts of the market which are too limited in size and potential to be of real interest to larger firms. By concentrating their efforts in this way 'nichers' are able to build specialist market knowledge and often avoid head-on competition with larger organizations.

Making use of examples, identify the criteria for effective market niching and discuss whether it is a strategy suited only to small organizations.

December 1992

(**See** Activity debrief at the end of this unit.)

Positioning problems

If the organization or the strategist fails on any of the steps involved in positioning strategy this is likely to lead to one of three common problems:

1 *Confused positioning* This happens when buyers are unsure of what the organization stands for and do not clearly see how it is different from the competitive companies and products in the choice presented. British banks continue to suffer from this.

2 *Over positioning* This occurs where customers perceive the organization's range of products and/or services as being simply expensive. The implication here is that the organization has either mis-identified or badly communicated the additional benefits inherent in the range. This is the area of the glittering but brief product appearances. Examples can be found from the Ford Edsel to many of today's glossy magazines that are launched and fold within months.

3 *Under positioning* A common problem, it happens where the message is simply too vague and customers have little real idea of what the organization stands for and exactly how it is different from the competition. Middle market tabloid newspapers suffer from this problem. The Daily Mail and the Daily Express fight constantly for the same market.

These three positioning problems are always evident in examination answers to case study questions. Look at your past exam attempts and identify where you have fallen into these traps. What could you have done to avoid them?

Remember, bad positioning can only lead to bad marketing mix answers!

Summary

In this section we have seen that market segmentation, targeting and positioning are essential ingredients to a modern practical marketing strategy. The mass market is an outdated concept in the vast majority of business areas and segmentation is an essential ingredient for any business which needs to understand customer needs in order to make profits. In the area of market segmentation we have seen:

- Segmentation is about improving the effectiveness of marketing activity.
- Segmentation is about better market penetration and better profits.
- Organizations don't segment markets, markets segment themselves.
- Segments must be based on motivation not description.
- Segments need to be tested.

Segmenting the market is only the first step. Once you have identified the segments that make up your marketplace you must:

- Plot where the segments are going.
- Decide which segments you are going to attack.
- Decide how you are going to market it to them.

Once decisions have been made on the structure of the market (in its segments and the ideal targets that the organization should focus upon) the marketing strategist needs to consider how best to position the organization, product range and brands within the marketplace. Positioning and identity are key strategic factors which will enable the organization to stand out in an ever more competitive marketplace. Segmentation and positioning, like marketing itself, are as much an art as a science; feel your way carefully. Do not go faster than others in your organization can understand and therefore can implement. Do not go faster than the market can understand, it also prefers evolution to revolution.

As a check on your understanding of what has been covered in this unit, consider the following questions:

1 What is meant by market segmentation?
2 Why is market segmentation becoming an ever more important part of marketing?
3 In what ways might you segment:
   - consumer markets
   - industrial markets

   What are the pros and cons of each method?
4 What are the nine tests of segmentation?
5 What problems are typically encountered when segmenting markets?
6 What is meant by market targeting?
7 What factors should be taken into account when targeting?
8 How might you decide upon which segments to enter?
9 Explain what is meant by undifferentiated marketing, differentiated marketing and concentrated marketing.
10 Why is positioning strategically significant?
11 How might you go about positioning?
12 What problems are often experienced in attempts to position? Give examples of companies that have made these mistakes.

Having read this unit, look in detail at how a variety of organizations segment, target and position. What lessons might be learned from them? Look then at organizations which seemingly have little understanding of how to segment or the benefits that can emerge. What appear to be the competitive consequences of this?

To supplement your understanding of the subject you should also read: Wilson and Gilligan with Pearson (1992), *Strategic Marketing Management,* Chapter 8, and Fifield (1992), *Marketing Strategy,* pages 122–134.

Activity debrief

Question 4.1 December 1994 Market segmentation is a key method of developing a detailed understanding of any organization's markets. It helps the marketing manager identify the range of different needs that exist in the market and the reasons (motivation) for the existence of those needs. The beginning of a successful marketing plan. Has your answer explained briefly what lifestyle and geodemographic segmentation is and, most importantly, how it can be applied to improve understanding of a market? What examples have you used? Do they support the question and demonstrate how better understanding of markets can be acheived in practice? If you have not included the examples asked for you will be unlikely to pass!

Question 4.2 June 1991 In your answer have you used clear examples (that will be recognized by the examiner) to illustrate your points? Have you used the 'hierarchy of needs' model as a base and explored the different ways that markets might be segmented? Your answer should have discussed what is meant by lifestyle segmentation with the rationale and general direction of research in this area. You should then have shown how lifestyle measures can be used to improve our knowledge of consumers and how this information can contribute to the formulation of effective marketing strategy.

Question 4.3 December 1992 In your answer have you 'evaluated the proposition'? You're not asked how to segment industrial markets! Your answer should argue both sides of the proposition – and then either support or reject the proposition, with justification. Does industrial segmentation lag behind consumer? Why – or why not? Examples could be useful.

Question 4.4 December 1991 Has your answer clearly demonstrated the link between developments in market segmentation and a broader understanding of consumer markets? Have you described the recent developments in segmentation? You have been asked to make reference to examples – have you done this? – you can sacrifice marks needlessly if you have not.

Question 4.5 December 1992 Your answer should succinctly explain market niching. You should have described (and briefly explained) the criteria for niching. Examples have been requested so must be included. Don't forget the last part of the question, you should have discussed (shown the arguments for and against) the proposition that market niching is a strategy only suitable for small organizations.

Formulating the marketing strategy

In this unit you will examine the various dimensions of marketing strategy and the ways in which an appropriate strategy might possibly be formulated. As a result of this, you will understand:

- What is meant by a strategic perspective and why a strategic perspective is important.
- The rationale for portfolio analysis.
- The various models of portfolio analysis.
- Porter's three generic strategies.
- How market position influences and needs to be reflected in strategy.

By the end of this unit you will:

- Be able to analyse a product portfolio.
- Appreciate the need for a clear competitive strategy.
- Understand how market forces influence strategy.
- Be capable of formulating a marketing strategy.

Within this unit we focus upon an important element of Stage 3 of the Planning and Control syllabus and one which feeds in very obviously to the Analysis and Decision case study. Given that the Diploma has become far more strategic in its orientation over the past few years, it is essential that you understand the sort of frameworks within which strategic marketing decisions are made and the sorts of models that can be used.

To support the content of this unit, you should read the specialist marketing press with a view to identifying, as clearly as possible, the sorts of strategies that firms are using.

Although this unit covers only about 12–15 per cent of the syllabus, its importance cannot be over-stated. You should therefore spend 4–5 hours on this unit, but supplement this with as much reading as possible, and discussions with managers to find out how they go about developing their strategies. You should also spend time reading the maxi case studies for the Analysis and Decision examination with a view to identifying the linkages between the material covered here and the maxi case.

The growth of strategic perspectives

The widespread growth of corporate and marketing strategic planning can be traced back to the early 1970s when managers, faced with the consequences of a series of major environmental changes and upsets, began searching for stronger and more analytical frameworks that would help them to identify opportunities and threats more readily and manage their businesses more effectively. This new planning process, which became known as portfolio analysis, was based on three main ideas:

1 An organization should be managed along the same lines as an investment portfolio with the interdependencies and interrelationships between different parts of the business being recognized and decisions on their development or deletion being made on this basis.
2 Detailed attention should be paid to each element's short and long-term profit potential.
3 A *strategic* approach to the management of the business should be adopted with emphasis being paid to such issues as the industry structure, business opportunities, organizational resources and levels of capability.

However, if such an approach is to be adopted, managers need to recognize – in detail – the nature of the interrelationships that exist between different parts and levels of the organization. In the majority of organizations there are three principal levels that need to be considered. In commenting on this Wilson et al (1992, page 224) suggest:

> At the *corporate level* the decisions made are concerned principally with the corporate strategic plan and how best to develop the long term profile of the business. This, in turn, involves a series of decisions on the levels of resource allocation to individual business units, be it a division or a subsidiary, and on which new potential businesses should be supported. Following on from this, each *business unit* should, within the resources allocated by corporate headquarters, then develop its own strategic plan. Finally, marketing plans need to be developed at the *product level*. Plans at all three levels need then to be implemented, the results monitored and evaluated and, where necessary, corrective action taken.

This is illustrated in Figure 5.1.

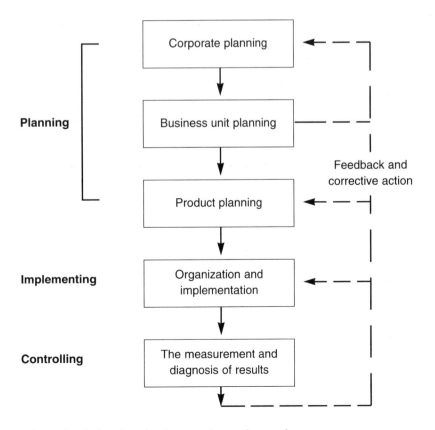

Figure 5.1   The cycle of planning, implementation and control

Approaches to planning

There are, in essence, three principal approaches to planning:

1 *Bottom-up planning* in which individual business units are given considerable freedom to develop their own objectives and strategies, with corporate management requiring only that the targets set are then achieved.
2 *Top-down planning* in which corporate management sets the objectives and maintains a close involvement with both the development and the implementation of strategy and tactics.
3 *Goals down/plans up* planning in which corporate management establishes the broad planning parameters in terms of targets and then allows the business units to decide how these will be achieved.

QUESTION 5.1

What do you think are the major advantages and disadvantages of each of these three approaches to planning? Which approach predominates in your own organization?

Regardless, however, of which approach is used, corporate management has the responsibility for the four principal dimensions of the planning process:

1 Defining the business mission.
2 Establishing the organization's strategic business units.
3 Conducting an evaluation of the existing portfolio.
4 Identifying areas for development.

EXAM TIP

It is often very apparent both in the Planning and Control and the Analysis and Decision examinations that candidates have only a hazy idea of the sorts of factors that should influence marketing strategy. You should therefore make sure that you understand the sorts of models that can be used and how market position is capable of exerting a powerful influence on strategy.

The role of strategic business units (SBUs)

Planning on the basis of strategic business units (SBUs) was first developed in the 1960s and was designed to give explicit recognition to the way in which the vast majority of organizations operate across a variety of market sectors with a variety of products or services. Because of this, any approach to planning needs to reflect the significance of each market sector and the very different opportunities and threats that exist. Without this, it is likely that managers will fail to appreciate the complete picture and concentrate instead upon particular parts of the portfolio at the longer term expense of the others.

A strategic business unit (SBU) is:

- A single business or a collection of related businesses which offer scope for independent planning which might feasibly stand alone from the rest of the organization.
- Has its own set of competitors.
- Has a manager who has responsibility for strategic planning and profit performance and who has control of profit influencing factors.

Source: Wilson and Gilligan with Pearson, *Strategic Marketing Management*, page 226.

We said earlier that portfolio analysis involves taking account of the interrelationships and inter-dependencies that exist between the organization's various SBUs. An important aspect of this is concerned with identifying the scope for development and the profit potential of each SBU and where, therefore, investment should be directed. A variety of frameworks to help with this have been developed, one of the earliest of which was proposed by Peter Drucker in 1963 who suggested labelling products as follows:

- Tomorrow's breadwinners.
- Today's breadwinners.
- Products that are capable of making a contribution assuming drastic remedial action is taken.
- Yesterday's breadwinners.
- The also rans.
- The failures.

Using Drucker's framework, conduct an initial analysis of your organization's SBUs. What picture emerges? Is it one that senior management can be happy with?

ACTIVITY 5.1

Although it has been argued that Drucker's classification of products in this way is too simplistic, it is potentially useful as a starting point for portfolio analysis in that it highlights the sorts of interrelationships that exist between the different parts or SBUs of an organization and the patterns of cash generation and cash usage that are likely to exist. Without this sort of understanding, it is likely that decisions on SBUs will be made with at least a degree of insularity with the result that the net long-term outcome will be rather less than it might otherwise be.

Using this sort of framework as a base, a number of rather more detailed and specific models, which collectively are labelled models of portfolio analysis (PA), have been developed.

Models of portfolio analysis

One of the earliest and best known approaches to portfolio analysis was put forward by the Boston Consulting Group (BCG). This model involves SBUs being plotted on a matrix according to:

- The rate of market growth.
- Their market share relative to that of the largest competitor.

The thinking behind the model is straightforward and based on the idea that, in making investment and marketing decisions, managers need to give specific thought to the market's future potential (the annual growth rate) and to the SBU's competitive position (relative market share); this is illustrated in Figure 5.2.

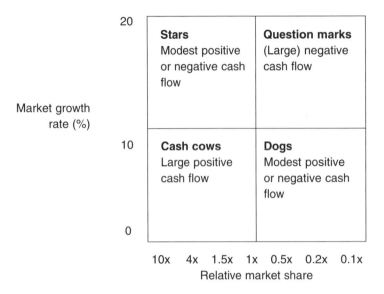

Figure 5.2 The Boston Consulting Group's growth-share matrix

The undoubted success of the BCG's growth-share matrix and the way in which it has subsequently been the forerunner for a number of other models of portfolio analysis can be attributed to several factors, including the apparent ease with which the model can be applied and the prescriptive strategies that were seemingly associated with each of the four cells. In the case of cash cows, for example, it was suggested that they should be milked or managed for their large positive cash flow. Dogs, it is argued, should either be phased out (shot) or, if they have a modest positive cash flow, managed to maximize this. Stars need the support of a well-formulated investment policy, whilst question marks need either substantial investment in order to strengthen their position or, if they offer little real long term potential, phased out.

An apparent attraction of the BCG matrix is the way in which it provides the strategist with an initial picture of the shape, health and balance of the organization's portfolio. Having this enables the strategist to make a series of decisions relating to the objectives, strategy and budget for each SBU. Typically, this then leads to a choice of one of four broad strategies involving:

1   Building market share in order to strengthen the SBU's position.
2   Holding the share at the current level to ensure that the maximum amounts of cash are generated.
3   Harvesting as much cash as possible in the short term, even if it weakens the SBU's long-term future.
4   Divesting by getting rid of the SBU so that it no longer acts as a drain on resources.

ACTIVITY 5.2

Using the BCG growth-share matrix, plot the position of your organization's SBUs. What sort of picture regarding the balance and health of the portfolio emerges? To what extent can you identify *explicit* strategies for each of the SBUs? In what ways do they correspond with the four strategies identified above? (Examiner's tip: in plotting the position of the SBUs, always start with the market growth rate. In the case of Figure

5.2, this goes from 1–20 per cent, although you may have to change this to reflect the specifics of your market; the key issue is that you distinguish between low and high growth. Turn then to the horizontal axis which focuses upon relative competitive position. This is measured logarithmically against the market share of the firm's largest competitor. If you have half the share of this firm, your relative position is 0.5x. If you are joint leader you have 1.0x. If you have the biggest SBU and your next biggest competitor has half the share that you have, you would position yourself at 2.0x.

In evaluating the shape of any portfolio, several factors need to be taken into account. In essence, a balanced portfolio exhibits certain characteristics including a mixture of cash cows and stars. By contrast, an unbalanced and potentially dangerous portfolio would have too many dogs or question marks and too few stars and cash cows, since this would lead to insufficient cash being generated on a day-to-day basis to fund or support the development of other SBUs.

The mini case study for the December 1994 Planning and Control examination was based upon an organization called RTJ Engineering Ltd. The case study included details of five SBUs. Candidates were required to comment upon the apparent state of the firm's portfolio and recommend how it should be developed. You should therefore turn to this mini case in Unit 9 and try to answer the question posed; the solution appears at a later stage in the unit (see pages 175–7, 204–5).

The limitations of portfolio analysis

Although models such as the BCG matrix are capable of providing the strategist with a picture of an organization's overall portfolio, the reader needs to recognize this is simply a snapshot at one particular point. In order to arrive at a clearer and more strategically useful picture, the strategist needs to think about how the portfolio is likely to develop over the next few years and what the implications of this probable shape are for the future of the organization. One way of doing this is to plot the portfolio not just for the current time period but also for, say, three and/or five years ahead. In doing this, you do of course have to make a series of assumptions, one of which might be that the current product/market mix will stay broadly the same. A second assumption might be that competitors will not make any major changes to their strategies. Given this, it should then be possible to identify the sort of strategic action that is needed in terms of decision on new products, marketing support, and possibly product deletion. The picture can then be made richer still if portfolio analyses are conducted for each of the firm's major competitors both for t0 and t+3 (t0 is today whilst t+3 is three years ahead), since this will provide the strategist with a greater understanding of each competitor's current and probable future portfolio strengths and weaknesses, as well as any portfolio gaps that might emerge.

What characterizes:

- A balanced portfolio?
- An unbalanced portfolio?

Although the Boston Consulting Group matrix has proved to be enormously useful in helping many managers to think far more strategically about the nature of their portfolio and the decisions that need to be made, it needs to be recognized that the real value of portfolio analysis is influenced very firmly not just by the quality of the basic data inputs, many of which have proved to be difficult to find and measure, but also by the broader environment within which decisions are made. It was very largely in an attempt to overcome these sorts of problems and to give recognition to a greater number of factors that a variety of other approaches to portfolio analysis have been developed. Included within these are the General Electric multi-factor matrix, the Shell directional policy matrix, the Arthur D Little strategic condition matrix, and Abell and Hammond's 3x3 investment opportunity chart.

In the case of the General Electric multi-factor model the thinking is based on the idea that it is often too limiting to set objectives and develop strategies simply on the basis of the BCG's market growth rate and relative competitive position. Instead, it is argued, success (and hence the basis on which decisions should be made) is determined by the *attractiveness of the SBU's markets* and the degree to which the SBU possesses the sorts of *business strengths* needed to operate and succeed in each of these markets; the GE matrix is illustrated in Figure 5.3.

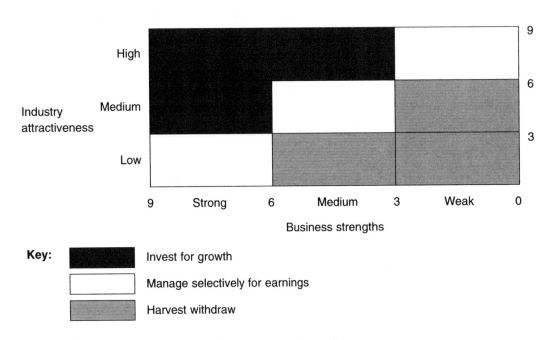

Figure 5.3 The General Electric multi-factor portfolio model

What sorts of factors do you feel contribute to:

- industry attractiveness?
- business strength?

Although the titles of the axes of other portfolio models such as Shell's directional policy matrix and Abell and Hammonds 3x3 matrix differ slightly from those used in the General Electric model, the thinking in each case is broadly similar.

Very deliberately, we have focused upon just two portfolio models. For a far more detailed discussion of portfolio analysis, the variety of models that have been proposed, and an examination of their areas of strength and weakness, refer to pages 233–236 of *Strategic Marketing Management* by Wilson and Gilligan with Pearson.

The current status of portfolio analysis

Although it is generally recognised that portfolio analysis (PA) has been useful in helping managers to think more strategically about their businesses, a variety of criticisms of PA have emerged over the past few years. Amongst the critics has been Douglas Brownlie who has argued that portfolio analysis:

- Is over-simplified.
- Often offers a misleading representation of strategy options.
- Makes use of inappropriate and overly general measures.
- Rests on an assumption that market leadership invariably offers benefits.
- Ignores the real potential and the benefits of marketing niching.
- Ignores a series of important and strategic factors in the competitive environment.

Others have suggested that far too many managers have failed to recognize that, if portfolio analysis is to be carried out meaningfully, the data inputs are often considerable, the exercise time-consuming, and the implications for strategy far more subtle than is often suggested by the almost knee-jerk idea of milking cash cows, shooting dogs, and so on.

Although a considerable amount of attention has been paid to the development of techniques of portfolio analysis, it is increasingly being recognized that managers still make only limited use of them. Comment upon the possible explanations for this and discuss how portfolio analysis might be applied more widely.

(Planning and Control, June 1994, Question 8.)

Porter's three generic competitive strategies

One of the major contributors over the past few years to the ways in which we think about competitive strategy has been Michael Porter who has argued that there are, in essence, only three generic types of strategy:

- Overall cost leadership.
- Focus.
- Differentiation.

He suggests that in order to compete effectively, strategists need to select a particular strategy and then pursue it consistently. In practice, of course, there is no one 'best' strategy, even within a particular industry. The choice therefore needs to be made so that the firm maximizes its relative competitive strengths, something which can only be done against the background of a clear understanding of five factors:

1   The bargaining power of suppliers (in other words, how strong relative to you are your suppliers and to what extent are they capable of influencing or determining your strategy?)

2 The bargaining power of customers (are you, for example, dealing with a whole series of small customers who individually have little bargaining power, or are you dealing with a small number of large, powerful and individually influential customers?)
3 The threat of new entrants to the industry.
4 The threat of substitute products.
5 The rivalry amongst current competitors.

It is the combination of these factors which determines the nature, level and intensity of competition within an industry and which, Porter argues, should influence or determine the choice of strategy.

Cost leadership: the achievement of the lowest cost base within the industry. Although this would typically then be reflected in a low price strategy, this is not always the case and the firm may opt instead for higher levels of investment in areas such as R&D, manufacturing, or marketing.

Focus: the concentration of the marketing effort upon one or more narrow market segments.

Differentiation: an emphasis upon the one or more elements of the marketing mix which are perceived by customers to be important and which, if performed particularly well and distinctively, offer scope for distancing the organization from its competitors and creating a competitive advantage.

A summary of the ways in which each of the three strategies might be achieved, together with the benefits and possible problems that are associated with each of the three strategies, appear in Figure 5.4.

Type of strategy	Ways to achieve the strategy	Benefits	Possible problems
Cost leadership	• Size and economies of scale • Globalization of operations • Relocating to low cost parts of the world • Modification/simplification of designs • Greater labour effectiveness • Greater operating effectiveness • Strategic alliances • New sources of supply	The ability to: • Out-perform rivals • Erect barriers to entry • Resist the five forces	• Vulnerability to even lower cost operators • Possible price wars • The difficulty of sustaining it in the long term
Focus	• Concentration upon one or a small number of segments • The creation of a strong specialist reputation	• A more detailed understanding of particular segments • The creation of barriers to entry • A reputation for specialization • The ability to concentrate efforts	• Limited opportunities for sector growth • The possibility of out-growing the market • The decline of the sector • A reputation for specialization which ultimately inhibits growth and development into other sectors

Type of strategy	Ways to achieve the strategy	Benefits	Possible problems
Differentiation	• The creation of strong brand identities • The consistent pursuit of those factors which customers perceive to be important • High performance in one or more of a spectrum of activities	• A distancing from others in the market • The creation of a major competitive advantage • Flexibility	• The difficulties of sustaining the bases for differentiation • Possibly higher costs • The difficulty of achieving true and meaningful differentiation

Figure 5.4   Porter's three generic strategies

Although Porter argues very firmly that success comes from identifying and pursuing the generic strategy that is most suited to an organization's capabilities and position within a particular market sector, many strategists either fail to recognize this or fail to achieve what they set out to do. The result of this is that the organization has no particular strategy and instead drifts into what can loosely be termed the strategic abyss or wilderness which is typically known as being 'stuck in the middle'. This is illustrated in Figure 5.5 and is a reflection of the organization not having a clear, distinctive or appropriate strategy.

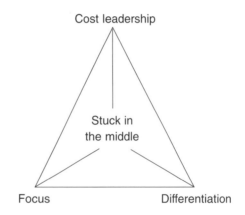

Figure 5.5   The three generic strategies (and the strategic wilderness)

In Porter's terms, which of the three generic strategies is being pursued by each of your organization's SBUs? Which strategies are your competitors' SBUs pursuing? Is there any evidence in your own organization of a 'middle of the road' or a 'stuck in the middle' strategy?

ACTIVITY 5.4

Making reference to examples, discuss how Michael Porter's ideas of generic competitive strategies can be used by the marketing planner.

(Marketing Planning and Control, December 1992, Question 5.)

QUESTION 5.5

Issues of competitive advantage

The development, pursuit and exploitation of competitive advantage is at the very heart of marketing strategy and was first discussed on pages 37–8; you might therefore briefly return to these.

Competitive advantage is achieved whenever you do something better than competitors. If that something is important to consumers, or if a number of small advantages can be combined, you have an exploitable competitive advantage. One or more competitive advantages are usually necessary in order to develop a winning strategy and this, in turn, should enable a company to achieve above-average growth and profits.

Source: Hugh Davidson (1987), *Offensive Marketing*, Penguin, page 153.

Davidson, the author of the definition above, has identified what he sees to be the eight most significant potential bases of competitive advantage as being:

1 *Superior product benefits.*
2 Advantages in the product or brand that, by virtue of the brand's advertising, its country of origin, and so on, are *perceived by customers* to be important.
3 *Low cost operations* which offer scope for aggressive pricing.
4 *Legal advantages* such as patents and copyright.
5 *Superior and influential contacts* with those within the industry or government.
6 *Greater knowledge* as the result of market research, experience or information systems.
7 *Economies of scale.*
8 *Competitively offensive attitudes* and a determination to succeed.

ACTIVITY 5.5

Which of Davidson's eight bases of competitive advantage does your organization appear to have? To what extent are these exploited? Which competitive advantages does each of your competitors have?

Market position and strategy

EXAM TIP

In discussing marketing strategy, candidates often treat all organizations as broadly the same; they are not. You should make sure therefore that your answer reflects the size and market position of the organization.

Marketing strategy is typically influenced by a spectrum of factors including:

* The organization's relative size.
* The existence of competitive advantages.

- What the organization has done in the past and the types of strategy that it has pursued.
- Previous levels of performance.
- Perceptions of risk.
- Stakeholders' expectations.
- Managerial objectives.
- Perceptions of market opportunities and threats.
- Competitors.
- Market, product and brand life cycles.

In addition, of course, strategy is also influenced – often to a very high degree – by the organization's market position. Is the firm, for example, a market leader, a market challenger, a market follower, or a market nicher?

Market leaders typically, but not invariably, have the largest market share and, by virtue of their position, are able to determine the nature, bases and intensity of competition.

Market challengers have a rather smaller share of the market and adopt an aggressive position by attacking the market leader or others in the industry in an attempt to strengthen their position and perhaps gain the leadership position.

Market followers pursue less aggressive strategies, avoid direct confrontation and are generally willing to accept current market structures and the status quo.

Market nichers concentrate their efforts upon small and often specialized parts of the market and in this way avoid head-on fights and develop a detailed but specific market knowledge.

Select a market sector and identify the position that each firm *appears* to occupy. What type of strategy is each of these firms pursuing? To what extent can you find evidence of a challenger's strategy? How successful does it appear to be?

ACTIVITY 5.6

Strategies for market leaders

It has been recognized that market leadership has a number of significant attractions, not the least of which is the competitive power that it gives a firm. At the same time, however, leaders are an attractive and a natural target for others in the industry and often therefore find themselves subject both to direct and indirect attacks. It follows from this that if a market leader is to remain a market leader it needs to follow a distinct and often proactive strategy. Without this it is likely that the firm will see its share of the market being eroded. The guidelines for the marketing strategist in these circumstances are therefore straightforward and involve focusing upon three areas:

1 The various ways in which the total market might possibly be expanded.
2 Ensuring that the firm's current market share is protected.
3 Identifying how, if at all, the firm's market share might possibly be increased.

These are illustrated in Figure 5.6

Market leadership

Expansion of the overall market	Guarding the existing market share	Expansion of the current market share
• Targeting groups that currently are non-users • Identifying new uses for the product/service • Increasing usage rates	• Strong market positioning • The development and refinement of meaningful competitive advantage • Continuous product process innovation • A generally proactive stance • Heavy advertising • Strong customer relations • Strong distributor relations	• Heavy advertising • Improved distribution • Price incentives • New product development • Mergers • Takeovers • Geographic expansion • Distributor expansion

Figure 5.6 Strategies for market leaders

The first of the three dimensions – *the expansion of the overall market* – can generally be achieved in one of several ways, including:

- Finding new users for the product or service.
- Finding new uses.
- Finding ways in which current and potential users of the product might use it more frequently and/or in greater quantities.

ACTIVITY 5.7

Select an organization which is very firmly a market leader and identify which of these three approaches to the defence of its position is being used. How successful does the strategy appear to be?

The second major need for market leaders involves ensuring that the firm's *existing share of the market is guarded* as effectively as possible. Given our earlier comment that leaders are often an attractive target for other firms, it follows that leaders need to be constantly vigilant so that any areas of vulnerability are minimized as far as possible. In practice, of course, this can be a difficult exercise, since it involves strength across a series of geographic, market and product sector fronts. Insofar as it is possible to identify how this might best be done, it is in terms of continuous innovation and the development of ever stronger competitive advantages and stronger selling propositions.

The third major dimension of a leadership strategy involves trying *to build market share* yet further. However, in doing this the issue of monopoly power needs to be considered and how the monopoly legislation which exists in the majority of the developed countries can prove to be a constraint.

Strategies for market challengers

Organizations which currently are not market leaders have a straightforward strategic choice: either they try to build share in an attempt to become leaders themselves (market challengers), or they adopt a less proactive and offensive approach by accepting the general status quo (market followers).

For those organizations which decide to challenge for leadership, there are several ways in which a challenge can be mounted, including:

- A direct attack on the current market leader.
- An attack upon firms of similar size to itself but which for a variety of possible reasons such as a lack of finance or a weak management team are vulnerable.
- An attack upon smaller firms.

The wisdom of a direct attack on an established market leader will depend very largely upon the sort of market in which the organization is operating and, very obviously, the sort of firm in the leadership position. When the leader shows signs of being over-stretched and vulnerable, a direct attack may well work. More frequently, however, a direct attack is likely to prove costly, time-consuming and, ultimately, self-defeating. There are several reasons for this, the most obvious of which is that, by virtue of being market leader, the firm under attack will generally – but certainly not invariably – have the advantages of size, economies of scale and greater financial resources. It is because of this that many astute challengers opt for a different approach and try to build their position by attacking firms of a similar size to themselves or a series of smaller firms.

Insofar as it is possible to identify a series of lessons which have emerged from the activities of successful – and unsuccessful – market challengers over the past few years, it has to be that the challenger must have a sustainable and meaningful competitive advantage; without this, any attack, regardless of whether it is upon a market leader or simply another player in the market, is likely to prove of little real value.

With regard to the specific ways in which an attack can be launched, Wilson et al (1992, page 264) have identified ten possible strategies:

1 Price discounting.
2 A different price-quality combination.
3 Product innovation.
4 Improved service levels.
5 Distribution innovation.
6 Intensive advertising.
7 Market development.
8 A more prestigious image.
9 Product proliferation.
10 Cost reduction.

Identify examples of market challengers for each of the ten bases of a challenge that are listed above. How successful does each one appear to have been?

ACTIVITY 5.8

Market leaders have often proved to be a natural target for ambitious, growth-oriented companies. Identify the marketing strategies that experience has shown to be the most effective in challenging market leaders, and discuss how market leaders might fight off such a challenge.

(Marketing Planning and Control, June 1991, Question 6.)

QUESTION 5.6

Strategies for market followers

As an alternative to challenging for leadership, many organizations opt for a rather quieter life by remaining as market followers. For those who do so, there are three distinct positions:

1 *Following the leader or challenger closely* by offering a similar market mix and operating in broadly similar market segments, but taking care not to pose any real threat or challenge to the leader.
2 *Following at a distance* so that whilst there are obvious similarities, there are also areas of difference.
3 *Following selectively* so that in some instances, there is little to choose between the leader and the follower, whilst in others there is a major gap.

Executed carefully, a market following strategy can prove to be highly profitable, since it is likely to mean that virtually all of the costs and risks of product and market development are borne by the market leader or challenger, with the follower then learning from their experiences. It is also a strategy which in mature markets in particular makes a great deal of sense. In such a market, organizations are often faced with what is referred to as a zero-sum game. Because there is little scope for overall market growth, an individual company can only increase its sales at someone else's expense. Given this, it often makes sense to recognize that higher, longer term profits are most likely to be made by avoiding challenging the market leader.

At the same time, of course, followers can prove vulnerable, particularly if market challengers see the basis for their challenge to be that of taking over the smaller and seemingly less aggressive firms in the industry. Recognizing this highlights that, if a follower is to succeed, it requires a distinct strategy on their part reflecting:

- Careful market segmentation.
- The efficient use of (limited) R&D budgets.
- An emphasis upon profitability rather than sales growth or market share expansion.
- A willingness to challenge conventional wisdoms.
- A distinct competitive strategy rather than a set of largely implicit actions.

QUESTION 5.7

In what circumstances would you recommend that an organization pursues a market follower strategy?

Strategies for market nichers

As an alternative to leadership, challenging or following, some organizations pursue a market niching strategy. Although often associated with smaller organizations, niching – if performed well – can often prove to be an attractive and profitable strategy for divisions or SBUs of far larger businesses. The principal attraction of niching is that it enables the organization to concentrate its efforts upon a particular segment of the market and in this way avoid concentration and competition. The criteria for niching are straightforward and have been identified by Kotler (1988, page 342) as being:

- The niche must be sufficiently large to be profitable.
- It must have growth potential.
- It must be of little interest to larger competitors.
- The firm must have the skills needed to serve the niche effectively.
- The firm must be able to defend itself, at least initially, against competitive inroads.

There are, of course, problems with niching, not the least of which is that the firm may outgrow the niche and ultimately find it to be too small. Equally, organizations can find themselves in a vulnerable position if for one reason or another the niche contracts or if a major competitor decides that the niche offers sufficient long-term potential to justify an attack. It is for these sorts of reasons that it is often strategically far more sensible to operate in several niches simultaneously in order to spread the risk.

With regard to the bases for niching, we can identify seven principal ways. These involve niching or specializing:

1 Geographically.
2 By the type of end user.
3 By product or product line.
4 On a quality/price spectrum.
5 Service.
6 Type of customer.
7 Product feature.

Identify an example for each of the seven bases for niching.

Making use of examples, identify the criteria for effective market niching and discuss whether it is a strategy suited only to small organizations.

(Marketing Planning and Control, December 1992, Question 10.)

For a detailed treatment of how market position influences strategy turn to Chapter 10 of Wilson and Gilligan with Pearson (1992) *Strategic Marketing Management*. The chapter also discusses how thinking on business strategy has been influenced by military strategy.

Summary

Within this unit we have focused upon a variety of the factors that need to be taken into account in developing a marketing strategy. As a check on your understanding of this, consider the following questions:

1 Why did an increasing number of managers begin to develop strategic perpectives from the 1970s onwards? (See page 95.)
2 What is meant by portfolio analysis? (See pages 97–8.)
3 What are the three levels of planning? (See page 95.)
4 Draw a model of the cycle of planning, implementation, control and feedback. (See page 95.)
5 What are the three main approaches to planning? (See page 96.)
6 What is an SBU? (See page 97.)
7 What purpose do SBUs play in the planning process? (See pages 96–7.)
8 What are Drucker's six categories of product? (See page 97.)

9   Draw the BCG framework. (See page 98.)

10 What are the apparent attractions of the BCG framework? (See page 98.)

11 What strategies does BCG lead to? (See page 98.)

12 What are the limitations of portfolio analysis (PA)? (See pages 99–100.)

13 Identify at least one other model of PA. (See page 100.)

14 What is the current status of PA? (See page 101.)

15 What are Porter's three generic strategies? (See pages 101–3.)

16 In what circumstances is each strategy appropriate? (See pages 101–3.)

17 What are Davidson's eight bases of competitive advantage? (See page 104.)

18 What factors should influence marketing strategy? (See pages 104–5.)

19 Define market leaders, challengers, followers and nichers. (See page 105.)

20 Identify the key elements of the strategies appropriate to each market position. (See pages 105–9.)

Activity debrief

Question 5.1: Although the appropriateness of any particular approach to planning will depend, at least in part, upon organizational structure, size, geographic coverage, and the type of products and markets, it is also influenced significantly by the type of staff. How well trained they are, how capable they are, their experience, and so on. You should therefore think about issues of motivation and control. Bottom-up planning gives staff freedom but reduces corporate management's control. Top-down planning is the opposite. Goals down/plans up planning is therefore often an attractive proposition for both sides.

Question 5.2: Refer to the discussion on page 99.

Question 5.3: Industry attractiveness is influenced by market size, its rate of growth, the degree of competition, the pace of technological change, the existence of any legal or governmental regulations and historical profit margins. Business strength is influenced by market share, product quality, image and reputation, the distribution network, production capacity, and production effectiveness.

Question 5.4: Refer to the discussion on pages 99–101.

Question 5.5: Refer to Figure 5.4 on pages 102–3.

Question 5.6: Refer to the ten points on page 107 and then turn to the discussion of strategies for leaders that appears on pages 105–6.

Question 5.7: Refer to the discussion on page 108.

Question 5.8: Refer to the discussion on pages 108–9.

Managing the marketing mix

In this unit you will examine the vehicle through which managers' ideas on marketing strategy are translated into a series of strategic and tactical moves. As a result of this, you will understand:

- The principal dimensions of the marketing mix.
- How an effective marketing mix can be developed.

By the end of this unit you will:

- Understand how the various elements of the mix can be managed strategically and tactically.

Within this unit we focus upon an important element of Stage 4 of the Planning and Control syllabus and, as with Unit 5, one which has obvious applications within the Analysis and Decision case study. To support the content of this unit, you should read the specialist marketing press with a view to identifying as clearly as possible how managers are making – and implementing – decisions concerning not just the individual elements of the marketing mix, but also how the overall mix is being managed, and to what effect.

The unit accounts for about 15–20 per cent of the Planning and Control syllabus, although in a number of ways its importance is far greater than this. Without a clear understanding of the mix and how it can be managed, it is unlikely that you will score anything other than the very minimum of marks in either of the Strategic Marketing Management examinations. Having worked your way through this unit, you should therefore look at a number of the mini and maxi case studies with a view to identifying how your knowledge might be applied.

Managing the marketing mix

The idea of the marketing mix and the 4Ps (Product, Price, Place and Promotion) was first discussed by McCarthy several decades ago. More recently, however, it has been recognized that there are several other elements that need to be taken into account in marketing mix planning and within this section we will therefore focus upon the 7Ps; these were first introduced in Unit 3 (page 46) and are illustrated again in Figure 6.1.

Given the pivotal importance of the marketing mix, it is not surprising that it has been the focus for a large number of questions in the Planning and Control examinations over the past few years.

Although the left-hand box in Figure 6.1 is labelled 'uncontrollable factors', remember that we said in Unit 3 that in practice many of these can be controlled or managed, particularly by large firms, if not in the short term, certainly in the medium to long term. The economy, for example, can be 'managed' by focusing upon areas of the world in which the economy is buoyant. Equally, competitors can be 'managed' by takeovers and alliances whilst political factors can be 'managed' by means of lobbying.

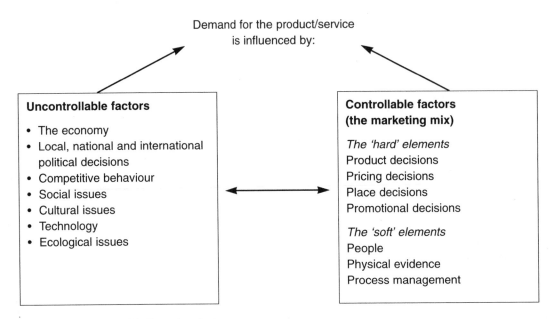

Figure 6.1 Demand influencing factors

What other factors should be added to the list of uncontrollable elements? Taking each point in turn, identify how it might be 'managed' through a marketing strategy.

Product decisions

The normal starting point for any discussion of the marketing mix is the product or service, since the majority of other mix decisions are directly influenced by what is offered. The product – and here we use the term to refer both to a physical product and to a service – is made up of three main elements:

1 *The product attributes* including its features, styling, brand name, quality, packaging, and the size and colour variations offered.
2 *The product benefits* that stem from its performance and image and which contribute to the 'bundle of satisfactions' that it delivers.
3 *The marketing support services* that are provided in addition to the product itself. These might include elements such as pre-sales services, delivery, installation, and after-sales support.

The *product mix* is the group of products sold by the organization. An example of this would be Ford with cars, vans, trucks, buses and tractors.

The *product line* is a group of broadly similar products targeted at a similar group of customers.

Select one of the products (services) offered by your organization and identify the three levels referred to above. In what areas do you appear particularly strong or weak?

Product management is based very largely upon the application of two major concepts:

- The product life cycle.
- Portfolio analysis.

Portfolio analysis was discussed in Unit 5 and you might therefore refer back to this unit to make sure that you fully understand the concept and how it can be applied.

The product life cycle (PLC) has been referred to as 'possibly the best known but least understood concept in marketing' (see *Strategic Marketing Management*, page 273). The reason for this comment is that only rarely does a marketing manager claim ignorance of the life cycle, but only a very small minority understand how, if at all, it might be used for marketing planning.

The thinking behind the PLC is straightforward and based on the idea that products have a finite life and that during this life they pass through a number of distinct stages, each of which demands a particular type of strategy. There are, however, several problems that are associated with using the PLC as a management tool, the majority of which stem from the difficulties of identifying the nature, length and precise shape that the life cycle will take. However, most discussions of the life cycle make use of a simple diagram of the sort illustrated in Figure 6.2.

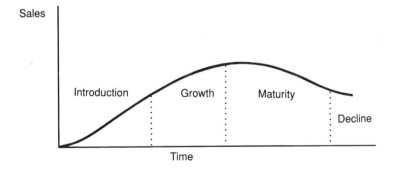

Figure 6.2 The product life cycle

In practice, of course, the length and shape of a life cycle is capable of varying enormously, since it is influenced by a whole series of factors, some of which are within the control of the marketing staff whilst others are not. The net effect of this is that numerous PLC shapes other than the simple S curve that is shown above have been identified. These include the four that appear in Figure 6.3, although to these we could add a further thirteen that have been identified by Swan and Rink.

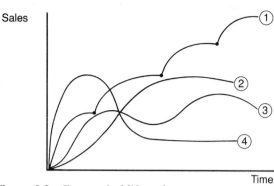

Sales

① Scalloped
② Conventional
③ Cycle – recycle
④ Growth – slump – maturity

Time

Figure 6.3 Four typical life cycle curves

It follows from this that using the life cycle in the neat and easy way that is often suggested in textbooks is only rarely possible and that the concept needs to be treated with a degree of care; it is certainly not, for example, the predictive framework that many have claimed it to be. However, it does have a value in that:

- It highlights the need for marketing strategy to change over time.
- It identifies the broad strategic issues that need to be considered at each stage.
- It can be used as a control tool in that comparisons can be drawn with broadly similar products in the past.

These points are examined in Figure 6.4.

Marketing mix strategies	Introduction	Growth	Maturity	Decline
Product	Basic product, limited range	Develop product extensions and service levels	Modify and differentiate Develop next generation	Phase out weak brands Consider leaving market
Price	Low price strategy	Penetration strategy	Price to meet or beat competitors	Reduce
Distribution	Selective Build dealer relations	Intensive. Limited trade discounts	Intensive. Heavy trade discounts	Selective. Phase out weak outlets
Advertising	Heavy spending to build awareness and encourage trial among early adopters and distributors	Moderate to build awareness and interest in the mass market. Greater word of mouth	Emphasize brand differentiation and special offers	Reduce to a level that maintains hard core loyalty. Emphasize low prices to reduce stock
Sales promotion	Extensive to encourage trial	Reduce to a moderate level	Increase to encourage brand switching	Reduce or stop completely
Planning time frame	Short to medium	Long range	Medium range	Short

Figure 6.4 The management of the product life cycle. (Adapted from Wilson and Gilligan with Pearson, 1992, *Strategic Marketing Management*, page 276.)

EXAM TIP

Many of the past Planning and Control exam papers have included a question on the life cycle and these have proved to be popular amongst candidates. However, many of the answers have proved to be disappointing in that candidates have simply regurgitated everything they understand or have ever heard about the concept. If you should be faced with a question on the PLC, look closely at what is being asked, since the question is likely to focus upon a *specific* aspect of the concept.

(i) The majority of products spend much of their life cycle in the mature phase of the product life cycle. To what extent does current thinking and research on the product life cycle provide marketing managers with worthwhile guidelines on how best to manage products during this phase?

(Marketing Planning and Control, December 1991, Question 5.)

(ii) To what extent does the product life cycle provide the marketing planner with worthwhile guidelines on how to manage products in the *introductory* and *decline* stages?

(Marketing Planning and Control, December 1992, Question 6.)

(iii) It is generally recognized that product life cycles are shortening. What are the implications of this for the marketing planning and control processes?

(Marketing Planning and Control, December 1993, Question 9.)

(iv) What problems would you be likely to experience in attempting to forecast the nature and shape of the product life cycle for an innovatory product aimed at a rapidly changing consumer goods market? How, if at all, might these problems possibly be overcome?

(Marketing Planning and Control, June 1994, Question 4.)

Managing the brand

An integral part of any product policy is the question of how the organization's brands are managed. In essence there are four types of brand strategy which can be pursued:

1 *Corporate umbrella branding* where the company's name is used to cover the complete spectrum of products and services offered (e.g. Heinz).
2 *Family umbrella names* to cover a range of products in a variety of markets (e.g. Marks & Spencer's use of its St Michael brand).
3 *Range brand names* which link products within a specific market sector (e.g. Mars with Mars bars, a Mars drink and Mars ice cream).
4 *Individual brand names* which are used for one type of product in one or more markets (e.g. Lucozade).

In managing brands, several factors need to be considered:

- What values are associated with the brand name?
- How can the brand be developed?
- How far can the name be stretched (in other words, to what extent does it lend itself to being moved into related or possibly new market sectors)?
- How much is it worth?

Valuing brands

The question of how to value brands has grown in importance in recent years as managers have come to recognize the significance of brand names as assets and how they might possibly contribute to the balance sheet. Although there is no one agreed method of brand valuation, there are several guidelines (see Wilson et al, 1992, pages 300–1). Included within these are:

1 The brand's market position (leaders are worth more than followers).
2 The age and stability of the brand.
3 The nature of the market (brands in market sectors such as food and drinks are less prone to fashion and have less unpredictable and fast-changing life cycles than, say, fashion or computers).

4 Geographic spread.
5 Sales trends in the market.
6 The trade marks or patents that give a form of protection.
7 The levels of advertising and the patterns of expenditure over the past few years.

QUESTION 6.2

Your company, which markets a range of biscuits and confectionery, is the target of an aggressive and unwanted takeover bid. As the company's marketing manager, you are required to prepare a report for the marketing director discussing how the firm's brands might be valued.

(Strategic Marketing: Planning and Control, December 1994, Question 2.)

Developing new products

An important element of any product strategy is the modification of existing products and the development of new ones. There are two ways in which new products can be added to the range:

- Internal new product development.
- Going outside and acquiring them from other organizations.

In the case of acquisition, this can include buying other firms, buying licenses or franchises, and buying patents. In the case of internal new product development, the process involves generating ideas, evaluating these ideas, disposing of those which seemingly offer little potential, and launching those which seem to offer the greatest promise.

But although NPD is an important dimension of strategy, almost inevitably it proves to be risky, time consuming and expensive. In an attempt to come to terms with this, a considerable amount of research on the causes of NPD success and failure has been conducted. The outcome of this research suggests that failure is typically associated with:

- Managers overestimating the size of the market.
- The product under-performing.
- Competitors being too firmly entrenched.
- The product being poorly positioned.
- Distributors lacking real commitment to the product.
- The product idea having been pushed through the NPD process by a senior manager, even though evidence exists to suggest that the product is likely to fail.

QUESTION 6.3

Why is NPD typically an expensive and risky activity? In what ways might these be avoided or minimized?

DEFINITION 6.2

certain: defin
lefinition *n.*
precise mea
distinct, cle
lefinitive *a.* fi
something:

Although we tend to use the term *new product* in a rather general way, there are several specific manifestations that need to be thought about, including:

116

- Products that are new to the world and which then go on to create a completely new market.
- Products that help the company to enter a new market.
- Additions to existing lines.
- Improvements to existing products.
- Repositionings which allow the organization to target new markets.
- Minor product modifications.

Why is NPD important?

NPD, if conducted effectively, is capable of performing several distinct roles, including:

- Ensuring that product obsolescence is avoided.
- Helping to ensure that the organization can compete in new and growing market segments.
- Reducing the dependence upon one or more (declining) market sectors.
- Matching or beating competitors.
- Helping to achieve long-term growth.

The NPD process

The starting point for any discussion of the NPD process is the work in the 1960s of the American consultancy firm Booz, Allen and Hamilton. Faced with clients who were experiencing high new product development failure rates, they developed a logical, analytical and sequential approach to NPD which was designed to ensure that managers did not miss out certain key stages; this is illustrated in Figure 6.5 on page 118.

QUESTION 6.4

What guidelines has research in recent years provided on how the new product development process might most effectively be organized?

(Marketing Planning and Control, December 1992, Question 8.)

Good practice in new product development has long been seen by many writers to be a linear process. Explain why, in today's environment, this is over-simplistic and inappropriate, and comment upon the nature of the approaches that might more effectively be used.

(Marketing Planning and Control, June 1994, Question 10.)

Although it has long been recognized that NPD is a potentially difficult, expensive, time-consuming and risky but, for many organizations, very necessary activity, these problems have in recent years been magnified as the result of seemingly ever faster changing market environments – something which is reflected in the second of the two examination questions above. To cope with this, managers have needed to become far more environmentally aware and have needed to respond far faster and in far more innovatory ways as opportunities emerge, possibly for a far shorter time than in the past.

The problems with test marketing

Although test marketing is often seen to be an integral part of the NPD sequence, many firms now avoid this stage, preferring instead to go straight from the detailed business analysis and product development/testing stages to the full launch. There are several reasons for this, including:

- The dangers of the test market alerting competitors.
- The problems of finding representative test areas.

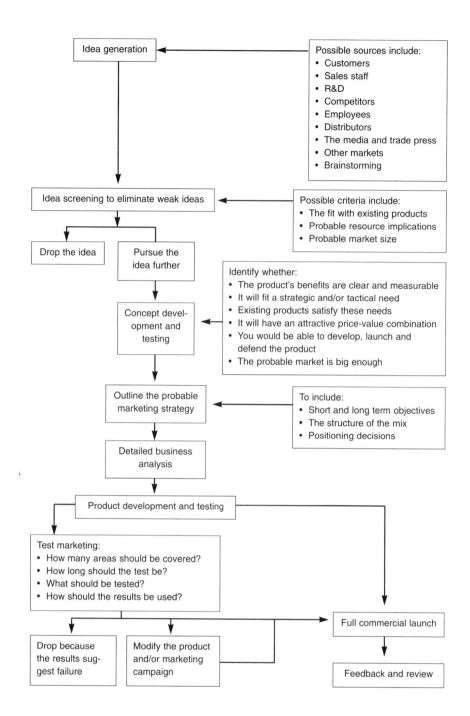

Figure 6.5   The new product development sequence

- The time needed to identify repurchase rates.
- Distributors being reluctant to become involved in test marketing costs.
- The difficulties of interpreting what is often an ambiguous results pattern.

These, together with the far faster pace of many markets, has led managers to argue that, if they are truly confident in the product, they should go ahead as fast as possible.

QUESTION 6.5

(i) Identify the types of information that might emerge from test marketing and discuss how this information might be used.

(Marketing Planning and Control, June 1992, Question 9.)

(ii) A succession of studies have shown that a majority of products which have generated encouraging test marketing results and which subsequently have been launched nationally, ultimately fail. Explain how this might be caused and how it might be overcome.

(Marketing Planning and Control, December 1993, Question 7.)

(iii) Identify the criteria that should be used in deciding whether to test market a new product and explain why so many test market results prove to be ambiguous.

(Strategic Marketing: Planning and Control, December 1994, Question 5.)

Pricing decisions

Organizations are essentially either *price takers* or *price makers*. In other words, either they have only a limited ability – or willingness – to control the prices they charge and therefore follow the lead set by others in the market, or because of their size, power or strong competitive advantages, are able to determine the prices which others then follow.

Looking at your own organization, identify whether a price taking or price making approach is adopted. To what extent is there evidence of a *strategic* approach to pricing?

Although prices are often influenced by a whole series of factors, the five most significant can be seen to be:

- The firm's corporate objectives and what it is trying to achieve in each sector of the market.
- The nature, structure and intensity of competition.
- The stage reached on the product life cycle.
- Consumers' response patterns.
- Cost structures.

Looking again at your own organization, what other factors appear to influence the prices charged? What about, for example:

- Distributors' expectations.
- Managerial fears about sparking off a price war.
- The cost and marketing interrelationships between different parts of the product mix.
- Price dumping by an overseas competitor.
- Collusion between firms in the form of cartels (whilst often illegal, implicit cartels exist in many markets).
- Prices that have been set in the past and a lack of willingness on the part of management to sit down with a clean sheet of paper and pose a series of fundamental questions about precisely what the price strategy is designed to achieve.

> Speak to one or more financial managers in the organization and identify how detailed an understanding exists of cost structures for:
>
> 1 Each product.
> 2 Each market sector that you operate in.

The sorts of factors that we have identified as influences upon price can be seen to act as the general framework within which specific pricing decisions are taken. In taking these decisions, the first major step involves setting in detail the pricing objectives. Although in practice the organization may well have a variety of objectives, the most common include:

- Survival: when the organization is faced with a particularly difficult market and cash flow is poor, prices can be slashed simply to increase the flow and maintain a base of working capital.
- Setting out to achieve a predetermined return on investment.
- Stabilization of the market.
- Attempting to gain market share.
- Minimizing competitive conflict by setting prices at the same level as competitors.
- Skimming the market by means of a high price strategy initially and then gradually lowering prices to attract new segments.
- Penetrating the market with a low price in order to capture as many sales as quickly as possible.
- Early cash recovery.
- Pricing to stop other firms entering the market.

EXAM TIP

Price is potentially an enormously valuable strategic and tactical weapon, although many managers try to avoid price competition by taking price out of the competitive equation. In preparing both for the Planning and Control and Analysis and Decision exams, think about the sorts of factors that influence price, how you might set a price, and the implications for pricing of more volatile and competitive market structures.

Having set the objectives, the marketing strategist can then go on to the question of *how* to set the price, something which involves a choice between cost-oriented and market-oriented techniques.

Cost-oriented techniques are, as the title suggests, based firmly upon a clear understanding of cost structures and include:

- Mark-up pricing (identify the costs associated with the product and add a previously determined mark-up).
- Target return on investment pricing (decide upon the ROI required and then price to achieve this).
- Early cash recovery pricing.

By contrast, market-oriented techniques involve focusing in far greater detail upon the market and, in particular, customers' response patterns, competitors, and opportunities. The techniques include:

- Perceived value pricing (what value does the market put upon the product?).
- Going rate pricing (what are the pricing norms in the industry?).

QUESTION 6.6

(i) What factors should be taken into account when deciding upon the price of a new product? In what ways might the relative importance of these factors be influenced by the type of industry in which the company is operating?

(Marketing Planning and Control, June 1991, Question 7.)

(ii) It has been suggested that pricing is the most difficult single marketing decision since so many variables are involved. Evaluate this contention making reference to the factors likely to influence the pricing of a new and innovatory machine tool.

(Marketing Planning and Control, June 1992, Question 6.)

(iii) What information would you require in order to set a price for an innovatory new product aimed at a consumer durable market? What particular problems might be experienced in obtaining this information and how, if at all, might they be overcome?

(Marketing Planning and Control, December 1992, Question 9.)

(iv) How would you attempt to predict the effects of a change in the price of a service in a competitive consumer market?

(Marketing Planning and Control, December 1993, Question 10.)

Any worthwhile pricing strategy must, of course, take explicit account of competitors, their costs and their probable patterns of behaviour. Without this, it is likely that sooner or later the firm will be taken by surprise by a competitor's moves.

QUESTION 6.7

What competitive information would you need when setting prices?

Hint: refer to pages 336–7 of Wilson and Gilligan with Pearson (1992) *Strategic Marketing Management.*

Promotional decisions

In developing a promotional strategy, the marketing strategist needs to begin by focusing upon the corporate and marketing objectives with a view to identifying precisely how promotional activity can contribute to their achievement. In doing this, you need to think about the complete spectrum of promotional activities; these are brought together in the idea of the promotions mix and its four principal dimensions:

- Advertising.
- Personal selling.
- Publicity.
- Sales promotion.

Advertising: any paid form of non-personal presentation and promotion of ideas, goods, or services by an identified sponsor.

Personal selling: an oral presentation in conversation with one or more prospective purchasers for the purpose of making sales.

DEFINITION 6.3

Publicity: the non-personal stimulation of demand for a product, service or business unit by planting commercially significant news about it in a published medium or obtaining favourable presentation of it upon radio, television or stage that is not paid for by the sponsor.

Sales promotion: those marketing activities, other than personal selling, advertising and publicity, that stimulate consumer purchases, such as displays, shows and exhibitions, demonstrations, and various non-recurrent selling efforts not in the ordinary routine.

In thinking about promotional strategy, seven questions need to be considered:

- What are we trying to achieve?
- How might we achieve it?
- How much will we need to spend?
- Where will we need to spend it?
- When will we need to spend it?
- What creative appeal is most likely to work?
- How can we best measure the results, feed these back into the decision-making process, and improve the strategy?

QUESTION 6.8

Identify the principal decisions that have to be taken in the development of an advertising campaign and discuss the contribution to these that marketing research might possibly make.

(Marketing Planning and Control, June 1993, Question 6.)

Because the CIM's Diploma includes a syllabus and examination paper dealing with Marketing Communication Strategy, it is not our intention within this workbook to look at the area in detail, but instead simply to highlight the main areas that you need to concentrate upon. The first of these is the question of objectives.

Promotional objectives can be categorized most obviously in terms of those that are sales related and those that are communication related. Thus, a sales-related objective would be designed to:

- Increase sales from A to B.
- Strengthen the competitive position.
- Generate N enquiries/coupon responses.
- Reduce the sales impact of a competitor's advertising.

A communication-related objective would be designed to:

- Improve the image.
- Help in repositioning.
- Raise levels of awareness.
- Change perceptions.

Having developed the objectives, attention needs then to turn to the question of the *promotional budget.* Given our earlier comments, the question of budgeting should be relatively straightforward: what are we trying to achieve and how much will this cost? In practice, however, the majority of organizations resort to one of a variety of other approaches, including:

- Affordable (how much can we afford to spend on promotion? In taking this approach, little account is taken of opportunities, objectives or indeed competitive threats).
- Competitive parity (how much are competitors spending? Having identified this, you spend broadly in line with their levels and in so doing avoid upsetting the status quo).
- Percentage of sales (setting the budget on the basis of a predetermined percentage of last year's or the forthcoming year's sales).

As an alternative to these techniques, all of which are inward looking, the budget setter can return to the idea outlined above which involves identifying your specific objectives, identifying in detail what will be needed in order to achieve them, and then calculating the costs. This approach, which is referred to as the objective and task method has an inherent logic but largely because of the amount of detailed information that is needed is often ignored in favour of a simpler approach.

Why, despite pressure upon costs and calls for an ever greater degree of accountability within marketing, do rule of thumb methods of advertising budgeting appear still to predominate?

(Marketing Planning and Control, December 1991, Question 7.)

Having set the budget, the planner needs then to think about *how the budget can best be allocated*. In doing this there is, of course, an element of iteration in that in setting the objectives and the budget thought should have been given to the contribution that each of the elements is capable of making to the achievement of these objectives and the costs that will be incurred. Nevertheless, within the constraints of the budget that has been agreed, the *detailed* allocation represents the next step. The *criteria for allocation* are, in one sense at least, straightforward: what is each of the alternative media and promotional vehicles capable of delivering?

In the light of the wide range of promotional vehicles and media that are now available, explain how you would plan the allocation of a promotional budget and how you might evaluate the success of this allocation.

(Marketing Planning and Control, December 1993, Question 6.)

Having made the allocation, the next question is concerned with *timing*. In other words, when will the money be spent? In deciding upon this, the planner has a choice between:

- Burst advertising which involves highly concentrated periods of heavy promotion.
- Drip promotion which involves spreading the campaign over a far longer period.

The issue of *where to spend the money* involves choosing between the variety of media available. What, therefore, are the benefits of the national press relative to the trade press or special internet magazines? What about posters or television?

Refer to the work that you are doing for Marketing Communication Strategy and identify the pros and cons of each of the major media.

The issue of the sort of *creative appeal* that is to be used needs to be considered against the background of a clear understanding of the image that the organization is attempting to create and its general positioning strategy. In essence, however, there is a choice between:

- The brand image approach which involves finding out what the brand means to the consumer and then emphasizing the product as a means of self-fulfilment.

- The unique selling proposition approach which focuses upon a highly specific and tangible benefit that the product is capable of delivering (buy this product, get this specific benefit).

The final stage is concerned with the measurement of results and here we have to go back to the objectives. What exactly has the campaign achieved and to what exent have the objectives been met? Given that we started this section by categorizing objectives as communication-related objectives and sales-related objectives, any measurement process needs to reflect this categorization. Thus, there are measures of:

- Awareness levels.
- Attitudes towards the product.
- The extent to which repositioning has been achieved.
- Image measures.

and

- Sales levels.
- Enquiry levels.
- Market share.

For many organizations, measuring the sales effect of a campaign is often difficult, largely because sales are typically affected by a spectrum of factors quite apart from advertising. Nevertheless, given the amounts of money that are spent on promotion, managers need to arrive at at least a broad measure of its impact.

In addition to post-testing, campaigns can also be pre-tested so that their probable effect can be gauged before the campaign is run and any necessary changes made. Amongst the pre-testing techniques available are:

- Direct rating tests whereby potential customers rate alternative appeals.
- Portfolio tests which involve customers listening or viewing a range of advertisements and then being asked to recall their content either on an aided or unaided basis.
- Laboratory tests which measure physiological responses to alternative ads.

QUESTION 6.11

Explain how an advertising campaign targeted at industrial markets might possibly be pre- and post-tested and how the test results might subsequently be used in the promotional planning process.

(Marketing Planning and Control, December 1994, Question 9.)

Although we have talked here about the various issues that are associated with the development of a promotional campaign, many of the decisions that need to be taken are taken in conjunction with an advertising agency. The question of the sorts of criteria that should be used in the selection of an advertising agency were the focus of the second of the two questions on the mini case study in the December 1993 Marketing Planning and Control examination. You should, therefore, attempt the question on the next page and then turn to the outline answer in Unit 9, pages 195–6.

What criteria should be taken into account in the appointment of an advertising agency?

Distribution and salesforce decisions

Distribution is the fourth of the 'hard' elements of the marketing mix and, it has been argued, amongst the most critical of the decisions faced by management. There are several reasons for this, although the two most significant stem from the way in which distribution decisions typically involve a series of long-term commitments to other firms and that the choice of channel affects all other marketing decisions.

Marketing channels can be viewed as sets of interdependent organizations involved in the process of making a product or service available for use or consumption.

(Source: Kotler (1991) *Marketing Management: Analysis, Planning, Implementation and Control*, Prentice Hall, page 508.)

Choosing the distribution channels

For many organizations there is often little real choice in terms of how the product is to be distributed and the type of distribution channel that is to be used. Instead, it is simply a case of plugging into an already well-developed – and often efficient – system that has been operating for some time; an obvious example of this would be the distribution system for foodstuffs. However, for other organizations there may well be a far greater degree of freedom, with the choice being between what is generally referred to as a 'short' or zero level channel (the producer sells direct to the user) or a 'long' and multi-level channel (the producer sells to a wholesaler network which in turn sells to a retail network which then sells to the consumer).

The role of the distribution network

Managed effectively, a distribution network is capable of performing several functions, including:

- The *collection of information* on customers, competitors, and the sorts of developments that are taking place within the market.
- The *promotion* of the product.
- The *financing* of inventories.
- The *delivery and physical transfer* of the product to the customer.
- A degree of *risk sharing*.
- An *ordering* function.

Infuences upon the channel decision

We said earlier that distribution channels can be categorized very broadly in terms of their length, that is the number of intermediaries that are used. In choosing between channel alternatives, there are several factors that typically influence the decision, including:

- *The product's characteristics:* Is it, for example, perishable? Is it of a particularly high value and does it need specialist installation and after-sales support?
- *The characteristics of the intermediaries* that might possibly be used. What particular skills and levels of sales expertise do they have? What geographic coverage are they able to offer and what particularly valuable sales contacts do they have? How

important would the product be to them and what level of effort would they put into the sales exercise? What profit margin would they expect and what level of promotional support would be needed?

- *Competitive characteristics:* How are the organization's direct competitors distributing *their* products? Do we want or need to adopt broadly the same approach so that potential customers are always faced with a choice between the alternatives, or is there scope for doing something completely different that would give us a competitive advantage?
- *Company characteristics:* What have we done in the past and what sorts of relationships have we developed with possible intermediaries? What level of resources do we have and what flexibility might this give us? What are the organization's long-term objectives and how might these influence the choice of network?
- *Environmental factors:* Are there any legal issues that might need to be taken into account? Is the economy generally buoyant or depressed and what are the implications of this for the costs, margins and prices?

Against the general background of these sorts of issues, the marketing planner can then begin to make a series of decisions, including whether to opt for *intensive, selective* or *exclusive distribution*.

Intensive distribution involves selling the product through as many types of distribution outlet as possible in order to maximize market coverage; examples of organizations which pursue this approach include cigarette and confectionery manufacturers.

Selective distribution involves choosing between the various types of outlet which would be willing to stock and sell the product and focusing the marketing effort upon those which it believes will offer the greatest potential and produce the highest long-term return.

Exclusive distribution involves the use of a very limited number of intermediaries in order to achieve a greater degree of control over how the product is sold and the sort of sales support that is given. Many exclusive distribution arrangements also go hand-in-hand with an obligation upon the distributor not to sell competing products; an obvious example of organizations which use this approach are the manufacturers of luxury cars.

Evaluating the channel alternatives

Having identified the channel alternatives that are open to the organization, the marketing planner needs to evaluate each of these against three criteria: *cost, control* and *flexibility*.

In the case of relatively low-priced items or where the scope for differentiation and competitive advantage is low, the *cost* or *economic* criterion is the most obvious and significant influence upon the decision. In taking this into account, the planner needs to identify the costs and sales that are likely to be associated with each of the channel alternatives and to weigh these against issues such as the segmentation and positioning strategy and the organization's long-term objectives.

Having done this, the planner needs then to take account of the implications for *control*. The company's own salesforce, for example, can be controlled in a direct way with the focus of their sales effort being channelled in order to reflect short- and long-term opportunities and priorites. By contrast, sales agents and intermediaries who are carrying large numbers of products, of which ours is just one small part, offer much less scope for being managed in a highly directed fashion. The planner may therefore be faced with what is often a classic trade-off between the levels of cost and control.

The third criterion that needs to be taken into account is concerned with *flexibility*. We made the comment earlier that distribution decisions often involve long-term commitments. Because of this, the degree of flexibility that exists is typically low; once decisions have been made, they offer little real scope for changes to be made, particularly in the short term. Given this, the planner needs to think at the outset about the ways in which environmental conditions might change, what the implications for the company's approaches to distribution might be, and how levels of potential flexibility might possibly be maximized.

Take a market sector and, in the light of what has been said so far, identify the *length* of the channels that are being used, the sorts of factors which appear to have *influenced* the choice and development of channels, the *role* played by the various channel members, and the apparent *efficiency* and *effectiveness* of the channel.

Managing the channel

Managing distribution channels involves four principal activities:

1. The *selection* of the appropriate channel members.
2. Their *motivation*.
3. Their *evaluation*.
4. When appropriate, the dropping of those channel members who are failing to achieve what is expected of them and their replacement with others.

The sorts of issues that influence the first of these has been the underlying theme of much of what we have said in our discussion so far and you might therefore try listing the factors that need to be taken into account.

Motivating the channel

Distribution channels can be motivated in a variety of positive *and* negative ways. Amongst the *positive* incentives are:

- The overall sales and profit potential that the product or product range offers.
- The extent to which sales support in the form of advertising and sales leads can be provided.
- Giving the distributor geographic sales exclusivity.
- The development of long-term co-operative relationships.
- A programme of sales incentives (the most obvious way in which this might be done would involve linking higher profit margins to certain levels of sales).
- Short term sales contests.

Included within the *negative* incentives are:

- A reduction in margins.
- A slowing down of deliveries.
- The threat to reduce or stop supplies altogether.

(i) By what criteria might you measure the efficiency of a distribution channel? Illustrate your answer with appropriate examples.

(Marketing Planning and Control, June 1993, Question 8.)

Evaluating the channel

At its most basic, the evaluation of channel members comes down to the simple question of whether each of the intermediaries is doing what is expected of it and achieving the performance levels that are required. If they are, the planner might possibly think about how these levels might be improved yet further. If, however, the expected levels of performance are not being achieved, thought needs then to be given to the reasons for this and how, if at all, the intermediaries might be supported and motivated so that their levels of performance are improved. If, however, the planner concludes that there is little real scope for their development and improvement, the decision needs then to be taken either to accept that the full potential of the market is not and will not be realized or that *modifications to the channel* will have to be made.

Channel dynamics

Only rarely do distribution channels remain unchanged for long periods. Instead, they typically evolve gradually over time as the responsibilities and performance levels of channel members fluctuate. Amongst the consequences of this is that the balance of power that exists within the channel also change; an obvious example of this in grocery retailing in most highly developed markets is the emergence of small numbers of large and powerful retail chains which are to a large extent able to dictate terms to the food producers.

Occasionally, however, we see the emergence of what is referred to as a 'category buster' which changes the entire industry and how the distribution task is carried out; an example of this would be the the entry into the market of an organization such as *Toys Я Us* which, by virtue of its size, scale of operations, the siting of its enormous stores and its general way of doing business, has radically altered how toys are sold.

ACTIVITY 6.6

Identify two examples of industries in which the approach to distribution has changed dramatically over the past few years or is currently going through a series of major changes. What has been driving these changes and what are the marketing implications for the suppliers within the industry?

Because the costs of distribution often represent a significant proportion of the final selling price of a product (anything between 20–80 per cent), the potential for making major savings – and gaining a competitive advantage – if the distribution process is managed more efficiently and effectively, are significant. Given this, the dynamic nature of many channels with the increasing development of vertical and horizontal marketing systems can frequently be seen to be a search for competitive advantage.

DEFINITION 6.6

A *vertical marketing system* involves the producer(s), wholesaler(s) and retailer(s) acting together in a unified way so that levels of conflict are reduced, and the operating economies and market impact are maximized. In this way, the profits of each of the members are increased.

A *horizontal marketing system* involves unrelated companies putting together the resources that are needed in order to exploit emerging market opportunities which, separately, neither would be able to capitalize upon.

Managing the salesforce

Managing the sales force involves a series of decisions that are concerned with its objectives, the way in which it is to be structured, and how the individual members are to be selected and motivated.

Managed effectively, the sales force is a powerful and highly visible part of the organization which is capable of performing a series of roles in addition to that of selling on a day-to-day basis. These include:

- *Prospecting* for new customers and markets.
- *Communicating* with customers and distributors.
- *Providing technical advice* and servicing distributors and customers.
- *Gathering market information.*

The *type* of salesforce that a firm uses is influenced by a variety of factors, including the nature of its products and their technical complexity, the types of customer that exist and their needs, the geographic location of its markets, the numbers of customers and their relative importance, the breadth of the product range, the scope for cross-selling, and so on. The implications of these factors are then reflected in the choice that needs to be made between:

- *Territorial structures* in which each member of the sales force is allocated an exclusive territory and expected to represent the company's full product line. The advantages of this approach, which is best suited to a relatively straightforward sales task, include its simplicity and the lack of ambiguity in reporting lines and issues of responsibilities. Insofar as problems with this approach are encountered, they stem from the question of the size and shape of the territories that should be used so that workloads and market potentials are allocated fairly.
- *Product-structured salesforces* in which individual members of the salesforce are given responsibility for a particular product or product line which they then sell across a far wider geographic area. Such an approach is best suited to markets in which the product is technically rather more complex and the buyers' needs more specialized. Although the costs of a product-structured salesforce tend to be rather higher than those of one structured around territories, the benefits are seen to be those of a more specialized and knowlegeable salesforce.
- *Market-structured salesforces* in which the salesstaff concentrate upon specific types of end user. It might therefore be the case that there are various types of customer for what is broadly the same product, but that their application needs differ. Recognizing this, the salesforce would be divided up on this basis; an example of this would be the computer firms which struture their salesforces along the lines of those who sell to the banks, those who sell to manufacturing industry, and so on.

Approaches to salesforce motivation

The question of how best to motivate the sales force is one that preoccupies many managers. If they are paid too much, costs rise unneccessarily. If they are paid too little it is likely that morale and performance will be low. Achieving the right balance is therefore important not just in terms of motivation, but also for the recruitment and retention of the best people. However, motivation should not be seen just in financial terms, since sales staff – in common with most employees – are motivated by a variety of other factors, including the potential for personal development, recognition by senior management of what they are achieving, opportunities for promotion, ego, drive, fringe benefits, and being part of a winning team.

In practice, these sorts of points translate into a choice between three main approaches to remuneration:

1   *Straight salary* in which each member of the salesforce is paid a fixed amount, irrespective of performance levels. The advantages of this are essentially that management can realistically expect members of the sales team to focus upon aspects of the business which will produce a return only in the long term, since this will not affect their immediate salary. However, if the sales team is guaranteed a certain level of income irrespective of their sales performance, their motivation to push harder, it is argued, will be reduced.

2   *Straight commission* in which the earnings of each of the sales staff are linked directly to their individual sales performance. Although this is an approach which can work well, it almost inevitably leads to a focus upon the very short term, with little attention being paid to longer term issues such as market development. Sales teams that are paid on this basis also tend to suffer from a high turnover of staff, since if the sales levels drop, individuals are perhaps understandably tempted to go elsewhere.

3   *Salary plus commission* in which sales staff are paid a basic salary which is then supplemented by a commission which is related to the individual's or the sales team's performance during a given period. Of the three approaches discussed here, it is this which tends to be seen as the fairest and most useful, since not only do the individual members of the team have a degree of security from their guaranteed income, but there is also a potentially powerful incentive to achieve high levels of sales performance.

QUESTION 6.14

(i) To what extent has research in recent years improved our understanding of how field sales staff can most effectively be motivated and controlled?

(Marketing Planning and Control, June 1992, Question 8.)

(ii) Making reference to examples, discuss the factors that should be taken into account when deciding how best to motivate and control a sales force and explain why so many firms experience problems in this area.

(Strategic Marketing Management: Planning and Control, December 1994, Question 10.)

Evaluating the salesforce

There are several ways in which the performance of sales staff individually and the salesforce overall can be evaluated, including:

- The levels of sales that are achieved and how they compare with the targets that were set and agreed at the beginning of the period.
- The number of new accounts opened.
- Sales calls per day.
- The average time per sales call.
- The average cost per sales call.
- The cost per sale.
- The number of lost customers.
- Sales person to sales person comparisons.
- Comparisons with previous time periods.
- Customer feedback and evaluations.

ACTIVITY 6.7

Speak to your sales director and discuss the sorts of issues raised within this section of the workbook. Ask about the sorts of problems that the company faces in managing its sales force and how it attempts to overcome these.

The 'soft' elements of the marketing mix

Our discussion so far has focused upon the traditional idea of the marketing mix and the 4Ps. Over the past few years, however, it has been argued that marketing management is concerned not just with product, price, place and promotion, but also with a series of rather 'softer' elements. The three most significant of these are, it is suggested:

- People.
- Process management.
- Physical evidence.

The *people* dimension is concerned with the types and skills of your staff, their ability to get things done, and – very importantly – how they interact with customers and suppliers.

The second 'soft' dimension – *process management* – is concerned with the ways in which customers are dealt with from the moment of the initial contact right through to the sales follow-up and the after sales service, whilst *physical evidence* relates to the surroundings in which the other elements are delivered and the sorts of messages they send to the customer.

Look at your own organization and assess the strengths and weaknesses of each of the 'soft' elements of the mix. To what extent does there appear to be a conscious effort to manage them? How does each of your competitors perform on these dimensions?

It follows from this that the marketing planner needs to think not just about the obvious dimensions of marketing (the 4Ps), but also the less tangible aspects, since for many organizations it is these which can play a powerful role in determining how the rest of the marketing programme is perceived. Their importance can also be understood by recognizing that, as market expectations of customer service levels increase, so the differentiating point between one organization and another will shift towards the 'softer' elements that are associated with the delivery of the product or service.

When analysing the major case study in the Analysis and Decision paper, make a conscious effort to identify how the 'soft' elements might contribute to the more effective performance of the organization.

Internal marketing

In 1982, Peters and Waterman published their book *In Search of Excellence* in which they focused upon high performing organizations and attempted to identify the sorts of characteristics which contributed to above average and excellent performance. Included within their findings was the way in which high performing organizations recognized the real value of their staff and made a conscious and sustained effort both to maximize and make full use of their potential. In doing this, it appeared that managers placed emphasis upon issues such as the careful selection of staff, the development of their skills, the pursuit of a clear and appropriate management style and – perhaps most importantly – the creation of shared values.

These ideas have, in turn, led to the idea of internal marketing.

Internal marketing refers to 'any form of marketing within an organization which focuses attention on the internal activities that need to be changed in order that marketing plans may be implemented.'

(Source: Christopher A., Payne A., and Ballantyne D., 1991, *Relationship Marketing*, page 79, Butterworth-Heinemann.)

Internal marketing is therefore concerned with creating the sort of culture and climate within an organization in which there is a far clearer understanding amongst all staff of the objectives, the key values and the sorts of implementation issues that need to be addressed. It follows from this that you should recognize that there is a need to focus not just on external customers, but also on a series of internal customers:

> The approach aims first to get a better understanding of the importance and performance of various activities within a particular work area which might be contributing to an internal quality group. The department then identifies by working with its internal customers and internal suppliers the key opportunities for improvement. Small problems are best tackled first to build mutual confidence through results.
>
> Source: Christopher et al, page 80.

QUESTION 6.15

Explain what is meant by 'internal marketing' and why it has been the subject of increased attention over the past few years. What factors should be taken into account when developing a programme of internal marketing for an organization?

(Marketing Planning and Control, June 1994, Question 5.)

Summary

Within this unit we have examined the various dimensions of the marketing mix. As a check on your understanding of this material, consider the following questions:

1 What are the 7Ps of the marketing mix? (See pages 111–12, 131.)
2 How might 'uncontrollable' elements be managed? (See page 112.)
3 What are the three elements of a product? (See page 112.)
4 Define 'product mix' and 'product line'. (See page 113.)
5 Of what value is the PLC? (See pages 113–14.)
6 How should marketing strategy change over the life of a product? (See page 114.)
7 Identify the four types of brand strategy. (See page 115.)
8 How would you value a brand? (See pages 115–16.)
9 Why is NPD important? (See page 117.)
10 What problems are typically associated with NPD? (See page 117.)
11 Draw a model of the NPD process. (See page 118.)
12 What problems are associated with test marketing? (See pages 117–19.)
13 What is a price taker and a price maker? (See page 119.)
14 Identify nine possible pricing objectives. (See page 120.)
15 How would you set a price? (See pages 120–1.)
16 What is the promotions mix? (See page 121.)
17 Define each of the elements of the promotions mix. (See page 122.)
18 Distinguish between sales-related and communication-related promotional objectives. (See page 122.)
19 How might you set the promotions budget? (See page 123.)
20 How would you measure the effect of a promotional campaign? (See page 124.)
21 Why are distribution decisions so important? (See pages 125, 128.)

22 Distinguish between intensive and selective distribution. (See page 126.)

23 What should be taken into account in measuring distribution efficiency? (See pages 126–8.)

24 What are the 'soft' elements of the marketing mix? (See page 131.)

25 What factors should be taken into account when managing the 'soft' elements? (See pages 131–2.)

Very deliberately, within this unit we have highlighted the key issues associated with the management of the marketing mix. For a more detailed discussion of each of these elements turn to Chapters 11–14 of *Strategic Marketing Management* by Wilson and Gilligan with Pearson.

Activity debrief

Question 6.1 (i): Refer to the discussion on pages 113–14.

Question 6.1 (ii): Refer to the discussion on page 114.

Question 6.1 (iii): Refer to the discussion on pages 113–14 and think about the need for faster and more frequent new product development, more flexible structures and a greater degree of proactivity.

Question 6.1 (iv): The problems include identifying the speed of take off, the speed of diffusion, the entry of competitors, repurchase rates and the length of the curve. to overcome these problems, think about drawing parallels with other products, previous experience with similarly innovatory products and lessons from other markets

Question 6.2: Refer to the discussion on pages 115–16.

Question 6.3: Refer to the discussion on pages 117–19.

Question 6.4: Refer to the discussion on pages 117–19.

Question 6.5 (i): Refer to the discussion on pages 117–19.

Question 6.5 (ii): Refer to the discussion on pages 117–19.

Question 6.5 (iii): The criteria include the cost and risks of launching the new product, the degree of managerial confidence in the product and what test marketing might be expected to generate. The second part of the question is covered by the discussion on page 118.

Question 6.6 (i): Refer to the discussion on pages 119–21.

Question 6.6 (ii): Refer to the discussion on pages 119–21.

Question 6.6 (iii): Refer to the discussion on pages 119–21 and think about managerial expectations, competitive response patterns, buyers' responses and issues of risk. The difficulties of getting this information are the typical market research problems.

Question 6.6 (iv): Small scale experimentation, focus groups and managerial experience. It will also be affected by the size of the change that is proposed.

Question 6.7: See pages 336–7 of *Strategic Marketing Management* by Wilson and Gilligan with Pearson.

Question 6.8: Refer to the discussion on pages 16, 122.

Question 6.9: Refer to the discussion on pages 123; in essence, it is the simplicity of the rule of thumb techniques.

Question 6.10: Refer to the discussion on pages 123–4.

Question 6.11: Refer to the discussion on pages 122, 124.

Question 6.12: Refer to the discussion on pages 195–6.

Question 6.13 (i): Refer to the discussion on pages 126–8 and think about absolute and relative costs, speed to market, spoilage levels, flexibility and the levels of marketing support needed.

Question 6.13 (ii): The direct and indirect manufacturing costs, any cost interdependencies, the shape of the experience curve, new product spending patterns, revenues, the total costs of distribution, costs by *type* of network, marketing support costs, salesforce costs, sales profitability, promotional costs and pricing issues.

Question 6.14 (i): Refer to the discussion on pages 129–30.

Question 6.14 (ii): Refer to the discussion on pages 129–31.

Question 6.15: Refer to the discussion on page 132.

Strategic evaluation and appraisal: which way is best?

Evaluation and appraisal are key issues in strategic marketing. Nothing the manager does can remove risk completely from business decisions but proper evaluation and appraisal can reduce these risks to levels more acceptable in highly competitive situations.

In this unit you will learn how to evaluate and appraise strategy and to choose among strategic options available. You will see:

- What criteria are available and how to choose between them.
- How to choose between options.
- What constitutes a 'good marketing' company.

By the end of this unit you will be able to:

- Initiate appraisal systems for marketing planning.
- Apply financial and non-financial criteria to choice evaluation.
- Identify the resource implications of mix decisions.
- Conduct feasibility studies and risk evaluation.

There are strong links between this unit and Unit 6 which focuses on the management of the mix and the development of marketing strategy.

This unit is primarily concerned with choice. It is an essential step between the previous stage of analysis and the following stage of decision.

In the major case study, especially, decision plays an important role and marks can be lost in the examination if clear recommendations for decision and action are not given.

In this section you should work carefully to master the various tests and approaches so that you are able to see easily the advantages and disadvantages of the strategic options that analysis reveals.

You should spend some time talking to senior managers in your organization with a view to identifying the criteria used in a real business setting to appraise strategy.

Also, you should look beyond your organization to other industries to discover the different criteria and/or tests that are used there.

The primary consideration in this unit is the evaluation of alternative strategic options open to the organization. Previous units have considered the options and methodologies open to strategic marketers and have shown the number of different routes that the strategist might consider in his or her planning. Once you have uncovered all the options, how do you decide which is the best way to go?

Many questions require an explicit or implicit understanding of choice criteria, be they marketing specific or financial.

Considering both broad business and marketing strategies as well as more detailed marketing programmes, the marketer is faced with two separate but related problems:

1   What choice criteria should be used?
2   How can we appraise and evaluate alternative options that appear to be open to the organization in question?

Short versus long term

Before considering the best way to evaluate and appraise marketing strategy, it is probably wise to stop at this point and consider just what we mean by strategy. Since strategy is about marshalling the gross resource of the organization to match the needs of the marketplace and achieve the business objective, this cannot be a short-term activity. Every organization is complex and any change takes time to accomplish. Strategic decisions, like the general choosing his battleground, will have long-term implications. Strategic decisions, such as which business area to enter, cannot be reversed at a moment's notice – momentum has to be built up over a planned period of time.

Neither is strategy just yet another word for important tactics. Tactics can be likened to manoeuvres on the field of battle and can be changed as often as required in response to the changing situation faced by the organization in its markets. No matter how important or critical the tactic under review, this does not make it strategy. For the want of a nail the horseshoe, the horse, the knight, the battle and the war were lost – agreed, but once a thousand soldiers have found a nail each they should all know the reason why they were there was to win the war.

The choice of evaluation and appraisal methods are critical because very quickly they become the main reasons for the organization's activities. We have to be careful that the evaluation and appraisal methods are aimed at assessing how well the war was won not how many nails were collected!

Marketing strategy is about the long-term success of the organization. Its success or failure must be measured by control systems which take into account this long-term view. A practical evaluation and appraisal system should note any short-term set-backs in the plan – but more importantly – should be capable of setting these within a long-term context.

Financial versus non-financial measurement

In marketing and business texts generally there is surprisingly little discussion over the difference between those measures which assess efficiency and those which assess effectiveness. Efficiency is defined as 'doing things right' and effectiveness is defined as 'doing the right things'. Efficiency and effectiveness were discussed in Unit 1. You might like to return there for a moment to refresh your memory.

Looking at your work, how much of your time each day is spent on activities which are primarily aimed at improving 'efficiency'? 70 per cent, 80 per cent, more?

How much of your work, as a marketer, is spent on 'effectiveness' activities – that add direct value to your customers? How might you improve this balance for the good of the business?

Efficiency measures are by far and away the most common in business generally and tend to evaluate, often on an ongoing basis, the efficiency or precision with which actions are carried out by the organization – mostly internal. When we look at effectiveness measures – and these are much less common in most organizations – we will be looking at how well the organization is doing the right things. In other words, how well the organization is meeting its external customers' needs.

Figure 1.5 (page 8) showed just how important the differentiation of these measures can be. For the rare organizations who manage to be both effective and efficient, that is they are efficient in their operations and also are delivering what their customers want, the future looks very rosy. For those organizations who are neither effective nor efficient then it is just a matter of time. In the middle, however, the situation is quite interesting. It is clear that organizations can become more and more efficient, leaner and leaner in their operations, but if they still fail to supply to the market what the market wants and needs it is only a matter of time before they are supplanted by eager competition. On the other hand, as long as an organization continues to supply what the market wants, the demand remains rather buoyant. They may not be very efficient in their operations and the way they supply the marketplace, but they are likely to survive.

More worryingly for organizations, however, is that the majority of measures which are used to evaluate and appraise strategy tend to be of the efficiency rather than the effectiveness nature. The majority of financial and accountant-driven measures also fall into this category. While, of course, there must be a point of inefficiency beyond which no organization can survive, efficiency of itself is no guarantee of the organization's survival. Unless the organization delivers what the market wants it will die – albeit slowly.

Strategy is always about balance. In this case, balance between efficiency and effectiveness measures. Ensure that your answers to questions and cases deal with and show this balanced thinking.

By what criteria might you measure the efficiency of a distribution channel? Illustrate your answer with appropriate examples.

June 1993

(**See** Activity debrief at the end of this unit.)

The answer, as in most strategic issues, is one of striking the elusive balance between these two apparently opposing forces. An organization's survival over the long term depends upon it being both effective and efficient. We should be searching out the evaluation and appraisal measures which allow us to pursue both these goals simultaneously. The problem is further compounded when we look in a little more detail at what effectiveness probably means. If we simplify the model of the firm down to its absolute basics we can see that the task of management is to satisfy the opposing needs of its two major publics:

Figure 7.1

The organization's most important two publics are its shareholders – who provide the finance and capital that the organization needs to continue, and its customers – who supply the revenue which pays for the product and produces the returns for the shareholders. We can see that these two publics require quite different things from the organization. Whatever the problems, it is the management's job to ensure that it satisfies both of these key publics if it is to survive over the longer term. How then can we evaluate our strategy within this context?

The financial requirements, and so the demands on marketing, can be strongly affected by an organization's stakeholders and what they require from this investment.

Can you identify the most important stakeholders in your organization? What do they require from your organization? What are the financial implications? What are the marketing implications?

Identify the areas to which you would need to pay attention in conducting a review of marketing effectiveness. How might the results be used to improve methods of planning and control?

December 1993

(**See** Activity debrief at the end of this unit.)

Financial measures
The more usual measures of evaluation under this heading will include:

- Profit.
- Profitability.

- Shareholder return.
- Cash flow/liquidity.
- Share price.
- Earnings per share.
- Return on net assets.
- Return on sales.

These were defined in more detail in Unit 2.

The interrelationships and working of these various measures can be seen in the extremely simplified diagram below.

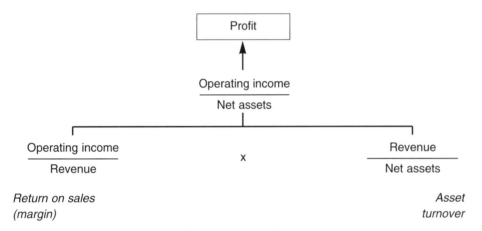

Figure 7.2

Most of these traditional measures concentrate on profit and it goes without saying that profit is essential to the long-term survival of any business no matter what size or shape. However, as Levitt said 'profit is a requisite not a purpose of business'. Profit is essential to any business but is not the only reason why we are here. Also, far more importantly, evaluation and appraisal processes which rely exclusively on profitability can overshadow the fact that the only way we make profits is by satisfying customers!

Equally important, if somewhat shorter term, liquidity/cash flow evaluation is essential. Lack of long-term profitability is not a major reason for the demise of businesses but cash flow problems can even eliminate companies with a rising order book. Despite everything we have said about strategy being longer term, the one thing we have to bear in mind is short-term cash flow. Without this there is no longer term.

QUESTION 7.3

What forms of financial control can most usefully be employed in marketing?

June 1994

(**See** Activity debrief at the end of this unit.)

Non-financial measures

The non-financial measures of performance tend to measure the effectiveness rather than the efficiency side of the equation, although not exclusively so. Non-financial measures may include:

- Market share.
- Growth.
- Competitive advantage.
- Competitive position.

- Sales volume.
- Market penetration levels.
- New product development.
- Customer satisfaction.
- Customer franchise.
- Market image and awareness levels.

EXAM TIP

The major case study often includes appendices with financial data. Be sure you also look at the non-financial data for measures of performance too.

Two things should be readily apparent from a review of the above list. Firstly, that any one of these measures taken in isolation is unlikely to be sufficient to guarantee the long-term survival and development of the organization. Secondly, implicit (although more often than not unstated) is that growth is always a good thing. The growth aspect to strategy is very much a development of the heydays of the 1970s and remains largely unquestioned in most texts.

ACTIVITY 7.3

There are times when a rapidly rising order book can be dangerous to the financial stability of a company. 'Overtrading' is a major cause of business failure – especially after a recession.

Do you understand what overtrading means?

Talk to a manager from the finance section of your company and find out what 'selling too much' can mean.

Certainly the organization must develop if it is to continue to adapt and remain in touch with its marketplace. But growth? Growth of what? Growth can be a good and healthy influence but if pursued for its own sake can lead to problems. Sales maximization and volume growth can often lead to serious declines in profitability, especially in static or highly competitive marketplaces. Directed and controlled growth based on a qualified and detailed analysis of the marketplace and potential business opportunities can lead to a flourishing organization. However, as Ed Abbey has noted, 'growth for the sake of growth is the ideology of the cancer cell.'

QUESTION 7.4

Making reference to examples, discuss the factors that should be taken into account when deciding how best to motivate and control a sales-force and explain why so many organizations experience difficulties in this area.

December 1994

(**See** Activity debrief at the end of this unit.)

EXAM TIP

Growth is just one example but there are a number of examples of marketing ideas that are just accepted as 'good things'. At Diploma level, examiners are looking for evidence of students being able to think for themselves, not just for regurgitated theory straight out of the textbooks.

Before you answer a question, do you understand why you are recommending a given course of action? Or is it just conventional wisdom again?

Multiple criteria

In almost every situation the dependence upon a single criterion for evaluating and appraising strategy is likely to be dangerous. As Wilson, Gilligan and Pearson note there are two extremely good reasons why we should consider using more than one criterion in our evaluation of strategy. This is because:

- Organizations behave ineffectively from some points of view if a single criterion is used.
- Organizations fulfil multiple functions and have multiple goals, some of which may be in conflict. It would be inappropriate to assess strategies purely on the basis of any one criterion.

EXAM TIP

Many questions require an explicit or an implicit understanding of evaluative criteria. You should therefore be aware of them and the circumstances in which they can be applied.

The major case study requires a clear demonstration of an evaluation among strategic options and a clear decision based upon this analysis.

Organizations and their strategies can best be regarded as living entities. If they follow their markets they will also need to be dynamic and evolving entities just to be able to survive, let alone flourish. Time, if no other reason, will always act to make certain measures redundant and other measures important in new situations.

We have also seen from the discussions above that conflicts naturally arise in the management of any organization. These require that different performance measures need to be traded off in different situations, for example:

- Customers' need for value versus shareholders need for return.
- Cost of achieving market share versus need for profitability.
- Organizations' need for efficiency versus customers' need for service.
- Production efficiency requirement for long runs versus the market's need for choice.
- The organization's drive to standardization versus the consumer's need for individualism.

The choice of the most appropriate measures for evaluation and appraisal will depend entirely on the organization's situation and the strategist's ability to balance internal and external needs.

Choosing the right criterion

How then can we make sure that we are choosing the right criterion against which to evaluate our longer term marketing strategy? Although there are no hard and fast rules for this selection the application of simple common sense can take us a long way forward. The judicious use of some selective models could also shed light on this problem. For example, if we consider the well-known product life cycle as a concept it is worthwhile trying to plot our organization's position on this cycle. Whether we consider this cycle applicable for the organization, the industry, the product or service category or even the particular brand, it will help us to select those criteria which are of most relevance to the situation at hand.

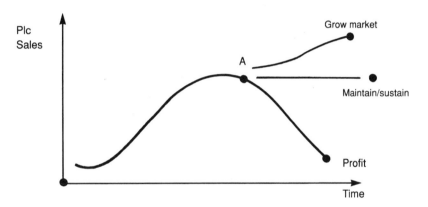

Figure 7.3

From the example above it can be seen clearly that an organization which plots its position at point 'A' and still decides to evaluate its long-term strategy according to either market share growth or maintenance, is only likely to be able to do this at the expense of profitability. Looking beyond the product life-cycle model to another popular model, the Boston Matrix, we can see that the same form of guidance is also available for those who wish to look.

	Net present value	Sales
Market Growth Rate	Return on investment	Net free cash flow

Relative Market Share

Figure 7.4   BCG Matrix

Although there is much debate about the continuing validity of the BCG matrix, and much care must be taken in its use, it can still be useful for conceptually placing products or businesses in the overall organization's portfolio. The diagram above shows that different forms of evaluation need to take place depending on the market and business situation of the product or the business considered. For example, 'dog' products or businesses need to be measured according to the net free cash flow which they generate. On the other hand 'question marks' are best evaluated by the sales volume and revenue which they are able to generate in their particular market situation. 'Stars' are best evaluated by an assessment of net present value while the all important 'cash cows' need to be assessed, evaluated and managed to generate the maximum return on investment.

GEC matrices and other models can also be used, with a little common sense, to ensure that we are measuring the right indicators in the right way.

It has been argued that one of the main reasons for the demise of the British motorcycle industry was their dependence on one key measure of performance – gross margin. As the Japanese advanced they retreated from one sector after another as margins were squeezed. The rest, as they say, is history.

Critical success factors

Much has been written about critical success factors (CSFs) although not all of it is in agreement. CSFs can be a useful way of focusing the attention of the organization onto those things, amid the wild array of important daily activities, that are really important. CSFs are not the same thing as performance measures and are not the same thing, strictly, as methods of evaluation and appraisal of long-term strategy.

CSFs need to be capable of measurement – obviously. This, however, can lead to organizations choosing 'quantities' rather than 'qualities' although the latter are no less important than the former. Also CSFs should not be based on variables that have only short-term importance. Nor should they be based only on internal variables. A study conducted in 1990 showed that companies which concentrated on achieving CSFs that were related to the external environment (e.g. customer needs, demand growth) were markedly more successful than those companies where CSFs were related to aspects of the internal environment.

Ideally CSFs are a short and pithy list of the key activities which, if the organization concentrates on and achieves, will go a long way towards achieving the long-term strategic aims of the business. CSFs are often a derivative of evaluation criteria and should always be causally linked to them. Examples of CSFs will tend to be very specific to the organization in hand and may even vary between organizations in the same industry depending upon their competitive situation.

CSFs can relate to, amongst other things:

- The speed of introduction of new products.
- Product and market profitability.
- Improving customer service.
- The development of creativity in management activities.
- Identification of new product opportunities.
- The achievement of critical mass in production or distribution channel throughput.
- Achievement in product or market leadership.
- Achieving a position of good corporate citizen.

> What are (or should be) the six most important CSFs used in your organization?
>
> How does your marketing activity relate to these CSFs?

The good marketing company

Considering the area of evaluation and appraisal of marketing strategy, the question always arises, 'so what would one of the best marketing organizations be doing?' Always a difficult question to answer since much depends upon the environment, the industry and the prevailing competitive situation of any particular organization.

However, as far as it is possible to answer such a general question, recent research carried out by the CIM and Cranfield School of Management have identified the following factors as those evidenced by the successful marketing company:

1 Start at the top.
2 Involve everyone in the organization in the marketing philosophy.
3 Be prepared for structural change.
4 Use the new structure to feed a 'customer facing strategy'.
5 Review marketing tactics (4Ps), do they work from the customer's point of view?
6 Accept that change is a way of life.
7 Understand the difference between 'quality systems' and quality products and services.
8 Focus on the customer, not the competition.
9 Look 'end-to-end' not piecemeal, customers expect seamless service.
10 Keep the end user in sight, don't be distracted by the middleman.
11 Measure the success of the marketing approach and be able to demonstrate the link between customer focus and profit.

This review gives good guidance to the types of evaluation criteria that can/should be used to drive practical marketing strategy.

> How well does your organization measure up against these points? What changes would you propose?

Summary

In this unit we have looked at how you should evaluate and appraise alternative strategic options that may be open to the organization.

We considered the pressures upon the organization that must be considered before attempting any evaluation, including the time period, outside factors, market conditions and internal factors.

The unit compared financial and non-financial measures and the case for using multiple criteria. The case is rarely clear cut and will normally be dependent upon the question posed in the exam or the nature of the company described in the case study.

Finally, we considered how to choose the right criteria and the particular role of CSFs. The unit concluded by looking at what constitutes a 'good marketing company' and the types of evaluation criteria that can be used to achieve this position.

Having completed this unit, consider the following questions as a check on your understanding.

1   How might the timescale (short versus long term) influence your choice of evaluative criteria?
2   Distinguish between efficiency and effectiveness.
3   Why should financial and non-financial measures be taken into account in deciding between alternatives and evaluating performance?
4   Identify the common financial measures of performance and evaluation.
5   Identify the common non-financial measures of performance and evaluation.
6   Why should multiple evaluative criteria be used? What problems are associated with this?
7   How might you go about selecting the 'right' criteria.
8   What are 'critical success factors'?
9   What is meant by 'a good marketing company'?

For a more detailed treatment of the sort of criteria that can be used in choosing between alternative strategies and evaluating performance, read:

Strategic Marketing Management, Wilson and Gilligan with Pearson, Chapters 15 and 16.

Marketing Strategy, Fifield, pages 27–38 and 174–189.

Activity debrief

Question 7.1   June 1993   To obtain maximum marks on this question, your answer should be well structured and clearly presented. Distribution can be considered for industrial, consumer goods and services – all are equally valid. However, have you clearly demonstrated the 'cost–benefit' approach that evaluates channels by what they cost the organization compared with what the organization gains. Has your answer also considered that efficiency needs to be measured against something – marketing/distribution objectives. Examples have been requested and must be included.

Question 7.2   December 1993   Has your answer considered the critical difference between 'effectiveness' and 'efficiency'? Have you highlighted specific 'areas' of marketing as you were asked? What are the critical areas that should be reviewed? The question had a second part – has your answer considered how the results of the review might be used to improve methods of planning and control. Analysis without a demonstrated ability to apply the findings can only achieve pass grades at Certificate level – diploma passes demand more.

Question 7.3   June 1994   This is a very straightforward question. Your answer should have presented the alternative methods of financial controls and briefly described their functions. To pass, your answer needed to describe exactly how these controls can be used to help marketers and how they support the marketing planning and control process. Examples would be useful.

Question 7.4   December 1994   As well as testing your knowledge and ability to apply theory in the area of salesforce activity, this question also tests your ability to select and apply relevant control mechanisms. Has your answer used examples as requested – they are essential to pass. Has your answer considered the role of the salesforce in the marketing activity of an organization and how it needs to be co-ordinated with other promotional methods? The key to motivation and control of a salesforce is the selection of objectives. Most organizations seldom look further than sales' ability to sell and reward on turnover acheived. Marketing is about satisfied customers and profits. Has your answer looked at how salesforces can be motivated and controlled to bring in the right quality of sale not just ever increasing quanitiy?

Strategic implementation and control: how do we ensure arrival?

In this unit you will consider the practical implementation of marketing strategy. Before strategy can be turned into reality you will need to understand:

- The barriers to stragtegic implementation.
- The drivers for strategic implementation.
- Control systems.

By the end of this unit you will:

1 Have an understanding of the issues associated with effective implementation and control of marketing plans.
2 Understand the principal barriers to implementation.
3 Be capable of showing how these barriers might be overcome.

This unit covers Section 5 of the Planning andf Control syllabus and part of Sections 4 and 6 of the Analysis and Decision syllabus.

It is important that, no matter how good, elegant or sophisticated the marketing strategy which you have developed is, unless it is executed in an equally sophisticated manner it remains just a document which will gather dust. Much has been written in the literature about marketing tactics and the methods by which implementation of strategy is to be achieved, but far less attention has been paid to the barriers which stand in the way of successful implementation.

Implementation and control systems are now key features on both strategic marketing management papers and you are urged to prepare this section fully and be able to explain or propose appropriate measures in the exam.

One way of find out what happens in practice is to discover what happens in your own organization. Many barriers will be present and control systems in place. How many can you identify?

Barriers to implementation

There are many barriers that stand in the way of successful implementation of marketing strategy, some evident, some not so. The barriers fall broadly into three separate categories; external pressures on the organization, internal pressures on the marketing function and pressures within the marketing function itself. We will consider these three forms of pressure independently.

To consider the external pressures on the organization first, these are best described under the traditional PEST or SLEPT headings to describe the environment. (These are described in more detail in Unit 3.)

Social factors Changing demographic and social patterns such as an ageing relation, fewer school leavers, and the shift in emphasis from manual to white collar skills will have a major impact on any strategic plans which require implementation over the next 5 to 10 years. British society is also undergoing some level of fundamental change and trends such as ecology, class structure and individualism need to be accounted for in your plans. Customers and consumers are also part of the social element of the environment but these will be considered in more detail under the heading 'drivers for strategic implementation' on page 151.

Legal There are an increasing number of laws which are affecting business activity on a wider and wider scale. Laws now cover employment, pay and price policies, health and safety as well as specific acts to control particular industries such as financial services and telecommunications. Also, as time progresses we can expect more impact on British activity from European based laws.

Economic factors The past 10 years have witnessed an unparalleled level of change in the British economy, and this change is unlikely to slow down. Strategic implementation of plans needs to take into account the changes which are likely to occur in the marketplace and you should consider aspects such as changes in your own marketplace such as mergers, joint ventures, share price movement and investment as well as any trade union activities. Suppliers' actions and changes to include vertical integration and disintermediation (the disappearance of intermediaries in the process). Distribution channels are also undergoing a radical change in a number of industries and successful implementation will depend upon a good forecasting of likely change in areas such as distribution infrastructure as well as in transportation and channel management and control. Internationalization is a major factor in all economic situations and is likely to affect your customers' perceptions of your offer, and the whole nature of competition. Competition itself is one of the most important factors to forecast in strategic implementation since no marketing strategy ever operates in a vacuum. You should be attempting to analyse not only the direct (own industry) competition but also the important and often more difficult to predict indirect competition from outside your traditional industry base. Competition is expected to increase in all sectors over the next 10 years, driven primarily by the internationalization of business and the fragmentation of so many markets.

It has been suggested that one of the most fundamental challenges likely to be faced over the next few years by manufacturers of consumer goods will stem from the seemingly inexorable increase in levels of retail concentration. Citing examples, comment upon the implications of this trend both for retailers and manufacturers, and suggest how branded manufacturers, intent on retaining the strength of a brand franchise, might possibly respond.

June 1991

(**See** Activity debrief at the end of this unit)

Political factors   There is a general trend in most western markets for Government to take an increasingly active role in business. Political activities include taxation, lobbying, as well as the ability to pass laws which affect not only your organization's ability to act in a free market, but also affects customers' ability to buy your products or services. In all markets political activities are often aimed at influencing competitive activity. Whatever the intention behind political actions, the result is always some form of restriction over the organization's activities in a marketplace and these restrictions need to be forecasted and attempts made to modify implementation of the strategic plan within this new framework.

Technological factors   Technology generally has had a massive effect over the past 10 years and we can expect this influence to continue if not to accelerate. Technology has made radical changes in manufacturing technology possible and has perhaps been a major catalyst in the recent proliferation of new products and services. A major factor in the development of technology has been its ability to reduce, if not sometimes eliminate, barriers to market entry. The application of modern technology has enabled small and medium-sized organizations to operate at cost levels previously the exclusive preserve of much larger organizations. Economies of scale are no longer the barriers they used to be.

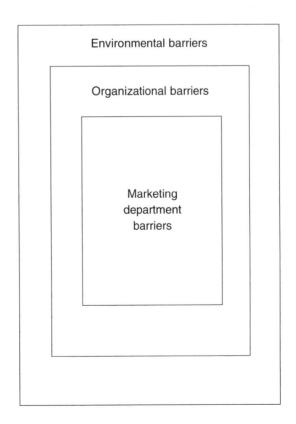

Figure 8.1 Barriers to implementation

Carry out a PEST analysis on your organization.

- What are the three most significant items under each heading that might block the implementation of marketing strategy?
- What can be done to avoid or reduce the effect of these factors?
- What is currently being done?

Identify the principal strategic challenges that marketers are likely to face over the next decade and comment upon their implications for approaches to marketing planning.

December 1992

(**See** Activity debrief at the end of this unit.)

As well as external pressures acting upon the organization that will affect the successful implementation of marketing strategy, there are a number of factors which are internal to the organization which will also affect its ability to implement its strategic plans successfully. All of these factors act as significant potential blockages to implementing marketing strategy and unless these blockages can be overcome inside the organization the marketer has little choice but to amend the goals and strategy to those which the organization is able to implement. To look at some of these factors in more detail:

Leadership There is little doubt that the ultimate success and implementation of any strategic plan will depend upon the degree to which top management buys into the process. This is especially evident where the strategic thrust of the plan involves any form of significant change. The organization's leadership may be opposed to the objectives of the plan for any number of reasons. For example, they may be from non-marketing disciplines, may feel that the need for change is not yet apparent or simply be more comfortable with 'steady state' management style. Whatever the reasons, unless the leadership has bought into the plans completely and feels that it owns these plans, little progress is likely to be made.

Organizational culture There are many forms of organizational culture and, in truth, few of these are customer or market focused. In the organization with a non-market oriented culture, chances of successfully implementing a truly customer-focused strategic marketing plan must be severely limited. Marketing in this type of organization tends to be all about marketing services, often linked or even subservient to the important sales function. In the product or production-oriented organization the marketer's role is to provide sales materials, product information and market analysis to support the sales and production functions of the organization. The market or customer-oriented organization is the only one which sees the marketer's role as that of catalyst and change agent to focus the rest of the organization's activities on the one activity that really matters – the customer. Changing the culture of an organization is never a short-term task. However, as today's markets become more and more competitive the option is becoming clearer – change the culture or the organization may not survive beyond the medium term. If the culture will not change in the short to medium term then goals and strategies will need to be amended to something which the organizational culture can assimilate.

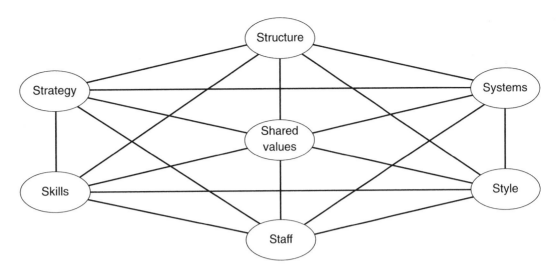

Figure 8.2 McKinsey 7-S framework

Organization design In many organizations the existing organization structure is simply not designed to be able to deliver the proposed marketing strategy as is intended. Too many organizations are designed for the convenience and administrative ease of those who work in them rather than being designed to deliver satisfaction to customers. It is simply unrealistic to design a customer-focused marketing strategy without spending some time looking at the organization's ability to deliver on the promises which you may be making to your customers. If organizations are so rigid that they cannot be redesigned, then your marketing strategy may need to be modified accordingly. 'Re-engineering' or 'Business Process Redesign' initiatives may be successful in this regard but only if they are directed at redesigning the organization in customer terms and not simply aimed at restyling the IT processes.

When dealing with organizations (culture and design) it is important to consider the 'soft' elements such as style, skills, staffing and shared values as well as the traditional 'hard' values. Remember, an organization is nothing without the people who work inside it. The 7-S Framework places these elements together (see Figure 8.2).

Functional policies A subset of organization structure, most functions in an organization (finance, operations, human resources... and marketing!) tend to grow up and produce a number of functional policies and procedures which determine how their part of the organization and their staff manage the day-to-day business. The intended marketing strategy may fall foul of these procedural processes and will encounter a blockage on the path to implementation.

Resources The proposed marketing strategy may require that either significant additional resources be allocated to certain functions or even the reappropriation of resources into different areas of the organization. Successful implementation will depend upon either these resources being available for implementation of the plan or making the appropriate resources available so that the plan can be implemented fully. The potential blockage here is likely to be either in the resources simply not being available or that senior management considers that other causes are more deserving. In any case this could provide a significant blockage to implementation.

Evaluation and control procedures The lack of appropriate monitoring and evaluation procedures in an organization will be a significant block to the successful implementation of any strategy. This potential blockage can be less of a problem than those outlined above in that you are not necessarily faced with overcoming perception or resource problems. As long as the proper control measures are installed there need be no problems in implementation. Control measures will be considered in more depth later in the unit.

Critically review your organization (or one that you are familiar with) for internal blockages.

- What blockages to marketing implementation can you identify?
- Why are these blockages present?
- How might they be overcome?

Given the scale and complexity of the blockages and pressures upon the marketing function from inside its own organization, the importance of internal marketing starts to become apparent. An integral part of successful strategic implementation, internal marketing involves all the processes necessary to carry the message of the strategic marketing plan inside to the various audiences that comprise the organization. We can see from the list of possible blockages which exist in the organization above, that success or failure of strategic marketing strategy can depend upon people and functions inside the organization not only believing the message but putting their weight behind the effort too. Internal marketing means more than just promotions, it means the same as it does in the external environment, the application of the full marketing mix to achieve some predetermined behaviour change. Internal marketing, like external marketing, to be successful requires a good understanding of the needs and motivations of the target audiences. The above review should start to give the marketer a reasonable understanding of where people in the internal organization currently stand and the measures needed to gain their full and willing support for the proposed marketing strategy (see also Unit 6, page 132).

Explain what is meant by 'internal marketing' and why it has been the subject of increased attention over the past few years. What factors should be taken into account when developing a programme of internal marketing for an organization?

June 1994

(**See** Activity debrief at the end of this unit.)

Not only are there a number of issues internal to the organization which can act as blockages to developing and implementing quality marketing strategy, there are a number of aspects of the marketing department or function which can also act as potential blockages to the development and implementation of your plans.

Marketing's interface with other functions   Delivering satisfactions to customers may be the responsibility of the marketing function but it is not a job that marketers can carry out on their own. In order to deliver customer satisfaction and thereby improve the organization's position against competition, the entire organization needs to operate as an effective partnership and deliver seamlessly. In order to do this marketing needs to interact positively with other functions within the organization, such as production, purchasing, personnel and finance. Unfortunately some of these functions may consider that they have competing responsibilities and may not fix the priorities in exactly the same way as marketing. Once again the solution is not in 'telling' other functions what to do, but in involving them in the process. The marketing manager must find means of securing better co-ordination amongst the various functional sub-systems that are not directly under his or her control. This may be achieved by improving communications and inter-organizational understandings about what is in the interests of the organization as a whole.

The role of marketing/marketer   The role of the marketer will depend largely upon the organization culture and structure. In the non-market-oriented organization marketing tends to be synonymous with 'advertising and promotion'. The marketing manager is often taken on as a necessary (and expensive) evil because the competition seems to be making inroads into the organization's markets by advertising. Other managers in the organization often have little understanding of the marketing concept and don't realize their role in satisfying customers. The role of the marketer in the production or product-oriented organization is two fold – to give his or her internal customers what they want and, secondly, to act as a catalyst for change toward a more customer-oriented position. In the case of a customer or market-oriented organization the role of the marketer and the marketing function is quite different. Rather than concentrating on advertising and promotion, the marketer's function is to identify, anticipate and satisfy customer needs profitably. To do this needs much more than a depth knowledge of advertising and promotional methodology and techniques. In this type of organization the marketer's key area of responsibility is to understand the organization's customers and to feed this information back into the organization and other functions so that people may act upon it profitably.

Marketing feedback   How effective a marketer is in his or her job and how well the strategic marketing plan is implemented will depend, to a great extent, on how much and how relevant and how good his or her information is and how well it is interpreted and acted upon. Information is critical. Information and feedback on a plan's progress is never 100 per cent accurate but it does act both to reduce uncertainty in planning and to improve the quality of action. Critically the marketer may not be in complete control of the information sources and the speed at which they are delivering quality information back to the marketing function. A great deal of data is often raised elsewhere in the organization but often not in a form which will provide adequate information for the marketer's use. The marketer has two main flows of data. One from the environment and the other from internal operations. Some, but not all, is likely to be under the marketer's direct control, for the rest, other departments need to understand the importance of quality and timely information flows and internal marketing can help this process.

The final, crucial area of marketing and market feedback is market research. In many organizations some market research is carried out but invariably it is insufficient to meet the organization's needs. Market research should not be regarded as a crutch to support weak decision making but as an essential 'investment' in the marketplace and future prosperity of the organization. Unfortunately many organizations, often product, production or planning oriented, do not see the investment aspects of market research but rather consider it as a cost. As competition increases and markets continue to fragment, it is unlikely that investment in market research will decline in the most successful organizations, rather we can expect it to increase as market circumstances become more and more involved.

Drivers for strategic implementation

Rather than simply paint a completely negative picture, organizations and the current market can actively support the implementation of marketing strategy. The astute marketer should be able to use these drivers for change, to enlist help and active co-operation within the organization to implement his or her plans.

Customer expectations   Customers in all markets are now starting to demand the 'impossible'. As their needs and wishes are met in very competitive markets such as groceries, consumer goods and motor cars, they see no reason why these expectations should not be met in unrelated fields such as banking, telecommunications and travel. As customer expectations continue to grow, so concepts like 'brand loyalty' tend to diminish with the passage of time. Customers are becoming less and less loyal to brands and organizations if these fail to provide what is wanted, when it is wanted and at a reasonable price. The astute marketer can use the changes in customer demand and forecasts of future demand to drive through changes inside the organization at a rate which internal departments would otherwise possibly consider to be uncomfortable. At this point, customer information and projections are invaluable and form the basis of the marketer's key strength in the organization.

Revenue Revenues and profits are the life blood of any organization. The past four or five years of deep recession in the British market (and a slightly lighter variant in other European markets) has meant that many organizations have cut costs dramatically in order to continue flows and returns to shareholders. As the movement out of recession is somewhat slower than expected the potential well of returns from cost savings starts to grow ever more shallow. The only source of continued revenue and profit growth for many organizations is now the marketplace. Customers are the source of all revenues and profits for any organization and satisfied customers have now started to top the agendas of more and more organizations. The marketer needs to use this trend and to drive through the message inside the organization that long-term profits do not come from a numbers game (adding more customers at any price) but from a quality game that involves constantly offering customers a solution which meets their needs better than the competition can.

Competition As technology drives down the barriers to entry into many markets; and markets are beginning to fragment in many and devious ways, competition is intensifying in practically every business sector. Not only are existing players fighting to gain and retain customers but also new entrants from outside the sector are being attracted by more substantial profits than they can gain in their home markets. Brands and products are proliferating and customers are now faced with a greater choice in most markets than they have ever experienced in the past. The only way through this maze for most organizations is to be able to establish a clear and differentiated image and position in the market in which they operate and to give customers good, simple and relevant reasons why they should come to them rather than the competition. Effective market positioning is not achieved solely by product quality but requires the deft application of all the elements of strategic marketing.

Innovation A by-product of the increasingly competitive nature of most markets and the application of modern technology, innovation has become the norm in many industry sectors. Innovation for its own sake is unlikely to gain market share or profitably but innovation directed at supplying more relevant products to customers will. In the future, innovation in both product or service delivery and processes and service will be the norm rather than the exception. Unfortunately, many organizations tend to find innovation an uncomfortable experience and many prefer the 'steady state' environment to work in. It is unlikely that such environments will prove profitable in the future and the marketer's role now is to use this tide of innovation to get his or her organization on stream to match, if not to exceed, the competition's offering.

ACTIVITY 8.3

Under the headings for the drivers for strategic implementation, can you identify how these factors are influencing your organization?

Are the drivers being properly harnessed to produce real changes? What can be done?

Control systems

Control systems form the second part of the expression 'planning and control'. If planning is defined as 'deciding what to do' then control is defined as 'ensuring that the desired results are obtained'. Planning without control simply means that the organization has a nice, sophisticated document. The control systems are essential to make sure that the organization drives through the content of the plans and achieves its objectives in the marketplace.

Control systems are many and various and selecting the right method of control will depend very much upon the market that the organization is addressing, the particular goals and objectives which the organization has set itself, as well as the particular organization structure, design and culture. In simple terms the control process can be described as in Figure 8.3 below.

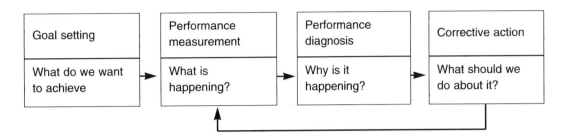

Goal setting	Performance measurement	Performance diagnosis	Corrective action
What do we want to achieve	What is happening?	Why is it happening?	What should we do about it?

Figure 8.3 The control process

Control systems then are a matter of balancing four primary issues.

1 Standard setting.
2 Performance measurement.
3 Reporting results.
4 Taking corrective action (if required).

In the major case study you may not be asked specifically to illustrate suitable control systems. You will, however, be asked for your recommendations on marketing strategy.

Any recommendation on strategy will be considered incomplete without suitable control systems and valuable marks will be lost if you do not include this area.

EXAM TIP

Setting the standards is the role of the planning element of the process and the goals and objectives which fall out of the strategic marketing plan are then translated into standards which drive through the organization and which, if implemented, will determine the successful implementation of the project. Ideally the standards will have been set within an understanding of what the organization is currently able to deliver.

Performance measurement and reporting of results are the key areas of most control systems. Most discussion then will centre around which performances should be measured and how results should be reported. The measurement activities of the planning achievements can simply be broken down into three broad areas.

1 *Quantity* How much was achieved? How much should have been achieved?
2 *Quality* How good was that which was achieved? How good was it meant to be?
3 *Cost* How much did the achievement cost? How much was it planned to cost?

These basic parameters of the plan can then be quantified through an analysis of one or more of five distinct areas of operation which are:

- Financial analysis.
- Market analysis.
- Sales and distribution analysis.
- Physical resources analysis.
- Human resource analysis

Audits One method of assessing strategic marketing effectiveness is by the use of constant and regular marketing audits. The marketing audit (which is described in detail elsewhere) is a robust method of monitoring the successful implementation of marketing plans and policies. No matter which form of marketing audit is taken, marketing management should ensure that all areas of marketing activity are regularly monitored and their performance measured against pre-set standards which, once achieved, will guarantee the successful implementation of the plan.

QUESTION 8.4

?

'Marketing Planning is a generally straightforward exercise; the marketer's real problems are those of effective implementation.' (Anonymous).

Identify the nature of the barriers to effective implementation that marketers typically encounter and suggest how, if at all, these barriers might be reduced.

December 1992

(**See** Activity debrief at the end of this unit.)

Budgets Budgeting is probably the most common form of control mechanism in most organizations and, although developed for financial housekeeping and management, is often applied to marketing implementation as well. There are a number of advantages as well as disadvantages to using the budgeting process. Many budgets tend to be short term, typically based on the annual plan for the achievement of that year's profit and turnover forecasts. Short-term budgeting of this nature is not always the most relevant for the measurement and control of long-term strategy. The strategic marketer should note that short-term deviations from plans may require only short-term tactical alterations, but no longer term strategic shifting in direction. Where the budgeting process is longer term and/or continuous rather than periodic in nature the feedback results may be more relevant to longer term strategic proposals. When dealing with budgets it is vitally important to understand that budgeting is not the same as management. Budgeting is an important aid to management decision making but budgets are always based on estimates rather than reality and are always, at best, someone's idea of how the future will happen. Therefore, when deviations from budgeted figures arise marketing must ask itself not only whether the deviations are significant and require corrective action but also how valid were the original estimates incorporated into the budgeting at the outset.

Variance analysis Another analysis and control procedure which falls out of the budgeting process is the detailed analysis of the variance (difference between actual and expected results) that arises from the organization's activities. Variances of a number of different items can be measured and assessed, much will depend upon the key parameters used by the organization to assess its performance overall. Typical variance measures will include sales-price variance, sales-quantity variance, sales-volume variance, profit variance, market-size variance, market-share variance, etc.

Whatever the method of analysis and evaluation that is deemed the most appropriate by your organization and the strategic marketing plans which you have compiled, it is important to recognize that analysis on its own is rarely sufficient to monitor and implement plans properly. As well as identifying the actual variances or differences from expected results, equal attention has to be paid to understanding the reasons for the variance in the first place. Before any corrective action can be taken (if indeed it is required) the reasons for the variance need to be identified. Corrective action needs to be taken against the reasons for the shortfall (or the overrun!) if it is to be effective. At this point additional feedback is required from marketing intelligence and assessment of the external and competitive situation which may give some clue as to the reasons for the deviation from the expected plan. At the very least it needs to be established whether the reasons for the divergence from the plan have been caused by internal problems or external problems.

Evaluate the contribution that marketing auditing is capable of making to the marketing planning and control process, and comment upon the problems that are typically encountered in auditing.

June 1992

(**See** Activity debrief at the end of this unit.)

Taking corrective action

Once the control system has been established, and then during the implementation phase of the plan, divergences or deviations from the estimated results have been highlighted, the marketer's role is to decide whether corrective action is required and if so how to implement this action in time to bring the plan back on to target. The options open to the organization in terms of corrective action fall into a number of separate categories:

Environmental changes If the reason for the divergence is caused by unpredicted changes in the external environment of the organization the marketer has a number of options open to him or her at this stage. If the environmental factors are deemed to be of a short term nature then a modification in the tactics needed to implement the strategic plan can be considered. If the changes in the external environment or the marketplace are deemed to be fundamental or structural in nature then the marketer may need to revisit the overall strategy and aims and objectives of the plan itself.

Internal problems If the non-delivery on the estimates of the plan are caused by internal problems the marketer has to decide whether this is a shortfall in performance or is caused by active blockages in other parts or functions of the organization. Corrective action will need to be directed at these points.

Faulty estimating It may be apparent from a deeper analysis of the variances that the problem lies not in the market nor in the organization's ability to deliver, but that the original estimates set against which the plan was going to be judged were erroneous. In this case the marketer needs to re-estimate the rate at which the organization will achieve its strategic objectives.

One final note of warning. This book and the two CIM papers are all concerned with strategy – not tactics. Strategic decisions will have long-term implications and organizational momentum has to be built over a planned period. Constant change produces uncertainty, confusion, misdirection and wastage – not results. Tactics are designed to change on a weekly or even a daily basis in response to changes in the marketplace caused by customer needs or competitor response. Tactical change causes no problems of uncertainty as long as the strategy, the broad overall direction of the organization, remains constant. Control systems which drive regular tactical changes to keep the strategy on course are a positive boon to any organization. On the other hand, if the control systems allow managers, through ignorance or panic, to make constant changes to strategy and direction the organization will end up achieving nothing and going nowhere.

Summary

In this unit we have looked at the all important step of strategic implementation. We have considered the two main areas critical to implementation, firstly the barriers and drivers to strategic implementation that exist and secondly the control and measurement procedures needed to ensure safe arrival at our destination.

First we considered the barriers to successful strategic implementation that exist for the marketer. These can be seen as originating from the external environment within which the organization must operate and from within the organization, from functions other than marketing itself. We also looked at some of the variables which can, if harnessed properly, actively promote implementation of strategic marketing.

Secondly, we considered the control mechanisms which are necessary to ensure that the strategic plan is implemented and the objectives are achieved. We considered the wide range of analysis and control mechanisms which are used in different organizations, including auditing, budgeting and variance analysis.

Finally, we considered the nature of corrective action that can be taken by the marketer and the form that this should take.

Having completed the unit, consider the following questions as a check on your understanding.

1   Why is implementation so often the cause of strategies proving to be disappointing?
2   What are the three principal causes of poor implementation?
3   Identify the major external pressures on the organization. What are the major internal pressures?
4   How might the internal barriers to implementation be reduced?
5   What is meant by 'drivers for implementation'? Identify the four principal drivers.
6   Why are control systems so important? How would you devise a control system?

EXTENDING YOUR KNOWLEDGE

For a more detailed explanation of implementation and control systems within Strategic Marketing refer to *Strategic Marketing Management*, Wilson and Gilligan with Pearson, pages 499–615 and *Marketing Strategy*, Fifield, pages 190–204, 240–243.

Activity debrief

Question 8.1   June 1991   Your answer, to reflect the question, should be in two parts. First, has your answer considered the trend of retail concentration and its implications for both retailers and manufacturers. Have you used a model (e.g. Porter), if so, have you integrated and applied it to the answer? What are the effects of, e.g. increasing buyer power and price resistance? Is the phenomenon widespread or concentrated in certain sectors? Have you used examples to demonstrate the situation and support your points? Part two of the question asked you to propose how manufacturers should respond to this in order to protect brand strength. Have you used examples again here?

Question 8.2   December 1992   Your answer needs to do two things: first, you should have identified what you believe to be the principal strategic challenges facing marketers in the 1990s (e.g. new technology, changing demographics, new values, increased competition, Europe, changing organizational structures). Secondly, your answer should describe the implications of these events for marketing planning and control. What can marketers do about it? What measures should be taken?

Question 8.3   June 1994   Your answer should include a clear examination of what internal marketing involves (it is not a good idea to attempt a question without the basic knowledge) and the reasons why it has become popular in organizations. Have you considered the benefits from internal marketing for the planning and control process? The question has a second part. Your answer should have included a detailed summary of those factors which you think are important. What are the problems with internal marketing? What barriers exist to prevent its successful implementation, how can these barriers be overcome?

Question 8.4   December 1992   Again, the question is in two parts and your answer should reflect clearly the division set by the examiner. Has your answer properly enumerated and explained the barriers to the implementation of marketing planning? Have you considered both the hard and the 'soft' (psychological) barriers that exist? The second part of the question asks for ways that these barriers might be reduced. Has your answer covered the methods available for reducing or avoiding the barriers?

Question 8.5   June 1992   Another question that comes in two parts. Has your answer responded to both parts of the question? Your answer should have included an explanation of the audit process, and the contribution that auditing can make to the marketing planning and control process. The second part of the question asks you to consider the problems involved in the auditing process (collecting data, data quality etc.). Remember you will have difficulty passing if you only answer half of the question!

The mini case study

A mini case study is the first part of the Strategic Marketing: Planning and Control examination. It is a compulsory part of the examination and designed to provide you with an opportunity to apply your knowledge to a particular situation. The purpose of this unit is therefore:

- To help you understand how best to approach the mini case study.
- To highlight the sorts of mistakes that are commonly made.
- To give you an opportunity to prepare a number of practice solutions.

By the end of this unit, you will:

- Be familiar with the sorts of mini case study that have been used over the past few years.
- Have an understanding of the issues that they raise.
- Have gained some practice at approaching these cases.

Although with each of the previous units, it has been a relatively straightforward exercise to identify how long you should spend working on the unit, it is far harder to do this with the mini case. Instead, you should recognize that the more practice you get with the mini case, the more likely it is that you will approach it in your examination with a degree of confidence and an understanding of what is required from you. You should, therefore, spend as much time as you can familiarizing yourself with the format of the mini cases and the sorts of questions that are asked. Practise preparing solutions to the questions and then compare your answers with the solutions that we have included at the end of the unit.

It needs to be recognized that the type of short case (popularly called the mini case) set in the examinations cannot be treated in exactly the same way as the extremely long case set for the subject of Strategic Marketing: Analysis and Decision.

However, far too many students adopt a maxi-case approach, using a detailed marketing audit outline which is largely inappropriate to a case consisting of just two or three pages. Others use SWOT analysis and simply re-write the case under the four headings of strengths, weaknesses, opportunities and threats.

Some students even go so far as to ignore the specific questions set and present a standard maxi-case analysis, including environmental reviews and contingency plans. Others adopt a vague and far too superficial approach. In each case, students are penalized. You should recognize therefore that the mini case is simply an *outline* of a given situation whose purpose is to test whether candidates can apply their knowledge of marketing operations to the environment described in the scenario. For example, answers advocating retail audits as part of the marketing information system for a small industrial goods manufacturer confirm that the examinee has learned a given MIS outline by rote and simply regurgitated this with complete disregard of the scenario. Such an approach cannot be passed. A more appropriate approach to the scenario involves a mental review of the areas covered by the question and the selection by the candidate of those particular parts of knowledge or techniques which apply to the case. This implies a rejection of those parts of the students' knowledge which clearly do not apply to the scenario.

All scenarios are based upon real world companies and situations and are written with a full knowledge of how that organization operates in its planning environments. Often, the organization described in the scenario will not be a giant fast-moving consumer goods manufacturing and marketing company but is instead an innovative, small or medium-sized firm faced with a particular problem or challenge. The cases are often, but not invariably, written from the viewpoint of a consultant and include an extract from a consultant's report.

The examination as a whole lasts for 3 hours. Including your reading time, you therefore have, $1\frac{1}{2}$ hours for the mini case.

EXAM TIP

> On opening the examination paper, read the mini case at your normal reading speed, highlighting any issues that appear to you to be particularly significant. Having done this, read the questions in Section 1 and then read the mini case again, identifying and highlighting those issues which are particularly relevant to the questions posed. Remember that both questions in the section need to be answered and that the examination paper will indicate the split of marks. Allocate your time accordingly and do not make the mistake of spending more than 90 minutes on Section 1.

The mistakes that candidates make

We have already touched upon some of the mistakes that candidates make in approaching the mini case. We can, however, take these further with the list of the ten most common errors that candidates make.

The ten most common mini case errors

1 Ignoring the specific questions posed and providing instead a general treatment of the case.
2 Thinking that every mini case study demands a SWOT analysis; it doesn't.
3 Not answering in the format asked for. You will normally be asked for a report, a memorandum or a marketing plan and should answer using one of these frameworks.
4 Making unrealistic assumptions about the extent to which organizations can change their working practices.
5 Assuming that unlimited financial resources will be available to you.
6 Failing to recognize the difficulties of implementation.
7 Introducing hypothetical data on costs.
8 Rewriting the case and ignoring the questions.
9 Failing to give full recognition to the implications of what is recommended.
10 Not spending sufficient time on the second of the two questions.

The past cases

Although for the majority of the Diploma papers, Syllabus 94 represented at least a small change in direction and emphasis, for Planning and Control it simply confirmed the sorts of changes that had been made to the syllabus and examination over a three-year period. It is for this reason that we have included eight of the past mini case studies within this unit. These are:

Portland Promotional Products Ltd	June 1991
Phoenix Telecom Ltd	December 1991
Penton Ltd	June 1992
New Directions plc	December 1992
Anderson Marine Construction Ltd	June 1993
Kanko Ltd	December 1993
Watergate Pumps Ltd	June 1994
RTJ Engineering Ltd	December 1994

In reading these case studies, several points should become apparent. The first is that the questions posed cover a spectrum of areas, although in nearly every instance we have a company which has one or several problems. The implication of this is that you will be concerned with addressing all or some part of the solution. The second point that should be apparent is that, in December 1993, we moved away from 2–3 pages of text and introduced some information in the form of tables and figures. There are several reasons for this, the most obvious being that marketing analysts and marketing managers are almost invariably faced with figures on a day-to-day basis and it is not unreasonable therefore for the Diploma examination to require candidates to demonstrate their powers of interpretation. It is perhaps worth emphasizing that you will not be required to *manipulate* any of the data, but instead need to *interpret* it. In other words, what specific and general messages does it convey and what conclusions can you draw?

The questions on the mini case study can realistically be drawn from any part of the syllabus, although insofar as it is possible to identify a general theme, it has to be that of identifying what is wrong with the organization, and what needs to be done in order to overcome these problems. The specific issues covered by each of the mini cases' questions is illustrated in Figure 9.1.

Quite deliberately, although we have included eight mini cases, we have not included solutions for every case. Instead, with some of these we have provided guidelines which should help you to structure your answer.

EXAM TIP

The mini case study accounts for 50 per cent of the marks available for the examination. If you do badly in the mini case, the pressures upon you to perform at a much higher level in Section 2 are obviously far greater. Make sure, therefore, that you identify clearly and precisely what the examiner is looking for and do not waste time by including unnecessary information.

The mini cases

Portland Promotional Products Ltd
Phoenix Telecom Ltd
Penton Ltd
New Directions plc
Anderson Marine Construction Ltd
Kanko Ltd
Watergate Pumps Ltd
RTJ Engineering Ltd

Case study	Question areas
Portland Promotional Products Ltd	• The implications of the consultant's report for the future marketing strategy • The information needed for a marketing plan
Phoenix Telecom Ltd	• An outline of a marketing plan • The nature of any control problems and how they might be managed • Selection criteria for franchisees
Penton Ltd	• The development of a marketing orientation, a stronger planning culture and improved new product process • The implication of these suggestions for control
New Directions plc	• A SWOT analysis • Suggestions for overcoming the organization's problems
Anderson Marine Construction Ltd	• An outline marketing plan • Implementation problems associated with the plan and how to overcome these
Kanko Ltd	• Criteria for how the product and sales and distribution networks should be evaluated and rationalized • Criteria for the selection of a new advertising agency
Watergate Pumps Ltd	• The development and implementation of an environmental monitoring system • Recommendations for future marketing action in order to overcome the organization's problems
RTJ Engineering Ltd	• Portfolio analysis and the implications of the analysis • The development of a customer care programme

Figure 9.1   The mini case question areas

Having read the case study, spend a few minutes trying to identify any underlying and fundamental issues. In particular, think about issues of cause and effect. Very often, the sorts of problems that are referred to in the case are the manifestations of something more fundamental. In other words, they are the 'effect', with the 'cause' being something such as a shortsighted management team or an inappropriate managerial culture (this is particularly so in the Portland, Penton, New Directions, Kanko, Watergate Pumps and RTJ Engineering case studies). The significance of this is that any solutions you recommend need to be made against this background and with a full recognition of the implications. In the Penton and New Directions cases, for example, you might think about whether any meaningful and long-term solution can be arrived at with the existing management team still in place.

EXAM TIP

THE CASE STUDIES

Portland Promotional Products Ltd (June 1991)

Established in the late 1970s, PPP specializes in the manufacture and supply of business and advertising gifts. Based in the West Country, the company employs a total of thirty people. The company's proud boast is that it supplies promotional products 'From a few pence to the limit of your imagination'. These products, which amongst other items include pens, key rings and desk accessories, are printed with the client's name and designed as giveaways to customers.

The business and promotional gifts market has become increasingly competitive over the past few years partly as the result of buyers becoming more demanding in their purchasing patterns, and partly because the number of companies within the industry has increased dramatically; the barriers to entry have traditionally been relatively low.

Having experienced a decade of sales and profit growth, PPP's management was concerned to find that the sales performance in 1989 was static, and that in 1990 it declined. This was despite an apparent general increase in demand within the industry as a whole. More worryingly, profits had by the end of 1990 virtually disappeared. At the same time, average order size and levels of repeat buying had both declined. With no sign that the next twelve months would see an improvement, a long delayed decision to begin exporting was made. Following discussions with a local businessman who, having been made redundant, had set himself up as an export consultant, the company began supplying several Dutch and West German business gift houses with products. With no previous experience of exporting, the responsibility for handling this was given to a relatively new and inexperienced sales administrator, who was one of the very few within the company with any language ability.

At the same time, a local market research agency was commissioned to conduct what PPP's Managing Director referred to as 'a bit of image research' in order to find out why the company's performance in its domestic market was so disappointing. The research findings suggested that:

1   Although levels of awareness of the company amongst buyers of business and advertising gifts are high, the company is generally viewed as old fashioned.
2   There is nothing distinctive about the company or its products.
3   It is seen as having a strong regional base and has only a limited ability to service clients outside this area.
4   The company's advertising material and catalogue are unadventurous.
5   Prices are perceived to be slightly above the industry norms.
6   The company's attendance at trade shows is spasmodic and its stands at exhibitions are generally uninspiring and inexpertly staffed.
7   The company rarely appears to launch anything new or innovative.
8   The staff do not have a reputation for being able to generate new ideas for clients' promotional campaigns. Instead, they tend to recommend ideas that have been tried and tested over the years.
9   Deliveries are often a day or so later than promised. Whilst in the majority of cases this does not cause real problems, it is a source of annoyance to clients. In other cases, however, when deadlines are tight and the product is tied to a specific promotion, this does create major difficulties.
10 In an industry in which timescales are often short, the company does not seem to be able to respond either quickly or effectively to unexpected demands.
11 Customer complaints tend to be handled unsatisfactorily.

When respondents were asked how likely it was that they would do business with PPP over the next twelve months, the mean pattern of responses suggested 'Fairly unlikely'.

The summary of these findings concluded with a comment that a small but arguably significant number of respondents had believed the company had gone out of business within the preceding six months.

PPP's four senior managers – the Managing Director, the Finance Director, the Sales Director and the Marketing Manager – were, despite the poor sales performance, seemingly surprised by these findings and were inclined to dismiss them. However, a copy of the report was also given to a non-executive director who had joined PPP three months previously. He insisted that the report be taken seriously and has recommended that a marketing consultant be employed to make recommendations on future strategy.

Questions

1   As the Marketing Consultant employed by PPP, prepare a report examining in detail the implications of these findings for the company's future marketing strategy. In doing this you should also make reference to the implications for approaches to management control.   (35 marks)
2   Identify the other types of information you would require before drawing up a medium-term marketing plan.   (15 marks)

Note the split of marks (35/15) and plan your time accordingly.

Required

The first of the two questions requires you to prepare a report in which you examine the company's current position (i.e. what is going wrong) and how this should be overcome (i.e. how the future strategy needs to address these issues in order to move ahead). Whatever you suggest will have obvious implications for the organization's control processes and your answer therefore needs to consider these.

The second question is relatively straightforward and requires you to identify the additional information that you would need before developing the marketing plan.

What do you think the key issues are in this case?
(The suggested solution appears on pages 178–80.)

Phoenix Telecom Ltd (December 1991)

Phoenix Telecom was established in 1986 by a husband and wife team to take advantage of the apparent opportunities offered by the Government's deregulation of the telecommunications market. The company began by operating from a single site selling small telephone systems, mobile phones, facsimile machines, telephone call loggers and answering machines to small and medium-sized businesses. In competing against British Telecom, Phoenix, in common with the other small independents in the industry, gave emphasis in its marketing to its price competitiveness, greater flexibility, its levels of personal service, and to the fact that it was an alternative to the market leader, British Telecom.

By the end of the fourth year of trading, the annual turnover had reached £4,500,000, the company employed 58 staff and operated from twelve high street retail outlets covering the North and East Midlands. These retail outlets sold telephone and security systems to domestic customers and acted as a convenient base and demonstration point for a local field sales-force selling telecommunications products to commercial customers.

At this stage, the company's Managing Director, Michael Greene, approached a marketing consultant for advice on the further development of the business. The consultant began by conducting a detailed marketing audit. Amongst the points that emerged from the environmental analysis were:

1 The telecommunications industry is becoming ever more competitive, although demand is increasing and seems likely to remain buoyant for the foreseeable future.
2 Margins are being eroded as more companies enter the market and place greater emphasis upon price as the major basis for competition.
3 The structure of the industry appears to be changing with a series of takeovers having led to the emergence of two big independents who, by buying in bulk, are also able to act as wholesalers to smaller companies.
4 Buyers of telecommunications equipment are becoming more knowledgeable and it therefore seems likely that, in the future, greater emphasis will be placed upon service levels.

5   Few of the smaller independents appear to demonstrate any significant commercial expertise. Rather they tend to reflect a strong technical bias which inhibits their growth after the initial 12–18 months.

With regard to the company itself, the two biggest problems identified by the consultant were those of control and how best to manage future growth. The problems of control were being manifested in a variety of ways and included periodic cash flow problems, an upsurge in the number of customer complaints, an apparent reduction in staff morale which was leading to higher labour turnover, and a lack of forward planning with a consequent dependency upon a firefighting style of management. The consultant also suggested that the organization still reflected a strong sales rather than a marketing orientation. On the positive side, he highlighted the positive and high profile image as a fast-growing and forward-looking company enjoyed by Phoenix throughout the region.

With regard to the future development of the business, five options were identified. These were:

1   To pursue a strategy of slow organic growth by continuing along broadly the same lines as for the last four years, adding and deleting products as appropriate.
2   To take over one or more smaller companies in the industry.
3   To diversify into an as yet unidentified area.
4   To develop a franchise scheme.
5   To sell out. Greene had already received one tentative offer for the company and felt that it would not be difficult to find a serious buyer. The downside of this was that he would probably be required to sign a two or three-year service contract and that the final price would be determined by the profit performance during this period.

Although Michael Greene's knowledge of franchising was limited, it was this option that had the most immediate appeal for him, since he felt that if handled properly, it would allow for rapid growth without any loss of control. He therefore asked his marketing consultant to look at the area in greater detail.

The consultant's subsequent report made a series of recommendations. In essence, he suggested that Phoenix should develop a franchise package whereby franchisees, in return for an initial payment of £40,000 and an 8 per cent royalty on sales, would be helped to establish retail outlets in town and city centres under the Phoenix Telephone banner. These retail outlets would be used to sell a range of telecommunications and security equipment both to domestic and commercial customers.

Phoenix would then train franchisees and their staff, provide advice on site location, supply shop fascias and fittings, negotiate with suppliers, advertise and initiate sales promotions campaigns. Franchisees would be obliged to buy stock from Phoenix for a least the first five years. The report went on to suggest that by the end of the second year of trading, franchisees could expect to turn over at least £450,000 annually at a 35 per cent gross margin. Rent and rates would be in the region of £14,000 and each retail outlet would require the equivalent of four full-time staff.

Questions

1   Prepare an outline of the marketing plan which Greene will need to develop and operate the proposed franchise scheme.   (20 marks)
2   Identify the nature of the control problems that are likely to be faced in establishing a franchising network of up to forty outlets by year three and suggest how these problems might best be managed.   (20 marks)
3   What selection criteria would you recommend be used in selecting franchisees?   (10 marks)

Required

(**Note**: The setting of three questions for the mini case study was an experiment which has not been repeated since. You should not therefore, expect to see three mini case questions in your exam.)

The questions require you to:

- Prepare an outline of the marketing plan.
- Identify the franchising, control problems and suggest how these might be overcome.
- Suggest selection criteria for the franchisee applicants.

The issue of the marketing plan's structure is straightforward and for guidance on this, you might usefully turn to the solution of the Anderson Marine Construction case (see pages 187–90).

The question of how to control franchisees is a little more complex and here you need to think about issues such as how to motivate and control self-employed business people who would have expectations of you in terms of central support. (**Hint**: reverse the positions and think about what *you* would expect from Phoenix.)

The third question requires you to make specific suggestions for deciding between those who are applying for a franchise. What would you look for?

What do you think the key issues are in this case?
(An outline of the suggested solution appears on pages 180–1.)

Penton Ltd (June 1992)

Penton is a medium-sized company which manufactures and markets a range of DIY (Do It Yourself) products under the Easi-Way brand name. Its performance over the past ten years, a period during which the market for do-it-yourself products has grown rapidly, has been viewed by those within the industry as steady, but generally unimpressive. In particular, its critics have pointed to performance levels that are below the industry norm, a reliance upon its long-established and now old-fashioned distribution networks, low levels of advertising spend, a failure to exploit the potential strength of the brand name, and a poor profit performance.

Towards the end of 1991, the company was the subject of a takeover bid from a smaller but more aggressive and far more successful competitor. Although Penton's board managed to fight off the bid, the sudden awareness of their vulnerability to further bids has led to a reassessment of their entire manufacturing and marketing strategy.

The problems being faced by the organization were exacerbated by the downturn in retail sales which began to affect the economy at the end of the 1980s. Faced with what was proving to be a static sales curve and a reducing profit margin, the decision was taken to bring in a firm of marketing consultants to conduct a detailed audit of the organization and make recommendations for future strategy. The consultants' initial report highlighted a number of areas of concern which, they suggested, should be the focus of attention:

1 The organization's strong production orientation and a lack of marketing representation at board level.
2 A largely reactive managerial philosophy.
3 Little long-term product or market planning.
4 An over-reliance upon a small number of ageing products.
5 A poorly structured new product planning process.
6 The generally disappointing performance and high failure rate of new product launches over the past few years.
7 A failure to exploit the potential strength of the brand name.
8 Increasing pressure upon margins.

The environmental analysis proved to be more encouraging, with the consultants giving prominence to the size and long-term growth potential of the DIY market, and the major profit opportunities offered by new products. They also pointed to the high level of retail concentration in the market, the need for organizations in this sector to be proactive in their new product development, and for new products to be supported by a strong promotional campaign. In a separate section, the consultants spelled out in detail the implications of the seemingly ever-greater degree of retail concentration, summarizing this with a comment that highlighted the strategic importance of relationship marketing.

The evaluation of the organization's manufacturing capabilities suggested that there was a need for investment in new plant. With regard to the research and development area, the conclusion was that 'whilst the area has potential and the R&D staff are enthusiastic and highly qualified, the activity has suffered from a lack of direction. As a result, the majority of new products have not been related sufficiently directly to market demands.'

Against the background of these findings, the board has attempted to identify the areas of greatest priority and has decided to focus upon the three areas which they believed require the most immediate attention. These are the development of:

- A marketing orientation.
- A far stronger and more effective planning culture.
- A structured and proactive new product development process.

Questions

1 As a member of the team of consultants, you have the responsibility for making recommendations as to how the organization might most effectively achieve this. You are therefore required to prepare a report showing how this might be done.
(35 marks)

2 What are the implications of your suggestions for approaches to management control?
(15 marks)

Required

This is a case study that requires you to be very clear about what is meant by a marketing orientation and how one might be developed within an organization that previously has been product led. Your suggestions must therefore be specific. It is worth remembering that if you can develop the stronger marketing orientation, it is likely that the planning and new product development systems will improve as the result of the stronger external focus.

The second question requires you to think about the nature of the control process and how planning and control are two separate but highly interrelated activities. Again, however, your suggestions must be specific.

QUESTION 9.3

What do you think the key issues are in this case?
(The suggested solution appears on pages 181–5.)

New Directions plc (December 1992)

New Directions is a high-street fashion chain which was founded in the late 1950s. After twenty years of slow and generally unspectacular growth, a new Managing Director, Thomas Oakley, was appointed in 1978. Under his very different and aggressively entrepreneurial management style, the company underwent a decade of explosive growth. Many of the old staff left during this period and a far younger team was recruited. The new staff were given considerable operating freedom and high salaries, but were expected to achieve performance levels well above the industry average. By 1988, the company had 400 stores and had become one of the major players in the young (15–25), C1/C2, male and female fashion sectors. Their reputation in the City was that of an ambitious, design-oriented company led by an unconventional, abrasive and maverick figure who inspired considerable loyalty among his employees.

At the beginning of 1987 the company was bought out by a large and cash-rich conglomerate whose financial performance over the preceding decade had proved to be consistently strong. Despite this, the group's senior management was viewed by the City as being generally staid and unimaginative. The group overall was viewed as having a strong financial orientation with an emphasis upon systems and control. Strategy at the group level was perceived as being risk aversive.

New Directions' Managing Director and small senior management team quickly found that operating within a group in which they were accountable to the group's main board constrained their entrepreneurial style and traditional freedom. Not only were they faced with the need to make out a strong written case for anything other than a minor change in strategy but, as they saw it, major restrictions were placed on their ability to capitalize upon short-term opportunities. Profits were remitted to the centre and each division's MD was then required on an annual basis to bid for sums for capital expenditure.

After two years in succession in which his plans for development were rejected by the main board, Oakley resigned. At the heart of the disagreement was his belief that New Directions needed to move up the quality scale and both up and down the age scale. The demographic changes taking place would, he argued, lead to a reduction of at least 20 per cent in the size of the company's traditional target market over the next few years. They should therefore chase the demographic shift by targeting the 30–40 year olds, a sector in which annual growth of 12 per cent was being forecast. At the same time, he suggested, a new chain should be developed that would appeal to the childrens' market. 'Children,' he said, 'are the ultimate fashion accessory. We need to capitalize on this.'

He also pointed to the research evidence which suggested that buyers wanted better quality, something for which New Directions had never had a particularly strong reputation. Instead, they had concentrated on developing a strong fashion element at 'popular' prices. While this strategy had undoubtedly been successful, there was now a need to begin the process of making a series of fundamental changes. Oakley also argued for the need for a re-think in the approach to store design. Competition from other retail chains had become ever more aggressive during the 1980s and evidence existed to suggest that buyers were looking for new and more exciting shopping experiences. An essential element in this was the retail concept, something which had taken a significant step forward in the late 1980s in the repositioning and renaming of one of the company's major competitors. Oakley also pointed to the need to begin looking towards opportunities overseas. 'The British market', he suggested, 'offers only limited scope for growth. We need to get into some of the other European markets and particularly Spain.' He went on to point out that the Spanish market was growing at a faster rate than any other. Indeed, without telling the main board or getting their agreement, he had already gone ahead with plans to begin selling into one of the largest chains of Spanish fashion stores.

Each of these arguments was rejected by the group's main board on the grounds of their cost and the perceived risk.

Following Oakley's resignation, the group appointed as his replacement one of their fast-track corporate finance staff. With little direct retailing experience, he set about re-organizing the company. In doing this, he slashed Oakley's plans for development. Largely because of this, a significant number of the team who had worked with Oakley and who very largely saw themselves as his protegés left. In most cases they were snapped up by competitors who placed considerable value on the training and experience they had been exposed to.

As the recession of the early 1990s began to bite, turnover dropped. The new MD's almost desperate response was to pursue an aggressive price cutting policy and to reduce overheads as far as possible.

The annual strategic review at the end of 1991 (two years after Oakley's replacement had taken over) painted a dismal picture. Sales were down, market share was slipping, staff were demoralized and, as a market research report highlighted, the image of the chain in the 15–25, 25–30 and 30–40 age groups was confused. In short, New Directions was no longer a leader or even a serious player in the young fashion market.

1 Prepare a SWOT analysis of the organization both for the period before the takeover and for the period reached at the end of the case study. Having done this, discuss the implications of *one* of your analyses for methods of marketing planning and control. (30 marks)

2 As a consultant to the organization, and in the light of the findings of the strategic review, what course(s) of action would you recommend should be taken? (20 marks)

Required

Most Diploma candidates are adept at preparing SWOT analyses and the first part of Question 1 is therefore straightforward. Because of this, the differences between candidates tended to become apparent in the second part of the question when the implications for planning and control were discussed. What is required of you here is a discussion of the *specific* implications.

EXAM TIP

Refer back to Unit 2 for a discussion of how to conduct a *worthwhile* SWOT analysis.

The second question is perhaps a little deceptive since it is likely to lead candidates towards a set of recommendations which fail to come to terms with the real need to address the underlying managerial culture. It is therefore worth thinking about the extent to which any real change can be brought about as long as Oakley's successor is managing director.

QUESTION 9.4

What do you think the key issues are in this case?
(An outline of the suggested solution appears on pages 185–6.)

Anderson Marine Construction Ltd (June 1993)

Anderson Marine Construction (AMC) is a well-established and financially successful builder of medium-sized, high-performance yachts and power boats. Based on the south coast of England, the company's products have developed a strong reputation for quality and performance, and an intensely loyal and knowledgeable customer base.

The company has traditionally adopted a largely reactive approach to selling, justifying this partly on the grounds that for the past twenty years they have been able to sell everything they have been able to make, and partly because the firm's founder and Managing Director, Tom Anderson, saw the firm facing little direct competition in its principal target markets. At the end of the 1980s, however, sales began to drop as demand for expensive luxury goods declined. As a response to this, AMC cut its prices by 6 per cent in real terms for the 1991 season and then by a further 4 per cent for 1992. Despite this, sales remained sluggish.

Faced with this and with no sight of an upturn in demand, Tom Anderson called in a marketing consultant to advise on what AMC should do next. The consultant argued that further price cuts were likely to achieve little and that in the long term they would probably be detrimental to the image developed by AMC. Instead, he suggested, AMC should capitalize upon its reputation and the very strong brand values associated with its name by moving down the size and price scale by developing a new range of smaller and lower priced boats. Although this sector of the market had a greater number of direct competitors, the consultant suggested that patterns of demand would be more consistent and less susceptible to fluctuations in the economy.

Although the idea had an initial appeal, Anderson recognized that the firm's approach to marketing and selling would have to change. Previously, the firm's sales effort had been limited to very occasional advertisements in the boating press and a small stand every other year at a regional boat show. This, together with the strength of the firm's reputation and word of mouth recommendation, had, he felt, been adequate. Boats were made to order with a delivery time of 9–15 months and prices, which were negotiated individually with clients, reflected the specification demanded. Once completed, they were either delivered by AMC or the customer collected the boat himself.

The consultant emphasized that the new range would need to be targeted at buyers for whom the sailing skills and buying motives and processes would be very different from those of AMC's traditional customers. The implications of this were spelled out in a report.

1 Buyers within the proposed target group are less knowledgeable about boats and sailing and would expect a greater degree of what he referred to as 'active selling' of the product's benefits.
2 There would be a need for a structured distribution network with at least ten distributors throughout the country.
3 Buyers would not be prepared to wait for delivery but would expect boats to be available from stock.
4 A communications programme would be required.
5 A formal pricing and distributor discount structure would be needed.
6 Because the new range would bring AMC into more direct competition with other boat builders, a competitive monitoring system should be developed.
7 A marketing budget should be set as a matter of priority and the responsibility for the marketing effort clearly allocated.

Recognizing that these recommendations called for a far more proactive approach to marketing than had previously been adopted, Anderson decided to appoint a marketing manager. As the person appointed to this post, you have the immediate responsibility for developing the marketing plan to support the new range which is scheduled for launch for the 1994 sailing season.

Questions

1 Prepare an outline of the marketing plan for the launch and subsequent market development of the new range. In doing this, you should make specific reference to the nature of any additional information that you might require.   (35 marks)
2 In the light of AMC's previous approaches to selling, what, if any, organizational problems might you expect to encounter in implementing the marketing plan? In what ways might these problems be overcome or minimized?   (15 marks)

Required

The first question requires a clear understanding of the structure of a marketing plan, something which the answers revealed that far too few candidates have. Without this knowledge, any answer will lack conviction.

The second question addresses the issues of implementation and how a marketing orientation might be developed and fostered (refer to Unit 7).

What do you think the key issues are in this case?
(The suggested solution appears on pages 187–92.)

QUESTION 9.5

Kanko Ltd (December 1993)

Kanko Ltd is a wholly owned subsidiary of a highly diversified listed public company which has traditionally allowed its subsidiaries to operate with a high degree of autonomy.

Kanko markets a wide range of plumbing accessories, heating systems and small air-conditioning units both for domestic and industrial use. Its products are sold through ironmongers, specialist builders' merchants and, increasingly, very large do-it-yourself (DIY) outlets (see Table 9.1 below). The company's sales force of forty is split fairly evenly into three geographical regions, each of which is headed by a Regional Sales Manager who has the sales but not the profit responsibility for that region. This profit responsibility rests with the Sales and Marketing Director. Each member of the sales team handles the entire range of products and is expected to cover all types of sales outlet in his/her territory.

Table 9.1   Kanko's sales turnover by type of outlet (1987–93)

	1987 %	1988 %	1989 %	1990 %	1991 %	1992 %	1993* %
Ironmongers	28	27	25	22	19	20	20
Builders' merchants	64	63	62	61	63	63	63
Do-it-yourself	8	10	13	17	18	17	17
*Estimate							

Following the publication of the interim results in mid-1993 (see Table 9.2 below), the Managing Director, Finance Director and the Sales and Marketing Director were asked by the parent company to resign. A new senior management team was appointed and far higher levels of accountability than had been the case previously were introduced.

Table 9.2   Selected sales and profit data (1987–93)

	1987 %	1988 %	1989 %	1990 %	1991 %	1992 %	1993* %	1993** %
Sales turnover (£m)	57	63	62	63	55	56	28	53
Profit (loss) net of tax and parent company management charges (£m)	3.4	3.2	3.0	2.6	0.7	0.5	(1.3)	(3.1)
Net profit as a percentage of turnover	6	5.1	4.8	4.1	1.3	0.9	(4.6)	(5.8)
*First six months **Projection for the full year								

Under the new team, an initial review of the entire sales and marketing function was conducted. Although the clarity of the findings was clouded somewhat by the poor costing and control systems that existed, it appeared that the company had previously been run in a highly haphazard fashion. This haphazard approach was manifested in a variety of ways, including:

1   An unstructured and seemingly indiscriminate new product development programme which had led to numerous products being launched with seemingly little real attention having been paid to their sales or profit potential.

2 Poor day-to-day management of the product range with the result that some 30 per cent of the product range appeared to be unprofitable.

3 Rising costs of distribution and an apparent willingness to appoint distribution intermediaries regardless of their sales potential or ability to provide after sales support.

4 A failure to address the rising levels of complaints about variable product quality and inadequate levels of service support.

5 The generally poor sales and profits performance of the sales team, with little attention paid to market development.

6 Uninspiring and tired sales literature and advertising.

Because of this latter point, the decision to fire the existing advertising agency has already been taken.

In 1992, the nature and intensity of competition throughout the industry increased significantly as Kanko's two principal competitors, both of whom have a similar product range to Kanko, used aggressive price competition to gain market share.

In the same period, overall market demand remained stagnant as domestic buyers, affected by economic uncertainties, demonstrated a high degree of price consciousness, whilst sales to industrial buyers were constrained by the downturn in housebuilding and factory construction. In parallel with this, the structure of the distribution networks continued to change, with an ever greater proportion of sales being channelled through the major DIY outlets (see Table 9.3 below). Because of the strength of the latters' buying power, the terms that their centralized buying teams were able to demand from their suppliers, as well as the far higher levels of marketing support they required, meant that margins on the sales made by Kanko to these outlets were, at best, slim. Kanko's penetration of the major DIY outlets is currently lower than that of each of its two principal competitors.

Table 9.3 Industry Sales by Type of Outlet (1987–94)

	1987 %	1988 %	1989 %	1990 %	1991 %	1992 %	1993* %	1994** %
Ironmongers	25	25	23	20	18	15	10	8
Builders' merchants	65	57	52	52	50	50	47	47
Do-It-yourself	10	18	25	28	32	35	43	45
* Estimated ** Forecast								

It is against this background that the detailed review of every aspect of the company's sales and marketing operations is taking place.

Questions

1 As a member of the new management team, you have been given the responsibility for recommending how the product and distribution strategies should develop. You are required to prepare a report detailing the criteria by which the current product range and sales and distribution networks should be evaluated and possibly rationalized. (35 marks)

2 You are also required to make recommendations on the appointment of the new advertising agency. You should prepare a short briefing paper identifying the criteria by which agencies pitching for the account should be shortlisted. (15 marks)

Required

The first of the two questions requires you to identify a set of *specific* criteria for the evaluation and possible rationalization of the product, sales and distribution networks. Without this specific treatment, it is unlikely that you will gain more than a few marks.

Equally, Question 2 requires you to identify the *specific* factors that should be taken into account. Vague generalizations are simply inappropriate.

QUESTION 9.6

What do you think the key issues are in this case?
(The suggested solution appears on pages 192–6.)

Watergate Pumps Ltd (June 1994)

Watergate Pumps Ltd manufactures and markets a range of water pumps and control systems for domestic and industrial central heating systems. For the past three years total industry sales of domestic pumps have been stable at an average of 1.3 million units per annum (£40 million at manufacturers' average selling prices). Sales are forecast to grow only slowly over the next few years and are expected to reach a peak of 1.55 million units p.a. in 1998.

Within the domestic sector, there are four principal markets for the product: local authorities; the public utilities such as British Gas; regional/national building companies; and small firms of builders/plumbers and individuals repairing their own heating systems.

The company, which is a subsidiary of a far larger organization which has interests throughout the building supplies industry, has three competitors. Selected market data collected from various sources appear in Tables 9.4, 9.5 and 9.6.

Watergate has been taken by surprise by a variety of developments in the marketplace over the past few years, including:

- The entry into the market in 1991 by Pump Suppliers, a Dutch-owned company which set up a factory in southern England.
- The launch by B G Industrial (BGI) and Northern Pumps of several modified and new products.
- A general competitive repositioning (see Figure 9.2).
- An extension by all three competitors of the guarantees offered on their products from one to three years.
- The three-year stagnation of the market.
- A significant shift in customers' buying motives, with quality and ease of fitting having become increasingly important.
- A series of improvements by all three competitors in their control systems.
- The move by BGI and Northern Pumps into a number of profitable overseas markets.

Because of this, there is now recognition that the company's understanding of the market is poor and that some form of structured external environment monitoring is needed.

Watergate Pump – selected market data
Table 9.4

	Market shares within the domestic pumps sector (1990–93)				Total manufacturing capacity (000 units)	Total output in 1993 (000 units)	UK overseas split of sales in 1993
	1990 (%)	1991 (%)	1992 (%)	1993 (%)			
Watergate Pumps	35	29	27	24	475	320	100/0
BG International	50	50	48	48	850	830	75/25
Northern Pumps	15	13	15	16	300	280	74/26
Pump Suppliers	0	8	10	12	300	300	52/48

Source: Trade Figures

Table 9.5

	Sales in 1993 by type of buyer (000 units)	Expected percentage increase/ (decrease) by 1998	Market position of each company by type of buyer (1993)			
			No 1	No 2	No 3	No 4
Local authorities	400	(25)	WGP	NP	PS	BGI
Public utilities	300	66	BGI	PS	WGP	NP
Regional/national builders	400	25	BGI	PS	NP	WGP
Local builders/ plumbers and private individuals	200	25	BGI	NP	PS	WGP
Key: WGP – Watergate Pumps BGI – BG International NP – Northern Pumps PS – Pump Suppliers						

Source: Trade Data

Table 9.6 Rank order of the principal buying motives of different customer groups

	Local authorities	Public utilities	Regional/ national builders	Local builders/ plumbers and private individuals
Price	1	3	3 =	3
Availability off the shelf	N/A	N/A	3 =	1 =
Reliability	3	1	1	4
Ease of fitting	2	2	2	1 =
N/A: Not applicable, since supplies are delivered in bulk to regional warehouses				

Source: Compiled from trade data

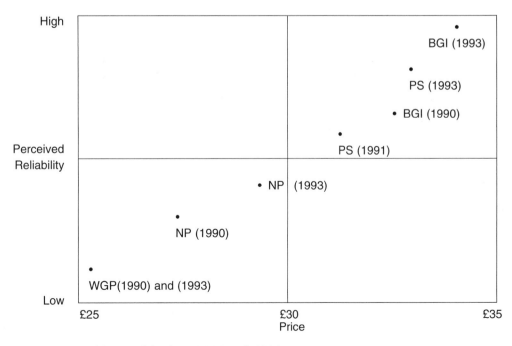

Figure 9.2 Competitive positioning (1990 and 1993)

173

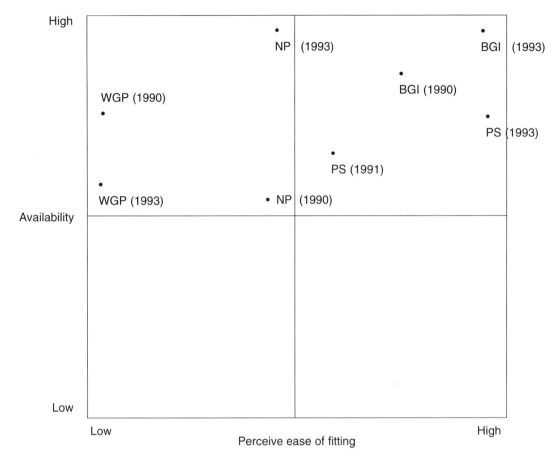

High

NP (1993) •   BGI (1993) •

                      BGI (1990) •

WGP (1990)
•

PS (1993) •

PS (1991) •

WGP (1993)
•

• NP (1990)

Availability

Low

Low   High

Perceive ease of fitting

Figure 9.3

Questions

1. As the company's newly appointed market analyst, you are required to prepare a detailed report for the marketing director recommending how an effective external environment monitoring system for the company might best be developed and implemented. Included within the report should be your suggestions on the structure of the system, the expected inputs and outputs, the probable organizational and resource implications, and the nature of any benefits that should emerge.   (30 marks)
2. In the light of the information contained in the mini case, what recommendations for future marketing action would you make?   (20 marks)

Required

The first of the two questions requires you to recommend how an environmental monitoring system might be developed and implemented. In your answer you need therefore to be specific about its structure and how it might be introduced into the organization. The second sentence in the question was designed to provide candidates with guidance on the principal issues that need to be included.

Diagrams can play a useful role in your answer, since if they are used properly they can be an effective way of communicating your ideas. This question provides you with an opportunity to draw an environmental monitoring system and illustrate the inputs, outputs and interrelationships that exist.

The second question is one that we have come across before in a variety of guises and requires you to recommend how the organization should overcome its problems.

What do you think the key issues are in this case?
(The suggested solution appears on pages 196–200.)

RTJ Engineering Ltd (December 1994)

Established in 1952, RTJ Engineering is a fabricator of highly specialized engineering components. Selected sales and financial data appear in Figure 9.5. The company's operations are divided between five strategic business units: Nuclear, Aerospace, Defence, Marine and General Engineering (see Figure 9.6 on page 176).

The firm has an international reputation for engineering excellence and prides itself on the very high quality of its work and its ability to tackle projects of extreme technical complexity. However, the sales department within the organization has traditionally operated with a highly reactive approach to selling, relying heavily upon word-of-mouth and repeat business from its established customer base.

In 1992 and 1993, total sales declined partly as the result of a downturn in its core markets, but also because of the loss of three medium-sized and long-standing customers to competitors. Because of this, the managing director hired a marketing consultant who, as part of a programme of activities, conducted a study designed to reveal current and potential customers' perceptions of the firm's three principal SBUs (see Figures 9.4(a) and 9.4(b) for a selection of the results). The consultant's report gave full recognition to the depth and breadth of the firm's technical expertise, but was highly critical of the approaches to marketing and selling. In particular, he pointed to the results of the customer study, arguing that unless a series of changes were made, the company would almost inevitably lose sales and market share to its ever more numerous and aggressive competitors. Against this background, it has been agreed that a far more proactive approach to customer care will be introduced.

	Nuclear		Aerospace		Defence	
	RTJ	Others	RTJ	Others	RTJ	Others
Design skills	8	6	8	7	6	7
Sales expertise	2	4	3	5	3	5
Customer management	3	5	3	6	4	5
Quality of literature	1	4	2	4	2	4
Production flexibility	7	7	7	7	7	7
Ability to cope with complex specifications	9	7	9	8	8	7
Adherence to promised delivery schedules	4	7	4	6	3	6
Price competitiveness	4	6	3	6	4	7
Quality of work	9	6	9	7	9	6
Unprompted technical support	4	6	3	6	3	5
Helpfulness of sales staff/sales support	3	5	3	6	2	5
(1 = Low, 9 = High)						

Figure 9.4(a) Customers' perceptions of RTJ Engineering and its principal competitors

'They work at their speed rather than ours.'

'Technically, they're the best in the industry but they haven't got the first idea about marketing or selling.'

'Do they ever deliver on time?'

'They are the most frustrating company that I've ever dealt with, but nobody can match their quality.'

'Have their sales staff ever had any training in anything other than being rude to customers?'

'Have you seen their sales literature? It's a joke.'

'I'd never go anywhere else when I've got a complex job that needs doing.'

'Superb quality, but very expensive.'

Figure 9.4(b)   Selected quotations that emerged from the customer research

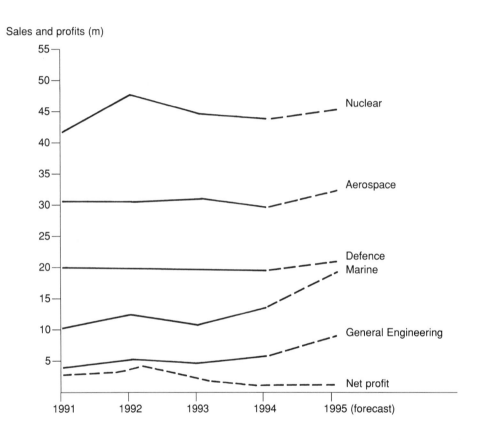

Figure 9.5   Selected sales and financial information

	RTJ's sales 1994 (£m)	Number of direct competitors	Sales of the three largest firms in the sector (£m)	Forecast annual growth rate (%)
Nuclear	13	5	13*, 13, 8	3
Aerospace	12	8	12*, 9, 6	4
Defence	9	12	15, 12, 11	(6)
Marine	6	7	18, 12, 6*	15
General Engineering	4	16	15, 14, 10	8
	44 (forecast)			

Note: Figures asterisked represent RTJ's sales within the sector

Figure 9.6   Selected SBU market data

Questions

1 Using a model of your choice, comment upon the apparent state of the firm's portfolio. In doing this, you should specify any assumptions that you make, the limitations of the model and any other information that you would require before recommending how the firm's portfolio should be developed. You should also identify briefly any other approach to portfolio analysis that might be used to evaluate the portfolio. (25 marks)

2 In the light of the research findings, prepare a report for the managing director identifying the key dimensions of a customer-care programme and how such a programme might be introduced into the organization. In doing this, you should pay particular attention to issues of implementation. (25 marks)

Required

The first of the two questions asks you to analyse the firm's portfolio. There are several frameworks that can be used for this, but whichever is used, there is a need to make use of the data in the case. Equally, in the second of the two questions, the recommendations for the customer-care programme need to be made against the background of the market research findings rather than in a generalized way.

What do you think the key issues are in the case?
(The suggested solution appears on pages 200–4.)

QUESTION 9.8

SUGGESTED SOLUTIONS

Within this section of the workbook, we have included full solutions to six of the cases: Portland Promotional Products Ltd, Penton Ltd, Anderson Marine Construction Ltd, Kanko Ltd, Watergate Pumps Ltd and RTJ Engineering Ltd. It needs to be emphasized that these are solutions which have been prepared by the Senior Examiner without the sorts of constraints of time and examination pressure that the candidates will have faced at the time. They are not designed to be seen as 'ideal' solutions but rather as relatively full answers to the questions so that you might gain an insight into the sorts of issues that might possibly be included.

Deliberately, we have not included solutions to the Phoenix Telecom and New Dimensions cases but have instead listed the sorts of issues to which you might usefully pay attention in the answer that you prepare.

(**Note**: the solutions to the mini cases appeared initially in the specimen answer booklets that are produced by Marketing Education Consultants on behalf of the Chartered Institute of Marketing. All of the answers were written by the Senior Examiner for the Planning and Control module, Professor Colin Gilligan.)

To gain the maximum benefit from this section of the workbook, read one of the case studies (the Portland Promotional Products is as good a starting point as any) and then prepare an answer under examination conditions (make sure that you are not interrupted, do not make use of books, and spend no more than 90 minutes answering the two questions on the case study). Having done this, compare what you have written with the suggested solution and think about how your answer might be improved. Having done this move successively through the other seven case studies.

EXAM TIP

Portland Promotional Products: a suggested solution

This case study puts you in the position of being the marketing consultant who, having identified what is wrong with the company, now has to suggest what should be done to put things right. You are also required to identify the additional information that would be needed before a marketing plan can be developed.

Question 1

As the marketing consultant employed by PPP, prepare a report examining in detail the implications of your findings for the company's future marketing strategy. In doing this you should also make reference to the implications for control.

From: Marketing Consultant
To: The Managing Director, Portland Promotional Products
Date: June 1991

CONTENTS
Foreword
Part A: An analysis of the implications of the market research findings.
Part B: The implications for control.

Foreword

The market research findings have highlighted a number of issues, all of which need to be examined in greater detail with a view to identifying how the problems might be overcome. Taken together, however, they point to the far more fundamental problem of poor management over a sustained period. In identifying the future direction of the organization, consideration needs to be given to the ways in which this can be tackled, since in the absence of this, the company runs the risk of addressing the symptoms of a managerial malaise rather than the cause. It is recommended that the move into overseas markets be delayed until such time that the major problems faced in the domestic market have been overcome.

Part A: The implications of the research findings

The picture painted by the eleven principal findings is quite obviously worrying and attention needs to be paid to identifying both the immediate cause and solutions. However, as we comment above, these elements point to a more fundamental failing within the organization and highlight the need for:

- A far better approach to planning.
- Improved methods of implementation.
- Better methods of control.

Arguably the most worrying single finding is the suggestion that the mean pattern of responses suggested that it is 'fairly unlikely' that the respondents would do business with PPP over the next 12 months. Acknowledging this suggests that any changes within the organization need to be significant, well planned, and to take place within a short time scale.

With regard to the eleven individual points of the research report, it is of course possible to go through each of these and recommend the sort of change required. Before doing this, we do however need to address the question of changes in the managerial structure, with particular attention being paid to issues of responsibility for planning, implementation and control. It is obvious that the approach currently reflects a complacent managerial philosophy and the management team needs to consider in detail whether the magnitude of the changes required can be achieved with the existing team. The problems identified by the report point specifically to weaknesses in the areas of marketing and sales, although the failure to adopt a stronger approach to control points to weaknesses on the part of the managing director. It is therefore recommended that the next stage of my work focuses upon issues of managerial capability and the need for change.

The eleven specific findings of the market research on page 162 suggest underlying weaknesses in several areas:

- Operational problems (points 2, 9, 10 and 11).
- A lack of creativity (points 4, 6 and 7).
- Perceptions of the organization (points 1, 2, 3, 4 and 5).

The implication of the operational problems is relatively straightforward and highlights the need for operating targets to be set far more clearly, for these targets to be adhered to, and for stronger control mechanisms to be implemented.

The lack of creativity is arguably more fundamental and is likely to require the appointment of a new advertising agency (point 4), a considerable amount of staff training, and possibly the recruitment of some new staff.

The current perceptions of the organization are the most worrying findings for a number of reasons:

- Overcoming a poor image typically takes a considerable amount of time, effort and money.
- The poor image is very largely the result of inadequate planning and control by the current management team. The question of whether they are capable of making the changes needed has to be considered.

In the light of these comments, it can be seen that the nature and magnitude of the changes required is significant. However, as a prelude to making any changes, management needs to consider in detail the objectives and image it wishes to project in the future and its ability then to deliver on this. It is therefore recommended that a detailed audit of the organization be conducted with a view to determining the true level of corporate capability and the resource base. This can then be developed within the following framework.

1 Assess the level of corporate capability.
2 Determine the short and medium-term objectives.
3 Identify the strategic imperatives.
4 Determine the costs involved.
5 Develop the action plan.
6 Identify the control mechanism required.
7 Identify the managerial changes required.
8 Implement the action plan.
9 Monitor the progress.

It should be apparent from this that whilst change is needed in the eleven areas of weakness identified in the research report, we are not recommending that a simple individual problem–individual solution approach be adopted. Rather we are arguing that these weaknesses are the result of a more fundamental malaise which needs to be addressed. If management fails to do this, any solution is likely to be temporary.

Part B: The implications for control
With regard to the issue of control, it is essential that strong control mechanisms are introduced so that future deviations from the plan can be identified quickly and corrective action taken. It is therefore recommended that use be made of:

- Sales ratio analysis.
- Market share ratio analysis.
- Market expense to sales ratio analysis.
- Financial ratio analysis.

Responsibilities need to be identified far more clearly than appears to be the case currently. Feedback mechanisms need to be formalized and a far more proactive stance adopted in which there is a willingness both to recognize the need for change and to make the changes needed.

This examination led to some very good scripts, although far too many candidates failed to answer the first of the two case study questions in report format. Make sure therefore that you are familiar with a variety of formats such as a report, a memorandum, a briefing paper and a marketing plan.

As with many of the examinations, a great many candidates spent very little time on Question 2; in some instances they simply wrote a paragraph. Remember that with a 35/15 marks split, you have 20–25 minutes available.

Phoenix Telecom: issues to think about

The first of the three questions asks you to prepare an outline of the marketing plan. If you are unfamiliar with the structure of a marketing plan, turn to the solution to the Anderson Marine Construction case that appears on pages 187–190 and look at the framework that is outlined on the first page. Although there is no one agreed format for a marketing plan, this covers the major areas and is one that we have used successfully with a variety of clients. Using this as your background, you should therefore be able to answer the first question.

In total, you have 90 minutes for Section 1. If we allow 10 minutes as reading time and for collecting your thoughts, you have 80 minutes in which to answer the three questions. The allocation of marks for these is 20/20/10. You should therefore spend about 30 minutes on this first question.

Having prepared the outline of the plan, think about the control problems that are likely to be faced (you might at this stage usefully turn back to pages 152–5 of Unit 8). Begin by listing the particular issues of control that are likely to be encountered in a franchise operation in which you are asking people to make an initial payment of £40,000 and then the payment of a royalty of 8 per cent on their sales. Quite obviously, the problems of control (and within this we would include the issues of motivation and co-ordination) are likely to be significant. The sort of people who take a franchise will typically be highly motivated and expect a considerable amount from Phoenix. It will not therefore be a simple matter of telling the franchisee what to do and how to do it, but instead will involve ensuring that a co-ordinated marketing programme is developed and implemented within a marketplace that is becoming ever more competitive.

Recognize also that the organization has no experience of franchising and that the learning curve for you will be steep. Any approaches to control will therefore have to take account of this. Think also about issues such as geographical coverage and the problems of delivering what is being promised in the final paragraph of the case study. (Again, give yourself about 30 minutes to answer this question.)

The third question asks you to identify the franchisee selection criteria. What sorts of people would *you* be looking for? Quite obviously, they need to be able to raise £40,000, but this is not necessarily the major issue. Instead, you need to think about issues such as their product knowledge, their sales abilities, their willingness to work as part of a franchise operation, their previous experience and so on.

Remember that you only have 15 minutes for this question and that you will therefore have to get your ideas onto paper in an ordered and structured manner as quickly as possible. Try therefore to categorize the key points. Are some of the criteria, for example, broadly financial in nature? Are others personal qualities, whilst others relate to product/market knowledge?

One thing that became very apparent when the scripts were being marked was that too few candidates were familiar with the structure of a marketing plan and as a consequence scored badly. Given that this is the Diploma stage, we were surprised that so many candidates appeared not to be able to outline what is one of the most common marketing documents.

The other common mistake made relates to Question 2. Far too many candidates identified the control problems, but did not then go on to suggest how they might be overcome or managed. REMEMBER that many questions have two parts and that both must be answered.

Penton Ltd: a suggested solution

This case requires you to suggest how the organization might be changed so that a stronger marketing orientation, more effective planning culture and a more proactive new product development process might be developed. It is therefore a useful vehicle for the second of the two questions that underpin many of the mini (and indeed maxi) case studies: knowing what is wrong with the organization, what can we do to improve things?

Question 1

As a member of the team of consultants you have the responsibility for making recommendations as to how the organization might most effectively achieve a stronger marketing orientation, more effective planning culture, and a proactive NPD process. You are therefore required to prepare a report showing how this might be done.

For the Attention of the Main Board of Penton Ltd.

1.0 Management summary

1.1 It has become apparent from our work with the organization that a series of major changes and actions are required. These may be summarized in terms of the need for:

    a   The appointment of a senior marketing person.
    b   A stronger and more obvious focus for the business.
    c   A programme of internal marketing.
    d   A full internal and external audit.
    e   A stronger top-down approach, particularly in the short term.
    f   A clarification of objectives.
    h   A programme of market research.
    i   A more structured planning process which incorporates a mission statement.
    j   Decisions on the competitive stance that is to be adopted.
    k   A programme of monitoring and feedback.

l   Increased accountability throughout the organization.

m   A detailed assessment of new product development capability.

n   Greater exploitation of the brand name.

2.0 Introduction and background

2.1   The suggestions and recommendations made here are based on our findings to date. There is, however, a need for further work with the organization, particularly in the area of implementation.

2.2   The success of much of what is recommended here rests firmly on the appointment of a new senior member of the management team who will have explicit responsibility for marketing activities.

3.0 A marketing orientation

3.1   Penton Ltd has become overly reliant upon a small number of established but ageing products. For the change that is required to take place, there is need for the development of a far stronger marketing orientation which will give greater explicit recognition both to the needs of the customer and to the ways in which, within a changing market, the company might gain – and retain – a significant competitive advantage. This will require a major change in corporate culture. This can best be achieved by:

- The appointment of a marketing specialist at a senior level with the responsibility for the development of a more proactive stance.
- A refocusing of the business.
- A programme of internal marketing so that staff are fully aware of the new direction for the organization and the contributions that they will be expected to make.
- An audit of current activities.
- Market and product development.
- A programme of promotion including public relations and advertising.

3.2   Any change of culture in these circumstances will only be achieved by a 'top-down' approach, with members of the board demonstrating their explicit commitment to customer satisfaction. The marketing and sales departments, led by the new marketing direction, must therefore become the basis from which the organization moves ahead.

3.3   An important part of this will be an understanding of customer and distributors' needs. There will therefore be a need for a programme of market research in order to identify:

- Levels of customer satisfaction.
- Areas of market opportunity.
- Distributors' expectations.
- Competitors' probable moves.

3.4   A degree of refocusing will be needed so that Penton's positioning becomes more meaningful and explicit. The decision on positioning can, however, only be taken following the programme of research referred to in 3.3 above. The refocusing will be designed to achieve several objectives, but most importantly will help to clarify the company's offer.

3.5   A programme of internal marketing will then be needed in order to ensure that staff are made and kept aware of the new direction, the reasons for this, the nature of their expected contribution, and the levels of success being achieved.

3.6   An audit of the current methods of operation underpins all of what has been suggested so far. This will be designed to improve levels of effectiveness and efficiency.

3.7   A programme of market and product development is needed which will reflect changing market needs and corporate capability. Assuming this is conducted effectively, the organization will more effectively be able to develop and sustain a meaningful competitive advantage.

3.8 There will be the need for a programme of advertising and public relations in order to increase levels of market awareness and to support the launch of new products.

3.9 Underpinning all of this should be the development of a mission statement which encapsulates the changed values of the organization (see also Section 4.2).

4.0 A stronger and more proactive planning culture

4.1 The management philosophy has traditionally been reactive. The development of better plans and a stronger and more proactive planning culture will be designed to ensure that:

- Opportunities are more readily identified and capitalized upon.
- Threats will be perceived more readily and action taken to minimize their impact.
- Lead times are reduced.
- Levels of effectiveness generally are increased.
- Levels of accountability are increased.

4.2 This planning process should begin with the development of a mission statement which incorporates the changed values of the business. This will, in turn, require a series of decisions on the direction that the business is to take and the market position to be adopted.

4.3 Other areas in need of clarification are the primary and secondary corporate and functional objectives that are to be pursued.

4.4 A full environmental analysis is required.

4.5 An internal audit designed to identify the true level of corporate capability should be conducted as a matter of some urgency.

4.6 Decisions are required on a variety of areas including:

- The competitive stance to be adopted.
- The product development programme.
- Pricing postures.
- Distribution issues.

4.7 Following on from 4.6, it is essential that work begins shortly on the first drafts of the plans for all key areas, with this being led by members of the board after decisions have been made on the corporate objectives.

4.8 A programme of monitoring and feedback should be instigated with responsibility for co-ordination and ensuring that corrective action is taken being the specific responsibility of main board members.

4.9 Levels of accountability throughout the organization need to be increased.

4.10 Given changes in all of these areas, the development of a more effective and proactive planning culture should begin to emerge. It does, however, need to be emphasised that levels of commitment to planning are only likely to increase if the plans themselves prove to be realistic rather than broad and generally unrealistic statements of intent.

5.0 The new product development process

5.1 The planning process referred to in Section 4 must provide the rationale and direction of any changes to the new product development process. It is, however, apparent from our work so far that the R&D team currently lacks direction. It is therefore essential that the environmental analysis referred to in 4.4, and the clarification of objectives referred to in 4.3, are used as the basis of the development of the new product development strategy.

5.2 Further work is needed on the organization's true NPD capability so that a fuller assessment can be made of:

- What NPD activity might realistically be carried out in the short and long term.
- The particular problems being encountered currently in the process. This can then be set against the background of the findings of the environmental analysis and, in particular, the opportunities that are likely to emerge over the next few years.

5.3 Clarification is also required of the competitive stance that the company wishes to adopt in this area and in particular whether the company, at this stage at least, wishes to be proactive or instead intends to adopt a market follower's approach.

5.4 Given decisions in these areas, work can then be done in order to improve the various stages of new product development, including:

- Market evaluation.
- Prototype development.
- Business evaluation.
- Test marketing.

5.5 It is essential that responsibility for NPD rests firmly at board level and is seen as part of the remit of the new marketing director (see Section 3.2).

6.0 Summary

6.1 A series of changes have been recommended in this report. Deliberately we have not put costings next to them, since these will be the focus of subsequent work. However, for our suggestions to be worthwhile, it is essential that levels of accountability are increased and stronger direction is given from the top.

Question 2

What are the implications of your suggestions for approaches to management control?

The implications for management control of our recommendations are significant and can be seen in terms of the need for changes both in attitude and operating practice.

With regard to attitudes, the key issue is the need for management to recognize that previous approaches to planning and control have been unsatisfactory and that this is due largely to failings in areas such as:

- The setting of objectives.
- The implementation of plans.
- Feedback and follow-up mechanisms.

The attitudinal change required is therefore concerned with recognition of the current inadequacies and a willingness to adopt a more structured and demanding approach to management. Included within this is the willingness to accept the discipline of regular and detailed market analysis and the establishment and implementation of more firmly structured plans throughout the business.

This attitudinal shift can be seen to overlap with the second dimension referred to above, that of changes in operating practice. If the recommendations made in the report that forms the answer to Question 1 are to be implemented, there is therefore the need for a fully integrated planning and control process since the control dimension is meaningless if the planning dimension has not been properly developed. Thus, as we observed above, there is a need for the following:

- A clear statement of objectives.
- A clear statement of the competitive stance.
- A firm positioning statement with an attendant clarification of the target markets.
- An unambiguous and realistic plan which covers both the corporate and the departmental activities.
- A firm allocation of responsibilities and structured delegation.
- A clarification of timescales.
- A programme of staff training.
- An improvement in communication patterns.
- A more collaborative ethos.

Underlying all of this is a far more definitive statement of accountability.

The specifics of the control process follow logically from this and centre around the establishment of intermediate objectives and the development of feedback and control mechanisms. In this way performances can be compared with targets and, where appropriate, corrective action taken.

Against this background, it can be seen that in many ways the implications of our earlier suggestions for the control process are relatively straightforward and can best be summarized in terms of far stronger process of monitoring, feedback, accountability and corrective action. With regard to specific activities, these include:

- Regular customer surveys.
- Trade surveys.
- Competitive monitoring.
- Performance monitoring of both financial and marketing measures.
- Performance against plan.

Although this case study led to some very good answers, far too many candidates produced answers that were unrealistic in that they assumed:

- Unlimited financial resources would be available.
- That management behaviour and customers' perceptions can be changed over night.

The other mistake made involved failing to come to terms with the underlying issue of managerial weakness and adopting what we can call a 'knee jerk' response to the eleven points raised in the consultant's report. In other words, if prices are perceived to be above industry norms, cut them. Only rarely is the answer so simple and instead you need to recognize that the issue of price is a manifestation of a more fundamental problem. Think therefore about whether a solution can realistically be arrived at with the existing management team.

New Directions plc: issues to think about

Question 1

Prepare a SWOT analysis of the organization both for the period before the takeover and for the period reached at the end of the case study. Having done this, discuss the implications of ONE of your analyses for methods of marketing planning and control.

SWOT analysis underpins a great deal of thinking on marketing planning. This case study provides you with an opportunity to construct two SWOTs and discuss the implications of one of them for the planning and control process.

The two questions that you have to answer have a 30/20 mark split. Allowing for 10 minutes of reading time, this means that you have about 50 minutes for the first question and 30 for the second.

The SWOT analyses are relatively straightforward and we have therefore mapped these out on page 186. We have not, however, identified the key features and so you might begin by comparing your SWOT with those on page 186 and then highlighting the points that you feel are the most significant. Having done this, turn to the very significant issue of the implications of one of the SWOTs for planning and control. Probably the best one to use is for Period 2 in which major changes have taken place. Think about the sorts of constraints that the new managerial climate would produce and how this would influence how the organization operates.

Against this background, turn to the second question and map out your recommendations for change.

Do you really feel that the organization has a future under the new MD? If so, what is it likely to be? If not, what are the implications for your recommendations?

Period One	
Strengths <ul><li>Oakley's entrepreneurial style</li><li>A decade of growth</li><li>Size (400 stores)</li><li>A young, high-performing team</li><li>A major player in high-growth markets</li><li>The firm's reputation in the City</li><li>Employee loyalty and motivation</li><li>A proactive managerial culture</li><li>High levels of performance</li></ul> *Opportunities* <ul><li>Scope for further growth both geographically and in emerging market sectors</li></ul>	*Weaknesses* <ul><li>20 years of slow and unspectacular growth before Oakley's appointment. In certain circumstances Oakley's style might be a disadvantage</li><li>A possible lack of managerial experience?</li></ul> **Threats** <ul><li>General competitive threats</li><li>An attractive target for a takeover?</li></ul>
Period Two	
Strengths <ul><li>The parent company's financial resources and performance</li></ul> *Opportunities* <ul><li>Oakley's perception of the scope for improving quality and shifting the demographic focus</li><li>The development of a new chain</li><li>Store redesign</li></ul> Repositioning New overseas markets Customers' expectations for new shopping experiences	*Weaknesses* <ul><li>Scope for conflict between Oakley's management approach and that of the new parent</li><li>The risk aversive approach of the parent in a fast moving and growing market</li><li>Greater bureaucracy</li><li>Managerial frustration</li><li>Oakley's resignation</li><li>Loss of direction</li><li>The emergence of a new and seemingly desperate strategy</li><li>Reduced turnover</li><li>Firefighting (slashing of overheads)</li><li>Increasingly demoralized staff</li><li>Confused image</li><li>Loss of confidence</li><li>The loss of staff to competitors</li></ul> *Threats* <ul><li>A reduced ability to capitalize upon short-term opportunities</li><li>Demographic changes and the decline of existing markets</li><li>A reputation for price rather than quality when research shows that quality is becoming more important</li><li>A stagnating UK market</li><li>The competitors' recruitment of New Direction's staff after Oakley's resignation</li><li>Competitive inroads (share slipping)</li><li>Loss of market leadership</li></ul>

Anderson Marine Construction: a suggested solution

This is a case study of an interesting organization which, because of a series of fundamental environmental disruptions is now faced with the need to make a series of major strategic changes. The decision on which way to go has already been made by the company's owner and the marketing consultant, and the issue that candidates therefore need to address is concerned with the structure of the marketing plan.

Question 1

An outline of a marketing plan covering the launch and subsequent market development of AMC's new range of boats.

The reader should recognize that this is an *outline* of the marketing plan for a new range of boats and, as such, identifies a series of issues without necessarily addressing each in depth. The final and detailed plan can only be produced after further research has been conducted; the areas in which this research is required are referred to in the appendix on page 190.

Structure of the plan

 1 Background.
 2 Situational analysis.
 3 Strategic imperatives.
 4 Principal assumptions underlying the plan.
 5 Preliminary marketing objectives.
 6 The target market.
 7 Positioning statement.
 8 The marketing mix.
 9 Implementation and control.
 10 Budgets.
    Appendix: areas for further research

1 Background

The recent report submitted by the marketing consultant has highlighted the gravity of our current position and the need to adopt a proactive stance by developing a new range of boats which will broaden our trading base and reduce our vulnerability to the downturn in the custom-built and high price sector of the boat market. With the board having accepted this recommendation, this plan outlines the steps that must be taken to ensure the new range is developed and launched in time for the forthcoming selling season.

2 Situational analysis: a review of the business environment and the company's internal operations.

2.1 The business environment

Market demand for medium-sized, high-performance, power boats and yachts is currently depressed, with sales having dropped steadily over the last four years. Despite a series of price cuts, demand for our products has not risen and this, plus other evidence, suggests that the market is not price sensitive. Instead levels of demand are determined by more fundamental factors such as levels of confidence in the economy. Economic and industry forecasts indicate few signs of an upturn in demand in the premium priced sector of the market over the next two years. Anecdotal evidence and casual observation suggests that our competitors are similarly affected.

By contrast, demand for lower-priced boats appears currently to be rather more buoyant, with forecasts indicating that sales patterns in this area over the next few years are likely to be relatively stable. A larger number of firms operate in this part of the market and a greater emphasis upon prices and costs is inevitable. Preliminary evidence does suggest, however, that with careful positioning, scope exists for AMC to establish itself in this part of the market.

(**Note**: these points are summarized as a series of opportunities and threats in the SWOT analysis.)

2.2 Strengths and weaknesses

2.2.1 Strengths

- Well-established manufacturer of high-quality and high-performance yachts and power boats.
- Loyal and knowledgeable customer base.
- Financially successful.
- Skilled workforce with a strong craft orientation.
- Reputation for quality and performance.

2.2.2 Weaknesses

- Reactive selling approach.
- Absence of a proactive marketing culture.
- Recent reductions in margins.
- Absence of a formal distribution network.
- No previous presence or experience in the lower-priced and higher-volume sectors of the boat market.
- Little experience of advertising and promotion.
- Workforce with a strong craft orientation and little experience in volume production.
- Seemingly little emphasis upon cost control and working to a particular price.
- Delivery schedules.

2.2.3 Preliminary assessment of strengths and weaknesses

Although the company undoubtedly possesses a series of strengths, questions must be raised about the management's ability to capitalize upon these in the short term on entering the higher volume sector of the market. It is therefore essential that attention be paid to the issues of managerial expertize and culture, so that gaps might be filled and a more proactive approach developed. Equally, the workforce has a tradition of producing high-quality products but little real experience of volume production in which a strong adherence to cost control is fundamental.

2.3 Opportunities and threats

2.3.1 Opportunities

- Market and sales growth.
- A reduction in the organization's exposure to one sector of the market.
- Scope to capitalize upon the firm's reputation for quality and performance.

2.3.2 Threats

- A greater number of competitors.
- The difficulty of establishing a worthwhile market position.
- Possible problems in establishing a firm presence within the distribution network.

2.3.3 Preliminary assessment of the opportunities and threats

Our ability to capitalize upon the opportunities which undoubtedly exist in the higher volume sector of the market will depend to a very large extent upon our ability to move along the learning curve. The threats identified, whilst significant, are very largely predictable. Again our ability to cope with these will depend upon *how* we move into the market and our ability to establish a distinct presence in the short term.

3 Strategic imperatives arising from the SWOT analysis

Given the nature of the findings of the SWOT, it is essential that we address several issues in the immediate future. These include:

- The skills gap in the workforce.

- The absence of proactive marketing skills within the firm's management.
- The development of an appropriate distribution network.
- The development of a communications programme.
- The financial implications of the proposal.

4 Principal assumptions underlying the plan

A number of assumptions underpin this plan, the most significant of which are:

- Demand for the current range will remain depressed.
- AMC will be able to establish itself profitably in the new target sector.
- Sales within this sector will continue to improve over the next 12–18 months.

5 Preliminary marketing objectives

- To capitalize upon AMC's current very strong reputation by developing a new range of smaller and lower price boats offering higher performance levels than the competition.
- To position the new range as *the affordable high quality small yacht and power boat range.*
- To achieve distribution coverage of x per cent (note that this figure can only be finalized in the light of further research).
- To achieve sales in year one of _____*, in year two of _____*, and in year three of _____*, These will translate into the following market share figures:

  Year one _____.
  Year two _____.
  Year three _____.

  * Again these figures can only be determined in the light of further research.

6 The target market

A considerable amount of research is still needed to clarify the size and detail of the buying patterns of the target market (see Appendix, page 190) and at this stage it is therefore possible only to provide a broad picture of the market. In essence, however, the range is designed to appeal to sailing enthusiasts who have several years of experience and who now wish to buy a boat which offers greater performance, albeit within a relatively restricted budget.

Given this, and as the consultant's report has highlighted, the market will require:

- A greater degree of active selling by the distribution network.
- Delivery from distributor's stocks.
- Exposure to an advertising campaign to raise levels of awareness and interest.

7 Positioning statement

The new range will be positioned as *'the affordable high quality alternative'* in the mid-priced sector of the market. In achieving this position, full emphasis will be placed upon the broad values and heritage of our traditional range. The selling propositions will reflect both the performance of and linkages with our current range.

8 The marketing mix

- The product range will consist of small high performance yachts and boats that reflect a high value for money offer.
- Initial distribution will be through a carefully selected number of existing boatyards throughout the south, south east and south west of England. In the light of our experiences in the first year, consideration will be given to broadening this network in years two and three. Distributors will be selected on the basis of their:
  - Current image.
  - Ability to provide sales and technical support.
  - Current sales levels.

- Geographic location.
- Existing franchises.

Emphasis will be placed upon the development of long-term relationships with distributors, with this being reflected in the high levels of marketing support provided by AMC and the margins offered.

- Prices will be set at the upper end of the sector in order to reflect the brand values associated with AMC, the quality of the product and the product's performance.
- Advertising and promotion will give prominence to the links with the existing range and will concentrate initially upon creating high levels of awareness and interest amongst the trade, the media and the target customer groups.

9 Implementation and control

Responsibility for refining and subsequently implementing this plan will rest with the marketing manager, reporting in to the main board. Given the significance of the proposed development, it is essential that the necessary level of resources and commitment are allocated to the project. Control will be achieved through monthly and quarterly reports with a series of measures of performance against target.

10 Budgets

These will be set in the light of the findings of further research. At this stage, however, it is possible to indicate several areas of major expenditure including:

- Modifications to the production facilities.
- The recruitment and/or retraining of the workforce needed to produce the new range.
- The development of an appropriate distribution network, including funding of stock levels.
- The funding of the principal dimensions of the marketing plan, including the advertising and research that will be needed.

Appendix

Areas for further research

In order to prepare a detailed marketing plan, a substantial amount of additional information is needed. Included within this is information on:

- Accurate and detailed sales forecasts for the short and medium term.
- The financial implications of the proposed action.
- Competitors: who are they, their size, location, patterns of ownership, resource availability, model ranges, strengths and weaknesses, selling propositions, positioning strategies, levels of advertising, pricing strategies, and patterns of distribution.
- Customers: probable size of each market sector, geographic location, buying motives, sailing skills, approaches to buying and expectations regarding sales support, price sensitivity and readership profiles.
- Distribution: major patterns of distribution network in existence currently, locations, distributors' selling skills, levels of sales support needed, and expectations regarding levels of inventory, terms of payment, margins and advertising support needed
- Trade shows: their relative importance, location, costs of appearance, visitor patterns and levels of media coverage.
- Media availability, areas of specific interest and copy dates.

Question 2
In the light of AMC's previous approaches to selling, what, if any, problems might you expect to encounter in implementing the marketing plan? In what ways might these problems be overcome or minimized?

Given the nature of the business in the past and in particular the relatively informal approaches to marketing that have predominated, I would anticipate a series of problems in implementing a plan which not only targets a new and very different set of customers from those served previously, but which also reflects an infinitely more proactive stance. For convenience, these problems can be categorized on the basis of whether they are essentially internal or external to the organization. Those that are internal are concerned primarily with issues of culture, expertise and resource allocation, whilst those that are external are largely concerned with areas such as customer perception, the nature of the distribution network and the responses of those companies with which AMC will now find itself competing.

Beginning with the internal problems, the most immediate of these is likely to be the question of how best to develop a culture which is more suited to dealing with a higher volume and less specialized market than the one that AMC has previously been concerned with. Because AMC will still be producing boats for its traditional market and can not afford to compromise its methods of operating within this sector, it may well prove to be appropriate to split the organization in such a way that scope exists for a clear focus upon each of the two sectors. Assuming this is done, there will then be a need to begin the process of developing a managerial culture that gives full recognition to the rather different long-term development of the business. It would appear that the current workforce is heavily specialized and, assuming this to be the case, a degree of retraining and/or recruitment will be needed in order to ensure that the firm has the production skills needed for the new range.

At the same time, a rather different set of selling and marketing skills will be needed in order to develop the new product, launch it onto the market and subsequently ensure its success. A question therefore needs to be raised about the ability of the current management team to do this. Where gaps exist, and from a distance it seems most likely that this will be in the market and sales development areas, expertise will of necessity have to be recruited.

Other internal problems that are likely to be encountered include:

- Whether AMC will have sufficient production capacity and flexibility.
- Identifying new suppliers and hence implementing a rather different purchasing policy from that of the past.
- Controlling costs rather more tightly. Given the nature of the comments in the case, it appears that price has not previously been a significant issue. Because of this, it seems likely that elements of tight cost control will not have been important. The new product and market will, however, demand a different approach if the venture is to prove profitable.
- The development and cultivation of new and possibly tighter controls, including those upon the sales and distribution networks.
- The establishment of a more proactive approach to selling, including the development of an internal and external sales team, the advertising campaign and the appearance at selected boat shows.
- A decision on the positioning strategy that is to underpin the market effort.

The probable external problems will stem very largely from coming to terms with the very different market which the company will be dealing with and in particular the characteristics of the new customer base and competitors. Without doubt, one of the most significant issues will be concerned with the company's image, since AMC cannot afford to compromise this in the eyes of its traditional customers, but needs to capitalize upon it for its new market.

In order to overcome these problems, a number of distinct changes will be needed, the most significant and immediate of which involves overcoming the lack of marketing expertise. Perhaps the easiest and fastest way of doing this involves recruiting one or more marketing specialists to support the new marketing manager. Together, these will have the responsibility for:

- Market development.
- The identification and development of an appropriate distribution network.
- The further development and implementation of the marketing plan.
- The recruitment and management of a sales team.

Other areas for action and change include:

- A formal assessment of production capability.
- The development of a modified purchasing policy.
- Instituting a more rigorous climate of cost control.
- Retraining of the appropriate staff.

It is obvious from this that a considerable amount of change is needed if the organization is to capitalize upon the opportunities that seemingly exist. However, without the active support of Tom Anderson and other members of the board, few changes in culture and direction will be achieved, and the effort will have little real payoff.

This case required candidates to prepare an outline of the marketing plan and, as with the Phoenix Telecom case that we referred to earlier, too many candidates demonstrated that they have little real understanding of what a marketing plan looks like. You should therefore make sure you are familiar with the plan's structure and where the information that the plan needs might come from.

The second question focused upon an issue that has cropped up on several occasions previously: how might you most effectively change the culture of an organization? We commented at an earlier stage that many candidates underestimate the difficulties of changing managerial cultures and well-established methods of operating and you should therefore give detailed thought to the various ways in which this might be achieved. In doing this, you might usefully refer back to pages 146–52 of Unit 8 in which we discussed both the barriers to implementation and the sorts of factors that encourage it.

Kanko Ltd: a suggested solution

This was the first of the mini cases to include a number of tables. You should therefore spend time looking at these tables, and indeed those in the subsequent cases, identifying the messages that they are designed to communicate.

It is very apparent from the case that the company has lost touch with its rapidly changing market. The changes that are needed both to the marketing mix and how the organization operates are therefore significant. The questions put candidates in the position of being a member of the new management team that is faced with the need to evaluate the current offer and decide how to move forward.

What significance do you feel that being part of a larger organization (what the case study refers to as being 'a wholly owned subsidiary of a highly diversified listed public company') might have?

Question 1

As a member of the new management team, you have been given the responsibility for recommending how the product and distribution strategies should develop. Prepare a report detailing the criteria by which the current product range and sales and distribution networks should be evaluated and possibly rationalized.

1.0 Management summary

This report highlights the company's current position and the rationale for a detailed review of the product range and sales and distribution networks. It identifies a wide range of criteria that can be used in the evaluation process and, against this background, explains the basis for possible rationalization of the organization's approach to the market.

2.0 The current position

The initial review of the sales and marketing functions, together with the other information and data available to us, has highlighted a variety of issues that need to be addressed. These include:

- The breadth and depth of the current product range.
- The appropriateness of existing patterns of distribution (refer to Tables 9.1 and 9.3 in the information that was supplied on the company).
- The significance and probable causes of sales and profit decline over the past few years (refer to Table 2 in the information supplied).
- The approaches to new product development.
- Levels of product quality and service support.
- Levels of sales force performance.
- Approaches to advertising and promotion.
- The failure of the advertising agency to capitalize upon our potential brand strengths.

3.0 The criteria for evaluating the product range

Given the nature and magnitude of the problems faced by the organization, it is essential that a full and detailed review of the product range be carried out as a matter of urgency. In doing this attention needs to be paid both to individual products within the range and to the range as a whole. In this way, we will gain a clearer understanding both of the potential of the individual components and of the degree of cohesion across the range. Having done this, we will then be in a far better position to recommend how the range might possibly be rationalized.

3.1 The criteria for the evaluation of individual products

A wide variety of criteria should be used to evaluate individual products within the range, the most important of which are as follows:

(a) The current level of sales by sector, area and region as well as nationally via each form of distribution network.
(b) The current levels of profit or loss and breakeven points.
(c) The levels of gross and net contribution.
(d) The scope that exists for product/market development and the costs associated with this.
(e) The length of time for which each product has been on the market, its apparent position on the product life cycle and the scope, if any, for extending the life cycle.
(f) The levels and costs of sales, service and after sales support needed.
(g) The strengths of any selling propositions and the scope that exists for their further development.
(h) End users, and distributors' perceptions of the product.
(i) The manufacturing, product handling and distribution costs.
(j) The levels of advertising support needed.
(k) The product's comparative competitive position.

(l) The product's position within the product portfolio (refer also to the later comments on the Boston Consulting Group's product portfolio matrix).

(m) The scope that exists for cost reduction.

(n) The product's price sensitivity.

(o) Whether scope exists for increasing the value added component within the product and hence any opportunities for price increases.

(p) Any competitive disadvantages that the product might have, the scope that exists for overcoming these and the costs that would be incurred in doing this.

(q) The level, nature and significance of complaints.

(r) Forecasts of future sales.

(s) Where appropriate, market share and/or position in the market.

(t) The attractiveness of each market served.

(u) Warehousing needed.

3.2 The criteria for the evaluation of the product range

Having evaluated each of the products within the range, we need then to evaluate the range in its entirety. The criteria that should be used for this include many of the points referred to above, although in addition should include:

- The degree of sales and cost interdependencies across the range.
- Issues of synergy.
- The nature of the product portfolio when plotted using a matrix such as that suggested by the Boston Consulting Group.
- Levels of market attractiveness.

3.3 The criteria for the evaluation of the sales and distribution networks

It is apparent from the information made available, and in particular Tables 9.1 and 9.3, that a number of the problems being experienced by the company stem from the ways in which the patterns of distribution that are being used are increasingly at odds with distribution trends within the market. Analysis of Tables 9.1 and 9.3 highlights both the degree of divergence that exists currently and the extent to which this mismatch will increase over the next few years. Given this, the detailed evaluation of the distribution and sales networks should make reference to the following criteria:

Distribution

- Distribution trends. Table 9.3 illustrates the growing strength of the DIY stores and the (continuing) decline of ironmongers and builders' merchants. These trends can be contrasted with the information contained in Table 9.1 which highlights Kanko's traditional presence in and commitment to builders' merchants. Although sales via DIY stores doubled in the period 1987–93, this compares with a 450 per cent increase of industry sales through DIY outlets and a decline of approximately 30 per cent through builders' merchants.
- The costs of distribution via each type of outlet. This should include issues of:
  - Order size.
  - Levels of sales, service and after-sales service support that is required.
- The importance of Kanko's individual products and full product range to each distribution outlet.
- The degree of commitment to Kanko that exists currently and the scope that exists for its development.
- The level of support and exposure that each distributor is willing to give to part or the whole of the range.
- The margins obtained within each type of outlet.
- Distributors' expectations.

Sales

- The costs of the sales force.
- Levels of sales force efficiencies.

- The degree of overlap between territories and/or responsibilities.
- Levels of sales force capability and the scope that exists for their development.

4.0 The application of these criteria

This report has so far identified a considerable number of the criteria that might be used to evaluate the product range and sales and distribution networks. However, although each criterion is undoubtedly of value, they need to be placed within the context of a framework which will allow for any rationalization that is needed to take place. The key dimension of this framework can be seen in terms of the sort of organization that it is intended that Kanko should become and should therefore include:

- The nature of the corporate objectives that are to be pursued.
- The competitive stance which it is felt that Kanko should attain and is capable of retaining.
- Levels of financial availability.

In deciding upon these, reference must also of course be made to competitors' stances. It is against this background that the shape of the future organization can then be decided.

Given this, decision on rationalization can then begin to be made, but should be based upon a clear understanding both of customer needs and distribution trends. It is a knowledge of these that will then provide a platform for a far greater degree of organizational focus and clarification of purpose. Thus in the case of the sales force, scope might well exist for rationalization by the development of key account managers to service the major DIY outlets.

Question 2

Make recommendations on the appointment of the new advertising agency. Prepare a short briefing paper identifying the criteria by which agencies pitching for the account should be shortlisted.

Background

Having operated with the same advertising agency for several years, the decision to fire the agency and appoint a replacement has been made. The basis for dispensing with the services of the old agency was primarily the uninspiring and tired sales literature and advertising that they were producing and hence the failure of the organization to capitalize upon the potential strength of its products and brand name. In appointing a new agency it is therefore essential that we develop a relationship with an organization that is capable of developing a promotional strategy that will contribute firmly to the overall marketing campaign and reflect a far higher degree of creativity. In this way, we are likely to restore some of the brand values that have been eroded over the past ten years.

The shortlisting criteria

Although a wide variety of criteria might be used in shortlisting potential candidates, arguably the most significant are:

- The *type* of agency that we require and the breadth of services needed. The alternatives open to us range from a full-service agency that is capable of handling all aspects of any promotional campaign, through to creative hot-shops which will concentrate upon the development of any creative appeal leaving us to organize, either directly or indirectly, other elements of the promotional task such as media buying. Given the size of our organization, it is recommended that we opt for a full-service agency, since this will allow us to concentrate upon more pressing issues.
- The agency's size and the relative importance of our account.
- Their current and past client portfolio, since this will give us an understanding not just of the breadth of their client range, but also the types of promotional work that they have undertaken.
- Their understanding of the marketing problems that we face and their views of the ways in which a new promotional campaign might possibly contribute to their resolution.

- Their apparent levels of creativity. These can be assessed, in part at least, by reference to previous campaigns.
- Their reputation.
(g) The nature of their pitch and the extent to which it appears to reflect an understanding of the organization and its market.
- The costs that are likely to be incurred.

An additional and possibly very important factor which should be taken into account is *the degree of empathy* which exists between the agency and Kanko, since it is essential that we develop a fruitful and profitable relationship. Other factors to which consideration might possibly be given include any areas of specialist expertise and their financial stability.

However, in doing this, we need to be very clear about the role that we expect advertising and promotion to play, the marketing and promotional objectives that will be pursued, and the levels of spend that we are willing to make.

EXAM TIP

Marketing strategists are often faced with the need to rethink their strategies, tactics and methods of implementation. This case study proved to be a useful vehicle for getting candidates to identify the sorts of criteria by which the product range and sales and distribution networks might be evaluated and possibly rationalized. Many candidates handled this well, but too many focused just upon marketing criteria rather than a series of marketing, financial, production and general organizational criteria.

Question 2 focuses upon the criteria for shortlisting potential advertising agencies. Recognize, however, that similar criteria might also be used for appointing, say, a new market research agency.

Watergate Pumps Ltd: a suggested solution

This case focuses upon an organization which, in common with others such as Kanko, Anderson Marine Construction and Penton, has lost touch with its market. It has been decided therefore to develop an environmental monitoring system so that the management team might gain a greater – and ongoing – understanding of the marketplace. Candidates were put into the position of having to suggest how such a system might be structured and implemented.

QUESTION 9.9

What pictures emerge from the tables and figures? What is their significance?

Question 1

As the company's newly appointed market analyst, you are required to prepare a detailed report for the marketing director recommending how an effective external environmental monitoring system for the company might best be developed and implemented. Included within the report should be your suggestions of the structure of the system, the expected inputs and outputs, the probable organizational and resource implications, and the nature of any benefits that should emerge.
(30 marks)

A report recommending the development and implementation of an environmental monitoring system for Watergate Pumps Ltd.

1 Management summary

This report makes a series of recommendations concerning how an effective environmental monitoring system might be developed and implemented with Watergate Pumps. It makes reference to:

- The structure of the system.
- The expected inputs and outputs.
- The probable organizational and resource implications.
- The nature of the system's likely benefits.

It does not include a costing of the system.

2 Introduction and background

It is apparent from the information provided that Watergate Pumps currently has an insufficiently detailed understanding of its external environment. The implications of this have been highlighted by the way in which the company has been taken by surprise by a series of market developments (for the detail of these, refer to page 172 of the information supplied and the series of bullet points) and by the subsequent decline in our market share (see Table 9.4). In addition, we have a heavy presence in the declining local authority market and a weak market position in the three other sectors of the market (see Table 9.5). Additional evidence of our poor understanding of the market is reflected in Table 9.6 (the buying motives of the different customer groups) and our failure to reposition between 1990 and 1993.

3 The purpose and benefits of the system

The proposed system will be designed to provide the management team with a clear and ongoing picture of the market. It will focus upon a number of areas, including:

- Competitors' strengths, weaknesses, resources, strategies and performance levels.
- Customers (existing and potential) and their current and developing demands.
- The general trading environment.

The benefits of the system should be seen in terms of a far clearer understanding of the market and, in particular, of customers and competitors. This should in turn lead to the development of far clearer, more focused and appropriate strategic and tactical behaviour. Given this, it should then be far less likely that the organization will be taken by surprise by developments within the market (see, for example, our failure to anticipate the entry of Pump Suppliers in 1991, the launch of new and modified products by BG International and Northern Pumps, the general competitive repositioning, and so on). In addition, the system should provide a basis for a more proactive approach and a general strengthening of our competitive position.

4 The structure of the system

It is proposed that the system consists of four principal dimensions:

- Internal records.
- Marketing research.
- Marketing intelligence.
- Marketing decision support analysis.

The relationship between these areas and the overall structure of the system are illustrated in Figure 9.7 on the next page.

To ensure that the system is of the greatest value to the organization, it will be based very firmly on an analysis of managers' information needs. It is therefore recommended that we begin by examining in detail:

- Information needs.
- Information gaps.
- The ways in which information generated by the system might best be used.

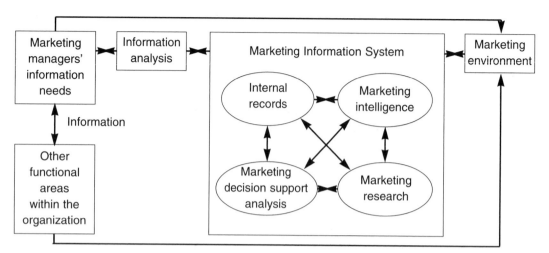

Figure 9.7 The marketing information system

It is essential, therefore, that in developing the system we ensure that we satisfy a number of conditions, including:

- The system must be user friendly.
- It must be manageable.
- It must provide the information that is needed for effective marketing decision making.
- It must avoid the problems of information overload.

Recognizing this, it is proposed that the system be developed and implemented over a predetermined time period. Given that the organization has not had such a system in place previously it is unrealistic to expect that the full system can be developed and introduced to the company in one move. It is therefore recommended that a timetable be established with the system being introduced over a 12 month period. As part of this, it is essential that the responsibility for the system is clearly allocated and that this is at a senior level in the organization. The progress of the system's development will also need to be monitored.

5 The expected inputs and outputs

Although brief reference has already been made to the inputs and outputs, they can be identified more specifically as being:

Inputs

- Competitive information.
- Customer information.
- General market information.

These inputs will be obtained from a spectrum of sources including the trade press, the sales force, exhibitions, and distribution intermediaries. In order to collect this information, it is essential that staff are made aware of the nature of the information needed and how it will be used. It is recommended that, initially, a relatively unstructured approach is used (i.e. collect whatever information we can) and that this is gradually refined over time.

A fundamental part of the system is, of course, that of the analysis stage; again, it is imperative that the responsibility for analysis *and dissemination* is clearly allocated.

Outputs

The output from the system will take the form of a monthly report summarizing the key market developments and highlighting the apparent opportunities and threats. The monthly report will be supplemented by a weekly briefing paper.

It needs to be emphasized, however, that these reports need to form the basis for subsequent marketing action and again, the responsibility for this will rest at board level. The circulation list for the reports will therefore need to be carefully determined.

6.0 The organizational and resource implications

The costs of the system cannot be determined at this stage. However, it needs to be recognized that the costs of *not* developing such a system are already apparent. It is therefore essential that there is a full commitment to the system – and its use – at senior management level. In terms of the immediate resource implications, it is evident that, as the newly appointed marketing analyst, I will need to spend a considerable amount of my time over the next few months developing the system. However, perhaps the most significant organizational implication can be identified in terms of the need for a far more obvious, a stronger and much more consistent external focus on the part of management, with a commitment to use the outputs. Without this, the system is likely to be of little value. This can perhaps best be summarized in terms of the need for a new and much more market-oriented management culture.

7 The benefits of the system

These have been alluded to in Section 3, but are in essence related to the scope for a far more proactive stance. This should be reflected most obviously in terms of:

- Better market positioning.
- A clearer and more focused new product development process.
- Better pricing.
- Clearer market targeting.
- Higher levels of customer satisfaction.
- A far stronger competitive stance.

8 Summary

Within this report, I have highlighted the need for an environmental monitoring system and the form that such a system might take. It must be emphasized that the development of the system will take considerable time and effort but that the benefits will be considerable. The consequences of *not* developing the system are likely to be significant and reflected in a further worsening of market position.

Question 2
In the light of the information contained in the mini case, what recommendations for future marketing action would you make? (20 marks)

It is apparent from the case study that the organization's market and competitive position has weakened considerably over the past few years. It is therefore essential that the current decline in market share is stopped and that the organization begins targeting those parts of the market which offer significant growth opportunities (see Table 9.5, page 173 in the mini case). Other issues which need to be addressed include the following:

1 The price/perceived reliability relationship (see Figure 9.2).
2 The issues of availability and perceived ease of fitting (see Figure 9.3).
3 The significance of the different buying motives of each of the customer groups (see Table 9.6, page 173).
4 The failure to make full use of the company's manufacturing capacity (see Table 9.4, page 172).
5 The possibilities for exporting (see Table 9.4, page 172).
6 Product modification and new product development.
7 The quality of the products' control systems.

Underlying these points is the question of the competitive stance that the organization wishes to adopt over the next few years. It is evident from the information in the case that the three principal competitors have all given greater emphasis to the issues of price, perceived reliability, ease of fitting, and availability. Watergate's management needs to decide whether it will adopt a broadly similar stance or deliberately adopt a low-price posture in order to achieve a degree of differentiation. There is, however, a danger in this in that evidence from the market suggests that price is not an important factor in the growing market sectors (see Table 9.6, page 173).

It is therefore recommended that the company increases its price, but only against the background of a series of product modification/new product actions designed to:

- Improve reliability.
- Improve the ease of fitting.
- Improve the control systems.

Without these three supporting actions, the company's sales will inevitably suffer. However, taking action in these areas is unlikely to prove sufficient by itself, since the improvements will need to be communicated to the market. It is therefore recommended that a clearly focused advertising campaign be developed, with emphasis being given to these improvements. The target markets for the campaign will be the growing market sectors.

At the same time, attention needs to be paid to issues of availability (see Figure 9.3, page 173). The information supplied provides little information on the sales and distribution approach and it is therefore difficult to make firm recommendations. It is, however, essential that a stronger, more proactive and more firmly focused approach be adopted in order to reach buyers and the appropriate decision making units (DMUs).

Table 9.4 illustrates the extent to which competitors are operating in markets other than the UK and this, coupled with Watergate's failure to use its full manufacturing capacity, suggests that exporting might well be attractive. It is recommended, however, that the company views this as a medium to long-term development rather than something for the short term. The reason for this is that the firm has really consolidated its domestic market, it is likely to overstretch itself by moving overseas. Thought might therefore be given to how costs might be reduced and revenues increased by alternative usage of the excess capacity (one measure, of course, might be to sub-let this part of the premises).

The success of the recommendations made so far will, of course, be heavily dependent upon a clear programme of implementation and a question that must therefore be asked concerns the quality of Watergate's management. Given that the current management team has been responsible for the organization's competitive decline over the past few years, reservations might possibly be expressed about issues of commitment and/or ability. However, without a far more proactive stance, it is unlikely that the recommendations made here will be implemented to the extent that is needed.

EXAM TIP

Question 1 was written in such a way that it provides a framework for the answer. It did this by stating that the report should make reference to the structure of the system, the expected inputs and outputs, the resource implication, and the nature of any benefits. Where these guidelines are provided, make full use of them. In the event, many candidates chose to ignore them.

RTJ Engineering Ltd: a suggested solution

The company operates with five strategic business units, three of which – nuclear, aerospace and defence – are in market sectors which, because of changed government and social thinking, are unlikely to grow at any real speed over the next few years. At the same time, three long-standing customers have been lost to competitors. The text of the case highlights several of the issues faced by the management team, but much of the information is in the form of the three figures.

What pictures emerge from the figures on pages 175–6? What is their significance?

Question 1

1 The state of the firms portfolio

A variety of frameworks can be used to evaluate a firm's portfolio, including the following:

- The Boston Consulting Group's growth-share matrix.
- The General Electric multifactor portfolio model.
- The Shell Directional Policy Matrix.
- Abell and Hammond's 3x3 matrix.
- The Arthur D Little strategic condition matrix.

Given the information that appears in Figure 9.6 of the case study (see page 176), we will use what is in many ways the most straightforward and probably the best known of these, the Boston Consulting Group's growth-share matrix; the results are illustrated below.

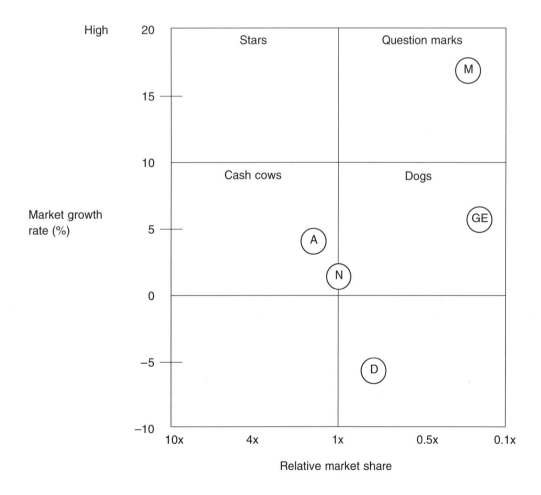

N: Nuclear   M: Marine
A: Aerospace   GE: General
D: Defence   Engineering

Figure 9.8   RTJ Engineering's product portfolio based on the BCG matrix

It can be seen from this, that there is a degree of imbalance within the portfolio and that given how the various markets are moving, the organization is likely to find itself exposed and potentially vulnerable over the next few years. The justification for this comment is that:

- Defence, which currently accounts for 20 per cent of RTJ's turnover, is forecast to decline at 6 per cent.
- The marine sector is growing at 15 per cent and it is therefore likely that large sums of cash will be needed to fund the continued growth of what is currently a Question Mark SBU.
- General engineering, which with 8 per cent has the second highest growth rate, is a small SBU (9 per cent of turnover) and is faced with a large number of competitors.
- Aerospace and Nuclear, both of which are cash cows (although perhaps less obviously in the case of Nuclear) currently have relatively low growth rates and given what is happening to these sectors of the economy may well find themselves faced with negative growth over the next few years.
- There is an absence of stars.

2 The assumptions made

It can be argued, however, that the picture that emerges from BCG analysis is relatively limited, since it focuses upon just two factors: the market growth rate and the relative competitive position. A number of writers in recent years (see, for example, Kotler, McDonald, Stacey and others) have argued that portfolio analysis (PA) of this type can be criticized both on general grounds (it provides a very limited snapshot and, in the case of BCG, uses two dimensions which arguably are not the most relevant for true analysis) and specific grounds (a far greater spectrum of factors need to be taken into account). The results should, it is therefore argued, be treated with a degree of caution.

In the case of BCG analysis, however, its advocates claim that the two variables used are capable of providing a valid basis for assessment, and it is this thinking, together with the limited information that is available, which underpins our choice of this particular model. Given more information on the market, we might have used other approaches to portfolio analysis, including the General Electric model which uses the rather broader ideas of *industry attractiveness* and *business strengths* as the basis for plotting SBU positions.

Industry attractiveness is arguably a more valuable dimension than market growth rate, since it encompasses market size, the growth rate, the degree of competition, the pace of technological change, the nature and extent of legislative and/or government constraints, historic profit margins, and so on. Equally, business strength is influenced by factors such as market share, product quality, the brand's reputation, the distribution network, production capacity, and production effectiveness.

Quite obviously, however, for the GE matrix to be used, we would need access to far more information than is in the case. Because of this, it needs to be emphasized that the picture of the portfolio that emerges from our BCG analysis is likely to have some value, but that this value is perhaps limited.

3 Additional information and the development of the portfolio

It follows from what has been said that, before making recommendations on how the portfolio should be developed, we would need far more information of the sort that is identified above. In addition, we would require:

- Forecasts of how each market sector is likely to develop.
- The patterns of ownership of competitive organizations.
- Their probable response patterns.

The other types of information that would be useful include:

- RTJ's resource capabilities under the headings of finance, marketing, management, and so on.
- Stakeholders expectations and attitudes to risk.
- Market information highlighting the patterns of opportunity and threat.

4 Other approaches to portfolio analysis (PA)

Reference has already been made to other models of portfolio analysis, although in each case, the information needs are greater than is the case for BCG.

In calculation, it is perhaps worth commenting that major reservations have been expressed recently about PA, since there is an implicit assumption that the environment of tomorrow will bear at least some relation to that of today. Stacey, amongst others, questions whether such an assumption can indeed be justified.

Question 2

Subject: The development and implementation of a customer care programme for RTJ
Engineering
Prepared by: ABC Consultants
Circulation: RTJ's main board
Date: December 1994

1 Background

It is very apparent from the research that we have conducted that, whilst RTJ's design and manufacturing skills are highly regarded within the marketplace, the organization is perceived not to be sensitive to customers' needs and expectations; the details of these findings are summarized in Figures 9.4(a) and 9.4(b) of our report. It is for this reason that we recommend the development and implementation of a customer care programme.

2 The scope of this report

This report identifies the principal dimensions of a customer care programme and suggests how it should be implemented. Details of the costs are not included and will be the subject of a separate exercise.

3 The dimensions of the proposed programme

The research has highlighted several areas of concern, the most significant of which emerge from Figure 9.4(a) in the case and include the following:

- Sales expertise.
- The quality of the sales literature.
- The failure to adhere to promised delivery schedules.
- Price competitiveness.
- Unprompted technical support.
- The ways in which the sales staff and sales support functions are operating.

These areas of concern are reinforced by the comments that emerged from the programme of qualitative research that was conducted (see Figure 9.4(b)).

Given that the organization has a number of competitive advantages in its technical operations, it follows that if the 'soft' side of the operation can be strengthened, the competitive advantages enjoyed by the organization should increase substantially.

It is therefore proposed that a programme of research be conducted to identify in greater detail the specific needs and expectations of different customers and customer groups. With this information, the organization will then be in a position to identify the specific service levels that should be established and how stronger relationships might be developed in order to foster the idea of lifetime customers.

It is apparent that the organization's handling of enquiries is currently weak and that these weaknesses are continued through the chain of manufacturing (see, for example, late delivery rates) and into the levels of after-sales service. A fundamental reorganization is therefore needed in order to overcome these problems, although underpinning all of these is the need for the following:

- Senior management commitment.
- A willingness to change existing work practices.
- A significant degree of training.

In doing this, we will be aiming to develop what is loosely referred to as a right-side-up organization or a customer-led rather than a product-led business.

Quite obviously, this will require a major change to the organizational culture which currently focuses upon manufacturing excellence rather than customer needs. In arguing for this, we are not suggesting that the levels of design and manufacturing excellence are compromised in any way, but that they are refocused so that customers' needs are met far more directly and immediately than is the case at present.

It needs to be emphasized, however, that change is needed throughout the organization and not just amongst, for example, the sales staff. RTJ is currently failing to perform adequately across a spectrum of areas, but appears to be taking refuge in the quality of its products and its design skills. If, however, a totally integrated programme is to be developed, it will involve staff throughout the organization working in a far more concerted and co-ordinated fashion.

4 Responsibilities

Such a programme will only work if there is total and sustained commitment from the main board. Without this, any subsequent moves are likely to be of little value. The programme must therefore be driven by a named main board direction (ideally the Managing Director) who, together with the other directors, will be held responsible for its success.

Further down the organization it is recommended that we introduce the idea of account managers who will have both the responsibility and authority for working closely with customers and RTJ. In effect, they will act as the interface between the two.

5 Training

It is evident that a full programme of training and development will be needed to heighten the levels of awareness and consequences of customer dissatisfaction. Of necessity, this training and development needs to be a top-down programme.

6 Performance targets

Against this background, a series of performance targets needs to be established. These will be both qualitative and quantitative in nature. It is also recommended that as part of the programme we include a variety of initiatives such as quality circles.

7 Summary

In the light of the research findings, it is apparent that the failure to work closely with customers is creating an increasing number of problems for the organization. In order to overcome this there is a pressing need to develop a practice customer care programme, led by the board, in which RTJ works far more closely with its customers in order to develop long-term and more productive relationships. It needs to be recognized, however, that the negative perceptions that exist can only be changed over what will probably be a lengthy time period and the effort must therefore be sustained. Without this, it is likely that the consequences will be significant.

EXAM TIP

As with a number of the previous cases, think in detail about the significance of managerial cultures and the ways in which they might possibly be changed.

The major case study: marketing strategy – analysis and decision

OBJECTIVES

This final unit of the Marketing Strategy Workbook will look not at any specific part of the syllabus, but at the final question paper in the Diploma series. In this unit we will consider what the case study exam is and why the Institute uses this particular method of examination.

We will also look at what you can expect in the examination itself, how to prepare for the examination and, finally, how to answer the examination without throwing away marks! We will also look at current trends, both in the examination itself and in marketing more generally, that you might want to take into account in your preparations for this examination.

Finally, we will consider the last two examination papers in the series which you can treat as a mock examination process. The two papers will be followed by a review of the case against which you can assess your own individual answer.

STUDY GUIDE

The most important aspects of this unit of the book are the two past examination papers. As in all things there is no substitute for experience and you are strongly advised to prepare for and to sit the two papers under examination conditions – or as close as you can approximate to examination conditions. Try if you can to consider the cases without looking at the questions or the additional information which is included. This will give you a better understanding of the examination process and prepare you for the examination day itself.

As there is no right answer to a case study no specimen or ideal answers have been included in this unit. Instead, each case is followed by a short review section which highlights the main points which the examiners were looking for when examining the cases.

What is the case study exam?

Case studies as a method of learning an examination, have played a major role in management education since the method was first introduced in the Harvard Business School in America. The main reason for using case studies was, and still is, to create a scenario or context within which academic theory can be practically applied to a real life business situation.

Most students find case studies far more difficult to tackle than the more traditional examination papers with a number of questions. Case studies are not necessarily more difficult, but they certainly are different from the traditional methods of examination that perhaps we have all been used to since school days. Nevertheless, if you follow the rest of this chapter carefully it should cause you no undue problems.

Finally, candidates hoping to pass the Analysis and Decision paper should bear in mind that as the Institute of Marketing Diploma becomes more widely recognized as the premier marketing qualification in the UK and Europe, this final paper must be a true test of the holder's ability to practise his or her trade. In the interests of both holders and employers, the Analysis and Decision case will continue to strive to be a rigorous test of the candidate's ability to apply marketing theory in real business situations.

Don't panic!

EXAM TIP

The Analysis and Decision paper has no set syllabus as such. It is a test of the student's ability to apply marketing theory from its sister paper, Strategic Marketing – Planning and Control, as well as the other two Diploma subjects Marketing Communication Strategy and International Marketing Strategy. As well as testing the candidate's ability to apply theory in all these four related areas, the major case study will also expect a solid and practical understanding of various issues which are covered in the Institute's certificate and advanced certificate papers. Topics such as financial implications, organization structure and design and the broader human resource implications of marketing strategy will also be rigorously tested in the case study.

It should also be understood that the very nature of the case study examination means that there is never one single 'correct' answer. In any complex business situation there will always be a number of alternative scenarios and strategic directions which can be identified by a manager. In the real world clear-cut cases are extremely rare too! What the examiners will be looking for in the case study, as will be shareholders in the real world, is a sound understanding of the situation facing the company described in the case study, an analysis and review of the strategic options open to the company and a clear recommendation as to the route that you believe the organization should take – with clear and reasonable justification.

What to expect from the case

Case studies can be anywhere from half a page to a hundred pages including appendices and additional information. The CIM Analysis and Decision case study typically extends to between twenty and fifty pages and will normally contain a section of text describing the situation faced by the particular company portrayed, plus a number of appendices.

The case study is always based on a real life business situation but will often be disguised in order to protect commercial confidentiality. On examination day the examination paper will consist of between two and four questions related to the case, normally carrying unequal marks. The examiner also reserves the right to include some additional information with the examination questions on the day. There are two reasons for including additional information. They are:

- To stimulate new and creative thinking on the day.
- To prevent the presentation of pre-prepared group answers.

It is important to take account of the additional information and to incorporate it into your answer wherever possible. Remember that the application of the additional information can be worth up to 20 per cent of the total marks awarded.

The case itself will often contain a wealth of data and information. As in the real world it is unlikely that the case material will contain all the data or information that ideally would be needed in order to solve the situation. So some assumptions or intelligent gap filling will be required. Also, not all of the data will be either useful or relevant to the situation in hand. Not only that but you are likely to uncover some contradictions or anomalies in the data material. All this has been designed, not to trap students, but rather to force them to think independently and creatively about the company described. In the real world data is not always clear cut nor are the solutions self evident. The case study does its best to replicate the real world with all its problems and challenges.

How to prepare

As has already been stated there is no single correct answer to any case study. Neither is there one guaranteed way of analysing a case study. A number of processes have been recommended which lay out the logical sequence of analysis and decision steps. Some of the more popular approaches are:

Process 1

1 What is wrong?
2 What are you going to do to put it right?

Process 2

1 Problem identification.
2 Problem definition.
3 Solutions generation.
4 Solution choice.
5 Solution implementation.
6 Solution monitoring.

Process 3

1 Situation audit.
2 Problem/decision statement.
3 Alternative identification.
4 Critical issues.
5 Analysis.
6 Recommendations.

Process 4

1 Comprehend the case situation.
2 Diagnose problem areas.
3 State problem.
4 Generate alternatives.
5 Evaluate and select.
6 Defend implementation.

In addition to the above, two more detailed processes of case preparation and analysis are recommended by the Institute and the senior examiners. The first is a process which breaks down into 28 identifiable stages and is the suggested route for the group process applied to case studies. The second is a derivative of the first, but a less detailed approach which tackles the case in six separate stages and is useful for group work and candidates working alone.

RECOMMENDED METHOD ONE
SUMMARY OF THE 28-STEP METHOD

Step 1   Read the case.
Step 2   After an interval, re-read the case.
Step 3   Reflect on the instructions and candidates' brief.
Step 4   Think yourself into the role and the situation.
Step 5   Re-read the case and write a precis. Discuss with colleagues.
Step 6   Conduct a marketing audit. Discuss with colleagues.
Step 7   Do a SWOT analysis. Discuss with colleagues.
Step 8   Conduct analyses/cross-analyses of appendices. Discuss with colleagues.
Step 9   Reconsider your precis, marketing audit and SWOT analysis.
Step 10 Conduct a situational analysis. Discuss with colleagues.
Step 11 Decide key issues. Discuss with colleagues.
Step 12 Develop a mission statement. Discuss with colleagues.
Step 13 Decide broad aims. Discuss with colleagues.
Step 14 Identify and analyse major problems. Develop and analyse alternative solutions. Discuss with colleagues.
Step 15 Develop quantified and timescaled objectives. Discuss with colleagues.
Step 16 Consider alternative strategies and select those most appropriate. Discuss with colleagues.
Step 17 Draw up detailed tactical plans covering the marketing mix. Discuss with colleagues.
Step 18 Draw up a marketing research plan and MkIS (Marketing Information System).
Step 19 Consider organizational issues and make recommendations for changes towards complete marketing orientation as felt necessary. Discuss with colleagues.
Step 20 Consider the organization's culture and make recommendations for internal marketing programmes as felt necessary. Discuss with colleagues.
Step 21 Consider the financial and human resource implications of your plans/recommendations. Discuss with colleagues.
Step 22 Assess costs and draw up indicative budgets. Discuss with colleagues.
Step 23 Draw up schedules showing the timing/sequence of your plans/recommendations. Discuss with colleagues.
Step 24 Specify review procedures and control mechanisms. Discuss with colleagues.
Step 25 Outline contingency plans. Discuss with colleagues.
Step 26 Review your complete marketing plan.
Step 27 Draw up your examination plan.
Step 28 Practise writing in true report style.

The process in detail is as follows:

Step 1   Read the case.

When the case arrives read it at normal reading speed and simply try to gather the gist of the situation and what is going on. You should avoid trying to go through the case too slowly at this stage or even making notes. Let the subconscious do the work for you.

Step 2   After an interval, re-read the case.

After a decent interval re-read the case once or twice again, not making too many detailed notes but to try and cover anything you may have missed first time through.

Step 3   Reflect on the instructions and candidates' brief.

Now that the content of the case is bedding down gently in your mind, it is time to turn to the important page of instructions which come along with the case and give you a clear indication as to what is expected of you. There are two sections to read. Firstly, the candidates' brief and secondly, the important notes which accompany the case study. The important notes remind you what will earn marks and what will not earn marks in the examination and that the data contained within the case will be split into the useful and the irrelevant. The notes also remind candidates not to bother contacting companies in the industry as this is unlikely to result in additional marks on the day. The candidates' brief is important in that it describes the role that you will be expected to play when framing your answer.

Step 4   Think yourself into the role and situation.

Without re-reading the case at this point consider the role which you will be asked to take in the examination and start to look at the case and possible alternatives from this point of view. Sometimes candidates are positioned as an employee in the company and other times as an external consultant. The role described will give strong indications as to the nature of the recommendations which will be required in the examination questions.

Step 5   Re-read the case and write a precis. Discuss with colleagues.

Writing a precis (this means shorter than the original!) of maximum one page A4 typed will force you to condense the details of between 30 and 50 pages of data into a very concise form. Precis writing is a useful discipline for identifying the really important facts from the case. Remember that in a short precis you have no space for opinions or interpretations. Once you have prepared your precis you should discuss this with your colleagues or group members and see how your opinion of the most important facts compares with other peoples.' In the light of other people's precis you may wish to refine your view of what the most important facts are.

Step 6   Conduct a marketing audit. Discuss with colleagues.

Marketing audit is described as 'a situational analysis of the company's current marketing capability.' (McDonald)

The marketing audit is the primary analysis tool of the case and is directed at analysing the current state of the organization's marketing as described in the case. A robust marketing audit should consider both external/uncontrollable factors including political, economic, sociological and technological factors (PEST) but candidates should note that this external analysis also includes a review of the most important marketing variable – customers (their needs, wants and aspirations) and competition. The internal element of the audit should be an analysis of how well the organization currently meets the market's requirements and should review mission and statements as well as marketing objectives, strategies and mixes if these are described.

It may also be relevant in this audit stage to consider other audits such as human resource, production, and financial audits if there is sufficient data and the analysis is considered pertinent. Once the audit has been completed, it is invaluable to discuss your findings with colleagues and compare notes on the different analysis routes and results obtained.

Step 7   Do a SWOT analysis. Discuss with colleagues.

SWOT analyses are well known analytical tools and, while they can be quite powerful, they are also prone to misuse. The SWOT analysis allows the investigator to identify the key strengths and weaknesses of the organization (internal) and the opportunities and threats which the organization may face from its external marketplace. Unfortunately the SWOT analysis is essentially a subjective process so comparison with colleagues and peers is essential. Also a variable is likely to feature in more than one category depending upon your point of view.

Too many SWOT analyses stop at the point of listing the various factors under one of the four headings. The real benefit from a SWOT analysis comes from discussion about what the classifications mean for the organization and what can be done. Many, more elaborate strategies have sprung from the simple idea of converting threats into opportunities, converting weaknesses into strengths and matching strengths to opportunities.

ACTIVITY 10.1

- Have you ever carried out a SWOT analysis in your organization? Most organizations have.
- What use was made of the SWOT? Most organizations carry out the analysis and then move on.
- How might the SWOT be used strategically in your organization?

Step 8   Conduct analyses/cross-analyses of appendices. Discuss with colleagues.

Case study appendices normally come in a variety of forms, from financial statements through tables to memos and examples of current advertising. The task before you in this step is to analyse the various tables in their various forms and pull out the various data sets that could be useful information to add to your understanding of the main text. Cross analyses of appendices also tend to highlight facts that will not be evident by looking at one table in isolation.

A word of warning, when confronted with financial data in a detailed form, you should be aware of the indiscriminate use of computer driven spreadsheets and always look for the meaning behind any financial calculations or ratio analysis.

Step 9   Reconsider your precis, marketing audit and SWOT analysis.

Putting the various analyses you have carried out so far together what can be learned? Are there any anomalies which appear? Have some of your earliest thoughts now been either confirmed or rejected?

Step 10   Conduct a situational analysis. Discuss with colleagues.

Based on the analyses now carried out, you should be ready to place all of this within a situational analysis which is capable of positioning the company within the broader industry and economic environment in which it must operate. Using the detailed analytical models at your disposal as well as some creativity and intuition, now is the time to step back from the detail of the case and consider where the company really is. The marketing audit data which reviewed the internal and external analysis of the organization can be developed further and now is the time to step back to one of the earlier writings in the marketing area, 'Marketing Myopia'. You should now have a much better idea about what the organization is able to do particularly well (competence), and the nature of the customer needs, wants and aspirations in the market being served. Looking at the problem from a customer rather than an internal perspective, can you decide what business the organization is in and what real competition faces – including substitutional competition? At this point it is essential to discuss your findings and your conclusions with colleagues. You will need a frank exchange at this point in order to sharpen your understanding of the real marketplace opportunities and threats which face the company.

Step 11 Decide the key issues. Discuss with colleagues.

There has to be a point at which the analysis stops, remember that no amount of analysis on its own – no matter how elegant – will be enough to achieve a pass mark in the examination. Decision is the only reason for carrying out analysis and we are now moving into that stage of the process.

If you have carried out your analysis properly then the key issues confronting the organization will start to become apparent. Further discussion with peers and colleagues will start to crystallize these key issues.

Step 12 Develop a mission statement. Discuss with colleagues.

The mission statement is a key element of any marketing strategy for any organization. A good mission statement is one which works for the organization. It should be clearly understood by everybody in the organization and should provide a focus for everyone's activity within the business.

A mission statement typically is unquantified but should do two things:

1   Clearly define what business the organization is in. In customer benefit rather than product terms.
2   State the organization's desired position within that business, for example biggest, most innovative, most recognized etc.

---

1   What is your company's mission statement?
2   What are the mission statements of your principal competitors?

ACTIVITY 10.2

Step 13 Decide broad aims. Discuss with colleagues.

This step takes the previous stage of the mission statement and develops it forward within the context of the case with which you are provided. Looking at where the organization is now and the mission statement of the organization, the broad aims would show how the organization might get from 'A' to 'B'.

The advantage of looking at broad aims at this stage is that you can get a clear and uncluttered view of the organization and its strategy before you take on detailed analysis of the data. Obviously broad aims have to capable of being turned into objectives and milestones at a later stage (with quantification and timings) but this step helps put the various data provided in the case into context. Remember that not all of the data will be useful to the organization and its strategy!

Step 14 Identify and analyse major problems. Develop and analyse alternative solutions. Discuss with colleagues.

Bearing in mind the work you have done on identifying the organization's mission statement and broad aims, your job now is to identify those key and major problems which may stand in the way of the organization achieving what it wants to achieve.

You would be well advised at this stage to try and differentiate between 'problems' and 'symptoms'. Look at all the apparent problems in the case and try and identify what are the major areas of concern (the strategic problems) that the organization needs to tackle and to solve in order to find a way forward. Before you jump to tackle what appear to be the biggest problems always look behind these to find out whether there isn't a bigger, more strategic, problem behind what are, in fact, just simply painful symptoms.

Remember, when you a look at a flat tyre, the puncture is not necessarily to be found where the tyre is flattest!

Step 15   Develop quantified and timescaled objectives. Discuss with colleagues.

Marketing, in common with all other business functions, requires objectives and timescales in order to control and monitor its activity. Now that you have identified the most likely mission statement for the organization and have identified its broad aims and its major (strategic) problems, you must decide what the marketing function now needs to take the organization forward in order to achieve its aims. Without objective timescales no one in the organization will know what needs to be done, by when it needs to be done and how we measure success or failure.

Your answer should clearly define and differentiate between corporate objectives and marketing objectives (this has been covered elsewhere) and also between objectives and strategies. Marketing is essentially about harnessing the resources and capabilities of the organization to satisfy its markets/customers needs. In other words the marketing activity will tend to revolve around products and markets and the marketing objective ought to be couched in these terms.

The best way to understand the difference between objectives and strategies, on the other hand, is to always remember that an objective is an aim or a goal and therefore should be preceded by the word 'to'. Strategy, on the other hand, is defined as the means by which the objective is to be achieved, it should always therefore be preceded by the word 'by'.

Tactics then cover all the rest of the day-to-day activity in the marketing function and include the whole range of marketing detail from research and development, new products, market research, advertising schedules, training etc. Remember that no matter how important these various tactical activities may appear on the day (or even in the case study) they are only tactics. To pass the analysis and decision case study successfully you need to be able to step back from these tactics to be able to take a broader view of the organization, its strategic situation and develop a strategic solution for the future.

Step 16   Consider alternative strategies and select those most appropriate. Discuss with colleagues.

Having decided on the most appropriate marketing objective for the organization described in the case, your next step is to decide the most appropriate way of achieving that objective. The Ansoff Matrix often provides the most useful first step in this process and, usually (leaving out diversification) market penetration, market development and product development, will normally contain the broad strategic approaches open to the organization. After Ansoff consider Porter or GEC McKinsey.

Remember that Ansoff is only a tool to be used and you should make your selection of the most appropriate strategy for the organization based on your understanding of the case and the problems facing senior management.

Too many examination failures are caused by candidates' apparent inability to take into consideration competitor activity when selecting from strategic alternatives. No organization exists or operates in a vacuum and competitors' strategic positions need to be analysed and understood. There are two important aspects of competitor analysis which need to be brought into play at this stage:

1   Predicting competitor strategic action. Where is the competition going – what are they likely to be doing and what do we believe their plans are for the future?
2   Competitor response. How is the competition likely to respond to any strategic activity on our part?

EXAM TIP

'Analysis Paralysis' can be dangerous. Don't become obsessed with the minute detail in the case. Look beyond this to what the data is telling you. Search for the 'Big Picture'.

Step 17 Draw up detailed tactical plans covering the marketing mix. Discuss with colleagues.

Now that you have a broad strategic option which you have discussed with colleagues and agreed is the most sensible way forward for the organization, you should be able to expand this strategic approach into a more detailed marketing plan covering the basic elements of the marketing mix. You should consider both McCarthy's 4P approach to the marketing mix (product, price, place and promotion) but also the extended marketing mix proposed by Booms and Bitner (product, price, place, promotion, people, process and physical evidence). The latter is especially useful when considering services organizations.

It is vitally important at this stage that your detailed tactical plans (the marketing mix) are seen to support completely the strategic approach which you have devised as a solution for this organization's problems. A marketing plan is only practical and useful if it takes the organization towards the achievement of its strategic objectives. Try not to get carried away at this stage by particularly large tactical problems facing the organization, nor your particular desire to develop an elegant promotional strategy for the business. Remember the analysis and decision case study will be testing candidates' ability to think strategically not just tactically.

Step 18 Draw up a market research plan and a marketing information system.

At this point in the process you should have started to uncover critical information gaps that face the organization and without which it will find moving towards its strategic objectives much more difficult. It is also important at this stage to differentiate between strategic research and tactical or operational research.

You may find that strategic marketing often requires information which is not normally covered in regular day-to-day tactical market research activities. Research of a strategic nature may cover items such as customer needs, market segmentation and competitor analysis as well as distribution channel availability and various internal performance measures.

At this stage you should be able to define clearly what information the organization needs to move forward – where it might be obtained and how it might be gathered. It is unlikely in the examination that you will be asked to present a detailed market research plan itself. However, you should be very conversant with the particular methodologies open to the business.

Step 19 Consider organizational issues and make recommendations for changes towards complete market orientation as felt necessary. Discuss with colleagues.

Here you should review the organization's structure and design with particular emphasis on its current ability to satisfy customer/market needs. Having developed a mission statement, broad aims, marketing objectives and strategies etc., you need to be looking at the organization to identify potential blockages which may stop management delivering on market needs.

Many organizations, of all types, tend to be organized along functional lines for their own internal efficiency and convenience. Often these hierarchical structures make delivering customer satisfaction quite difficult. What changes would you suggest to this structure?

The second important area under this step is to try and identify the level of market or customer orientation which exists in the business. To what extent do the people in the organization (in all the functions) understand that the customer is king? To what extent is the focus of the organization on the internal activities or on the external (market) activities? What changes would you suggest are made to make the organization more market and customer focused?

Step 20 Consider the organization's culture and make recommendations for internal marketing programmes as felt necessary. Discuss with colleagues.

If the culture is not customer focused how does this need to be changed? You should be aware of recent emphasis in the business literature on TQM, BS5750/ISO9000 and Re-engineering. These are all useful activities but only if customer focused. (Remember that BS5750/ISO9000 is all about efficiency of process and makes little or no mention of customers and customer needs!)

All organizations can say they are changing and can even make changes to managers' titles. Real culture change is a long and complicated process but often necessary. If culture change is a major issue in the organization described in the case how might you go about this process?

Step 21 Consider the financial and human resource implications of your plans/ recommendations. Discuss with colleagues.

Marketing does not operate in a vacuum – much as many marketers would like it to do so! Whatever strategies and plans you propose for the organization they will always have both financial and human resource implications. It is unreasonable and unprofessional not to predict and understand these implications fully before such strategic plans are proposed.

Financial implications: whatever activities the marketing function undertakes, including strategic plans for the future, the objective is always to improve the profitability of the organization. Marketing strategy is not about buying market share but improving longer term return on the organization's assets. At the very least you will be expected to understand the financial implications of your proposed strategy in terms of a small number of key financial measures – for example, what effects will it have on revenue, gross margins, costs and cash flow?

Human resource implications: nobody should ever forget that whatever an organization decides to do has to be carried out by people. Your proposed marketing strategy will have implications on the human resource function in an organization as well as the culture of the organization. Your strategy will probably have implications on the skill base required by the organization and may even require the acquisition of completely new skills. At the very least you should understand the implications of your proposals in terms of training and of longer term recruitment. Any such measures require time and money both of which will need to be budgeted.

Step 22 Assess costs and draw up indicative budgets. Discuss with colleagues.

A period of four weeks is given and it is felt this is sufficient time for you to uncover most reasonable costs of the actions and activities of which you are proposing. It is also expected that candidates will be able to develop an outline marketing budget and therefore will be able to cost their proposals fully. Advertising and promotion is often a major marketing cost but it is not the only one. Don't forget to allow for and budget for the other marketing costs which will be implied within your strategic proposition.

Step 23 Draw up schedules showing the timing/sequence of your plans/recommendations. Discuss with colleagues.

This stage allows you to build in some realism to your strategic proposals by working out just how long the various proposed activities are likely to take. In some instances case studies show a situation where time is of the essence, in other case studies the organization may be less pressed by competition and have time to plan more carefully for the future. Whichever case, your planning needs to incorporate this data.

Again, any strategic proposition needs to be accompanied by more than a simple promotional plan. There are likely to be a wide range of activities which you proposed and some will be dependent upon other activities before they can be started. Your schedules will need to cover all such activities including new product development, market research, internal recruitment and training as well as advertising and promotion.

Step 24 Specify review procedures and control mechanisms. Discuss with colleagues.

The detail of control mechanisms is discussed elsewhere. It is essential with any plan or strategic proposal that management understands exactly how progress towards (and deviation from) the strategy is both identified and corrective measures taken as required.

Here you will need to decide exactly which measures should be used to control the progress of the plan and how they will be used in detail. Remember, a plan without a control mechanism is not called a 'plan' – it is called a 'hope'.

Step 25   Outline contingency plans. Discuss with colleagues.

In the real world nothing ever goes to plan. It is the one thing we can be certain of! In the real world customers change, competition changes and organizations change and, however we see the world at the moment, is likely to have changed by the time any strategic proposals start to get implemented. Therefore it is useful at this stage to run one or two 'what?' scenarios to test the rigour of your strategic proposals. For example, in the Purbeck case what would be the scenario if the Government decided to levy VAT on motor insurance?

In the modern world, with its uncertainties, no plan is complete without contingency thinking and some level of contingency planning. Remember you are never quite sure what the additional information will be on the day!

Step 26   Review your complete marketing plan.

Now is the time to go right back to the beginning. Look at all the elements of your plan from analysis of the problem through mission statements, broad aims, marketing objectives and plans – do they all make sense when put together?

You must ensure that where you started and where you finished still makes sense given the structure and situation outlined in the case study. If your overall strategic selection was in the area of market development make sure that in developing your market plans you haven't spent most of your time talking about product development!

Step 27   Draw up your examination plan.

Now that you have completed the main thinking work and have discussed your thoughts with colleagues and refined your ideas in the light of their observations, it is time to plan carefully how to use your available resources between now and the day of the examination.

It is probably fair to say that one of the major reasons for failure in the case study is lack of examination technique. You have some four weeks between the time you get the case study and the examination. You should use this time carefully to prepare, analyse, view the situation from different angles and to share your observations with peers and colleagues. On the examination day you have but a scant 3 hours to incorporate the additional information into your thinking and your analysis and to get all your thoughts and explanations down on paper in a form that will acquire the maximum number of marks. You should talk to your tutors and your colleagues about exam technique but in the end there is no substitute for practice, practice and more practice. Two of the most recent cases have been included in this book for you to test your approach. Other cases are available from other sources. You are strongly advised to take the cases as dry-run experience and to time yourself. Time on the examination day is strictly limited so use it wisely.

Step 28   Practise writing in true report style.

The answers to the major case study are required to be written in business report format. There is a clear difference between report style and essay writing and you should practise to make sure that you are able to write in a clear report format. As with examination technique there is no substitute for practice.

The 28 step method is a good, if detailed, approach to the case study and is ideal when working with a group of other students. This method relies strongly on gathering feedback from others and modifying your approach in the light of contribution from peers. Unfortunately, not all candidates wish, or are able to analyse the case with others. Whenever possible you are urged to do so. If you cannot work in a group with others taking the exam you should try to enlist the help of someone else to talk over the case with. Maybe a friend or a colleague at work.

For those candidates who are not able to tackle the case in the group process, or who only have a short amount of time in which to do so, the second method may be more appropriate.

> **RECOMMENDED METHOD TWO**
> **SUMMARY OF THE 6-STEP METHOD**
>
> Step 1   Where are we now?
> Step 2   Where do we want to be?
> Step 3   How do we get there?
> Step 4   How can we make it happen?
> Step 5   How can we ensure arrival?
> Step 6   Putting it all together.

The process in detail is as follows:

Step 1   Where are we now?

Begin with detailed audits and analysis of the case material to establish the current position as described. You should be able to produce a succinct summary highlighting the key strengths, weaknesses, and constraints affecting the organization.

Step 2   Where do we want to be?

At this stage you should critically review the organization's mission, forecasts of likely future demand, objectives and be able to calculate gaps in achieving the set goals. At the end of this stage you should be able to produce a short statement of objectives for the organization, quantified over time. These could be illustrated by market, product, image, activity and competitive gap analyses.

Step 3   How do we get there?

Step 3 involves identifying alternative ways (strategies) that the organization might have of achieving the objectives which it has set. You should also consider the key criteria for selection between these strategies – and you should make a choice. Once completed you should be able to write a brief summary of the organization's 'strategic intent'. Typically this could be illustrated by models such as Ansoff and positioning maps.

Step 4   How can we make it happen?

This step takes the analysis into the tactical and operational level of planning. Developing your strategic thinking into areas such as product policy, pricing, distribution, promotions, finance and organizational design. At the end of this stage you should be able to draft an outline marketing plan to support your choice of strategy.

Step 5   How can we ensure arrival?

This stage will include the important control measures required to monitor and modify (if required) the implementation of the plans. You should consider aspects such as budgets, timescales, management and marketing information systems and contingency planning. You should consider both financial and non-financial controls. Your report at this stage might include budgets, gantt charts and cash-flow forecasts to support the implementation of your proposed plan.

Step 6   Putting it all together.

This final step is essential. Although we have broken down the strategic process into separate steps, these are only to permit us to understand better how to approach the problem. The customer may be effected by our activities in different audits and in different situations. For the customer the presentation must be seamless. At this stage you must review the steps above from the customer's point of view. Does it make sense? When it is implemented will it appear sensible? Do all the plans/actions piece together in a way that makes sense to the marketplace? Will the totality of the approach make this a more attractive proposition than the competition?

If not you may need to modify elements at different steps. Marketing is an iterative process.

How to answer the case

The marketing strategy, analysis and decision paper is examined as a three hour 'open book' case study examination. Open book means you may take as much material into the examination room as you please to include pre-prepared material and text books in order to help you frame your answer. If you have any precise questions about what is allowed in the examination and what isn't you are advised to check with the CIM or your local tutors. You should remember though that open books examinations are not always the great boon that they appear to be. Three hours is a limited time and the more information and data which you take in with you the more time you could waste looking through it to find the last final quote or analysis that you require. It is far better to carry out analysis prior to the examination and take in a clearly marked binder or folder with all the pages that you might need in predetermined order.

Whilst the open book examination allows you to take in additional materials, you are expressly forbidden to append materials to your script which have not been produced during the examination on paper provided by the CIM invigilator. Any prepared pages or appended material will be treated as invalid by the examiners.

Read the questions and the additional information carefully: as soon as you see the paper on the day take time to read the questions carefully and the additional information to find out what new perspectives this might throw on the case and the analysis which you have carried out on the case prior to the examination. Remember the additional information can carry marks up to 20 per cent of the total for its inclusion in the answer so don't throw this opportunity away. Once you have read the questions re-read them another second and third time to make sure that you understand exactly what the examiner is asking from you in your separate answers to the various sections. Remember that examiners are not trying to trick you or mislead you with the questions but often a degree of anxiety makes interpreting the plainest of English a problem. Take your time.

Make notes   before you start to write the answer proper look at each of the questions in turn and the additional information and carefully plan out your answer to each one of the questions. Make sure that your answer follows a logical flow of argument and that it answers the question as stated as completely as possible. Make sure that wherever feasible you have managed to incorporate additional information into your answer. Once you have done this, review your notes and find out whether anything is missing and whether you need to add any additional thoughts at this stage. Now you may be ready to write.

Take on the role   in the case study you will have already been assigned a role to play, this might be as an internal manager or an external consultant. You are strongly advised to take the role and to frame your answer from this persons point of view.

Write in report format   if you have been successful and spent at least 15–20 minutes at the beginning of the examination understanding clearly and precisely what the questions are asking from you and you have made copious and logically ordered notes you should now be ready to start writing in clear, concise report format. Report format is not the same as essay writing and requires a logical flow of arguments and the use of headings and sub-headings wherever possible to support the sequence of argument. Clearly, logically thought out notes and a planned answer will make the report writing of the examination a fairly straightforward task.

While we are on the subject there are a number of things that you should certainly NOT do when answering the examination. If you wish to pass the examination the following should be noted:

Don't start writing as soon as you open the question paper.

Don't ignore all the planning and analysis which you carried out prior to the exam.

Don't write out the questions on the answer paper again (it just wastes more time).

Don't simply re-state the data contained within the case study.

Don't write pages and pages of essay text unbroken by headings.

Don't submit pages and pages of analysis (decisions gain marks).

Don't write beyond the allotted time on each question.

Don't forget to leave five minutes at the end of the examination to check your answer all the way through.

Don't run out of time.

Don't panic!

Trends in the examination

As with all areas of contemporary marketing, the analysis and decision case study tries hard to keep up to date with modern developments in the field. Since there is no set syllabus for the case study you can of course take advantage of many new developments and incorporate them easily into the required answers. Senior examiners also change over time but this should influence the tone of the case study less than the development of academic and practitioner thinking in the area of marketing generally. There are a number of key areas where the case study has changed over recent years and will continue to develop in the future. The following are worth noting:

Longer term thinking Despite a current emphasis on financially driven shorter term thinking, strategy is about the longer term. Managers must think beyond the short-term financial drivers of an organization and must have a clear driving vision or mission statement that looks at least five years forward. The case study will be looking for answers which take into account this longer term view and have a good understanding of what the organization needs to do in a longer time frame.

Financial awareness It is true to say that in the past one major criticism levelled at marketers was that they tended to be financially illiterate. If marketing is ever to achieve its destiny in organizations then it is clear that financial awareness is a skill that marketers simply have to acquire. The analysis and decision case study will continue to contain more and more searching financial analyses of an organization's situation and successful candidates will need to demonstrate a clear understanding of financial matters.

Organizational implications Apart from finance, human resource is a key area which will be affected by and will affect marketing strategy. Human resource is a key element in every organization and having the right people and organizational structure can often make the difference between a successful marketing strategy and a failure. Marketers in the future will need to be much more aware of the human resource implications of their proposed strategy as well as the role of people in implementing strategy into the marketplace.

Internationalization The world is shrinking, globalization is a major issue, fewer and fewer organizations are now able to survive in a purely local market facing local competition only. The UK is not outside but is a full member of the European Union (EU) and, as we move slowly towards a single market, European marketing will start to become the norm rather than the exception.

The importance of customers As the British and European economies continue to realign from the 1980s to the new realities of the 1990s it is clear that a major factor in organization success in the future will be the ability of senior management to focus their attention on customer needs as well as internal cost control and efficiency drives. Marketing strategy needs to be at the forefront of this movement and must ensure that the development of strategy is based on clearly defined and understood customer need. Scientific marketing, modelling and analysis are useful tools but are no substitute for empathy with our customers.

From analysis to decision Now that the two papers covering Strategic Marketing, Planning and Control and Analysis and Decision are both required compulsory papers for every candidate wishing to obtain the diploma, it has become easier to refine more closely the focus and objective of each paper. The Analysis and Decision paper will, in the future, concentrate much more on the practical application of marketing strategy within the real business world. All candidates should note that the use of marketing theory and analysis, no matter how eloquent and accurate, will not be sufficient to obtain a pass mark in the case study examination. The examiners place their emphasis clearly on the application of theory rather than simple analysis and this focus can be expected to increase over the coming years.

Trends in marketing

As the case study has no formal syllabus to follow it makes it a relatively easy task to incorporate new ideas and thinking into the appropriate case answers. For example, there has been much talk over recent years about issues such as 'quality', 're-engineering/business process redesign' and 'relationship marketing'. Wherever relevant to the case study in question, candidates should always attempt to bring this latest thinking into their answers and apply it in a relevant and practical manner.

A note of caution, however, needs to be made at this point. There is a difference between modern marketing thinking and management 'fads'. Answers to a case study which content themselves with a long exposé on the benefits of re-engineering (just because it happens to be current in the candidate's organization) are unlikely to gain a pass grade. If re-engineering or relationship marketing, for example, are seen as relevant activities given the overall approach proposed in a marketing strategy then they should be included – but always in context.

Past cases

This unit concludes with the two most recent case studies, Purbeck Financial Services and the Australian Tourist Commission. You are urged to use these two cases as practical, timed 'dry runs' for the case study you will face in your examination.

Since there is never a right or a wrong answer to a case study the cases and questions have been included as they were presented to candidates in 1994 but, rather than a specimen answer, each case has been followed by a series of notes against which you should mark your own answer. These notes are intended for guidance only but cover the main points which you should have included in your answer.

Case study

Purbeck Financial Services

PURBECK FINANCIAL SERVICES

CANDIDATES' BRIEF

You are Neil Hammond, the recently appointed Marketing Manager of Purbeck Motor Insurance, a division of Purbeck Financial Services. You report directly to the Sales Director who sits on the divisional board.

Before joining Purbeck you had previously worked as Deputy Marketing Planning Manager with a European multinational company in the consumer durables business.

You took up your position some three months ago in what is, to all intents and purposes, a newly created role. There had, previously, been a Publicity Manager reporting to the Sales Director but her role had related almost exclusively to the development of publicity material, brochures, advertisements, direct mail activities and other support functions.

Your working relationship with the Sales Director is good, although both of you have been trying separately to get to grips with the nature of the motor insufance business and Purbeck's particular position within it. Most of your colleagues are long-time Purbeck employees with many years of experience about what works and what doesn't in this particular industry.

Purbeck's Chief Executive, Gordon McRae, who chairs all of Purbeck's divisional boards, has asked you to prepare a presentation for the Motor Insurance Division's board meeting on 21st June. He emphasised that he would want you "to give an outsider's considered view of the division's position before you become absorbed by the culture". While, of necessity, you have had to look after your day-to-day workload, you have started to put together enough information to make the presentation. In doing so, you have talked with and/or had meetings with a good number of people, including Gordon McRae and Christopher Purbeck the Group's Chairman.

This case material is based upon actual organisations and existing market conditions. However the information provided and the real data has been significantly changed to preserve commercial confidentiality. Candidates are strictly instructed not to contact companies in the industry, and are advised that some additional information will be provided at the time of the examination.

The whole of this case study is copyright material, jointly held by the Chartered Institute of Marketing and Winchester Marketing Group and no part of it may be reproduced in any form without prior permission being obtained in writing.

Copies may be obtained from the Chartered Institute of Marketing, Moor Hall, Cookham, Maidenhead, Berkshire, SL6 9QH.

Neil Hammond stood by the window of his seventh floor office, gazing down at the cars in their apparently effortless and endless flow round the busy roundabout below. This time, he was not so much seeing, as looking without noticing - his mind was elsewhere.

As Purbeck's new Marketing Manager, he had plenty on his mind. He had spent his last few years working in a planning role in a very different industry. It seemed like a lifetime ago, or just yesterday, depending how you looked at it. Either way, he had some of the most serious decisions still to make and little time to reach his conclusions before presenting them to the Board.

As his mind nagged away at the core issues, his attention was suddenly drawn back to the road beneath him. With a screech of tyres, a Volvo estate managed to avoid colliding with a yellow, rather aged Ford Escort which had suddenly turned left across its path. Either unaware of the near miss or only too anxious to keep going, the Escort disappeared in a haze of blue exhaust fumes down the road to Horsham. The Volvo driver, adrenalin no doubt still pumping, sat stationary for a full thirty seconds before rejoining the traffic stream - but not before two cars, neither of whom had witnessed the accident, had blown their horns and another driver had shouted abuse through his open window. For Neil, it was a microcosm of his new world.

PURBECK FINANCIAL SERVICES

The business that was to become Purbeck Financial Services was founded in 1922 by two friends, Andy Downs and John Purbeck, as Downs, Purbeck & Partners Ltd, insurance brokers. During the 1920s and 1930s, while his colleague sold general insurance, such as house and contents insurance, John Purbeck had concentrated on the growing potential of the motor insurance business, as the number of drivers and cars expanded rapidly. At the time, motoring for many was still an enthusiast's activity and motoring organisations and associations sprang up to organise rallies, meetings and occasions for motorists to share their newfound pleasures and experiences. An early contact with a group of enthusiasts who had formed a motoring association called the Government Service Motoring Organisation (GSMO) had led to twenty-four of its members using Downs, Purbeck & Partners as their motor insurance brokers. Since Downs, Purbeck received 15% commission from the insurance companies that they placed the business with, John was a happy man.

1

This unexpected sale was to have a long term effect on the whole future development of the business. John Purbeck devoted his energies to first finding and then selling his services to membership of "affinity" groups like the GSMO. In each case he sought ways of becoming the "preferred supplier" and to establish good and close continuing relationships with both the associations' officers and, through the service he gave, their members. As a result, as membership grew, so did his business. His reputation with the GSMO gave him access to a number of trade unions, especially in the public sector - such as local government and the teaching profession, who saw the offer of a specialist insurance service as another benefit they could offer to their membership. They were also quick to see that by sharing some of Purbeck's commission they could create a valuable income stream for their organisations.

Andy Downs, who had looked after the firm's general customers, left the business in the early 1930s to take over his father's estate in Scotland. John Purbeck continued to concentrate on his affinity groups, but now offered a more complete range of insurance service products.

After the Second World War, the GSMO asked Purbeck Insurance Ltd - as the firm had now become known - to offer financial assistance to its members who wished to purchase motor cars. Purbeck obliged and formed Highton Securities Ltd to offer such help. This tentative step into banking and finance was to establish a precedent and between 1950 and 1985, Purbeck was to move into an increasing range of financial service products including life assurance. In 1982, its name was changed to Purbeck Financial Services Ltd, but motor insurance remained a crucial part of the organisation and its original customers, and many others, remained loyal.

In 1993, 314,000 GSMO members and 104,000 public service trade union members insured their vehicles through Purbeck. However, the total number of members in the associations and affinity groups with whom Purbeck now sustained a continuing relationship was 4,310,000 and this suggested that there was still a good deal of room for penetrating the existing customer base.

According to Christopher Purbeck, the present company's Chairman and nephew of one of the founders, the business's success was the result of carefully nurtured personal relationships between the "sponsors" or "affinity groups" and Purbeck - one that had to be worked at and maintained at all levels of management. He personally spent a great deal of time with the Chairmen and senior officers of the various associations who formed Purbeck's core customer base and felt that this both kept

2

him close to the customer and alert to any failings in Purbeck's service levels. "The great advantage is that we have a number of clearly identified people with whom we can keep close contact - the Group's or Association's officials - and a very identifiable body of existing and potential buyers who have quite a lot in common. They are accessible to us and know about us. The other thing is that we do not need a High Street presence and all the difficulty of trying to pull people in off the street - instead we can operate through direct marketing from an inexpensive location."

Gordon McRae, Purbeck's Chief Executive, was however quick to point out that since the whole group handled some 10 million internal or external insurance-related "transactions" a year it was very dependent for its profitability on cost-effectiveness. In fact, these transactions represented the servicing of 660,000 individual customers each of whom purchased an average of 1.1 products each. On average therefore there were 15 transactions each year for each customer and this yielded around £11 in pre-tax profit per customer average for the group. In his view, as a broker, Purbeck was "a high-volume and low-margin business and that was the critical issue - even more true of the motor business as it was of the whole Group". He was also concerned that Purbeck was awkwardly dependent on a relatively small number of big "customers" and this made the personal relationships sometimes more important than business issues.

Purbeck's origins and success were reflected in its Mission Statement which stated that it wished to be "The natural first choice provider of financial and insurance services to membership groups, of whatever kind, in such a way that the delivery of our service is an integral benefit to that membership." This, in turn, had led to the development of a set of Corporate objectives:

"Purbeck seeks to:

- retain and enhance our "Affinity Group" customer base

- expand our ability to cross-sell

- add real and genuine value to our customers' members

- extend the penetration of our existing products and services

- develop at least one conspicuously different new product/service each year

3

- continue our emphasis on cost efficiency"

Its strategic targets were defined as follows:

"We will:

- increase our "individual" customer base by 70% over five years

- increase average products sold per customer to 1.7

- increase average profitability to £15 per customer"

Purbeck believed that their core brand values were "friendliness, integrity, exclusivity and quality". There was little question but that Purbeck had been successful. By 1993 the group as a whole employed 1,700 people, had a turnover of £58 million and annual profits (before tax) of around £7,500,000. John Purbeck's strategy had worked well.

THE MOTOR INSURANCE BUSINESS

Purbeck are insurance brokers, the dominant distribution channel for motor insurance - a business currently worth some £6.8 billion a year in premiums. In the 1970s, brokers had accounted for around 70% of the premiums placed, with the remaining 30% being handled by other agents, such as the direct sales force of some of the large insurers, like Prudential. During the 1980s, the brokers' market share started to decline, as insurers won a greater proportion of their business direct. By the mid 1980s, the high street insurance brokers' share had fallen to 60%.

The main types of motor insurance cover are as follows.

1) Comprehensive (which means that in the event of an accident, for which the insured was to blame, both the insured's and the other driver's car are covered by the insured's policy)

2) Non-Comprehensive. This broke down into two further forms:

Third Party, Fire and Theft (which means that in the event of an accident, for which the insured was to blame, only the other driver's car is covered by the insured's policy. However in the event of accidental fire or theft, the insured's car is covered for loss)

- Third Party only (which means that in the event of an accident, for

4

which the insured was to blame, only the other driver's car is covered by the insured's policy. Nor is the insured's car covered in the event of accidental fire or theft)

In the UK, Third Party insurance is a legal requirement. Around 72% of those who insured themselves bought comprehensive cover.

CHANGES IN THE MOTOR INSURANCE MARKET

From the mid 1980s, the brokers' share of the market fell further until, by 1992, it represented only 45% of the market. The insurers' share of sales made direct had grown. When added to sales now being made through new channels such as garages and motor manufacturers (with new car sales) and banks and building societies, they accounted for 40% market share. The most impressive new entrants, the "direct writers" - that is organisations who established themselves as insurance companies (such as Arrowhead and Keystone) underwriting their own risks, but dealing with the public direct rather than through an intermediary (such as Arrowhead and Keystone) - had taken a 15% share.

During the mid 1980s, these direct writers, led by Arrowhead, had been seen as an irrelevance by both insurance companies and brokers alike, because the market believed that motor insurance products could only be sold over the telephone to a limited number of consumers. They were also quick to point out that the direct writers were only underwriting a narrow range of policies - for instance, for individuals aged 35-50 driving a limited group of car models.

Conventional industry wisdom was certain that products sold down the phone were hard to differentiate. In particular, the time span spent in client contact was dramatically less and it was hard to make the "experience" memorable. Brokers, who often had a High Street presence, felt that they provided a personal service.

The brokers' regular procedure was to use a panel of selected insurers who supplied them with "rating" questions to help assess the risk involved in each individual purchase. These rating questions had to be standard for the panel system to work. The broker completed the questions for each new customer and then used an on-line service to obtain quotes from the insurers. These were then provided to the potential consumer.

From the insurance companies' point of view, the standardisation of this approach precluded them from introducing new questions which, in turn, made it difficult for them to refine their underwriting. They all received

5

the same information and had to make their own assessment of the risk - based on experience - and then quote appropriately. A good broker would normally know which insurer would offer the best price on which risk. Over time there had been little pressure for change in the way things were done and the industry had a sense of stability about it.

The perception that consumers much preferred to deal face to face with their existing broker was gradually broken as it became clear that they were, after all, happy to deal with their insurer directly, over the phone. The ability to handle the client direct, and therefore carefully refine the ratings, meant that the direct writers could revolutionise the underwriting process. Arrowhead were able to ask far more detailed questions than a standard panel insurer and, by using good information systems, test their ratings' assumptions on a continuous basis. This, in turn, gave them the ability to revise their rates immediately, based on actual live experience rather than previous experience. In fact, it soon became apparent that it had moved the nature of the business from risk assessment, which the other insurance companies had to do (based on standard rating questions) to risk management: setting rates by analysing real time results. Arrowhead were able to introduce new questions, test results and revise rates at will and almost instantly. Its IT systems, new in comparison to the rest of the industry, and set up with this end in mind, were capable of fast adjustment and quick information feedback.

At first, this risk management approach was again dismissed because the industry argued that it would take large numbers of customers to make it effective, whereas initially Arrowhead restricted its customer base by limiting those whom they would underwrite. In fact, although they had intentionally picked low risk groups to start off with, the refinements it were able to apply through new IT systems and sophisticated software gradually enabled them to extrapolate its experience to increasingly wider groups of motorists, without meeting the forecast difficulties.

Arrowhead's approach also reduced costs. It did not need retail sites, of itself a considerable saving which was further enhanced by its ability to find labour and premises in low cost areas. Arrowhead was also able to extend the working day or week thus allowing those consumers with little time to spare during the working day to call on the telephone in the evening or at weekends. Its low fixed costs enabled Arrowhead to segment the market, be selective and turn down unattractive business - something brokers would have liked to do but never actually did, because there was always pressure to cover costs by bringing in new premiums.

6

Overall, direct writers, like Arrowhead were able to pass on the benefits to customers either through enhanced service or reduced pricing - or any combination of either.

Some in the market felt that the Automobile Association, who operated as a broker, had softened up the market for them by greater use of the telephone in offering motor insurance policies and dealing with their customers. Whatever the reason, there was, by 1993, little doubt that the direct writers had affected the market significantly. Research showed that since 1989, the level of "shopping around" that consumers did had increased by 300% and Purbeck's own research suggested that over 30% of their existing customer base now shopped around annually.

Arrowhead advertised in all main media, including posters and television. It had invested heavily in brand awareness from the start using a variety of direct marketing techniques. In 1993, its marketing spend was £4 million - representing 1% of gross turnover. When Arrowhead first entered the market, it took four years of renewals before a new customer paid back his or her acquisition cost. By 1993, Arrowhead were able to write off its acquisition cost in one year.

An initial belief that Arrowhead would fall down on its claims operation also proved to be ill-founded. Its new IT systems enabled them to respond well on two fronts. For their own benefit, they were able to run a sophisticated claims checking procedure, built up on experience. This enabled them to judge that, for example, a car theft from a public house carpark in Newcastle on a Saturday night might be a fraud and would merit being checked, while damage to a Range Rover on a farm gate in Hampshire was cheaper to pay out than investigate. From the customers' point of view, the speed with which they handled claims was impressive. Other insurers and brokers told stories of receiving letters from Arrowhead referring to an incident in the same post that they received the first notification of a claim from their own policyholder. Familiarity with using the phone and Arrowhead's same day response made a fast combination - and customers seemed to like it.

Arrowhead's success by the end of the 1980s and into the 90s had drawn a number of other direct writers into the market, including Keystone and GMP. By 1991, two of the large composite insurance companies, Kestrel Direct and Colonial Linkline, had opened "direct" operations, and others such as Basilica, Mercury & General and Mercantile Exchange were either planning to enter the market direct or extend their existing, and

7

rather limited, direct selling operations. Other brokers, such as AA Autoquote and Bradstock had national coverage and significant market share.

Industry forecasts varied, but Arrowhead forecast that it would have a 20% market share by the year 2000 and many felt that the direct writers as a whole would hold 35% of the market by that time, even though they had not existed twenty years earlier.

PURBECK MOTOR INSURANCE

As he had stood looking down at the roundabout, Neil's mind had been running through some of the key issues that had surfaced during his various meetings and discussions.

There was no doubt that Purbeck had strong loyalty among its consumer base within the affinity groups, indeed other brokers envied its reputation and standing. Inroads by competitors were only likely to be through pricing, but market research suggested that this was not the over-riding criterion, once consumers had experienced the package of services that Purbeck offered. The number of members of the various groups who were not yet Purbeck consumers seemed to indicate that it would be valuable to address the membership more directly. This would require sensitive management so that excellent "sponsor" relationships were maintained simultaneously. The various groups' committees and officials jealously guarded their roles and sought to protect their members from being sold to too hard. Another problem with this approach was that Purbeck was unable to focus, because it had to take most of the business which came out of the affinity groups - in the interest of maintaining good and successful relations. This contrasted strongly with Arrowhead's current ability to "cherry-pick".

As he saw it, the greatest difficulty was the need to expand outside the existing customer base. After years of keeping a low profile and building long-term loyalty among its "affinity group" customers, awareness of Purbeck was practically non-existent among the general public. A number of different brokers had, over time, moved into other affinity groups and Neil imagined that they would be as hard to dislodge as Purbeck would be in its sponsor groups - and new affinity groups were hard to find.

So, to expand its customer base as proposed within Purbeck's corporate objectives, it might need to approach the broader market-place and, more difficult, to identify new market segments. Particularly ones which contained the key characteristic of being prepared to purchase by direct

8

communication. Growth would need to be achieved by promoting Purbeck to this larger market because if Purbeck was not "on the shopping list" at the time of purchase, it could not expect to win new customers.

While seeking growth in new markets, Purbeck would need to ensure high degrees of customer retention. This meant that lapse rates (the rate at which customers ceased their existing policies or failed to renew) would need to be watched carefully. Better and more focused communications would need to be developed alongside any image building campaign. Market research appeared to indicate that consumers with more than one product or service from the same company were more loyal. Cross-selling was therefore a two-fold opportunity.

When Neil had spoken with Christopher Purbeck, he had seemed most worried about the rise of the new phenomenon, the "direct writers", who appeared to be changing the nature of the market for motor insurance and therefore potentially challenging the basic strength and core competitive advantage around which Purbeck had centred its success for some seventy years. He saw the effect of the direct writers success as two-fold. The market had become much more price sensitive and motor insurance was seen increasingly as a commodity product. In his view, the extension of the number of direct writers had simply meant that the customer has placed himself in the broker's role and now phoned around himself for the best product or price. After the conversation with Christopher Purbeck, Neil had pondered what he had said. He was less sure that it was a commodity market; from his previous experience of consumer durables, he knew that consumers did not always buy on price. Perhaps instead of it becoming a commodity market it was simply that the buyer of motor insurance was becoming more sophisticated.

It was the need to respond to this threat, by becoming a low-cost provider, that had caused Gordon McRae, in a separate discussion to emphasise the need for new systems and processes which maintained and enhanced service quality but ensured cost reduction. McRae clearly felt that the implications of being in a commodity market were that it was vital to become a low-cost producer, exploiting all and any economies of scale that were possible to find. This, in turn made size a crucial issue. He believed that operating direct, using telecommunications as a distribution channel, was one way of achieving growth and economies at the same time.

Neil was also aware that a body of opinion was forming at Purbeck that in effect, it was already a "direct writer", who simply re-insured 100% of

9

its business (by putting it out to other insurers). If that was so, should it start to think and act like Arrowhead? The leading proponent of this line of argument repeatedly stated the fact that in the United States nine of the top ten motor insurers were direct writers and that between them they controlled 55% of the US market.

If this was the case, mused Neil, then Purbeck would have to change its current marketing approach pretty quickly. At which point the near collision between the yellow Escort and the Volvo had occurred beneath him and Neil's attention had been brought back to the present. Only the night before, he had been talking to a friend who had just bought a Volvo. Apparently the friend had been offered a very good deal by the garage in terms of something called Volvo Owner's Insurance backed by one of the large insurers. It had been quite a sophisticated package and Neil's friend had said more than once that price wasn't the only factor.

Back at his desk, Neil picked up the file of background information that he had collected ...

NEIL'S FILE CONTENTS

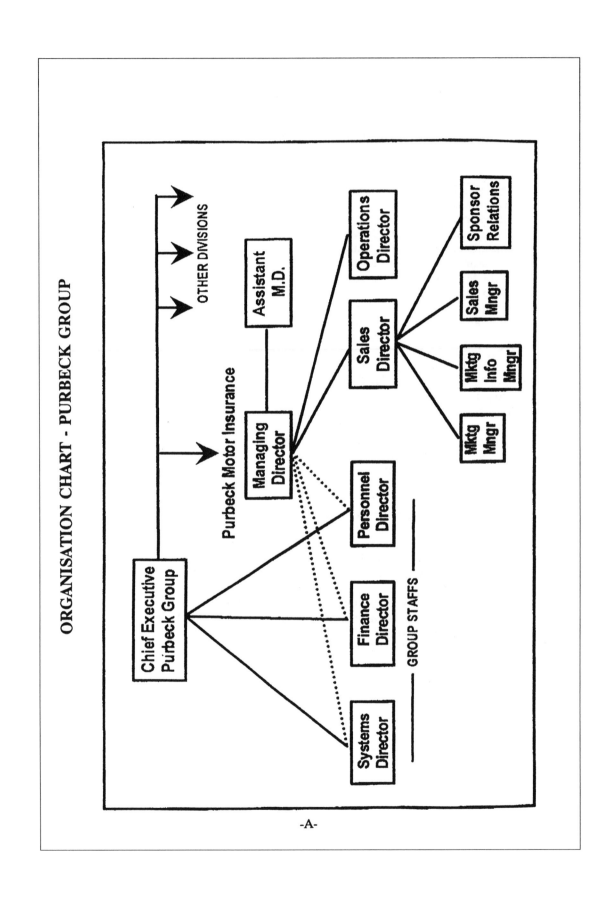

ORGANISATION CHART - PURBECK GROUP

-A-

PURBECK MOTOR INSURANCE - KEY FINANCIAL DATA

MOTOR INSURANCE	1993	1992	1991	1990
(£,000)				
Commission	23591	21271	16828	15018
Other Income	2333	1850	1664	1130
Total Income	25924	23121	18492	16148
Staff	10111	9248	7767	7105
Marketing	1296	925	592	436
Mail/phone/comms	2074	1618	1110	969
Computing	1037	763	573	44
Other	7259	6474	4993	4199
Total Expense	21777	19028	15035	13193
PBT	4147	4093	3457	2955
Staff Numbers	953	902	769	715
Portfolio Size (,000)	599	566	533	519
Average Premium (£)	267	243	206	179

PURBECK PRODUCT PORTFOLIO

Motor insurance
Buildings insurance
Contents insurance
Health insurance
Travel insurance
Pensions
Life assurance
Endowments
Retirement advice

and through Highton Securities:

Personal loans
Secured loans
Savings accounts
Deposit accounts
Continuous credit accounts
Credit card accounts

234

MEMORANDUM   24 March 1994

TO: NEIL HAMMOND

FROM: JOHN BAKEWELL
           MARKET RESEARCH

You were asking at the meeting the other day about what priorities the
consumer places on what elements of the decision making process. I
promised to look out the research we did eighteen months ago.

In fact, the priority they give to things changes depending on whether
they are buying for the first time or renewing, after having had some
experience of us (this can involve any form of contact - including making
a claim). The following are the priorities the research threw up:

New Business	**Those with experience of us**
Price (cheapest?)	Service Issues
Reputable	Price (value for money)
Service Issues	People
People	Reputable
Product	Product

It is interesting to note that product issues are the lowest in terms of
priority to the consumer.

The research also showed that consumers want a company that:

-       offers service (with a capital 'S')
-       pays claims quickly
-       treats the consumer fairly
-       has a good reputation or is one that they already deal with

Hope this helps

John Bakewell

-D-

MEMO

TO: Neil Hammond, Marketing Manager

FROM: Colin Jenkins, Assistant to the Managing Director

12 APRIL 1994

THE FUTURE ENVIRONMENT

Following your request last week for some broad figures on the future environment for Purbeck, I have looked through several reports on the Motor Industry and relevant Press Articles and noted down various figures below. Without knowing exactly what you want it is difficult to know if I have covered the aspects you were particularly interested in. If I can be any further help don't hesitate to let me know.

Best wishes

Colin Jenkins

THE FUTURE ENVIRONMENT FOR THE MOTOR INSURANCE INDUSTRY

1. INSURANCE MARKET VALUE

Expenditure by UK households on all types of insurance has increased at a rate well above inflation (RPI) since 1983. Some of this increase will be due to increased product ownership, but a significant amount will be from the substantial rating increases experienced by the market generally. Based on the Central Statistical Office, predictions for UK households (on which average annual expenditure is based) the total annual insurance market value stood at £17,370 million in 1991.

2. TRENDS AND ASSUMPTIONS IN NEW TARGET MARKETS

2.1. Employment Trends

Purbeck's existing affinity groups provide a potential audience of over 3.4 million consumers of whom just over 2.5 million are in employment, the rest are retired from their respective industries. Although certain industry sectors are experiencing a reduction in employee numbers the net effect of changes has produced a fairly balanced target audience over a seven year period (1985 - 1991). However it is generally agreed that the public and quasi-public sectors are undergoing significant reorganisation and will most probably decrease in size, but even a 10% decrease in employed numbers would still provide a potential target audience of over 3 million consumers.

However, the recession has had an effect on consumer confidence. All the Confederation of British Industry figures suggest a slow but fragile improvement, but it would not take much to knock it and the gradual fall in unemployment off the rails. It is expected that Purbeck's target markets will be affected in the same way as the rest of the UK community, and there is every likelihood that the public service market will be hit harder than the rest of the UK unemployment market especially when we consider the existing/planned:

-       local government expenditure capping

-       tight limits on public expenditure

- continuing health service reforms

- redundancies among organisations privatised in last five years

- further privatisation plans.

2.2 Motor Vehicle Ownership

The number of motor insurance policies in the UK is determined by the number of privately registered cars and the number of UK households with the regular use of a car. A couple of graphs are attached. As can be seen, the number of privately registered motor vehicles has increased steadily over the past 10 years with the accelerated growth in the late 80s tailing off in 1991. This tail-off is forecast to continue for the near future. The annual growth for private vehicle ownership had fallen from a 1988 high of over 5 % to a level of 1% in 1991.

The number of households with regular use of a car must also influence the motor insurance market. Based on the 1992 JICNARS data of 22.7 million households in the UK, with some 70% having a motor vehicle, we can see that approximately 15.6 million households have to purchase motor insurance. These 15.6 million households account for 17.8 million vehicles. Based on current trends, by 1995 16.6 million households will own 18.9 million private vehicles.

The cost of motor insurance has risen significantly over the last 20 years, premiums rose steadily until 1987 and then took a strong turn upwards. Current market expenditure stands close to £300 per insurance policy per annum; it is felt that the cyclical nature of the motor insurance market will lead to a slowing of the rate of premium increase - the market is back in alignment - with average premiums only reaching approximately £370 by 1997. Of course, this could well change if a couple of bad sets of results are turned in by the large insurers. All in all, consumers in Purbeck's target market can most probably look forward to a stabilising of their premiums over the next 4 - 5 years.

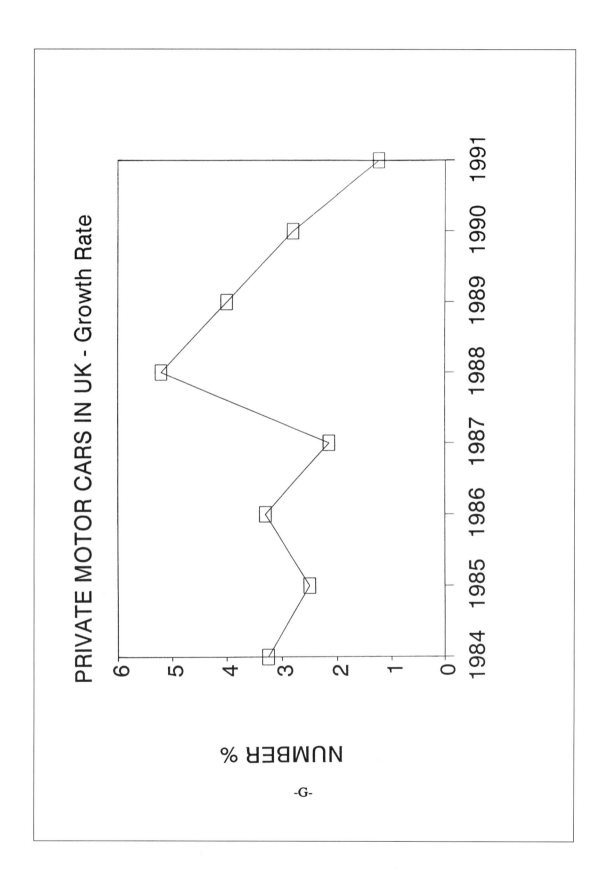

PRIVATE MOTOR CARS IN UK - Growth Rate

NUMBER %

-G-

239

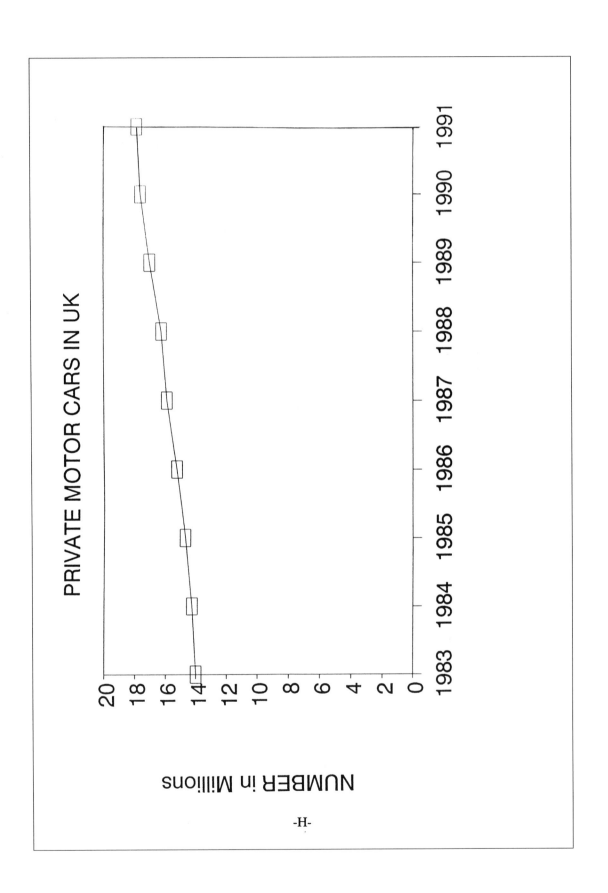

PRIVATE MOTOR CARS IN UK

MEMO

22 April 1994

TO: NEIL HAMMOND

FROM: CHRIS TAYLOR
             MOTOR SALES

OTHER KEY PLAYERS IN THE AFFINITY MARKET

You asked me to hunt out who else among the brokers were active in the "Affinity Group" market. The following all sell motor insurance to different affinity groups:

MILLS, SABLE

BULLRING

BLAIR PATTERSON

TE BEXLEY

CHERRY, ASH & LORD

Others who currently do not offer motor but do sell health, life or household insurance include:

RUSHMORE

GARDINERS

STEWART MUIR

We believe we are prominent in all categories but are the market leader in motor insurance to affinity groups. However, as you probably know, almost all of these others are very sizeable players - larger in most cases than us - its just that they have not concentrated as much as we have on this area.

Chris Taylor

-I-

22 April 1994

TO: NEIL HAMMOND

FROM: WENDY JONES

MARKET RESEARCH STATISTICS

You asked the other day for some background data. Attached are:

1) Competitive Market Shares for Private Cars. I cannot get figures for AA Autoquote or Bradstock, since both are brokers and therefore do not have to publish figures publicly. Also, the figures are somewhat out of date, being for 1991.

2) The growth of the direct writers. These are up to 1992 and show us in comparison to Arrowhead, Keystone and GMP both in terms of number of policies issued and the % annual growth.

3) Comparative Spontaneous Awareness. This was the result of some research which we conducted in 1993 among members of various of our affinity groups and the general public. I am afraid the figures for us look bad in the last category.

Wendy

COMPETITIVE MARKET SHARE 1992 - Private Cars

COMPANY	NUMBER OF VEHICLES	GROSS PREMIUM INCOME £M	AVERAGE PREMIUM £
AA Autoquote	N/A	N/A	N/A
Confederated Star	8.3%	281.49	£191
Colonial (incl Direct)	5.1%	258.63	£286
Monarch	6.4%	225.80	£198
Norfolk Insurance	4.8%	300.76	£353
Kestrel (incl Direct)	4.6%	272.10	£334
Victoria Group	3.2%	222.17	£388
Hillside	4.9%	190.70	£219
GMP	1.8%	83.53	£257
Neptune	3.7%	146.00	£219
Ryegate	2.9%	139.69	£272
Leeds & Bradford	3.0%	105.61	£197
Purbeck	3.2%	132.44	£234
Bradstock	N/A	N/A	N/A
Countrywide	1.9%	97.48	£288
Arrowhead	3.9%	158.20	£226

-K-

MOTOR INSURANCE PORTFOLIO SIZE AND GROWTH RATES

Purbeck compared to the main "direct writers"

Year	Purbeck Policies	Annual Growth	Arrow-head	Annual Growth	Key-stone	Annual Growth	GMP	Annual Growth
1987	480,000		120,000					
1988	499,000	4.0%	190,000	58.3%			30,000	
1989	510,000	2.2%	245,000	28.9%			85,000	183.3%
1990	519,000	1.8%	290,000	14.3%	56,000		150,000	76.5%
1991	533,000	2.6%	400,000	37.9%	137,000	144.6%	260,000	73.3%
1992	566,000	6.2%	700,000	75.0%	250,000	82.5%	325,000	25.0%

COMPARATIVE SPONTANEOUS AWARENESS

COMPANY	PURBECK MAIN AFFINITY GROUPS	PURBECK SECONDARY AFFINITY GROUPS	GENERAL PUBLIC
AA	46%	41%	38%
Kestrel	45%	41%	32%
Bradstock	43%	37%	41%
Colonial	42%	38%	29%
Norfolk Insurance	40%	33%	36%
Purbeck	35%	19%	2%
Mercantile Exchange	34%	28%	26%
Mercury & General	25%	28%	29%
Justice & Universal	24%	27%	32%
Confederated Star	24%	23%	22%
Arrowhead	22%	17%	20%
Lloyds	22%	23%	15%

-M-

NOTES OF THE BRAINSTORMING SESSION

Neil, these are a copy of the notes that summarise the main outputs of the brainstorming session that the Sales Director organised to identify issues of future importance to Purbeck's business. They are in no particular order.

- The increasing dominance of the direct writers, and more specifically Arrowhead, within our own markets.
- The significant reduction in the numbers of cars in the UK that are company owned
- The continued cost of commission payments to our sponsor or affinity groups
- The diverse number of IT systems in Purbeck, elements of which could impact on our ability to exploit economies of scale
- The increasing supplier-led commoditisation of the Motor business which may result in a price war.
- The identifiable trend we believe there is towards greater individualism
- The possible extension of indirect tax (VAT) to Financial Services
- Changing consumer expectations - especially in speed of response - as a result of increasing use of IT in service sector
- The mediocre quality of some of our front line and middle management
- Slowness and fragility of economic recovery in the UK
- Our ability to retain consumers in the light of highly visible, aggressive direct marketing by competitors
- Should we consider making acquisitions?
- The increasingly crowded "direct" market for insurance sales
- The growth of cable and other interactive technology for consumers
- The need to optimise our investment in marketing in order to deliver business volumes necessary to merit wholesale IT system replacement
- The need to expand our product range in highly competitive markets
- Our continuing high level of consumer loyalty may be under pressure
- The medium of direct mail, which we use heavily, is becoming increasingly tired
- The ability of our sponsors to be relevant to their members in the 1990s
- The danger of mergers between some of our affinity groups - especially trade unions
- Early signs of resistance to telemarketing techniques
- The continuing rise of car crime and its impact on rising premium levels
- The ageing population

-N-

RATING FACTORS

The commonly used rating factors are:

- Car group (One of 20 groupings based on ABI recommendations)

- Rating area (Based on the area the car is normally kept, identified by Postcode)

- Driver age (Age of youngest driver)

- Class of use (Social, business or commercial travelling)

- No Claims Discount

- Driving restrictions (Categories: any driver, owner only driving, or policyholder and spouse)

- Vehicle age

- Whether garaged

Other rating factors frequently used include:

- Value (used only for very high value cars)

- Sex of main or only driver

Factors not used for rating but which may be taken into account for underwriting include:

- Details of specific accidents (any driver)

- Details of motoring convictions or disqualifications

- Physical or mental disabilities

- Occupation

- Type of driving licence and how long held

- Period of recent, non-UK residence

- Imposition of special terms of refusal of cover by any insurer

- Access to other vehicles

- Vehicle modifications

-O-

MEMORANDUM   5 May 1994

TO: Neil Hammond

From: Ted Clarke
           Market Research Department

John Bakewell mentioned that you were looking for information on what
customers think of us. We conducted research some three years ago
which might be helpful. It was part of some research we did into
Purbeck's image - unfortunately, it was only conducted among existing or
recently lapsed motor insurance customers.

NAME ASSOCIATIONS

Positive Association   **Negative Association**

- Reliable   - Only for motor insurance
- Easy to deal with   - Only a broker
- Helpful   - Remote
- Friendly   - Old fashioned
- Excellent reputation   - Boring
- You can trust them   - Just "average"
- Understanding/Sympathetic
- Efficient and fast
- Competitive
- Understand needs

We all felt rather pleased with it at the time. The positives are how we
want to be seen and the first two on the negative side are not surprising -
especially since we asked people with motor policies. "Old fashioned"
and "boring" were the ones we worried about and addressed in
subsequent promotions and advertising.

Ted Clarke

MEMO

TO: NEIL HAMMOND   10 May 1994

FROM: CHRIS TAYLOR
           MOTOR SALES

LAPSE RATES

Following my last note on "Other Key Players in the Affinity Market" you asked for details about relative lapse rates.

Our lapse rate for motor is around 12%. Although it has been rising slowly this is still very good since Arrowhead claim 16% and are very proud of it! As we understand it some of the insurers have lapse rates of around 30% or more while some of the brokers have lapse rates at over 40%.

Hope this helps.

Chris Taylor

-Q-

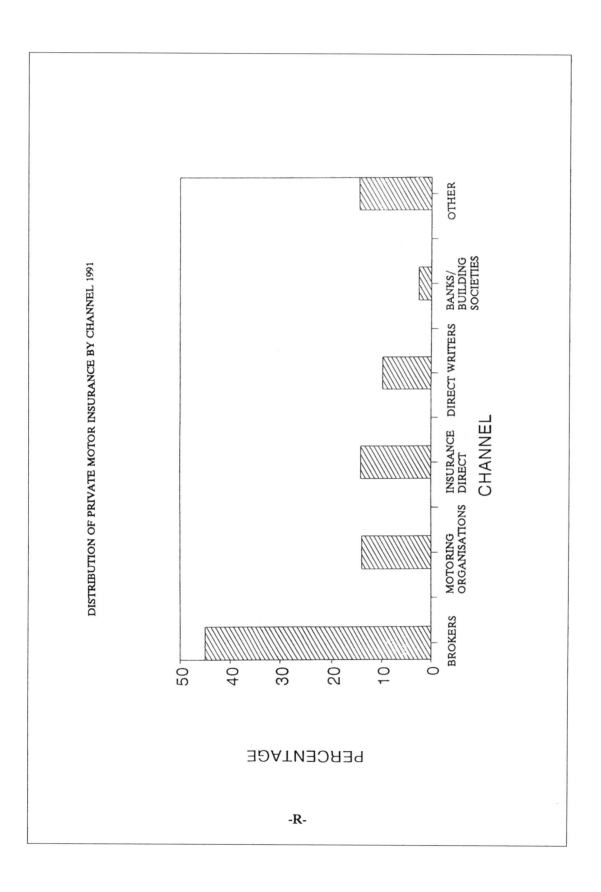

DISTRIBUTION OF PRIVATE MOTOR INSURANCE BY CHANNEL 1991

GARDNER PENROSE RESEARCH
22 Silver Close
Basingstoke
Hampshire

3 June 1994

Dear Neil

Attached you will find the Automobile Insurer magazine's annual analysis of the UK company motor market for 1992. Apparently it is compiled from DTI returns supported by other sources so I hope it is of some use. Purbeck is not mentioned, of course, because you are not an insurer.

Good luck with your research.

Yours sincerely

Alice

Alice Gardener
Partner

MOTOR INSURANCE MARKET

TABLE 1. Net Earned Premium and Related Statistics for Major UK Motor Insurers 1992

	Net Earned Premium £m		Underwriting Result		Expenses Ratio % NEP	
	1991	1992	1991	1992	1991	1992
Norfolk Insurance	665.84	578.08	-28.90	-4.08	23.92	25.00
Colonial	546.14	541.94	-25.24	-16.55	28.47	27.82
Kestrel	437.23	466.73	-18.38	-4.16	29.50	30.22
Monarch	448.02	450.84	-18.10	-1.71	26.73	25.76
Victoria Group	444.69	422.77	-35.38	-20.12	23.11	28.52
Confederated Star	403.20	414.76	-23.39	-19.69	31.86	33.66
Mercantile Exch	280.16	368.10	-7.44	2.12	28.41	26.16
United Insurance	197.79	203.46	-23.50	-8.36	24.74	24.82
Ryegate	174.50	201.24	-18.61	-4.42	27.15	25.37
Neptune	135.12	175.32	-13.81	-10.98	29.52	27.23
Elfin	108.17	134.64	-21.40	-11.80	30.10	32.20
Mercury & General	220.19	134.17	-23.20	-20.14	32.35	39.29
Countrywide	123.31	133.95	-17.28	-8.03	29.55	30.63
Leeds & Bradford	98.79	122.05	-15.08	-16.72	26.34	26.31
Shoreditch	100.24	121.25	-13.90	-17.05	21.92	19.70
St Justin	130.46	118.24	-35.54	-14.35	44.38	43.37
Arrowhead	64.18	113.78	1.59	5.82	28.65	20.47
Basilica	76.17	102.04	-27.60	-17.58	31.87	30.03
Deansway	34.38	66.27	-9.59	-4.96	27.19	25.64
Criterion	44.60	64.60	-12.44	0.55	27.81	26.18
Justice & Universal	53.59	63.72	-30.45	-22.91	32.88	30.91
Spear	52.73	61.87	-12.84	-11.96	24.88	24.13
British Union	46.46	60.73	-23.74	-8.20	29.74	27.68
Towerhill	50.00	50.19	-12.71	-24.28	18.03	31.04
Keystone	25.36	49.52	-36.80	-18.30	40.70	31.30

Net earned premiums (premiums earned during the calendar year) increased over those for 1991 for the majority of players, though this is more often a function of premium rate increases than volume of business. A negative underwriting result (effectively a loss, incurred when claims and expenses are greater than the premiums taken) is also the rule for most, though less dramatic than the previous year.

Expense ratios (business expenses as a ratio of net earned premiums) show a small downward trend, though there is no cause for complacency.

-T-

TABLE 2. Breakdown of Gross Motor Insurance Premium by Category 1992

£ million

Company Name	Private Car	Fleet	Comm'cial	M-Cycle	Other	Total
Norfolk Insurance	300.76	144.04	104.88	42.35	0.00	592.03
Colonial	258.63	115.38	65.89	4.87	0.00	444.77
Kestrel	272.10	139.88	41.42	3.96	0.00	457.36
Monarch	225.80	143.40	43.18	0.06	0.00	412.45
Victoria Grooup	222.17	80.01	35.02	0.00	0.00	337.20
Confederated Star	281.49	67.97	22.09	0.56	0.00	372.13
Mercantile Exch	181.81	106.53	28.29	0.18	0.00	316.82
United Insurance	157.09	0.00	19.22	3.04	15.19	194.54
Ryegate	139.69	54.06	7.31	0.69	0.00	201.75
Neptune	146.00	0.00	23.11	7.15	0.00	176.26
Elfin	86.64	42.49	5.21	0.00	0.14	134.47
Mercury & General	81.12	0.00	49.97	1.59	0.00	132.69
Countrywide	97.48	19.09	18.00	0.05	0.69	135.31
Leeds & Bradford	105.61	0.00	0.00	0.00	18.72	124.32
Shoreditch	67.81	0.00	54.78	0.60	0.00	123.19
St Justin	150.11	5.91	6.50	0.00	0.24	162.76
Arrowhead	158.02	0.00	0.00	0.00	0.00	158.02
Basilica	83.77	0.00	21.93	0.52	0.00	106.22
Deansway	57.14	0.11	0.00	0.00	0.00	57.25
Criterion	31.19	9.90	25.44	0.00	0.00	66.53
Justice & Universal	36.69	0.00	16.66	1.11	0.00	54.46
Spear	61.00	1.50	0.00	0.00	0.00	62.51
British Union	48.18	14.97	5.23	0.00	0.00	68.40
Towerhill	51.23	0.00	0.00	0.00	0.00	51.23
Keystone	50.56	0.00	0.00	0.00	0.00	50.56

-U-

253

TABLE 3. Accidents per 100 Vehicles (Comp only) UK Private Car Account 1992

Company Name	1987	1988	1989	1990	1991	1992
Norfolk Insurance	28.9	28.4	28.6	29.7	28.5	25.3
Colonial	24.5	24.8	24.7	26.6	25.3	24.9
Kestrel	26.7	26.9	26.8	29.0	28.8	27.1
Monarch	20.0	18.9	18.4	19.5	19.5	17.6
Victoria Grooup	26.3	26.3	28.7	24.8	32.8	29.6
Confederated Star	21.5	20.7	20.4	21.2	20.2	18.7
Mercantile Exch	27.0	26.1	25.3	27.1	27.3	25.6
United Insurance	24.5	24.7	23.1	24.1	24.2	22.7
Ryegate	23.9	22.8	21.3	22.2	23.4	22.5
Neptune	28.4	27.1	26.0	27.1	27.1	25.3
Elfin	17.0	16.1	15.9	16.7	16.7	16.8
Mercury & General	27.0	26.9	26.3	28.8	30.8	23.1
Countrywide	24.2	24.6	28.1	21.3	23.1	25.7
Leeds & Bradford	25.0	27.0	28.1	31.3	27.7	22.9
Shoreditch	25.6	22.0	21.9	23.1	23.3	21.4
St Justin	20.6	27.5	24.2	21.9	22.0	22.8
Arrowhead	19.3	22.3	23.8	24.2	25.5	24.8
Basilica	26.4	26.4	25.4	25.4	36.8	24.4
Deansway	21.0	21.2	18.8	21.6	22.5	23.7
Criterion	18.6	21.8	18.6	22.4	23.7	23.6
Justice & Universal	23.3	22.0	21.8	23.0	24.4	23.1
Spear	17.3	17.3	18.7	19.3	19.7	18.5
British Union	18.1	20.5	18.6	18.5	19.0	19.9
Towerhill	-	55.7	47.7	34.4	38.9	41.7
Keystone	-	-	-	30.5	35.9	23.6

There is a trend to slightly less accidents per 100 comprehensively insured vehicles than in 1991. Looking back over the six-year spread the picture shows less change than anecdotal reporting would suggest. However it must be remembered that these figures relate to comprehensive covered vehicles only - the addition of third party (including fire and theft) would doubtless show a sadder picture.

-v-

TABLE 4. Average Cost/Claim (Comp only) UK Private Car Account 1992

£ million

Company Name	1987	1988	1989	1990	1991	1992
Norfolk Insurance	759.00	822.39	894.16	1004.07	1109.30	1186.10
Colonial	593.13	659.84	750.94	839.67	930.64	1036.23
Kestrel	569.17	630.37	711.76	773.87	823.26	897.60
Monarch	579.08	636.28	688.53	789.64	753.88	844.51
Victoria Grooup	628.59	711.29	815.37	951.72	1025.15	1204.51
Confederated Star	561.76	608.88	678.37	739.94	808.42	935.48
Mercantile Exch	535.41	564.55	650.83	717.79	787.93	878.53
United Insurance	615.99	730.84	869.29	928.75	1051.42	1123.90
Ryegate	552.45	627.25	690.78	807.14	884.30	1000.72
Neptune	515.48	562.12	651.15	692.71	767.25	855.27
Elfin	630.00	756.00	834.00	869.00	985.00	1182.00
Mercury & General	585.21	600.82	666.70	715.33	826.31	907.10
Countrywide	547.86	606.62	642.90	706.10	784.87	853.16
Leeds & Bradford	721.68	812.90	947.74	983.67	1037.68	1091.61
Shoreditch	595.97	691.54	730.70	799.11	904.11	1040.07
St Justin	545.36	604.46	693.36	747.30	795.16	1000.00
Arrowhead	529.00	485.00	498.00	566.00	611.00	674.00
Basilica	556.74	614.07	704.69	774.00	822.82	899.09
Deansway	517.32	752.23	772.83	890.71	866.72	878.58
Criterion	560.90	654.68	675.80	703.75	794.23	845.45
Justice & Universal	585.48	654.53	682.27	765.12	825.33	944.92
Spear	453.06	508.47	550.45	620.97	722.47	826.91
British Union	558.66	589.46	672.73	764.73	814.41	958.87
Towerhill	842.00	871.00	981.00	1178.00	1294.00	1503.00
Keystone	-	-	516.00	654.00	717.00	793.00

The average cost of claims over the six year spread looks much more alarming - and inflation cannot wholly be blamed. Increased ownership of middle to higher-priced cars, inflated repair costs, "credit car hire", greater consumer awareness of their legal rights and higher levels of compensation for the catastrophically injured, even fraudulent claims; all these factors play a part.

-W-

TABLE 5. Average Premiums Charged per Private Car (£)

Company Name	1991	1992	Change %
Norfolk Insurance	310	353	15
Colonial	234	286	23
Kestrel	282	334	19
Monarch	177	198	12
Victoria Grooup	328	388	18
Confederated Star	160	191	19
Mercantile Exch	328	303	-8
United Insurance	234	268	14
Ryegate	227	272	20
Neptune	189	219	16
Elfin	192	232	21
Mercury & General	302	271	-10
Countrywide	187	288	55
Leeds & Bradford	181	197	9
Shoreditch	219	257	18
St Justin	-	214	-
Arrowhead	192	226	15
Basilica	208	236	17
Deansway	179	159	-14
Criterion	168	165	- 2
Justice & Universal	225	260	19
Spear	150	183	17
British Union	187	235	26
Towerhill	614	616	0
Keystone	189	206	9

-X-

TABLE 6. Vehicles Insured '000s (Comp and Non-comp) UK Private Car Account 1992

Company Name	1987	1988	1989	1990	1991	1992	% Change 1991/1992	Comp as % of Total 1991	Comp as % of Total 1992
Norfolk Ins	770	860	992	1225	1075	860	-21	74	78
Colonial	1138	1158	1130	1245	1311	900	-31	78	78
Kestrel	763	885	912	902	930	825	-11	66	63
Monarch	941	1035	1111	1210	1225	1128	-8	88	91
Victoria Group	890	757	862	925	765	579	-24	70	70
Confed Star	1558	1760	1762	1745	1689	1450	-14	64	63
Mercantile Exch	475	468	474	463	487	610	24	84	82
United Insurance	763	785	760	730	666	582	-12	78	76
Ryegate	512	520	548	521	545	524	-4	81	83
Neptune	560	592	690	675	592	653	11	54	51
Elfin	265	278	322	325	340	380	12	86	85
Mercury & Gen	480	435	415	397	290	298	3	77	76
Countrywide	315	272	287	380	452	336	-25	78	86
Leeds & Bradf'd	418	551	640	628	520	529	2	27	32
Shoreditch	225	238	243	252	260	271	4	85	83
St Justin	159	125	196	220	-	695	-	-	43
Arrowhead	120	190	245	290	400	700	75	90	90
Basilica	415	415	330	240	295	349	18	71	76
Deansway	112	85	122	132	240	369	54	61	65
Criterion	150	156	188	185	191	193	1	58	60
Justice & Univ	142	127	128	130	136	141	4	86	84
Spear	212	263	295	318	346	341	-2	99	99
British Union	440	255	148	127	185	211	14	73	70
Towerhill	-	-	25	35	52	86	68	74	76
Keystone	-	-		56	137	250	83	68	74

-Y-

257

MEMO

TO: NEIL HAMMOND   6 June 1994

FROM: CHRIS TAYLOR
        MOTOR SALES

Just one further thought after our conversation on affinity groups the other day.

One important point, which we must not miss, is that the perception of many affinity group members is that they are part of an "exclusive club" and party to a "well-kept secret" by being able to insure through Purbeck. Our low public profile reinforces this.

We therefore need to think very carefully about going public - certainly if there was any danger that our rates to ordinary (non-affinity group) applicants were lower than to affinity group members!

Chris Taylor

Purbeck Financial Services

Examination paper

Additional information to be taken into account when answering the questions set.

MEMO

TO: NEIL HAMMOND, Marketing Manager

FROM: COLIN JENKINS,
           Assistant to Managing Director

17 JUNE 1994

I tried to get hold of you on Friday evening to let you know that someone from Automobile Insurer's magazine had been trying to get Gordon McRae's comments on Arrowhead's latest figures. As you know Gordon's away, but I did manage to extract what Arrowhead's figures look like!

Apparently their latest figures show that they have now got a portfolio of 1.25 million customers. Since their figures last year were 700,000, this is even faster growth than last year. I make it 78%. As you know, we are expecting to have reached 600,000 – 6% growth!

I know you will want to have this information before your presentation – I am away on Monday, so I thought I would send you this note.

Best wishes

Colin Jenkins

Examination questions

The managing director has had time to reflect on the presentation he asked you to make to the board and has suggested that you make your recommendations *in report format* on the following, precise aspects:

1   Critically review Purbeck's current market position.   **20 marks**

2   Evaluate the alternative marketing strategies open to Purbeck. Your evaluation should conclude with an assessment of what Purbeck's competitors (new and existing) might do as the market situation evolves.   **40 marks**

3   Building on your analysis, propose and justify in detail your preferred marketing strategy for Purbeck which will enable it to achieve the stated corporate objectives.   **25 marks**

4   Identify the vital information gaps which confront the company and which will have to be filled before any action towards strategy implementation can be started.   **15 marks**

Purbeck Financial Services

Examiners' notes

Overview

The additional information

The additional information given on the day of the examination may have confused some candidates. Those who managed to gain a good understanding of Purbeck, however, should have no difficulty in making some easy marks. The additional information in terms of a memo from Colin Jenkins simply shows that the company *does not have the luxury of time* to spend on elaborate planning processes. Timely action is crucial.

Question one   20 marks

'Critically review Purbeck's current market position'

Approach

The important words here are: 'critically', 'review' and 'market'.

Good answers will show a systematic approach to the problem and headings to look for are:

- Internal issues
- Customers/market
- Marketing mix
- Competition/environment

The best answers will provide a good impression of the most important issues now facing Purbeck.

Has your answer considered the following?

Internal issues:	Declining profitability
	Increasing turnover
	Increasing costs
	Product orientation culture
Customers/market:	Reliant on small number of large clients (sponsors)
	Ageing customer base
	Shrinking customer base (decline in public service)
	No good segmentation base
	More 'shopping around' for good prices
	Lack customer motivation information
	Loyalty (lapse rates)
Product:	Commodity image – no differentiation
	Seen as 'add-ons' by sponsors
	Not 'benefit-led'
Price:	High enough to cover costs?
	Becoming main competitive weapon

Distribution:	Expensive channel
	Value-added?
	Disintermediation
Promotion:	Well-kept secret
	Not known outside affinity groups
Competition:	Direct-writers
	Telesales
	Price competition
	Macro-environment issues
Additional info:	Competition growing rapidly
	Purbeck slow response

Question two   40 marks

'Evaluate the alternative marketing strategies open to Purbeck. Your evaluation should conclude with an assessment of what Purbeck's competitors (new and existing) might do as the market situation evolves.'

Approach

Ansoff is the classical approach for strategic evaluation. Ansoff should however only be used as a guide and strategic options must be firmly linked into Purbeck's particular situation.

Pure Ansoff gains no marks, applied Ansoff to Purbeck's strategic situation does.

The second part of the question requires the student to take into account competitive strategies and perhaps competitive response models.

Good answers will deal with the sense of 'dynamism' in the market and will look at the full range of alternatives open to the organization.

Best answers will demonstrate an ability to look beyond Purbeck's current competition to possible new entrants.

Has your answer considered the following?

Market penetration:	Add extra value to customers
	Segment the market
	Motor to Purbeck non-motor customers
	Leverage suppliers
Product development:	Enhance core product (to customer needs/segments)
	'Bundle' products
	Service development
Market development:	New affinity groups
	A&M activity
	Geographic expansion (e.g. Europe)
Diversification:	Other insurance markets
	Become direct writers
	Allied 'motoring/leisure' markets
Competitor action:	Direct writers to grow?
	to saturate?
	to diversify into other areas?
	Increased pressure on prices
	Concentration of other insurers (A&M)
	Brokers – to contract?
	– to consolidate? (A&M)
	Technology: allows other/new entrants
	New competition from: – banks?
	– building Societies?
	– car manufacturers?
	– car dealers?

Question three   25 marks

'Building on your analysis, propose and justify in detail your preferred marketing strategy for Purbeck which will enable it to achieve the stated corporate objectives.'

Approach

Answers here can vary quite widely depending on the student's choice of strategy. Nevertheless there will be obviously 'inappropriate' answers.

Generally we are looking for a consistent flow of argument, preferably following a sequence such as:

- Understanding of the corporate objectives
- Marketing Plan: – objectives
    - target market (segments)
    - positioning
    - 4 or 7 Ps
    - timescales
    - budgets

It is important that the answer be related to the corporate objectives stated in the case and that all recommendations are justified.

Above all, the 4/7 Ps must be consistent with the target market's needs and company positioning.

Has your answer considered the following?

Marketing objectives:	e.g, market share/lapse rates/products per customer
Target market:	Affinity groups Segments
Positioning:	Differentiated position Market leader in...
Product:	Benefit packages Reflecting target market needs and positioning
Price:	Related to benefits Premium (eventually) Competitive environment
Distribution:	Routes to the customer Telesales?
Promotion:	Objectives/plans to meet above
Timescale:	Not long (Purbeck must act soon)
Budgets:	Indicative of scale of activities suggested and company resources

Question four   15 marks

'Identify the vital information gaps which confront the company and which will have to be filled before any action towards strategy implementation can be started.'

Approach

This question is not designed to be a 'catch-all' question for students to dump knowledge on market research. The answer should follow logically from the previous answers and the selected strategy route for Purbeck.

The word 'vital' has been included in the hope of producing a *short* but *relevant* list of information needed. Time is important to Purbeck so lengthy research programmes will clearly be inappropriate. Note that the question does *not* ask for sources of information or methods of collection.

Best students will prioritize the information gaps (well I can dream!).

Has your answer considered the following?

Strategic information gaps will probably include:

Competitor analysis:	Direct writers
	New entrants
	Strategic intentions
Customers:	Needs and wants
	Buying motives
	Segmentation possibilities
	Product selection criteria
	Sponsor motivations
	Power of 'affinity group' belonging
Internal:	Relative market profitability
	Sales/distribution costs

Case study

Australian Tourist Commission

AUSTRALIAN TOURIST COMMISSION

CANDIDATES' BRIEF

You are Chris Benson, Regional Director of the Australian Tourist Commission (ATC) Europe. You report directly to Doug McKenna, Joint Managing Director, based in Sydney.

You have recently been promoted to your current position for Trade Marketing Director, UK, as part of a recent world-wide reorganisation. Responsibilities have been reallocated along functional rather than geographic lines, with consumer and trade marketing roles clearly separated. Consumer marketing is concerned with increasing consumer awareness and desire to travel to Australia in order to make it the preferred long-haul holiday destination in priority markets. Trade marketing involves increasing the distribution of Australian holiday programs through new or existing channels, broadening the range of product to suit the needs of European customers and increasing the number of Australian incentive schemes and conferences booked from Europe.

Doug McKenna has asked you to prepare a presentation on strategic marketing in Europe in time for the board meeting in Sydney on 13 December. This is the first time that the marketing planning process has been implemented under the new organisation structure and the first time that you have been responsible for devising a marketing strategy which covers the whole of Europe. In previous years, each country director had submitted their marketing plan to a regional board which was responsible for producing a cohesive regional marketing plan and allocating resources amongst the countries.

Whilst you have a good working relationship with your colleagues in Europe, there is a degree of competition among European countries for marketing resources. This is likely to become intensified as the organisation focuses on the opportunities which will emerge during the run up to the Olympic Games which, in the year 2000, are to be held in and around Sydney.

PROLOGUE

"Sanctuary Cove, Bungle Bungle, Seven Spirit Bay, Cradle Mountain, Great Ocean Road, Lightening Ridge, Remarkable Rocks and Tidbinbilla - the very names have their own magic and Australia is one of the most romantic continents on earth. A paradise of endless soft white sands, the bluest of oceans, waving palm trees, quiet coves, moonlight feasts of shellfish and lobster and inimitable panoramas from the white caps of the Snowy Mountains to the sunset cityscape of Sydney, where the Opera House overlooks one of the world's most beautiful harbours...."

Chris Benson put down the latest draft of the 1995 Travellers' Guide, took off his glasses and, rubbing his eyes, looked out of his window at a grey south London landscape. It had just started raining and already the traffic was solid as far as the eye could see. "Should have stayed a bit longer" he muttered to himself, thinking of the perfect spring day he had left behind in Sydney.

Jet lag had not yet hit him - he could probably keep going until about four in the afternoon with a bit of luck. Just time to finish proof reading this draft of the Travellers' Guide before setting off for lunch with a friend, Joe Haslem, in the West End. Joe had just started in a position at Tourism Canada similar to his own, having previously held an administrative post in the Canadian High Commission.

After a hideous journey by tube, Chris ran through the rain to the restaurant. "So sorry Joe" he apologised as he arrived. "I still can't get used to this country - the weather, the traffic, the lack of infrastructure...."

"Don't worry Chris, I'm so grateful that you can spare the time to tell me about the ATC and tourism generally. I feel a little lost at the moment in this new job."

Chris began by filling in some detail about the history and aims of the ATC.

THE AUSTRALIAN TOURIST COMMISSION

The ATC was formed in 1967 to promote and market Australia overseas as a tourist destination. It is governed by a board of ten directors and is directly responsible to the Minister for Tourism. It is a statutory authority established under the Australian Tourist Commission Act 1987. The principal objectives of the ATC, as stated under the ACT are to:

- increase the number of visitors to Australia from overseas
- maximise the benefits to Australia from overseas visitors
- ensure Australia is protected from adverse environmental and social impacts of international tourism.

The ATC's overall corporate objective is to increase the economic and social benefit to Australia of inbound tourism by achieving a sustained increase in international tourist arrivals, yield and market share. In carrying out its objectives, the ATC undertakes marketing activities which are primarily directed at consumers and the trade in overseas markets.

THE TOURIST MARKET WORLDWIDE

During the 1970s and 1980s, tourism has changed dramatically from being a fragmented industry with a low profile to become an industry which is recognised by all governments as being a vital foreign exchange earner and employer of labour. During the early 1990s, the pattern of growth has been somewhat disrupted by economic and political factors such as the widespread economic recession and the Gulf War. It has become clear that GDP growth is a necessary condition for growth in international travel but it is not sufficient. After a recession it takes some considerable time for tourists to start travelling again - it seems that travel is less important to them than other purchases which they have been denied during the recession.

The economic situation has now stabilised and the outlook for international tourism is promising. GDP growth is forecast to improve in most of the world's major economies and because of demographic changes, leisure time is increasing internationally. However the rate of growth in international travel is expected to slow over the longer term compared with previous decades and the pattern is expected to change. Developed economies such as the USA and UK are expected to exhibit relatively modest growth while emerging economies have a strongly growing demand for travel.

Although the number of visitors from traditional markets will not be growing so rapidly, the quality of these visitors from the perspective of the tourist industry is high since they tend to be high-yielding independent tourists who disperse widely into the country they are visiting.

By contrast, the situation with the fastest growing outbound travel markets, such as Korea, Taiwan and Indonesia is quite different, with many visitors travelling on group tours because of their inexperience.

2

The Japanese also tend to travel together in groups and they tend to spend more than other tourists, although their purchases take the form of goods (which may have been imported) rather than services.

During the 1990s the tourist industry world-wide has faced a number of other crucial issues, apart from economic and political factors. Consumers have become more experienced travellers and tend to seek an "experience-based" holiday with individually prepared itineraries or at least a flexible package. the impact of new technology has been important, making the industry more flexible and efficient, as has the growing realisation that there are environmental limits to growth which must be taken into account.

Demographics also affect the tourist industry. For example, in the US, Japan and Germany, the group of over 55s (who have the resources and the time to travel) is increasing and this will have a major impact on tourism in the coming decade. Meanwhile the working population appears to find its available leisure time reducing, partly because of pressures in the working environment and partly because in some countries the under 30s generation are worse off than their parents.

Some interesting competitive moves have been made by several countries who have relaxed their visa requirements in order to promote tourism. For example, the US introduced the Visa Waiver Programme, when visas were no longer required for European visitors, at the same time as moving towards deregulating air access. The Australian government has not followed suit here having introduced increased visitor taxes, while maintaining the requirement for visas and failing to handle the increasing volume of visa issuance, resulting in frequent blockages.

Meanwhile, the competition to attract international tourists is intensifying. Around 175 National Tourist Offices (NTOs) actively promote their countries in order to receive economic benefits. Much of these efforts are directed towards the major travel markets where the propensity to travel is high. Traditionally, the largest NTOs come from the world's most established tourist destinations. The major markets most often targeted by NTOs are Australia, France, Germany, Italy, Japan, Taiwan, UK, USA and apart from Japan, these same countries have some of the largest NTOs.

However there is an active second tier of NTOs competing against the ATC who are marketing aggressively and investing significant sums of money to do so. These include Canada, Hong Kong, New Zealand, Singapore, South Korea, Spain, Thailand. Behind these is an emerging

3

list of new destinations which includes Brazil, Cyprus, Greece, Indonesia, Mexico, Philippines and Turkey.

World NTO expenditure is growing by between 5% and 10% per annum largely as a result of these newcomers rather than because of consistent budget increases in the traditional markets. The geographic spread of priority markets of each NTO is broadening and the emphasis is switching away from the traditional markets of Europe, North America and Japan to the emerging economic powers in Asia and South America. The growing focus on Asia in particular will mean significantly increased competition for the ATC in some of its fastest growing markets.

The ATC has recently opened offices in Taiwan, Indonesia and Malaysia and sees excellent opportunities in China, Vietnam, South Africa, the Middle East and parts of Central and South America. All NTOs view local offices as essential to the development of tourism from that region. Once established, the local office will develop links with the local tourism trade, concentrating first on trade activity and later on consumer promotion if appropriate.

THE TOURIST MARKET IN EUROPE

Holidays for Europeans are vitally important and with high disposable incomes, many are able to choose to escape the weather, overcrowding and social pressures.

However the economic situation in Europe is mixed and has changed significantly over the past few years. While Britain was depressed and is now showing strong signs of recovery, other important markets such as Germany are now in a state of turmoil.

The ATC has been highly successful in Europe and has managed to demonstrate strong growth both in terms of numbers of holidays, meetings, conventions and incentive journeys and in terms of market share. Furthermore the public perception of Australia is such that it is the most desirable travel destination in Sweden, and the second highest in the UK after the USA. Australia is perceived to be safe and offers a positively different holiday from other destinations. However, converting such desirability into firm bookings remains a challenge.

Australia particularly welcomes European tourists because they are the highest yielding, longest staying and widest travelling visitors. Also they tend to travel during the opposite seasons from Australian, Asian and Japanese tourists leading to a flattening of seasonal peaks. Europeans

4

tend to blend into the culture so that they are unobtrusive tourists, which is also welcomed by the locals. However, as a result, many Australians are unaware of the importance of European tourists to the economy, particularly outside the major tourist centres.

Long haul travel is increasing at the expense of short haul travel as products become available which Europeans find attractive because they offer new experiences at an affordable price. However the limitations on growth in the long-haul sector will be governed by developments in the air transport sector. Airfares and airline capacity are under pressure and demand is catching up with, and sometimes exceeds, supply.

The integration of the European Community (EC) is having an effect on the tourist market in many ways. There will be freer movement of people and money throughout the EEC. National laws, such as consumer protection laws, are being harmonised. Cross-border vertical integration is occurring, such as the running of charter services by tour operators and many airline operators are moving towards a pan-European organisation, presenting a formidable challenge to airlines outside the EC.

Considerable work has been done by the ATC in trying to identify the typical European traveller to Australia and this work will continue. Broadly speaking, two overall themes have emerged and within each there is an active and a passive element. The first theme is "Australia, Land of Discovery" and the active element is known as "Experience Australia". The triggers which decide people to book include "Adventure with a foreign flavour; Discovering, feeling, doing, hands on; Meeting local people and Aborigines; Unspoilt scenery, wildlife". The passive element, dubbed "See Australia", mention the following as triggers: "Foreign but safe and comfortable; Organised tours; Meeting people, exploring, learning; Seeing natural wonders, history and wildlife".

The second theme is "Australia, Endless Sun and Exotic Beaches" and within this the active element has been called "Sun, Sand, Surf and Sex". Triggers include "non-stop active resorts, hot and sunny; sexy company; fun, lots of night life; meeting young people, discos". Finally, the passive element is known as "Exotic Sun" characterised by "unspoilt natural beaches, hot and sunny; romance, sensuality, watching a sunset; spectacular scenery, cruising; luxury, beautiful people, fashionable".

The ATC know that more work should be done in this area, particularly bearing in mind the problems in turning top of mind awareness into bookings.

RECENT MARKETING INITIATIVES

The corporate restructuring of the ATC has in itself provided a major improvement in the efficiency of the organisation so that Europe is now treated as a single market, managed out of London, with responsibilities being clearly separated between consumer and trade marketing.

This restructuring has taken longer than expected to implement but some pan-European advertising campaigns have now been launched such as the very successful "Australia Now." "Let yourself go", which generated a strong consumer response and increased levels of interest and desire to travel to Australia.

Consumer Marketing

Consumer advertising remains the most important means of raising public awareness about Australia and desire to travel there. Although the budget for consumer advertising has been reduced in recent years, it still accounts for over half the consumer marketing expenditure and one third of the total budget for the region. Other programmes such as information distribution, direct marketing and industry list rental take their lead from the consumer advertising campaigns. The Travellers' Guide is the core publication of the ATC aimed at potential travellers and is published by the consumer marketing division.

The ATC is strengthening its PR activities throughout Europe in order to try to compensate for the lack of advertising "share of the voice" which has been the result of the rapid growth in advertising spend by competitive and new NTOs. One of the key initiatives here is the Visiting Journalist Programme, VJP, which revolves around showing journalists a broad range of activities which Australia has to offer catering for all kinds of special interests. Journalists are already being taken to Homebush Bay, which is twenty minutes from downtown Sydney and will be the site of the 2000 Olympics, although marketing of the Olympics may not take place formally yet.

Trade Marketing

The ATC has initiated an extensive programme of joint marketing agreements (JMAs) with wholesalers and retailers resulting in a broader variety of product being offered to the European customer. The idea of these schemes is to ensure that there is a good array of suitable products available in the market. It is not a subsidy scheme but one which provides established tour operators with incremental promotional

6

funding, allowing them to generate incremental traffic. One example of a JMA would be the ATC together with Qantas doing some short term tactical advertising such as the recent "Australia £499" promotion in the UK.

The JMA scheme has been further enhanced by the introduction of "Partnership Australia" (PA), a collaborative venture between the ATC, States and Territories. The Partnership Australia programme is one of joint promotional activities undertaken with the individual states and territories and includes the provision of centralised information handling services, development of distribution channels and tactical advertising very similar to the JMA scheme but in this case it is concerned with the marketing of State and Territory product.

PA activities include the consolidation of a pan-European information and distribution service to provide enhanced trade and consumer information servicing. Historically, the effectiveness of information servicing in Europe has been the ATC's weakest link and there has been an imbalance of product development with products other than Queensland and Northern Territory under represented.

The ATC has found that the training of the tourist trade plays an important role in effective marketing in order to overcome the lack of knowledge which restricts the agents' ability to sell. To this end, the ATC runs two training conferences: Operation Walkabout is a two day intensive training conference targeted to 130 independent UK agents. Multiple training targets the more important retailers, offering dedicated training days with a minimum of 40 longhaul agents within the retail sector covering at least 12 Australian products. A new training initiative will be launched named the Aussie Specialist Shop Network whereby selected retail agents are given in-depth training and are then supported through a database running on a CD ROM.

Trade and consumer information servicing is another important part of market development. "Aussie Helplines" have been established in seven locations across Europe to handle consumer and retail industry enquiries.

The travel trade is different through Europe. While the bulk of business in Continental Europe passes through tour operators and travel agents, the UK market is dominated by a handful of direct operations specialising in Australian holidays.

7

Meetings, Conventions and Incentives

The priority markets for meetings, conventions and incentives (MC&I) are UK, Germany, Italy and France, with the UK being the dominant market for this type of travel. The UK incentive body, ITMA, has 30 full members and is growing in importance. The ATC is beginning to implement JMAs with key incentive and conference organisers. Australia has been gaining market share in this market which is extremely sensitive to economic pressures. However distance and time remain the greatest barriers to long haul incentive travel and the perception that Australia is the ultimate long haul destination leaves the customer with the problem of where to take his clients next.

TRAVEL TRENDS

The changes in demographics have also led to a switch in the types of holidays people are undertaking. Whereas in the past, group travel was the norm, there is an emerging trend whereby tourists are planning their own itineraries to suit their own interests and budgets. Such travellers are known as FIT (Free Independent Traveller) and it is estimated that they represent 80% - 95% of the visitors from many of the ATC's key markets in Europe. When Kuoni in the UK abandoned package travel to Australia and introduced a modular style of programme, its sales increased six-fold.

There are two types of independent travellers from Europe - backpackers and the more mature, sophisticated and experience traveller. Backpackers tend to buy their airline ticket only and pay for everything else once they arrive. Their importance should not be underestimated - although they do not spend money on smart hotels they will happily spend AUD $500 on a scuba-diving package and they do travel to far-flung corners of the continent.

Most of the remaining independent tourists book through tour operators. In this market the UK tourists and, to a lesser extent those from the Netherlands, are different from other European markets in that they are often visiting friends and relatives (VFR) which means that they book much less hotel accommodation. Germans tend to be more independent still in that they frequently do not use a tour operator at all but book everything directly.

Another new type of tourist is the Special Interest Traveller who is looking for an experience-based holiday. There is still some uncertainty as to the definition of the term "Special Interest" and its potential. The

8

ATC, having commissioned research into this matter, launched a five-year programme - Special Interest Australia - which began in 1993 with a different theme for each year. The themes - Sport, the Great Outdoors, Arts and Culture, Festivals, Good Living - are designed to enrich the image of Australia as a holiday destination. The programme is targeted towards secondary travellers, that is those who add special interest products into their itinerary, rather than primary travellers who set out single-mindedly to pursue their own special interest.

Eco-tourism, or nature-based travel, is another new trend which the ATC is watching closely. This is hard to define, but the most widely accepted definition is travel connected with a "closeness" to and an appreciation of the environment, coupled with a strong responsibility to avoid environmental damage

Of course all these trends are intertwining but together they demonstrate how far the industry has evolved from the standard packages of the 1970s and 1980s.

THE OLYMPIC GAMES

In recognition of the importance of the Year 2000 Olympic Games the ATC has established an Olympics sub-committee from among board members, three of whom were on the Sydney Olympics Bid Committee. While the detailed strategies for the ATC approach to the games are still to be finalised, three broad approaches have been identified at this stage.

Firstly, the ATC will focus on the years before and after the Year 2000 to maximise on the full effects of the Games. The Olympic marketing campaign will begin immediately after the Atlanta Games have ended in 1996 and will continue until the Year 2000. From 2001 onwards it will require special strategies to avoid visitor arrivals falling sharply but the ATC is taking heart from the success of Spain in this respect, following the Barcelona Olympics in 1992.

Secondly, the ATC will endeavour to ensure that the full effects of the Games are spread throughout Australia. Partnership Australia will have a pivotal role to play here, by providing centralised information and through tactical advertising and promotion.

And finally, the ATC will make the most of the spirit of the Olympic Games because it is consistent with the brand image and positioning of Australia. In the promotion of the bid and the publicity surrounding Sydney's win, various national attributes were highlighted such as "a place

9

of spectacular and unspoilt beauty"; "a young, vibrant and capable country"; "a fun, festive and colourful location"; "a culturally active and multi-cultural community".

Research will be important in strategy formulation here, but the best estimate of potential arrivals for the Year 2000 is 6.82 million, which implies a contribution by international tourism to the Australian economy between now and the year 2000 of AUD $73 billion. A revision of targets and an analysis of the reported experiences of other Olympic host cities is underway.

EPILOGUE

Joe thanked Chris warmly for all the useful background information and insights which would help him in his new position and left wondering whether many of the marketing concepts had even occurred to Tourism Canada. Although he was not a marketing man himself, he felt that his new employers were probably years behind.

Chris returned to the office to collect his suitcase, still wondering why he had hurried back from Sydney so soon. After all, he could put together a presentation in no time about marketing in Europe - half the business came from the UK and he knew this market like the back of his hand. He admitted that Australia winning the Olympic bid was exciting but he felt there was so much time to plan, it was hardly a matter of urgency.

Sally Purvis, Chris's administrative assistant, appeared clutching a file of information which he had asked her to put together for him while he was in Australia. "I have just had an interesting call from Jan Lewis in Los Angeles" she said. "She wanted to talk to you about the re-focusing of the ATC that you had been discussing at the Regional Directors meeting in Sydney last week."

Chris remembered the session well. As part of the ATC's re-structuring, consultants had presented to the board and regional directors a very strong case for re-positioning the ATC from an organisation which concentrated on advertising and promotional activities to one which started to take full responsibility for all aspects of marketing. They had all seen the need to change and Doug McKenna had asked that the next set of plans would deal with full marketing strategy rather than just advertising or promotional plans.

10

Chris had managed to skim read a book on Marketing Strategy that the consultants had handed out at the briefing and was starting to understand what this might mean for his presentation. Different consumers, different needs - market segmentation of some sort was obviously the key but how he was going to implement that with a travel trade infrastructure based on countries he really didn't know.

He turned to Sally and said "I'll call Jan just as soon as I have had a chance to think through how I might approach the problem - what have you managed to put together to get me started?"

Sally handed over the file....

CHRIS'S FILE CONTENTS

12

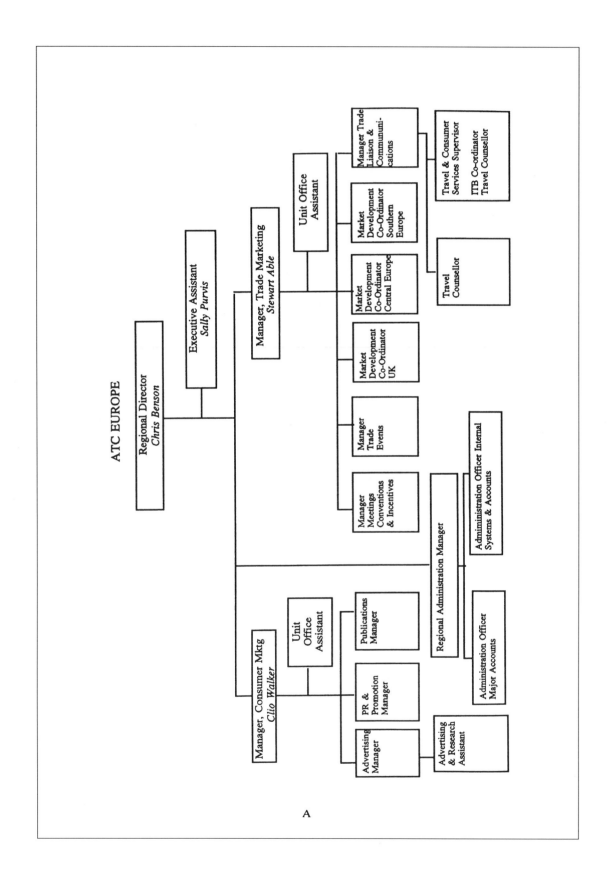

ATC EUROPE

Regional Director
Chris Benson

Executive Assistant
Sally Purvis

Manager, Consumer Mktg
Clio Walker

Unit Office Assistant

Advertising Manager

PR & Promotion Manager

Publications Manager

Advertising & Research Assistant

Administration Officer Major Accounts

Regional Administration Manager

Admimistration Officer Internal Systems & Accounts

Manager, Trade Marketing
Stewart Able

Unit Office Assistant

Manager Meetings Conventions & Incentives

Manager Trade Events

Market Development Co-Ordinator UK

Market Development Co-Ordinator Central Europe

Market Development Co-Ordinator Southern Europe

Manager Trade Liaison & Communications

Travel Counsellor

Travel & Consumer Services Supervisor

ITB Co-ordinator
Travel Counsellor

A

MEMORANDUM

To: **All Regional Directors**   From: **Doug McKenna**

Subject: **European Marketing Plan**

Date: **27 October 1994**

Just a couple of thoughts I have had on the 1995/96 marketing plan which I wanted to share with you:

Firstly on timing. We are prohibited from pushing actively for the 2000 Olympics until the Atlanta Olympics has ended in September 1996. However, our 1995/96 marketing plan must put us in a position to start the build-up to the Olympics from that date without losing any time. The advanced publicity is going to be as valuable as the event itself.

Secondly the marketing plan must put in place the foundations of a campaign which is going to sustain the new higher levels of tourists after the Olympics. To put this into perspective, we had 2.8 million visitors in 1992/93, we are expecting 3.8 million this year and this should grow to 6.8 million in the year 2000. If we achieve this, it will generate an **extra $75 billion** in export earnings and 160,000 new jobs between now and the end of the decade. This compares with total foreign exchange earnings from tourism in 1992/93 of $8.6 billion - a quantum leap!

I expect you have seen the consultant's report which is predicting an extra 1.3 million overseas visitors between 1994 and 2004 on the strength of the Olympic games. What we must do with this marketing plan is to make sure that people keep up the habit well into the next century

Spain has been very successful here - you may have seen the press coverage.

B

SUMMARY OF EUROPEAN MARKETING ACHIEVEMENTS   1993

UK/Ireland and Scandinavia

Key Consumer Objectives	Key Trade Objectives
• Increase Australia as a desired holiday destination among travellers with the greatest potential to travel • Increase the conversion rate from desire to actual travel	• Increase the European trade's commitment to marketing and selling travel to Australia and make their efforts more effective

	Activities	Inputs	Methods	Key Direct Outputs

Consumer	Advertising	• ATC exp $6,977,300
		• Industry contrib $2,003,000 (22%)
			• UK TVC - 60, 30 & 10 sec ads (476 spots)
			• Sweden TVC - 60,30 & 10 sec ads (99 spots)
			• UK print - 16 colour & 18 b/w ads
			• Sweden print - 12 colour & 37 b/w ads
			• Direct mail - to 50,000 consumers
			• JMA activity with co-op partners incl.:
			  • 30 & 10 sec TVC (54 spots)
			  • 50 col & 23 b/w print ads
			  • 373 b/w print ads in classifieds
			  • direct mail - to 114,000 consumers
			  • 176 travel agency window displays
				• TV reach - UK 25m, Sweden 5m
				• Press reach - UK 37m, Sweden 3.5m
				• Responses to TV & print ads - UK 50,000; Sweden 14,500
				• JMA activity (TV & print) total reach - 205m consumers

	Servicing	• ATC exp $156,000 • Industry contrib $938,800 (86%)	• Service inquiries & requests • Distribute promotional material • Produce 128-page full-colour Travellers Guide	• 44,000 inquiries • 136,000 Travellers Guides, 3,000 maps, 500 posters, 40 videos distributed
	Public Relations	• ATC exp $654,800 • Industry contrib $437,400 (40%)	• 44 journalists visits • 69 media releases & 112 interviews • 142 journalists to ATC functions	• Publicity generated $14.5m • PR yield $22:1 • 5 TV features in UK; 85 print features in UK & Scandinavia • 135 media requests generated
Trade	Advertising	• ATC exp $97,000 • Industry contrib $23,000 (19%)	• 22 colour print ads in UK/Ireland trade publications	• 19 features in national trade press (av. circulation 20,500 each)
	Promotions	• ATC exp $336,000 • Industry contrib $489,000 (59%)	• Trade shows (incl. World Travel Market, Walkabout, TUR) • 11 retail training sessions	• 2,533 agents at training sessions • 82 buyers at ATE; 41 at ITB • 87 co-op partners at trade events
	Servicing	• ATC exp $278,000	• Service inquiries & requests • Distribute sales material	• 36,000 inquiries • 261,000 Travellers Guides, 301 videos & films, 1,137 posters, 990 maps distributed • 3,000 slides loaned to trade
	Conventions & Incentives (All Europe)	• ATC exp $404,000 • Industry contrib $217,000 (35%)	• 23 full-page colour ads in UK, Germany, Italy and France • Full-page colour ad in EIBTM catalogue & stand at EIBTM (14 co-op partners) • 4 newsletters x 2,200 database contacts • Produce Contacts List (2,000 copies), Promotional Ideas Brochure (5,000), Incentive Brochure (5,000), Meeting Planners Guide (2,000) • Purchased lists (1,300 German incentive/meeting planners and 4,000 UK corporate end users) for direct mail of ATC newsletter	• Advertising reach - 339,000 meeting planners • 4,700 visitors and 354 direct contacts made at trade shows • 15 incentive buyers visited Australia • 220 Meeting Planners Guides to European associations • UK & German incentive workshops attracted 21 co-op partners and 30 buyers • 8,800 contacts reached via newsletter • 4-6% response rate to direct mail campaign

Key Consumer Results	Key Trade Results
• Number one desired travel destination in Sweden. Intention to travel rose 14% to 23% • Number two desired holiday destination in UK and gaining. Increased top-of-mind intention to travel	• Record trade contributions for ATC activities ($3.9m for joint marketing campaigns; $489,000 for trade shows; $216,000 for conventions/incentives)

Achievements
■ 7% increase in arrivals for 1992/93 (compared with only 2% growth in European long-haul travel)

C-1

Central and Southern Europe

Key Consumer Objectives	Key Trade Objectives
• Increase Australia's level as a desired holiday destination among travellers with the greatest potential to travel • Increase the rate of conversion from desire to travel • Expand knowledge of Australia as a travel destination	• Increase the European trade's commitment and effectiveness in marketing and selling travel to Australia

	Activities	Inputs	Methods	Key Direct Outputs
Consumer	Advertising	• ATC exp $5,967,000 • Industry contrib $1,400,000 (19%)	• Strategic co-op ads with Qantas in magazines and n/papers in Germany, Italy, France and Switzerland: - 37 double-page colour, 26 double 1/2 page, 10 b/w 1/2 page • Strategic co-op ads with Singapore Airlines - b/w inserts, 3 dailies in the Netherlands • JMA tactical ads with 35 partners in Germany, Switzerland, Italy, France, Netherlands & Spain	• Press reach - Germany 35m; Italy 16m; Switzerland 2m; France 13.5m • 25,000 responses to print ads • 52,000 consumers reached and Travellers Guides distributed
	Promotions	• ATC exp $25,000 • Industry contrib $43,000 (63%)	• Coordinate presence at 3 consumer fairs in Germany and 1 in the Netherlands	• 51,000 consumers reached • 80,000 brochures distributed, incl. 45,000 Travellers Guides
	Servicing	• ATC exp $850,000 • Industry contrib $840,500 (50%)	• Produce 132-page Travellers Guide in German, Italian, French & Dutch & 64-page Spanish Guide • Service 84,000 inquiries • Provide a second level fulfilment service for German-speaking countries	• 23 partners supported the tag-along mailing in 2 countries • 415,000 Guides distributed • 100,000 Visitor Maps and 22,000 Year of Sport Fact Sheets distributed
	Public Relations	• ATC exp $1,179,500 • Industry contrib $785,500 (40%)	• 63 consumer & 32 trade media releases in 5 languages • 100 journalists visits, incl. 8 TV crews & 14 trade journalists to ATE • 752 media requests & 517 interviews; 86 trade media requests & 13 interviews	• 21 cover stories/features, 480 articles & 6 supplements • 16 tv/radio programs on Spanish & German-speaking TV • $40m publicity generated • PR yield = $34:1 • 12 trade features & 79 articles
Trade	Advertising	• ATC exp $80,000	• 63 quarter-page and single column spot colour ads in selected media (Germany, Switzerland, Italy, France, Netherlands) • Advertising placed in 12 publications	• 850 coupon responses • 4730 Travellers Guides distributed
	Promotions	• ATC exp $315,000 • Industry contrib $208,500 (84%)	• Organise presence at trade events - Italy's BIT, Germany's ITB, Switzerland's TTW, France's TOP RESA and Netherland's Vakantiebeurs • Retail agents training programs incl.: DER Reiseakademie, Meier's Weltreisen, Asia/Pacific workshops, ATOS workshop • Select delegates for ATE • Australia pavilion at Expo 1992, Seville	• 45,000 trade visitors & workshop guests reached • 75,000 brochures distributed • 210 Australian delegates at ITB - reached 1121 trade visitors & 15,500 consumers • 91 tour operators attended scheduled workshops
	Servicing	• ATC exp $97,000	• Service and fulfil trade inquiries for information and promotional materials • Industry updates for Australian product suppliers in all priority markets • Produce point of sale material for travel agency use in all markets	• 81,000 inquiries serviced • 125,000 brochures distributed • 1,280 Australia window displays • 2,000 window display units, 4,000 poster sets, 85,000 shell folders distributed

Key Consumer Results	Key Trade Results
• Broader perception of Australia as a desirable, affordable and 'value for money' holiday achieved.	• Increased European tour operator involvement and commitment in ATC joint marketing programs • 8% increase in co-op marketing funds from industry

Achievements
■ Inquiry and visa application levels increased, especially in Germany, Spain and France ■ 9% increase in visitor arrivals in 1992/93 compared with only 2% growth in European long-haul travel generally ■ German visitors up 14%, France 20%, the Netherlands 10% and Italy 6%

C-2

REASON FOR VISIT

	1985				1989			
	Holiday		VFR		Holiday		VFR	
	Total	%	Total	%	Total	%	Total	%
France	3,929	(32.6)	2,183	(18.1)	8,600	(42.8)	3,800	(18.9)
Germany	18,143	(49.3)	8,125	(21.8)	43,800	(64.3)	11,800	(17.3)
Italy	4,171	(28.8)	5,813	(40.1)	8,100	(39.5)	7,000	(34.1)
Netherlands	3,469	(22.6)	8,158	(53.1)	6,600	(32.8)	9,500	(47.3)
Scandinavia	9,351	(49.4)	3,694	(19.1)	27,400	(63.6)	5,700	(13.2)
Scotland	8,821	(61.8)	2,275	(16.0)	19,000	(72.6)	3,500	(12.8)
UK	40,902	(25.7)	80,999	(51.0)	116,500	(40.9)	119,900	(42.1)

D

OVERSEAS VISA REQUIREMENTS

ENTRY VISAS NEEDED TO:

Travel From	USA	Canada	France	Germany	Italy	Spain	UK	Australia	N.Z.	H Kong	Japan	Malaysia	Singapore	Thailand
USA								X						
Mexico			X					X						
Canada								X						
France								X						
Germany								X						
Italy								X						
Spain								X						
U.K.								X						
Australia			X			X					X			
New Zealand														
Hong Kong				X		X		X	X		X	X		
Japan								X						
Malaysia			X			X		X			X			
Singapore	X							X						
Taiwan	X	X	X	X	X	X	X	X	X	X	X	X		X
Philippines	X	X	X	X	X	X	X	X	X		X			
Thailand	X	X	X	X	X	X	X	X			X			
Korea	X	X				X		X			X			
TOTAL	8	4	6	4	3	7	3	16	3	1	7	2	0	1

E

July 1994: Notes of meeting, internal marketing Chris Benson/
Clio Walker/Stuart Able

CRITICAL KEY ISSUES AND TRENDS

- The continuing barriers of perceived cost/time/distance

- Increasing pressures on airfares and airline capacity as demand catches
  up to (and in some cases exceeds) supply

- Short term airline pricing and scheduling decisions often lead to reduced
  consistency and reliability of competitiveness and accessibility

- Reducing consumer marketing funds by the ATC and increased
  competitor spend has severely reduced Australia's share of voice

- While there has been an improvement, there is generally still a weak
  branding of the destination and its product and a hazy perception in the
  minds of consumer

- To date, product and destination servicing for trade and consumers has
  been ad hoc, un co-ordinated, incomplete, reactive, and for the user, very
  difficult

- While registered "desire and intention" to travel to Australia is relatively
  high, conversion of this interest by consumers has not kept pace with its
  growth

- A substantial increase in consumer advertising by tour operators, airlines
  and retail chains, particularly for often discounted short/medium haul
  holidays

- Compared to other destinations there is virtually no consumer promotion
  or advertising by Australian product suppliers

- Corresponding with increased travel advertising spend there is an
  increase in consumer director travel editorial and specific travel media
  available

- Varying degrees of weakness in distribution channels (depending on the
  particular market), lack of retail presence and lack of Australian product
  knowledge by the retail trade

- Problem of visas - most competitive destinations do not require them -
  along with evidence of increasing inability of the Australian High
  Commission, Embassies and Consulates to handle increased demand

- Substantially increased spend particularly by Asian competitors in
  convention marketing

- Threat to increasing incentive business if Australia's consumer image and
  top-of-mind awareness is allowed to diminish.

F

IVS STATISTICS

The International Visitor Survey (IVS) gives some important facts about the European travellers:

- The majority of travellers to Australia from Europe, around 50%, fall in the age group of 25-49 years

- About 30% of European visitors are over 50 except in the UK where they account for 40% (VFR travellers)

- At the other end of the scale, the 20-24 year olds account for around 10-12% (except in Scandinavia where is it 18% backpackers)

- An average of 88% of European visitors to Australia classify themselves as 'non group independents'. The UK is the highest with 92% which is indicative of the high volume of VFR and "working holiday" travellers

- The percentages of visitors who bought arrangements other than the international airfare were:

  UK/Ireland 35%
  Germany 40%
  Scandinavia 27%
  Other Europe 34%

- 84% of all visitors who used backpacker hostels came from Europe

- 64% of all visitors who used campervans or who used tents came from Europe

- More Europeans than any other nationality rented self-drive cars or campervans

Source: IVS 1992

G

1993 TRACKING STUDY - GERMANY

Australia's position has eased since 1992. This is common to other major destinations although Thailand has held at similar levels to 1992. Australia is still second to USA as a preferred destination and follows USA and Canada in terms of intention/consideration for a holiday.

Intention to visit	1993 - 8% (-4%)
Intend or consider:	1993 - 17% (no change)
Ideal destination (first choice):	1993 - 8% (-2%)
Ideal destination (first three choices)	1993 - 20% (-4%)

Overseas holiday advertising has not had a wide reach (38%). Among these, Australia's is best remembered and best liked. However, our advertising has reached fewer people this year than in 1992; 15% of spontaneous recall and 18% prompted.

There has been relatively little movement of "The Images of Australia". Beautiful Beaches and Big, Airy & Spacious moved up slightly (3%); Adventure Holiday, Different to Other Countries, Unique Scenery, interesting things to do - all stayed more or less the same. The biggest positive shift was for Last Frontier 67% (+12%) and the most significant drop was for Exciting Holiday 68% (-9%).

Australia compares quite well to competitive destinations, however, there has been minimal movement since 1992.

"It is a country which is different from other countries"

> Australia 72% leads; Thailand is number two at 66%, followed by USA 64%, Kenya, Singapore and South Africa are equal fourth 59, 57, 56% respectively

"It is an exciting place to visit"

> USA 70% and Australia 68% are clear leaders. Thailand 56%, South Africa 55%, Kenya 54%, Singapore 48%

In the "safety" category Australia is clear number one at 64%. All other countries lie between 32% and 13%.

Australia 62% also leads with "friendly people", however most other countries follow closely; Thailand 61%, Kenya 54%, USA 50%, Singapore 49% and South Africa 32%.

H-1

1993 TRACKING STUDY - ITALY

Australia follows USA as the country Italians most intend to visit in the next three years. As a preferred destination, Australia (33%) is again second behind USA (40%) and clearly ahead of China (20%) and Thailand (15%). It was more strongly preferred by those who recognised ATC advertising (41%).

Intention to visit	1993 - 23% (+8%)
Intend or consider:	1993 - 29% (+4%)
Ideal destination (first choice):	1993 - 17% (+4%)
Ideal destination (first three choices)	1993 - 33% (+4%)

Spontaneous recall of Australian advertising has dropped slightly to 8%; total prompted recall was 24%.

Positive moves of "Images of Australia" include:

Unique Scenery:	84% (+26%)
Adventure Holiday:	78% (+5%)
Unique & Varied Lifestyle:	67% (+12%)
Unique Holiday:	65% (+7%)

The negative moves were minor such as Beautiful Beaches 88% (-2%); Modern Cities 85% (-5%); Interesting things to do 68% (-2%).

Compared to competitive destinations, Australia's positioning is not especially unique.

"It is a country which is different from other countries".
Australia 84% is second behind Thailand 88% and followed by South Africa 80%, Caribbean 78%, USA 75%.

"It is an exciting place to visit"
Australia 78% again second behind Thailand 81%, followed by Caribbean 74%, USA 68% and South Africa 61%.

"It has lots of different things to do"
Australia 68% lies third behind USA 89% and Thailand 71%. Caribbean follows at 58% and South Africa 45%.

In the "value for money" category Australia 60% is only ahead of South Africa 49%. Thailand leads 78% and Caribbean and USA are equal second 74%.

H-2

1993 TRACKING STUDY - SWEDEN

The potential for Swedish travellers to select Australia as a holiday destination has improved over the past 12 months. More people nominate Australia as a desirable destination; more people have put it on the consideration list; and more people have moved it up onto their "intended" list of destinations for the next three years.

Intention to visit:	1993 - 23% (+9%)
Intend or consider:	1993 - 34% (+12%)
Ideal destination (first choice)	1993 - 22% (+4%)
Ideal destination (first three choices):	1993 - 49% (+11%)

These figures strongly indicate an upsurge in arrivals over the next few years.

Awareness of Australian advertising is slightly lower than last year among the whole group (39%) but is at a higher level than any competitive advertising. Recognition of advertising was much higher than recall with 70% recognising some advertising, 52% recognised TV and 42% recognised some press ads. Recognition was much higher than 1992.

There were some very positive moves of "The Images of Australia":

Unique Scenery:	87% (+7%)
Interesting things to do:	77% (+7%)
Offers Variety:	73% (+6%)
Unique Holiday Destination:	69% (+12%)

On the down side, "The cost of getting me there puts me off" moved from 44% in 1992 to 54% in 1993; perhaps as a result of the devaluation of the Swedish Krona. Interestingly, another category "It is harsh and dry with a hot climate" moved from 56% in 1992 to 70% in 1993; possibly due to the popularity of "The Flying Doctors" in Sweden.

When comparing Australia to competitive destinations, we sit well on most attributes explored.

"It is an exciting place to visit"
> Australia is a clear leader at 85%, ahead of Caribbean 77%, New Zealand 74%, Thailand 73%, USA 60% and South Africa 49%.

"It has a lot of interesting things to do"
> Australia 77% is number two behind USA 79%. Thailand 70%, New Zealand 64%, Caribbean 47%, South Africa 30%.

In the "good value for money" category, Thailand is a clear leader at 77%; all other countries, including Australia 32%, are between 26% - 39%.

1993 TRACKING STUDY - SWITZERLAND

This is the first year in which a tracking study has been undertaken in Switzerland and, therefore, no comparisons year-on-year can be made.

Intention to visit	1993 - 17%
Intend or consider:	1993 - 24%
Ideal destination (first choice):	1993 - 16%
Ideal destination (first three choices)	1993 - 37%

Awareness of any overseas holiday advertising is low at 41%, of which 32% claimed spontaneously to recall Australia's advertising. This seems very high in view of the expenditure and both source and content recall suggest that information other than ATC advertising is being recalled.

"The Images of Australia" are quite well developed among Swiss potential travellers.

Big, Airy & Spacious:	92%
Adventure Holiday:	83%
Unique Scenery:	79%
Variety Holiday:	78%
Exciting Place:	75%
Interesting things to do:	73%

Compared to other destinations, Australia sits competitively on some attributes, however, we do not fare so well on others.

"It is a country which is different from other countries"
USA 74%, Thailand 67%, Singapore 65%, Australia 63%, Kenya 62%

"It is an exciting place to visit"
USA 84% and Australia 75% are clear leaders. Thailand, Singapore and Kenya score 62, 50 and 43% respectively.

"It is a safe place to have a holiday"
Australia 62% clearly leads this attribute with Singapore 38%, USA 34%, Thailand 28% and Kenya 22%.

"It has friendly people"
Australia 72% is almost equal to Thailand 73%, followed by USA 64% and Kenya and Singapore both at 59%.

"It has lots of interesting things to do"
Australia 73% again fares well although USA is clear leader at 92%. Thailand 66%, Singapore 56%, Kenya 51%.

H-4

1993 TRACKING STUDY - UNITED KINGDOM

Australia has improved its position in the UK tourism market in 1993 on all consumer tracking measures.

Intention to visit	1993 - 19% (+4%)
Intend or consider:	1993 - 25% (+4%)
Ideal destination (first choice):	1993 - 19% (+2%)
Ideal destination (first three choices)	1993 - 38% (+2%)

Of the 53% who recalled seeing any overseas holiday destination advertising, 43% recalled Australia's. This was the campaign most recalled, surpassing the US for the first time.

There were some significant moves of "The Images of Australia", both positive and negative:

Unique Scenery:	81% (+14%)
Beautiful Beaches:	90% (+5%)
Modern Cities:	71% (+5%)
Exciting Place:	68% (+4%)
Offers Variety:	57% (-5%)
Friendly People:	50% (-9%)

When comparing Australia to other competitive destinations, Australia has no unique positioning compared to USA, Canada, New Zealand, Hong Kong and Thailand.

"It is a country which is different from other countries":
Australia is equal to USA at 61%, rates higher than Canada and New Zealand (55 & 53%) and below Hong Kong and Thailand (78 & 79%).

"It is an exciting place to visit":
Australia (68%) is equal to Thailand (69%), rates higher than Canada and New Zealand (57 & 53%) and below USA and. Hong Kong (76 & 79%).

Australia (49%) rates third behind New Zealand (72%) and Canada (64%) as a "safe place to have a holiday". Hong Kong (26%), USA (23%) and Thailand (15%).

Australia (50%) has dropped its positioning in the "friendly people" category compared to the last three years (90 = 59%, 91 = 67%, 92 = 59%). USA, Canada and New Zealand all rate higher at 75,69 and 64% respectively.

All other destinations rate higher than Australia (33%) as a "good value for money vacation". USA tops the list with 69%.

PRESS COVERAGE RE: SPAIN

1. Spain is hoping 1993 will reap major benefits from tourism. The media exposure given to Barcelona (during the Olympics) and Seville (during Expo 92) created a high level of public awareness, while Madrid benefited to a lesser extent as European City of Culture. Tour operators are confident Spain will win back some of the ground lost in recent years. If 1993 is an anti-climax for Spain after the excesses of 1992, it is not evident when meeting Spanish Tourist Office UK director German Porras. Last year produced a modest increase of six per cent in UK arrivals to 6.5 million, spread fairly evenly throughout resort areas and the big cities of Madrid and Barcelona.
    But there was a marked slow-down after an 18% increase in the first six months. Overall visitors increased by 3% to 55 million. Even allowing for the many day-trip visitors across borders, more than 40 million people went to Spain.
    Barcelona received very favourable coverage during the Olympics, as did Seville during Expo 92.

2. While on the whole Europe bookings have been somewhat disappointing for some wholesalers, suppliers say that a number of European destinations are selling well this year. Not surprisingly, they are destinations in which the US dollar has gained the most against European currencies - Britain, Italy, and for many, Spain and Greece.

3. A number of operators report Spain is selling well following its post Olympics/Expo publicity, and several wholesalers point to Greece as making a strong showing this year. European fly/drives and fly/rail vacations are selling well this year, others note.

I

EUROPEAN PRODUCT/COMMUNICATIONS STRATEGY

1 — Basic Thrust/Overall Positioning:
2 — Executional Themes:
3 — Specific Executions (Cultural Nuances)

	Australia, Land of Discovery		Australia — Endless Sun & Exotic Beaches	
	Active — Experience Australia	Passive — See Australia	Active — Sun, Sand, Surf & Sex	Passive — Exotic Sun
UK	Exp Australia 10.7%	V.F.R 0.9%	Young Ragers 2.2%	Faraway Beaches 3.9% / Exotic Sun 1.6% / Upscale Resorts 0.6% / Package Resorts 3.9%
	Total UK 11%	Total UK 1%	Total UK 10%	Total UK 10%
Germany	Foreign Lands 10.9%	See Australia 13.6% / Germany V.F.R. 1.8%	Sun Seekers (Types I & II) 12.6%	Sun Resorts 8.1%
	Total Germany 11%	Total Germany 15%	Total Germany 13%	Total Germany 8%
Italy	Exp Australia 10.8%	See Australia 6.4%	Young Ragers 5.8%	Garaway Beaches 4.4% / Stylish Beaches 3.2% / Upscale Resorts 2.0% / Beach Resorts 2.0% / Package Resorts 3.6%
	Total Italy 11%	Total Italy 6%	Total Italy 6%	Total Italy 15%
Sweden	Foreign Lands 6.0% / Exp Australia 7.9%	Tour Australia 3.3% / See Australia 4.6%	Sun Seekers (Types I & II) 6.3%	NIL
	Total Sweden 14%	Total Sweden 8%	Total Sweden 6%	
France	Foreign lands 20.9% / Adventure Seekers 2.5% / Exp Australia 2.5%	See Australia 6.3%	Youthful Ragers 4.1%	Exotic Resort 2.0% / Package Resort 7.9% / Upscale Resort 2.5%
	Total France 26%	Total France 6%	Total France 4%	Total France 12%

J

CONSUMER PERCEPTIONS

European Consumer Profiles

UK

- Relatively mature market
- Strong VFR links and common language
- High level of awareness/knowledge of Australia through cultural links, TV, language
- Positive impact of TV soaps and films - sunny weather and beautiful beaches
- Negative impact of TV soaps and films - not foreign, exciting or different enough
- Four X adverts create rough, uncouth image - i.e. Australia is not a sophisticated destination
- Price-sensitive market - perception of Australia as a "too expensive destination" gradually being broken down by charters although Australia has lowest rating for "good value for money destination"
- Relatively high yield consumers - UK is 4th top spender after US, Germany and Japan
- High level of desire - Australia - 2nd most desired holiday destination
- Not such independent travellers - package holidays account for 60% of total outbound holiday travel
- High recognition of TV campaign

GERMANY

- High propensity and opportunity to travel
- High yield and length of stay
- VFR - 18%
- Seek soft adventure
- Interest in Ecotourism and great outdoors
- Independent travellers - small percentage of package tours
- Often educated and seeking "educational" experience
- Australia - perceived as being the most exciting and different place to visit with the friendliest people
- Australia - seen as safe/clean/under populated
- Strong desire - 2nd to US
- Australia's advertising is the most recalled and liked of all overseas advertising although overall awareness is beginning to drop
- Perceived time/distance/cost barriers
- Fuzzy and unfocused view of Australia
- New tourism opportunities

K-1

FRANCE

- Large but unfocused interest in Australia as a holiday destination
- French tourist to Australia - highly independent and adventurous
- Current market is moderately wealthy, well-travelled and 40+
- Good potential market is younger (20-35 years), well-travelled professionals
- Hardly any VFR market and no sizeable backpacker market
- Strong adventure bias - desire to experience and discover Australia in relative comfort
- Australia seen as new "Far West". Films like Mad Max and Crocodile Dundee symbolises Australia for many
- Interest in culture - especially Aboriginal art and history
- Language - not a barrier and often an attraction for English language study
- Perceived as being expensive
- Fear of being unwelcome

ITALY

- Fast growth market for long haul travel
- High spenders - majority of long haul passengers come from the richer mid and northern parts of Italy
- VFR links (although most VFR traffic is ex-Australia to Italy)
- Tendency to book individually tailored tours
- Becoming more adventurous and independent
- Becoming less intimidated by language and distance barriers
- Large interest in relaxation/beach holidays
- High desire to visit Australia - intention to visit 2nd to USA
- Expanding long haul holiday base
- Positive images of Australia include unique scenery, adventure holiday, varied lifestyle
- Not considered a value for money destination compared to other destinations

SPAIN

- High interest in Australia - positive images and perceived high value
- Long haul travellers - wealthy, self-made people
- Late booking market - even for long haul
- High spenders - about European average
- Poor knowledge of Australia
- Inclination towards Spanish speaking long haul destinations - South America and Mexico
- Outbound travel very seasonal, i.e. northern summer

K-2

SWEDEN

- Increasing interest in long haul destinations due to high disposable income and annual leave although current economic situation has meant a decrease in consumer disposable income
- Far East and USA - most popular long haul destinations
- Travellers are becoming more adventurous and independent
- Oct, Nov, Dec, Jan - prime travel months
- Tendency to take on long holiday (usually long-haul) rather than several shorter holidays
- Very high level of desire to travel to Australia/most desired
- Australia - large share of voice
- Swedish consumer = long stay, high yield
- Australia viewed as a unique and exciting holiday destination with a variety of interesting activities on offer
- Cost - a major factor

SWITZERLAND

- Consumer expenditure - at an all time low due to recession
- VFR market - relatively large
- Australia - seen as expensive
- Australia - viewed as less of a foreign country
- Travel to Australia - grown by 100% over last 5 years
- Well-developed awareness and image perceptions of Australia
- Australians seen as friendly people
- Desire to go to Australia - 2nd after USA
- High yield market
- Environmentally friendly nation - fear of ozone depletion in Australia
- Australia seen as "big, airy and spacious", unique, exciting and a place for safe adventure

CONSUMER BUDGET ANALYSIS 92/93 V 93/94 V 94/95

	1992/93 AU$	Local Currency	1993/94 AU$	Local Currency	% Change v 1992/93	1994/95 AU$	Local Currency	% Change v 1992/93	% Change v 1993/94
Germany	2,196,088	2,039,506	3,320,209	3,469,286	+70.10	2,500,000	2,938,275	+44.06	-15.3
UK	3,604,916	1,333,818	2,507,000	1,078,010	-19.17	2,087,789	939,505	-29.56	-12.84
France	1,045,299	3,300,035	1,006,000	3,581,762	+8.53	1,003,055	4,002,475	+21.28	+11.74
Italy	872,273	713,580,373	834,000	843,474,240	+18.2	794,166	910,476,375	+27.59	+7.94
Sweden	878,618	3,068,024	270,000	1,332,828	-56.55	226,102	1,244,037	-59.45	-6.66
Switzerland	260,071	214,825	-	-	-	-	-	-	-
TOTAL	8,857,265	3,277,188	7,937,209	2,795,000	-10.38	6,611,112	2,975,000	-25.35	-16.7
£ST at AU$ - £0.358	£ST at AU$ = £0.37	-11.05	£ST at AU$ = £0.43			£ST at AU$ = £0.45			

£ST: DM 2.51
      IL 2211
      SEK 9.4375
      SFR 2.2325
      FFR 8.5325

£ST: DM 2.43
      IL 2352
      SEK 11.48
      SFR 2.25
      FFR 8.28

£ST: DM 2.6118
      IL 2547.68
      SEK 12.2269
      SFR 2.2083
      FFR 8.8673

L

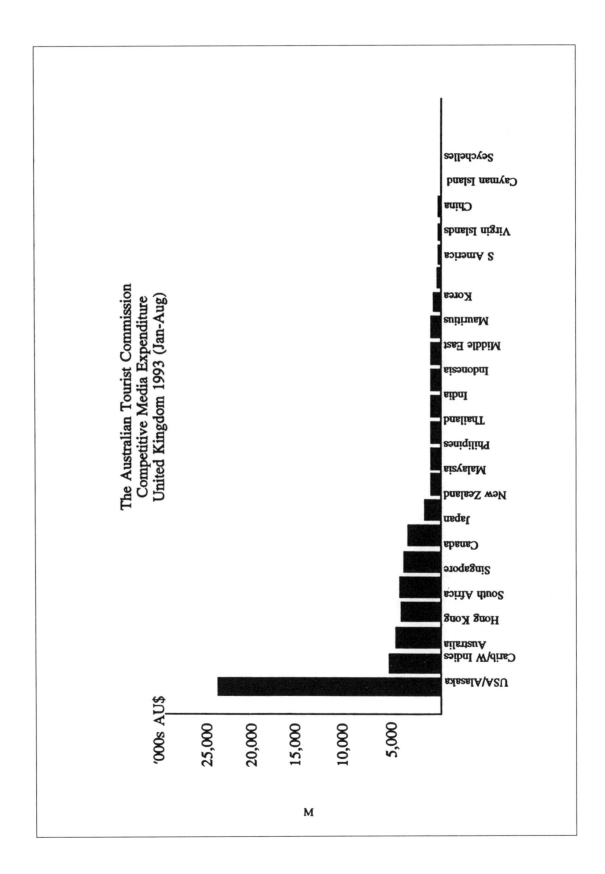

The Australian Tourist Commission
Competitive Media Expenditure
United Kingdom 1993 (Jan-Aug)

EUROPEAN ARRIVALS TO COMPETITIVE DESTINATIONS

1992 Arrival Figures (individuals) from Europe to competitive destinations and % increase from 1991

	Austria	France	Germany
Australia	10,000 + 5%	25,400 + 12%	89,900 + 16%
Kenya	14,041 - 9%	35,555 - 16%	109,973 - 13%
South Africa	11,897 + 5%	24,556 + 13%	91,362 + 5%
Carribean	23,391 - 10%	359,388 + 5%	182,861 - 1%
Canada	26,500 + 22%	310,000 + 1%	290,300 + 6%
USA	150,663 + 25%	795,444 + 3%	1,691,663 + 18%
South America	13,306 -	97,026 - 15%	174,595 - 5%
Hong Kong	22,104 + 13%	128,497 + 34%	172,200 + 26%
South East Asia	72,618 + 3%	368,311 + 4%	638,779 + 8%
New Zealand	3,507 + 24%	5,325 + 15%	45,705 + 33%
Egypt	47,157 + 108%	213,376 + 171%	356,178 + 117%
India	10,606 + 7%	74,304 + 7%	84,422 + 17%

N-1

EUROPEAN ARRIVALS TO COMPETITIVE DESTINATIONS

1992 Arrival Figures (individuals) from Europe to competitive destinations and % increase from 1991

	Italy	Netherlands	Spain
Australia	27,400 + 13%	23,500 + 10%	4,900 + 23%
Kenya	35,105 - 14%	12,628 - 20%	7,186 - 27%
South Africa	20,339 + 13%	21,007 + 16%	4,386 - 9%
Carribean	110,139 + 36%	120,240 + 1%	62,625 + 24%
Canada	94,800 + 9%	85,200 - 3%	27,700 + 13%
USA	589,837 + 23%	342,034 + 8%	343,922 + 18%
South America	148,361 + 2%	48,935 - 32%	131,976 - 9%
Hong Kong	80,634 + 15%	42,571 + 15%	24,525 + 35%
South East Asia	260,724 + 18%	254,945 + 3%	54,927 + 6%
New Zealand	3,766 + 5%	9,734 + 28%	1,528 + 65%
Egypt	169,962 + 117%		84,172 + 62%
India	51,138 + 24%	30,145 + 52%	24,850 + 82%

EUROPEAN ARRIVALS TO COMPETITIVE DESTINATIONS

1992 Arrival Figures (individuals) from Europe to competitive destinations and % increase from 1991

	Sweden	Switzerland	UK
Australia	19,100 -	29,000 - 2%	289,900 + 10%
Kenya	22,739 + 1%	26,883 - 9%	117,458 - 17%
South Africa	4,901 + 35%	20,300 + 4%	151,913 - 7%
Carribean	22,179 - 2%	32,654 - 18%	362,042 - 6%
Canada	25,900 - 2%	79,100 + 3%	536,400 + 1%
USA	261,728 + 1%	321,725 + 6%	2,823,983 + 13%
South America	10,842 + 3%	56,519 - 14%	85,286 - 9%
Hong Kong	24,648 + 15%	50,709 + 13%	314,231 + 14%
South East Asia	135,613 + 2%	208,872 + 18%	712,036 - 14%
New Zealand	6,700 - 16%	12,457 + 6%	96,523 + 10%
Egypt		57,415 + 100%	316,803 + 90%
India	13,305 + 26%	28,851 - 1%	244,263 + 15%

EUROPEAN ARRIVAL IN AUSTRALIA

ANNUAL	HISTORIC		AV INC	EXPECTED		AV INC
	1984	1989	PA %	1994	1999	PA %
Australia	3,600	9,200	18.3	14,300	22,900	10%
France	11,200	20,100	12.4	33,000	65,500	14%
Germany	34,200	68,100	14.8	129,000	260,000	15%
Italy	13,400	20,500	8.9	44,500	101,500	17%
Netherlands	14,100	20,100	7.3	30,500	46,500	9%
Scandinavia	15,600	43,100	22.6	61,000	107,500	11%
Switzerland	12,500	27,400	16.9	42,500	68,250	10%
UK/Ireland	150,000	286,000	13.8	405,000	627,000	9%

THE EUROPEAN LONGHAUL MARKET

The Biggest Seven Source Markets

RANK	COUNTRY	TRIPS - MILLION
1	Great Britain	4.1
2	Germany	3.9
3	France	2.1
4	Netherlands	1.0
5	Belgium	0.8
6	Sweden	0.7
7	Switzerland	0.7

Source: European Travel Monitor

O-1

THE EUROPEAN LONGHAUL MARKET

Destinations

COUNTRY	PERCENTAGE
USA	36%
Asia	20%
Africa (Sub Sahara)	13%
Latin America	12%
Caribbean	8%
Canada	8%
Australasia	7%
Australia	*5%*
New Zealand	*2%*

Source: European Travel Monitor

O-2

THE EUROPEAN LONGHAUL MARKET

Type of Business

TYPE OF BUSINESS	PERCENTAGE
Incentive	5%
Trade Fair	13%
Conference	13%
Traditional	69%

Source: European Travel Monitor

O-3

GNP EUROPE

	European Personal Disposable Income		% growth p/a Forecasts
	1986-1991	1991-1995	1995-1999
West Germany	2.9	2.2	2.0
Spain	3.4	3.5	3.0
Holland	1.9	2.0	1.7
Belgium	1.9	2.3	1.9
Italy	3.1	2.4	2.0
France	2.1	2.5	2.5
UK	3.7	2.0	2.5

The Single European Act forecasts a 6% benefit to economic growth as a result of the removal of trade barriers. The UK, nevertheless, will remain a less well-off economy.

P-1

POPULATION: EUROPE (1989)

	POP 1989 (M)	Forecast 1995 (M)	POP 2010 (M)	Adult Holiday Makers (M)	%M of Holiday Makers	Departs. Abroad
France	56.3	57.1	58.8	24.8	16	4.0
Germany*	76.1	78.3	81.2	30.0	60	18.5
Italy	57.4	57.4	55.6	25.3	13	3.3
Netherlands	14.9	15.3	15.7	7.4	64	4.7
Scandinavia	22.8	23.2	23.2	N/A	N/A	N/A
Switzerland	6.6	6.8	6.8	N/A	N/A	N/A
UK/Ireland	56.7	58.1	59.4	27.5	35	9.6

* including former East and West Germany

CORPORATE OBJECTIVES

The ATC's overall corporate objective is to increase the economic and social benefit to Australia of inbound tourism by achieving a sustained increase in international tourist arrivals, yield and market share. In carrying out its objectives, the ATC undertakes marketing activities which are primarily directed at consumers and the trade overseas.

The overall goal is supported by objectives in each of the following areas:

Marketing	To position Australia as the chosen destination in all major markets by creating awareness and desire to travel to Australia
Product Development & Distribution	To seek to influence all elements of the marketing variables that are involved in converting desires to travel into positive action
Strategic Market Research	To use market research to develop competitive and professional marketing programs, provide visitor arrival targets and to evaluate programs to ensure their effectiveness
Environmental and Social	To promote and encourage ecologically sustainable tourism development, increase the awareness and respect of international tourists and tour operators for Australia's natural, cultural and social environment and to assess the impact of major changes in inbound tourism
Corporate Direction and Support	To maximise the ATC's achievements through effective corporate management and support and by ensuring that the benefits to Australia of inbound tourism are appreciated by policy-makers and the wider community

Q

Australian Tourist Commission

Examination paper

Additional information to be taken into account when answering the questions set.

MEMORANDUM

To: All Regional Directors   From: Doug McKenna

Subject: Olympics 2000

Date: 9 December 1994

The local authorities in Sydney have just agreed to make grants available to hotel companies in the run up to the Olympics in 2000. It is estimated that an additional 3000 rooms will be needed in Sydney and the surrounding area to cater for the influx of visitors expected to attend the games. Although some of this grant will be taken up by local companies, we can expect the big international companies such as Holiday Inn, Marriott, Sheraton and Forte to take advantage of these grants too.

As you know, occupancy rates are currently running at about 65% so the hotels are making money – but not a lot.

With average break-even at about 55% occupancy and an additional 3000 rooms on stream, the Sydney hoteliers will be looking to us to help fill them after the Olympics' visitors have left. I hope your presentations next week will give some concrete ideas on how we will do this.

I look forward to hearing your presentations.

Best wishes

Doug McKenna

Examination questions

Based on the data you have collected and further consultation with your team you have decided to approach the strategic marketing presentation in three discreet parts. Your presentation, *in report format,* will cover the following:

1   Propose and justify an effective method of segmentation for the European Market that will form the basis of your strategic marketing plan.   **30 marks**

2   Present a detailed strategic marketing plan for Europe that meets the stated needs of the ATC and the Ministry of Tourism up to the year 2004. Your plan should be firmly rooted in identified consumer needs and should cover all aspects of marketing as well as the 'uncontrollable' elements of the environment (including competition) that you see as important.   **55 marks**

3   Based on your proposed marketing strategy for the ATC, prepare a brief action plan to show how your approach will meet the needs of Sydney hoteliers after 2000.   **15 marks**

Australian Tourist Commission

Examiners' notes

Overview

The case

The case is largely undisguised and represents a real organization with real problems. The case details broadly represent the marketing issues that the new Regional Director (they are currently recruiting) will face when he/she takes up the position.

Key points

1 The ATC has recently reorganized and has created the 'European Region'.
2 Chris Benson has been told to move from 'promotion' to 'full marketing' responsibility.
3 The ATC does not have an effective segmentation approach and needs one.
4 The Olympics is important only as a 'lever' to building the annual growth of visitors to Australia – before and *after* 2000.

The Additional Information

One comment from last year's paper (justified I think) was that it was difficult to see how and where the marks for using the additional information were awarded. This case has taken a different approach to the additional information and has devoted a question (Q3) uniquely to it.

The additional information also gives yet another strong hint that the strategy must be aimed at 2000+ and not just at the Olympics themselves.

Question one   30 marks

'Propose and justify an effective method of segmentation for the European Market that will form the basis of your strategic marketing plan.'

Approach

The important words here are: ... *an* effective method for the *European market* that will ...

What the ATC needs is a way through this jungle and a way of concentrating their marketing effort on to those segments where they will get the maximum response.

'Country' or 'national' segmentation is not acceptable. The opportunity of the reorganization and the EC is to break away from this and identify behavioural or motivational groups of customers. Remember, 'national segmentation' means breaking down the European market by historical differences in military power!

Good answers are likely to vary in their recommendations (because of the options available) but should include:

1 A critical assessment of ATC's current approach
2 Proposal of an effective segmentation method
3 Tests of segmentation
4 Justification of the recommendations

Has your answer included the following?

- Current 'segmentation' approach is:
  - Cumbersome
  - Too wide
  - Based on administrative convenience

- The proposed segmentation approach should:
  - Not be based on countries
  - Not be based on 'the trade'
  - Be based on consumer needs/motivations
  - Be related to 'reasons for travel/experience'
  - Differentiate between understanding motivations of customers and targeting them with marketing activities, e.g. you can use ACORN, *country,* etc. to 'target' but it is not because they are 'German' that they go to Australia
  - Be focused enough for the ATC to concentrate their marketing activity to have an effect
  - Inform the ATC what to do about:
    – the trade
    – national boundaries
    – the 'Australian product'
  - Inform the development of the ATC's marketing strategy

- Tests of segmentation:
  - Homogeneous
  - Reachable
  - Profitable
  - Recognized, etc.

- Justification:
  - How will it improve ATC's marketing effectiveness?

Question two   55 marks

'Present a detailed strategic marketing plan for Europe that meets the stated needs of the ATC and the Ministry of Tourism up to the year 2004. Your plan should be firmly rooted in identified consumer needs and should cover all aspects of marketing as well as the 'uncontrollable' elements of the environment (including competition) that you see as important.'

Approach

Ansoff is likely to be popular again but should only be used as a guide and strategic recommendations must be firmly linked into the ATC's particular situation. The same argument, of course, holds for PEST/SLEPT, PORTER, GEC or any of the other models.

Pure models gain no marks, applied to the ATC's situation does.

What the question is asking for is:

1 Links to the segments proposed in Question one. (Customers)
2 Detailed marketing plan:
   - What to do?
   - How to do it?
3 For Europe
4 For ten years (to 2004)

Good answers will follow a logical sequence of steps such as:

1 Apply environmental analysis to ATC
2 Identify target market and position ATC to meet them
3 Identify strategic options
4 Select and expand on strategic approach
5 Develop a marketing plan (7Ps) to deliver the strategy
6 Describe budgets and control systems

Has your answer considered the following?

1 Corporate objectives
   - Understand what the ATC's job is
   - Europe is part of ATC worldwide

2 Environment/situation analysis
   - PEST/SLEPT approach
   - What are the important factors that effect the plans between now and 2004?
   - Competition – who from?
                 – likely effects over following years

3 Target market
   - Related to Question one?
   - Who are we aiming at?
   - What are the key needs/wants/motivators/drivers?
   - Other 'stakeholders' and their interests

4 Marketing objectives
   - What are we trying to do?
   - Visitor numbers per year
   - Spend in Australia per winter/per year

5 Targeting and positioning
   - What is the key 'Product-Market Match'?
   - What is Australia to mean?
   - How different from the competition?
   - 'Umbrella' position and segment variants?
   - Different positions to different segments?

6 Market penetration[1]
   - Frequency of visits
   - Length of stay
   - Amount of spend
   - Competitive positioning[1]

7 Product development
   - Repackaging/repositioning
   - Interest or segment needs driven
   - Actions with 'inbound' tourist product producers
   - Other states/territories (beyond Queensland/NT)
   - Beyond Sydney (for Olympics)

8 Market development[1]
   - Segments (new)
   - 'New' aspects of Australia e.g. culture/arts[1]

9 Diversification
   - Can't see any opportunities here, although candidates may try to 'fill the box' with something

10 Product policy
   - Package/present/develop products to better meet identified customer needs
   - Activities
   - Mix 'n' match/modular
   - Use Olympics as lever

11 Pricing policy
   - To match benefits sought
   - To match segments
   - To select targeted customers

12 Place policy
- Strategic alliances with suppliers
- New distribution channels for segments?
- Trade motivation

13 People policy
- Structure (modification only?)
- Training and recruitment
- Trade training

14 Process policy
- Systems and procedures
- Booking process – variants for segments
- Travel in Australia
- Travel to Australia

15 Promotion/physical evidence policy
- Clear communications objectives to match rest of mix
- Broad split – advertising/promotion/PR etc.
- *Not* pages of detail!

16 Timetables
- Showing development of strategy over ten years
- Growth/development important
- Olympics as just one element

17 Budgets
- Estimated costings over the period
- Related to objectives/returns required
- Note opportunity costs and trade-offs made

18 Control
- What control procedures are recommended?
- How implemented?
- Contingency planning

19 Other (miscellaneous)
- Short/medium/long term divisions to plans
- Internal (ATC) factors for consideration
- Re-organization (not major!)
- Individual segment/market plans – OK but need to be combined into an overall 'European Plan'

Note ¹: This process uses 'Ansoff'. Other models such as Porter/GEC may be equally valid and, consequently, steps 6–9 will vary.

Question three   15 marks

'Based on your proposed marketing strategy for the ATC, prepare a brief action plan to show how your approach will meet the needs of Sydney hoteliers after 2000.'

Approach

This question is applied directly to the additional information provided at the time of the examination. Although no hint of the hotel application was made in the case study itself, a candidate who has properly prepared the case should have no problem in taking the proposed strategy one more step into practical application. It follows then that Question three must seem to follow on logically from what you have written in Question one and Question two.

Question three clearly focuses on the years post-Olympics and tests your ability to understand why *customer retention* is important.

Good answers will extend strategy into action and will include:

1   Build on the proposed strategy of Question one/Question two
2   Propose full marketing tactics that address the problem
3   Suggest control systems/contingency plans

Has your answer considered the following?

1   The 3000 additional rooms don't all have to be filled from Europe
2   Advertising, while important, is not the only solution
3   People need a reason to visit Australia (hence to need rooms) i.e. it is 'derived demand'
4   Whether people go back (re-purchase) will depend on how satisfied they were with the previous trip
5   Joint programmes with the hoteliers may be important – note that many of the larger groups will have European operations too.
6   Demand for 'out of season' needs to be managed/encouraged. The rooms will be available 365 days per year
7   If occupancy falls below a profitable level pressure will be brought to bear on ATC to do something about it

Index

Marketing planning, 6
Marketing report (study), 178–80
Marketing research system, *see* Market research
Marketing strategy, 5–7, 104–5
    evaluation and appraisal, 135
    for market challengers, 106–7
    for market followers, 108
    for market leaders, 105–6
    for market nichers, 108–9
Matrix structures, 19–20
Micro environment, 45
Mini case studies, 158–9
    common errors, 159
    past cases, 160–1

New Directions plc (mini case study), 166–8
    suggested solution, 185, 198
New product development (NPD), 116–17
    (study), 183–4
    test marketing, 117–19
Non-financial evaluation measures, 138–9

Objectives, definition, 6
Operational ratios, 30
Organizational culture, 148
    balance, 32–3
    changing, 191–2, 199
Organizational markets, 71–2
Organizational structures, 18–19
    buying process, 70–1, 73–5
    redesign, 149
    (study), 181–4
    vulnerability, 62

Penton Ltd (mini case study), 165–6
    suggested solution, 181–5, 198
People management, 131
Performance measurement, *see* Evaluation and appraisal
Performance-importance grid, 25, 33–4
Performance-importance matrix, 34–5
PEST analysis/framework, 49–50, 146
    changing environments, 51–2
Phoenix Telecom Ltd (mini case study), 163–5
    suggested solution, 180–1, 197
Planning, 4, 6, 10, 96
    approaches, 96
    contingency, 9
    and control cycle, 10–11
    corporate, 4, 6
    importance, 11–12
    obstacles to, 12
    scenario, 9
    strategic perspectives, 95
    (study), 183
Planning and implementation matrix, 39

Political/legal factors, 50, 51, 147
Portfolio analysis (PA), 95
    BCG approach, 97–8
    comparative approaches (study), 201–2
    current status, 101
    General Electric multi-factor model, 100
    limitations, 99–100
Portland Promotional Products Ltd (mini case study), 161–3
    suggested solution, 178–81
Positioning, 90–1
Positioning statement (study), 189
Price makers, 119
Price takers, 119
Pricing decisions, 119–21
Product dimensions, 112–14
Product evaluation (study), 193–4
Product life cycle (PLC), 113–14
    as evaluation criterion, 141
Product line, definition, 113
Product management, 113
Product mix, definition, 113
Product portfolio, 32–3
Profit evaluation, 138, 152
Profit margins, 29
Promotional decisions, 121–2
    budget, 123–4
    creative appeal, 124
    objectives, 122
    results measurement/testing, 124–5

Quick ratio, 30

Range branding, 115
Relationship marketing, 75–6
Resource audit, 25, 26
Resource utilization, 25, 28–9, 149
Result reporting, 153
Return on capital employed (ROCE), 30
Revenue, source, 152
RTJ Engineering Ltd (mini case study), 175–7
    suggested solution, 200–4

7-S framework, 40, 149
Sales force:
    evaluating, 130–31
    managing, 129
    market-structured, 129
    motivating, 129–30
    network, 194
    payment systems, 130
    product-structured, 129
    territorial-structured, 129
Scenario planning, 9
Segmentation, 80–2
    bases for, 82–3
    choice of, 86–8

    industrial markets, 83–4
    marketing activities, 89–90
    problems, 85
    testing, 84
Selective distribution, definition, 126
Shared values (7-S framework), 40
Shareholders (as stakeholders), 29, 137
Skills (7-S framework), 32, 40
SLEPT environmental factors, 146–7
Social and cultural factors, 50, 51, 146
Societal marketing concept, 2–3
Staffing (7-S framework), 40
Stakeholders, 7
Standard setting, 153
Stock turnover, 30
Strategic business units (SBUs), 32–3, 96–7
Strategic capability, *see* Capability, strategic
Strategic decisions, definition, 4–5
Strategic drift, 37–8
Strategic marketing management, *see* Marketing strategy
Strategic perspective, 8, 95
Strategic positioning, 90
    steps, 90–1
Strategic wear-out, 38
Strategy:
    (7-S framework), 40
    definition, 6
    development, 7
    generic types, 101–3
Structure (7-S framework), 40
Style (7-S framework), 40
Success factors, 143
Suppliers (as stakeholders), 29
SWOT analysis, 35–7, 168
    (study), 185–6, 188, 198
Systems (7-S framework), 40

Tactics, definition, 6
Targeting, market, 86
Technological factors, 50, 52, 147
Test marketing, 117–19

Umbrella branding, corporate, 115
Undifferentiated marketing, 89
Unique selling proposition approach, 124

Value chain analysis, 25
    primary activities, 26–7
    support activities, 27
Variance analysis, 154
Vertical marketing system, definition, 129

Watergate Pumps Ltd (mini case study), 172–5
    suggested solution, 196–200
Working capital ratio, 30

your chance to bite back
Strategic Marketing Management

Dear student

Both Butterworth-Heinemann and the CIM would like to hear your comments on this workbook. All respondents will receive a FREE copy of a CIM marketing book.

If you have some suggestions, please fill out the form below and sent it to us at:

Business Books Division
Butterworth-Heinemann
FREEPOST OF/1639
Oxford OX2 8BR

Name:

_____

College/course attended:

_____

If you are not attending a college, please state how you are undertaking your study:

_____

_____

_____

How did you hear about the CIM/Butterworth-Heinemann workbook series?

Word of mouth ❏
Through my tutor ❏
CIM mailshot ❏

Advert in _____

Other _____

What do you like about this workbook (e.g. layout, subjects covered, depth of analysis):

What do you dislike about this workbook (e.g. layout, subjects covered, depth of analysis):

Are there any errors that we have missed (please state page number):